Presented pursuant to the GRA Act 2000

Ministry of Defence Annual Report and Accounts

including the Annual Performance Report and
Consolidated Departmental Resource Accounts

2005-06

(For the year ended 31 March 2006)

Laid in accordance with the Government Resources and Accounts Act 2000

Ordered by the House of Commons to be printed
14 July 2006

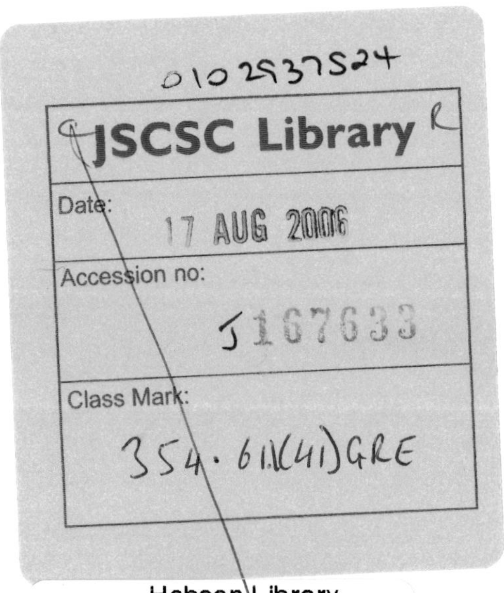

London: The Stationery Office
HC 1394

14 July 2005
£40.70

Contents

Ministerial Responsibilities

Secretary of State for Defence Rt. Hon. Des Browne MP

The Right Honourable Des Browne MP was appointed Secretary of State for Defence on the 5th May 2006. The Secretary of State for Defence is the Cabinet Minister charged with making and executing Defence policy, and with providing the means by which it is executed, the Armed Forces. As Chairman of the Defence Council and of its three Service Boards, (the Admiralty Board, the Army Board and the Air Force Board) he is responsible for the command, administration and discipline of the Armed Forces on behalf of the Crown. Although responsible ultimately for all elements of Defence, the Secretary of State is supported by three subordinate Ministers: the Minister of State for the Armed Forces; the Under Secretary of State and Minister for Defence Procurement; and the Under Secretary of State and Minister for Veterans. The Secretary of State assigns responsibility to them for specific aspects of the Armed Forces and the Ministry of Defence's business, but retains specific responsibility for policy, including nuclear issues and European defence; operations; personnel; finance and efficiency; oversight of major acquisition decisions and Defence industrial issues; and media and communications.

Minister of State for the Armed Forces
Rt. Hon. Adam Ingram MP

Responsibilities

Defence policy and planning, including:
- Arms control and disarmament; export licensing
- International organisations
- US visiting forces
- Size and shape of the Armed Forces
- Intelligence and security, including counter terrorism

Operations, including:
- Overseas commitments and garrisons
- Northern Ireland
- Military Aid to the Civil Authorities
- Nuclear accident response
- Military assistance overseas

The Armed Forces (Regular and Reserves), including:
- Readiness
- Sustainability
- Equipment support
- Performance
- Collective training
- Reputation

Defence Logistics Organisation, including ABRO and DARA, and logistics transformation

Regional issues and the Devolved Administrations

Under Secretary of State and Minister for Defence Procurement
Lord Drayson

Responsibilities

Acquisition, including:
- Policy
- The forward Equipment Programme
- Equipment and logistics support project approvals
- Equipment disposals
- Nuclear procurement and disposal (including the Atomic Weapons Establishment)
- Defence Procurement Agency
- Defence Logistics Organisation acquisition
- Defence industrial issues
- International collaboration

Defence science and technology, including:
- Policy
- International collaboration
- Defence Science and Technology Laboratories
- QinetiQ

Defence exports, including:
- Policy
- Defence Export Services Organisation
- Marketing campaigns

Defence issues in the House of Lords

Under Secretary of State for Defence and Minister for Veterans
Tom Watson MP

Responsibilities

Veterans affairs, including:
- Legacy veterans' health issues
- POWs
- War Graves
- Medals and memorials
- Commemorative events

Defence estates, including:
- Defence estates acquisition and disposals
- Service housing
- Heritage and historic buildings

Service personnel issues, including:
- Recruitment, basic training, and education
- Pay and compensation
- Equal opportunities
- Defence medical services
- Cadets
- Claims casework
- Service families, and Service Children's Education
- Armed Forces Bill

Other issues, including:
- Civilian personnel policy and casework
- MoD Police
- Health and safety
- Hydrographic Office and Meteorological Office
- Non-Departmental Public Bodies
- Low flying
- Visits by Peers and MPs/ Armed Forces Parliamentary Scheme

Foreword

by the Secretary of State

Right Honourable Des Browne MP,
Secretary of State for Defence

It was a great privilege for me to be appointed Secretary of State for Defence in May. Like most people in this country I have long admired the men and women of all three Services – and the civilians who work with them. They do a vital job, defending the UK and its interests and strengthening international peace and stability. Having seen them at work in Iraq, Afghanistan and the UK, I have been hugely impressed by their attitude, skills and determination, even in the most difficult and demanding of circumstances. They are a real force for good at home and overseas.

This has been a challenging year for Defence. Over the last year alone, nearly one fifth of our servicemen and women have been deployed on operations around the world, helping to manage the consequences, or prevent the intensification, of conflict.

Our operational commitment in Iraq has continued. This is a difficult task but we remain committed to seeing it through. There has been encouraging progress in the past year. Iraqis have taken significant steps towards taking control of their long term future and the Iraqi security forces continue to increase in professionalism and strength. On a practical level, over 5,000 schools have been rehabilitated and millions of new textbook distributed; sewage treatments plants are operating where none were under Saddam; there have been improvements in electricity and water supply, and of course democratic elections have taken place.

The UK is also playing a leading role in the UN-endorsed mission to Afghanistan, alongside many international allies. Our task is to support the democratically elected Government of Afghanistan to improve the lives of ordinary Afghans. British Armed Forces are defending the people of Afghanistan from the lawlessness and violence that have blighted their society for so long, and they are there to protect those who are rebuilding this devastated society. The UK is proud to be playing such a central role in a truly multinational operation; and with the support of the international community – NATO, the UN and EU among others – fully behind this mission, we cannot and will not fail.

Iraq and Afghanistan dominate the news, but we are extensively deployed on other important, but less heralded, operations. We have continued to contribute to safety and security in the Balkans, the Demoncratic Republic of Congo, Georgia, Sudan, Liberia, Sierra Leone, the Falkland Islands and elsewhere, while also helping with disaster relief in the aftermath of last year's earthquake in Kashmir. At home we have continued to support the civil authorities in Northern Ireland in addition to providing search and rescue, explosive ordnance disposal and other important assistance across the UK.

Looking beyond the challenges of today, we have made further progress already in delivering the capabilities and reformed force structure set out in the July 2004 Command Paper 'Delivering Security in a Changing World: Future Capabilities'. These changes will increase our ability to undertake expeditionary operations as well as investing in an advanced range of capabilities for the tasks of tomorrow. And we have delivered over £1 billion in efficiencies across Defence – freeing up more resources to support the front line.

We have achieved a great deal this year, but there is no room for complacency. We have huge challenges ahead. In Iraq, Afghanistan, the Balkans and elsewhere, we must build security for the longer term. At the same time, we have embarked on an important programme of modernisation and reform covering virtually all areas of Defence and an ambitious Defence Industrial Strategy transforming our relationship with industry. I am determined to carry this forward, investing in our people and their equipment, to ensure the continued effectiveness of the Armed Forces and success in achieving our tasks and building for the future. We demand a lot of our people, military and civilian. They are among the best in the world. I and my colleagues remain committed to ensuring they receive the support they need, and deserve.

Des Browne

Preface

Our purpose, as set out in the Defence Vision published in 2003, remains to defend the UK and its interests, strengthen international peace and stability, and act as a force for good in the world. We achieve this by working together to produce battle-winning people and equipment that are fit for the challenge of today, ready for the tasks tomorrow, and capable of building for the future. Our strategy is to match new threats and instabilities, maintain flexible force structures, seek to reach out to the wider world, and for this to be led by high performance headquarters, which consciously invests in their people.

This report sets out how we are doing against this Vision by: ensuring the operational success of the Armed Forces in Iraq, Afganistan and wherever else they are deployed; taking forward a major programme of change and efficiency at home to produce more flexible and effective Armed Forces supported by a more efficient organisation; meeting our responsibilities to our own people and to society; and working towards the Government's wider social and economic goals.

At the top level, we continued to meet our Public Service Agreement targets, at home and overseas. In particular we delivered our military objectives in Iraq, Afghanistan and elsewhere, achieved the required level of military readiness and, for the first time, met all our targets for equipment acquisition. We are still validating the efficiencies achieved during the year. On the information available at time of publication we look likely to have met our overall 2002 Spending Review value for money target from 2002-03 to 2005-06 and to be on course against our more demanding 2004 Spending Review efficiency target.

We made progress in a number of areas:

- We took forward the force structure changes set out in our July 2004 White Paper on future capabilities. The formation of the first operational Typhoon squadron in the Royal Air Force was a significant milestone. As part of the process of normalisation in Northern Ireland we continued to reduce the size of the garrison. The last roulement infantry battalion left Northern Ireland on 16 January 2006, and we announced in March 2006 a fair and appropriate settlement package for the home service members of the Royal Irish Regiment being discharged;

- We continued to improve the sustainability and efficiency with which we conduct our business in order to minimise unnecessary overheads and ensure that we can produce the greatest Defence capability from the resources available. We achieved significant further improvements in the effectiveness and efficiency of our logistics support, and completed the roll-out of regional prime contracts to improve maintenance of the Defence estate. Our finances remained firmly under control, with unqualified accounts for the third year;

- We are moving in the right direction on acquisition, but there is much yet to do. The successful implementation of the Defence Industrial Strategy, announced in December 2005, is fundamental. We are serious about following through the implications of the Strategy for Departmental reform within the MoD, and announced on 3 July 2006 a range of measures that will help us to do so. We look to Defence industry to match our commitment;

- Our people are central to all we do, but we must keep investing in them. This has many dimensions. We implemented the Armed Forces Pay and Review Body recommendations in full. We have continued to improve the standard of single and family accommodation for Service personnel. We have continued to work to ensure that Service personnel receive the training they need to ensure they are ready for military operations, to improve the care available for sick or injured Service personnel including Reserves, and to ensure that Service veterans receive the support they have earned. We are taking forward further proposals to meet the recommendations to improve the care we provide to young recruits in their initial military training. We have also introduced the new Armed Forces Bill to Parliament to bring Service law up to date in a coherent manner;

- Internationally the year saw useful further development of NATO and European deployable military capability, and its practical demonstration on the ground. We have consistently worked towards this end. It is essential if the burdens of collective military operations are to be properly shared. It will also over time reduce the call on UK forces to sustain such operations. The NATO-led force in Afghanistan, currently under UK command, has significantly expanded its operations. The European Union's military mission in Bosnia, under UK command throughout 2005, continued to provide the security underpinning political progress and demonstrated the effectiveness of practical NATO/EU cooperation arrangements;

- We are taking forward an interrelated series of programmes to improve the way we work. This includes both the introduction of the Business Management System to ensure that we maintain and implement key processes coherently and consistently across Defence, and the introduction of new Service and Civilian personnel management systems making best use of information systems to minimise transactional activity. The progressive roll-out of the Defence Information Infrastructure over the next few years will enable us to embed these changes and go further.

But there are continuing difficulties and challenges too. In recognising progress and success, we do not seek to underplay these. Sadly, 20 Service personnel lost their lives on operations during the year. For the fifth successive year we sustained a level of military operations higher than that we plan routinely to deliver. The proportion of the Armed Forces deployed on operations or other military tasks rose from 18% to 20% during the year, while readiness levels fell slightly at the end of 2005-06 after rising steadily for over a year. Both the Army and the Royal Air Force continued to breach harmony guidelines. We were also unable to conduct all the collective training we would have liked; and there continued to be some shortfalls in the provision of logistic support to the Front Line Commands. The reductions in the Armed Forces and the Defence Civil Service, and the relocation of Defence business from more to less ethnically and socially diverse parts of the country mean that, despite our good track record on diversity, meeting our already demanding targets in this area is becoming more rather than less difficult.

The targets we have set ourselves are not easy to meet. We are changing our organisations, systems and ways of working to create better Defence capability for the future at the same time as using them heavily to sustain current operations. We are encouraged that opinion surveys show that the Armed Forces continue to have the confidence and respect of the public. Our internal satisfaction surveys indicate that Service and civilian staff remain committed and motivated to what they do and we have noted the wide range of national awards and prizes they win, in such diverse areas as health and safety, conservation, communications, diversity and project management. We ask a lot of all our people, military and civilian. They are among the best and we are encouraged that, drawing on their deep rooted military traditions and lasting sense of public service, they continue to rise to the challenges we face.

Bill Jeffrey CB
Permanent Under Secretary of State

Air Chief Marshal Sir Jock Stirrup
GCB AFC ADC DSc FRAeS FCMI RAF
Chief of Defence Staff

Introduction

i. The Ministry of Defence's Annual Report and Accounts is a comprehensive overview of Defence, and how the Department has used the resources authorised by Parliament, from April 2005 to March 2006. It has two main sections. The first comprises the Department's Annual Performance Report for 2005-06, including performance against our Public Service Agreement (PSA) targets. The second comprises the Departmental Resource Accounts for 2005-06. There are also a number of Annexes containing background information on the Department, its organisation and administration. Further information is published in parallel on the Department's website at *www.mod.uk*.

SECTION 1: ANNUAL PERFORMANCE REPORT

ii. Since 2000 the Defence Management Board has used a Balanced Scorecard to assist in the assessment, reporting and management of Defence performance. The scorecard for 2005-06 (figure 1 below) encapsulates the Government's key objectives as set out in our Public Service Agreement together with the Defence Management Board's wider supporting objectives and priorities, as set out in the *Departmental Plan 2005-2009*. A more detailed explanation of how the Defence Balanced Scorecard works can be found at Annex D. The Annual Performance Report is set out on the same basis as the Departmental Plan, and reports performance against the targets set out therein. As in previous years it is divided into four main sections (Purpose, Future Capabilities, Enabling Processes and Resources), matching the top level structure of the scorecard. Each section contains separate chapters on the individual high level scorecard objectives, supplemented by an essay providing additional background on some relevant aspect of Defence business during the year.

iii. The *Departmental Plan* and the Defence Balanced Scorecard are designed deliberately to evolve over time to reflect emerging top level priorities and changes in the way the Department is organised. Consequently although the overall four-part structure has remained consistent for several years, there is inevitably a certain amount of change from one year to the next in the top level supporting objectives and the way they are brigaded and presented. In particular, the *Departmental Plan 2005-2009* placed particular importance on implementation of the Department's change and efficiency programmes and the work to develop future military and supporting capability, and this is reflected by the placement of this section immediately following that covering operations and policy.

Significant changes from the 2004-05 Defence Balanced Scorecard are:

- The Wider Government chapter under 'Purpose' has been expanded to reflect the importance of sustainability in Defence activity, in support of wider Government objectives;
- Chapters on Health and Safety and Business Management have been included under 'Enabling Processes', reflecting the priority the Defence Management Board attaches to effective health and safety management and efficient ways of working across Defence, and the previous chapters on Personnel Management and Training have been merged; and
- The 'Future Capabilities' section has been expanded to reflect the range and scale of the Department's investment, change and efficiency programmes. The chapter on equipment has been moved from the 'Enabling Processes' section and expanded to cover non-equipment investment, and change and development has been broken into separate chapters on Future Effects, which covers what we are doing to improve military capability directly, and Efficiency and Change, which covers what we are doing to make the organisations and processes that support the Armed Forces more flexible and efficient. This includes, but is not confined to, the work covered by the Department's efficiency commitment in the 2004 Spending Review.

Public Service Agreement Targets

iv. At the highest level the Ministry of Defence's objectives are set out in our Public Service Agreement. The Annual Performance Report therefore starts with a summary of performance as of 31 March 2006 against the targets for 2005-2008 set out in the 2004 Spending Review. It also includes a summary of performance against the outstanding 2002 Spending Review Value for Money PSA target, and the 2004 Spending Review Efficiency Target. Supporting detail is provided throughout the report. A full description of these targets and the way in which performance against them is measured, together with quarterly performance reports, can be found on the MoD website at *www.mod.uk*. We assess that we are on course or ahead in meeting our 2004 Spending Review PSA and efficiency targets. A final determination of whether we have met the 2002 Spending Review Value for Money Target will be made in the autumn on completion of validation work and reported in the Autumn Performance Report. On the evidence available at the time of publication of this report, we judge we are likely to have met it.

SECTION 2: DEPARTMENTAL RESOURCE ACCOUNTS 2005-06

v. The Department is required to prepare resource accounts for each financial year detailing the resources acquired, held, or disposed of during the year and the way in which it has used them. The resource accounts are prepared on an accruals basis in accordance with Treasury guidelines. They must give a true and fair view of the state of affairs of the Department, the net resource outturn, resources applied to objectives, recognised gains and losses, and cash flows for the financial year. The Accounts are audited by the Comptroller and Auditor General supported by the National Audit Office to ensure that they are true and fair and that they have been properly prepared. The Departmental Resource Accounts for 2005-06 together with the Comptroller and Auditor General's certification comprise Section 2 of the Annual Report and Accounts.

The 2005-06 Defence Balanced Scorecard

Are we fit for today's challenges and ready for tomorrow's tasks?

Purpose

A Current Operations: To succeed in Operations and Military Tasks today.

B Future Operations: Be ready for the tasks of tomorrow.

C Policy: Work with allies, other governments and multilateral institutions to provide a security framework that matches new threats and instabilities.

D Wider Government: Contribute to the Government's wider domestic reform agenda, and achieve our PSA and PPA targets.

Are we using our resources to best effect?

Resources

E. Finance: Maximise our outputs within allocated financial resources.

F. Manpower: Ensure we have the people we need.

G. Estate: Maintain an estate of the right size and quality, managed in a sustainable manner to achieve Defence objectives.

H. Reputation: Enhance our reputation amongst our own people and externally.

Defending the United Kingdom and its interests: acting as a force for good in the world

Are we a high performing organisation?

Enabling Processes

I. Personnel: Manage and invest in our people to give of their best.

J. Health and Safety: A safe environment for our staff, contractors and visitors.

K. Logistic support to the Armed Forces: Support and sustain our Armed Forces.

L. Business Management: Deliver improved ways of working.

Are we building for future success?

Future Capabilities

M. Future Force Effects: More flexible Armed Forces to deliver greater effect.

N. Efficiency and Change: More flexible and efficient organisations and processes to support the Armed Forces.

O. Future Capabilities and Infrastructure: Progress future equipment and capital infrastructure projects to time, quality and cost estimates.

P. Future Personnel Plans: Develop the skills and professional expertise we need for tomorrow.

Q. Science, Innovation and Technology: Exploit new technologies.

FURTHER INFORMATION

vi. The Annexes to the *Annual Report and Accounts* contain background information, mainly in regard to the administration of the Ministry of Defence. These include information on accounting to Parliament, the higher organisation of the Department, detailed conflict prevention assessments, a description of the Department's performance management system, summaries of the performance of Defence Agencies, Trading Funds and Non Departmental Public Bodies, performance against Government standards for efficient administration, and a summary of the major Defence equipment projects and international collaborative activity. Further information, including the Department's first annual report against the Code of Good Practice on *Corporate Governance in Central Government Departments* and the annual report of the Defence Audit Committee are published in parallel on the MoD Website at *www.mod.uk*. Other sources of more detailed information on specific aspects of Defence performance and activity are identified throughout the report at the end of every chapter.

SECTION 1: PERFORMANCE REPORT

Annual Performance Report

2005-06

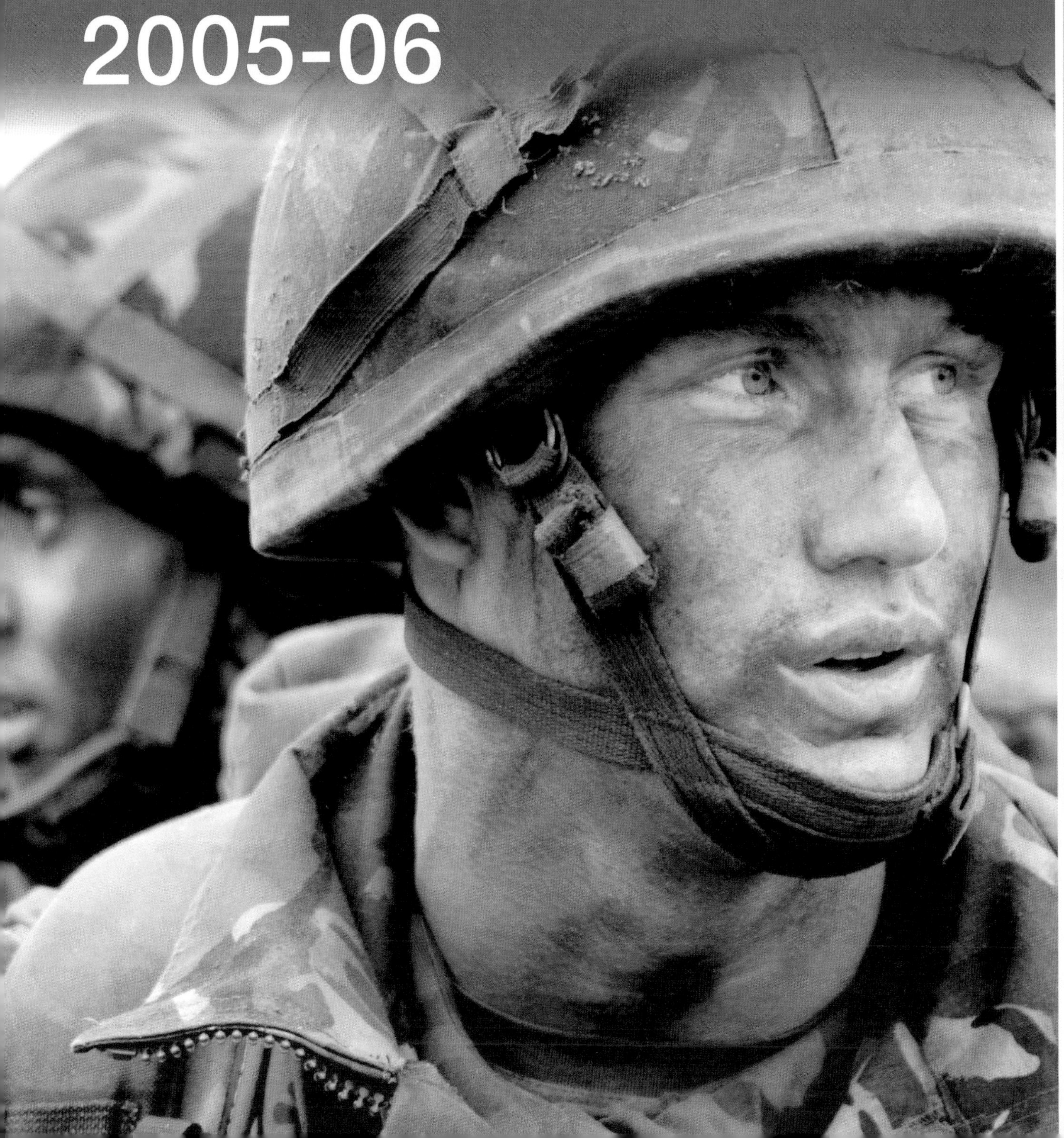

Performance against SR2004 Public Service Agreement Objectives and Targets

This section shows current performance against 2004 Spending Review (SR2004) Public Service Agreement (PSA) and Efficiency Targets (April 2005 to March 2008) and the 2002 Spending Review (SR2002) Value for Money PSA Target (which runs until March 2006).

2004 SPENDING REVIEW PUBLIC SERVICE AGREEMENT

The Ministry of Defence Vision is reflected in the three objectives and six targets of the Department's Public Service Agreement. The Agreement represent a contract between the Department and the taxpayer as to what we will, as a Department, deliver. The SR2004 PSA is shown below.

MoD Public Service Agreement 2005-06 to 2007-08

Aim: to deliver security for the people of the United Kingdom and the Overseas Territories by defending them, including against terrorism, and act as a force for good by strengthening international peace and security.

Objective I: Achieve success in the Military Tasks we undertake at home and abroad.

1. Achieve the objectives established by Ministers for operations and Military Tasks in which the United Kingdom's Armed Forces are involved, including those providing support to our civil communities.

2. By 2008, deliver improved effectiveness of UK and international support for conflict prevention by addressing long-term structural causes of conflict, managing regional and national tension and violence, and supporting post-conflict reconstruction, where the UK can make a significant contribution, in particular Africa, Asia, Balkans and the Middle East. *(Joint target with the Foreign and Commonwealth Office and the Department For International Development.)*

Objective II: Be ready to respond to the tasks that might arise.

3. Generate forces which can be deployed, sustained and recovered at the scales of effort required to meet the Government's strategic objectives.

4. Play a leading role in the development of the European Security Agenda, and enhance capabilities to undertake timely and effective security operations, by successfully encouraging a more efficient and effective NATO, a more coherent and effective European Security and Defence Policy (ESDP) operating in strategic partnership with NATO, and enhanced European defence capabilities.
(Joint target with the Foreign and Commonwealth Office.)

5. Recruit, train, motivate and retain sufficient military personnel to provide the military capability necessary to meet the Government's strategic objectives.

Objective III: Build for the future.

6. Deliver the equipment programme to cost and time.

Target 1

Achieve the objectives established by Ministers for Operations and Military Tasks in which the United Kingdom's Armed Forces are involved, including those providing support to our civil communities.

Overall Assessment
ON COURSE

Between 1 April 2005 and 31 March 2006 UK Armed Forces achieved the objectives for Operations and Military Tasks. Detailed information of Military activity during the year is set out in paragraphs 1-30. The proportion of regular forces deployed on Operations and other Military Tasks increased from about 18% in the first quarter of the year (including about 21% of the Army) to just under 20% in the last quarter of year (including about 25% of the Army);

Percentage of Regular Armed Forces undertaking Operations and other Military Tasks during 2005-06

	January 2006 to March 2006	October 2005 to December 2005	July 2005 to September 2005	April 2005 to June 2005
Navy/Marines	13.5%	12.1%	9.3%	11.6%
Army	25.1%	22.8%	22.0%	21.0%
RAF	13.4%	12.3%	11.9%	13.3%
Overall	**19.8%**	**18.7%**	**17.5%**	**18.0%**

Notes:
1. Percentages are quarterly averages and reflect the burden of activity imposed by the operations and military tasks undertaken by each service. Figures are based on man-day equivalents.
2. A list of Military Tasks can be found on the Department's website (www.mod.uk).

Target 2

Improve effectiveness of the UK contribution to conflict prevention and management as demonstrated by a reduction in the number of people whose lives are affected by violent conflict and a reduction in potential sources of future conflict, where the UK can make a significant contribution. (Joint target with Foreign and Commonwealth Office and Department for International Development).

Summary

Out of twelve performance indicators nine are on course. The UN peacekeeping target of a 5% increase in number of UN peacekeepers is ahead. The three reporting slippage – Middle East Peace Process, Nepal, and Sudan – are volatile conflicts frustrating UK conflict prevention efforts. Detailed Assessments against the Performance indicators for each target are at Annex C.

A – Afghanistan	E – Middle East Peace Process	I - Sudan
B – Balkans	F – Nepal	J – UN Peacekeeping
C – DRC	G – Nigeria	K – UN Peacekeeping
D – Iraq	H – Sierra Leone	L – African Peacekeeping

Key

On course, ahead	Slippage	Not met

Target 3

Generate forces, which can be deployed, sustained and recovered at the scales of effort required to meet the government's strategic objectives.

Overall Assessment
ON COURSE

Assessment against Performance Indicators

a. By 2008, ensure more than 73% of force elements show no serious or critical weakness against their required peacetime readiness levels.

Over the year as a whole an average of 77% of Force Elements reported no critical or serious weaknesses in achieving their peacetime readiness – achieving our PSA target of 73% two years early. Further information is set out in paragraphs 32-33.

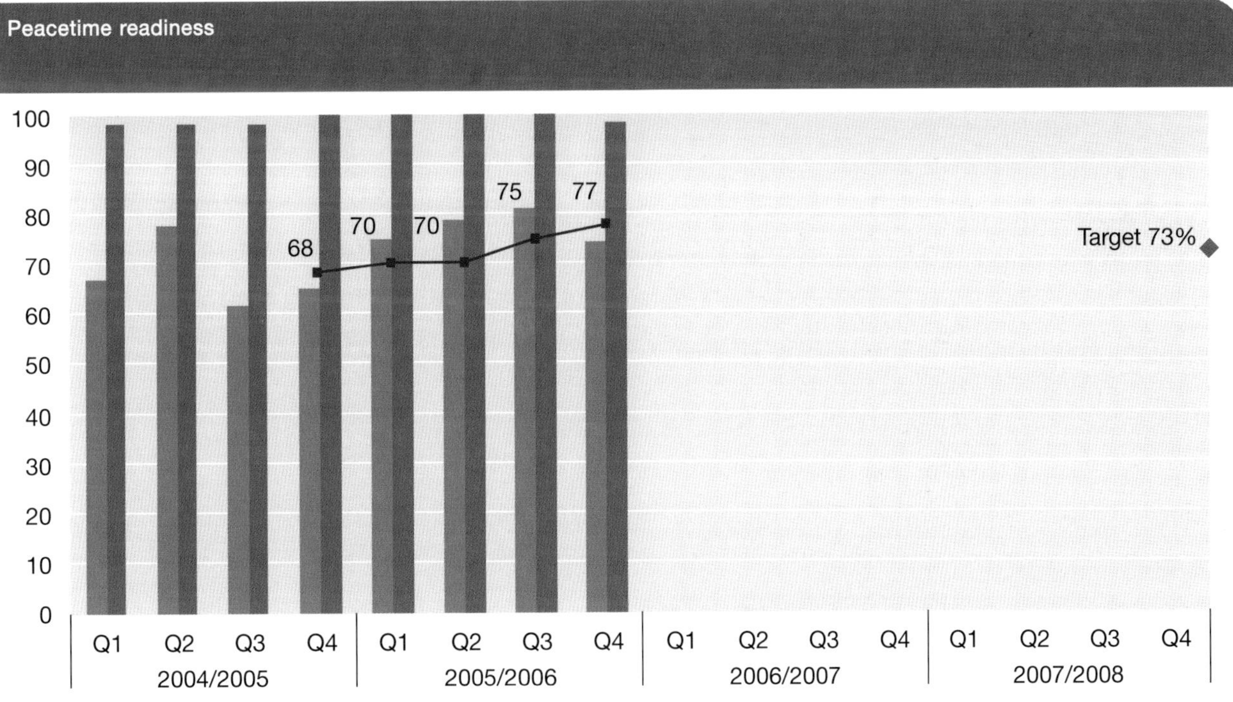

b. By 2008, ensure that more than 71% of force elements report no serious or critical weaknesses against the ability to generate from peacetime readiness to immediate readiness for deployment on operations.

Over 2005-06 an average of 70% force elements reported no serious or critical weaknesses. Further information is set out in paragraph 34.

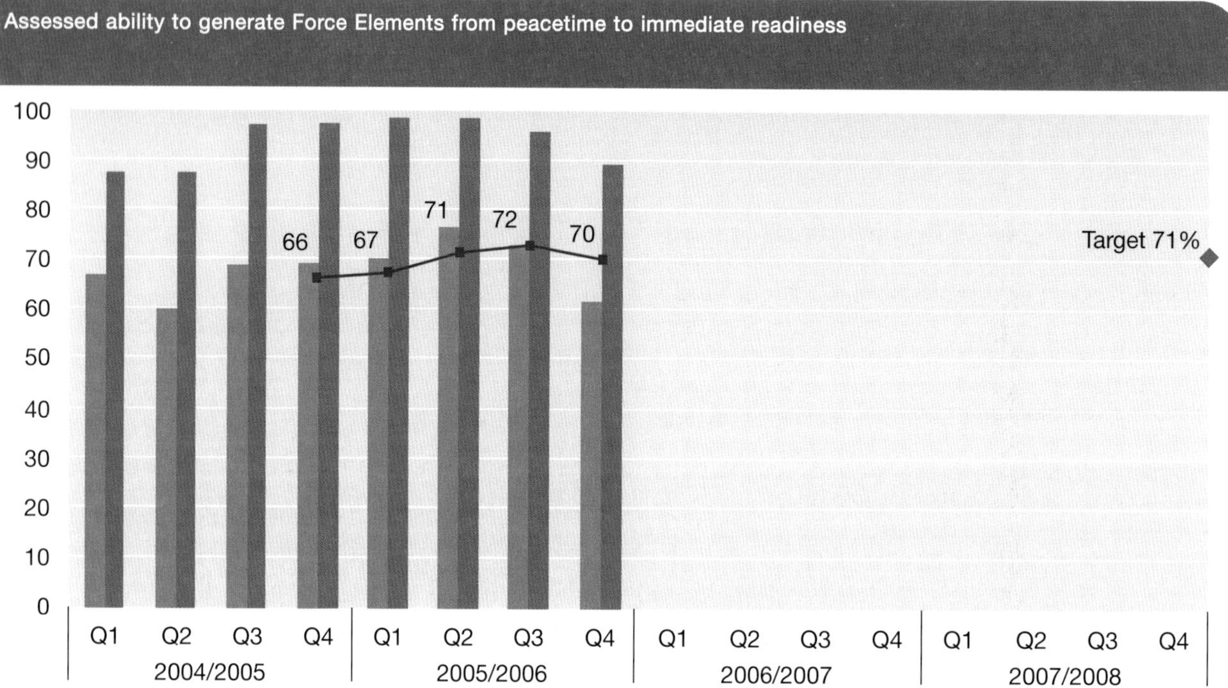

c. By 2008, ensure that the assessed ability of the Department physically to deploy its Force Elements, sustain them in theatre and thereafter recover them to their home bases shows a 5% improvement in the numbers of serious or critical weakness compared with the average reported in 2004-05.

Performance at 31 March 2006 is assessed as being on course to improve as required by our PSA target. Over the year there has been an improvement in the ability of Defence to sustain those Army force elements required in our most demanding likely deployments. We are developing a metric that will allow us to for report our ability to deploy, sustain and recover our force elements in a way that is consistent with the other reports against Target 3.

Target 4

Play a leading role in the development of the European Security agenda, and enhance capabilities to undertake timely and effective security operations by successfully encouraging a more efficient and effective NATO, a more coherent and effective ESDP operating in strategic partnership with NATO, and enhanced European defence capabilities. (Joint target with FCO.)

Assessment against Performance Indicators

a. A more efficient and effective NATO

- Expanded NATO commitment to Afghanistan;
- NATO training mission for Iraq;
- Progress towards achievement of NATO Response Force full operational capability and deployment of NRF elements to Pakistan for earthquake relief;
- NATO Agreement of Comprehensive Political Guidance for planning staffs.
- Further information is set out in paragraphs 50-51.

b. A more coherent and effective ESDP operating in strategic partnership with NATO

- Achievement of UK EU Presidency ESDP goals;
- EUFOR mission to Bosnia under UK command;
- Expansion of ESDP operations.
- Further information is set out in paragraphs 52-53.

c. Enhanced European defence capabilities.

- Further development of European Defence Agency;
- Implementation of EU Battlegroups complementary to NATO Response Force.
- Further information is set out in paragraphs 54-55.

Target 5

Recruit, train, motivate and retain sufficient military personnel to provide the military capability necessary to meet the Government's strategic objectives.

Assessment against Performance Indicators

a. Manning Balance[1]

Operational commitments and the changes in Service personnel numbers announced in the July 2004 White Paper mean that there is currently some slippage in meeting manning balance targets. In particular, the complexities of managing reductions in Service personnel inevitably produce short term imbalances against the overall personnel requirement. Graph 3 shows the manning balance since April 2005.

At 1 April 2006:

- The Royal Navy (including the Royal Marines) trained strength is 3.7% below the requirement – 1.7% below manning balance. The RN continues to forecast an improving position.
- Both the Army and Royal Air Force are within the target range.

There are continuing shortages within some specialist groups in all three Armed Services. Further information is set out in paragraphs 279-280.

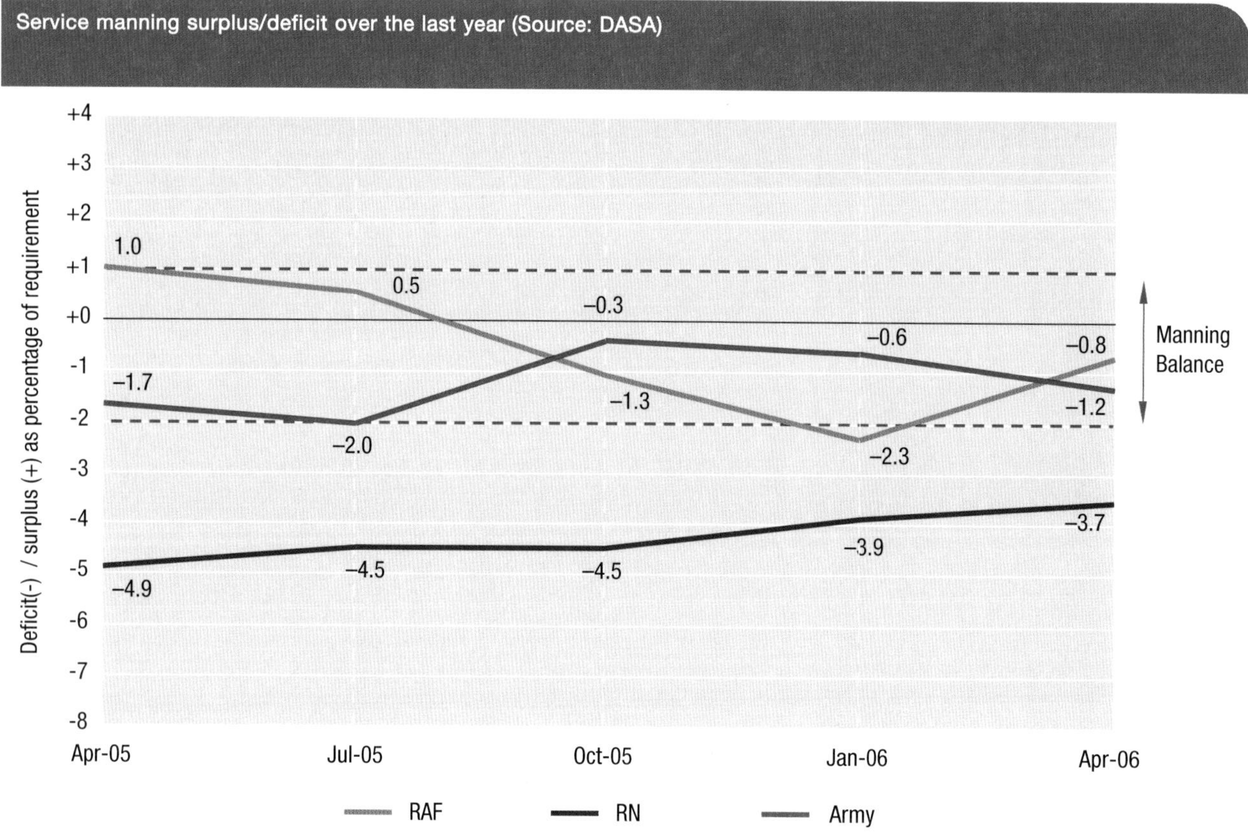

[1] Manning balance is defined as between –2% and +1% of the requirement, and is measured against the target prevailing at the time. Since the total requirement of Service manning is dynamic, this target will itself tend to fluctuate over the PSA period.

b. Gains to Trained Strength (trained recruits provided to the front line)

Gains to Trained Strength	Numbers achieved in 2005-06	Target (and % achieved)
Naval Service Officers	370	410 (90%)
Naval Service Other Ranks	2,330	2,700 (86%)
Army Officers[2]	750	810 (93%)
Army Other Ranks[2]	7,770	9,230 (84%)
Royal Air Force Officers	360 (P)	370 (98%)(P)
Royal Air Force Other Ranks	1,770 (P)	1,800 (98%)(P)

Notes:
1. Naval Service and RAF figures come from DASA. The Army figures come from Adjutant General TLB.
2. The Army numbers show officers completing the Royal Military Accademy Sandhurst and soldiers completing Phase 2 training. This metric is used for internal manning management and does not match the figures produced by DASA and published in Tri Service Publication 4.
3. 'P' represents that figures are provisional due to the introduction of the new Joint Personnel Administration system in the RAF.

c. Medically Fit For Task

The target is for at least 90% of Service personnel to be medically fit for task by 1 April 2007 – an increase of 1% from the performance at 31 March 2005.

At 31 March 2006 87.9% of the overall Armed Forces personnel were reported as fit for task. This reflects the current operational tempo and environment. The vast majority of those personnel unfit for task are working normally but their deployability is limited. Further information is set out in paragraphs 211-214.

d. Voluntary Outflow[2] Exits

The Voluntary Outflow exits for 2005-06 are shown in the table below. Further information is set out in paragraph 282.

Voluntary Outflow Exit Rates	Stable long term Voluntary Outflow goals	12 months ending 31 March 2006	12 months ending 31 March 2005	12 months ending 31 March 2004
RN Officers	2.0%	2.8%	2.5%	2.5%[2]
RN Ratings	5.0%	6.0%	6.4%	5.7%
Army Officers	4.1%	4.3%	3.9%	3.7%
Army Soldiers	6.2%	5.5%	5.7%	5.3%
RAF Officers	2.5%	2.5% P	2.4%	2.1%
RAF Other Ranks	4.0%	4.8% P	3.8%	3.7%

Notes:
1. Data from DASA and Voluntary Outflow goals from the Departmental Plan 2005-2009.
2. This figure is different to that published in the Annual Report and Account 2003-04 due to the introduction of a new exit code which was not correctly classified.
3. RAF figures for the 12 months ending 31 March 06 are provisional owing to the introduction of the new Joint Personnel Administration System for RAF.

[2] This was known as Premature Voluntary Release

e. Levels of Individual Separated Service against Harmony Guidelines.

The guidelines for individual separated service and performance against these guidelines are shown in the table below:

Levels of Individual Separated Service		
	Guidelines	**Performance**
Royal Navy/Royal Marines	In any 36 month period, no one to exceed 660 days separated service.	At 31 March 2006 less than 1% of the Royal Navy had exceeded the guidelines.
Army	In any 30 month rolling period no one to exceed 415 days separated service.	At 31 December 2005[3] 14.5% of the Army personnel on current trained strength had exceeded the guidelines.
Royal Air Force	Not greater than 2.5% of personnel exceeding more than 140 days of detached duty in 12 months.	At 31 March 2006 4.6% of the RAF had exceeded 140 days of detached duty in the last 12 months.

Data from DASA.

[3] Position at 31 March 2006 not available due to missing information from individual units

Target 6

Deliver the Equipment Programme to time and cost.

Performance against the PSA is measured against all Category A to C projects that have passed Main Gate and are yet to achieve ISD at the start of the financial year.

Assessment against Performance Indicators

1. **Achieve at least 97% of Key User Requirements for all Category A to C Projects that have passed Main Gate Approval, to be achieved throughout the PSA period.**

   97% of the customer's key requirements have been met. Further information is set out in paragraph 137.

2. **Average In-Year variation of forecast In Service Dates (ISD), for all Category A to C Projects that have passed Main Gate Approval, to be no more than 0.7 months in 2005-06, 0.5 months in 2006-07 and 0.4 months in 2007-08.**

   Average in-year variation of forecast ISD of 0.7 months. Further information is set out in paragraph 137.

3. **Average In-Year variation of forecast costs for Design and Manufacture phase, for all Category A to C projects that have passed Main Gate approval, of less than 0.4% in FY05/06, 0.3% in FY06/07 and 0.2% in FY07/08.**

   Average in-year cost increase of 0.2%. Further information is set out in paragraph 137.

2002 SPENDING REVIEW VALUE FOR MONEY TARGET

Increase value for money by making improvements in the efficiency and effectiveness of the key processes for delivering military capability. Year-on-year output efficiency gains of 2.5% will be made each year from 2002/03 to 2005/06, including through a 20% output efficiency gain in the DLO.

Overall Assessment
TO BE DETERMINED

Assessment against Performance Indicators

Subject to confirmation and validation, we believe we have met the overall target of 10%. Detailed information is at paragraphs 269-270.

Target	Weighting	Culumative Trajectory			
		2002-03	2003-04	2004-05	2005-06
Reduce by an average of 6% the per capita cost of training a successful military recruit to the agreed standard.	9	2%	4%	5%	6%
Achievement		1.7%	4.2%	Discont'd	Discont'd
Achieve 0% average annual cost growth (or better) against the equipment procurement projects included in the Major Projects Report, while meeting customer requirements.	6	0%	0%	0%	0%
Actual in-year cost growth		5.7%	3.1%	-4.6%	-0.1%
Reduce by 20% the output costs of the Defence Logistics Organisation, while maintaining support to the Front Line	68	2%	6%	10%	14%
Achievement		3.1%	6.6%	9.8%[1]	13.7%
Reduce MoD Head Office and other management costs by 13%	5	5%	9%	12%	13%
Achievement		6.3%	10.6%	12%	12%
Identify for disposal land and buildings with a net book value of over £300M	12	£84M	£134M	£258M	£300M
Achievement		£135M	£230M	£395M	£456M
Overall Target	**100**	**2%**	**5%**	**8%**	**10%**
Overall Achievement		**2.3%**	**5.0%**	**7.3%**	**10.0%**

Notes:
1. The 2004-05 achievement against the Logistics target and the overall achievement have been amended from that reported in the Annual Report and Accounts 2004-05 to reflect subsequent checking and validation. See paragraph 231 for futher information.
2. Logistic performance is subject to validation by Defence Internal Audit.
3. The net book value of land and buildings reflect their valuation in accordance with the Department's accounting policies. The actual income from the sales could vary significantly from this value and will be dependent upon market conditions at the time of sale.

2004 SPENDING REVIEW EFFICIENCY TARGET

As part of Spending Review 2004, the Department agreed that it would realise total annual efficiency gains of at least £2.8 billion by 2007-08, of which three quarters will be cash releasing. As part of this programme the MoD will by 31 March 2008:

- Reduce its civilian staff by at least 10,000
- Reduce the number of military posts in administrative and support functions by at least 5,000
- Be on course to have relocated 3,900 posts out of London and the South East by 2010.

Performance Assessment

By 31 March 2006 between £1,323M and £1,398M of efficiencies had been delivered, including £200M of sustainable efficiencies realised in 2004-05. Detailed information is set out in paragraphs 126-133.

Programme	Planned Efficiencies by 31 March 2006	Achievement by 31 March 2006	Future Planned Efficiency gains	
			2006-07	2007-08
	£M	£M	£M	£M
Force Structure changes	**106**	**106**	**298**	**388**
Corporate Services	**131**	**343**	**254**	**309**
Military Personnel Management	5	16	43	85
Civilian Personnel Management	21	24*	49	107
Finance Function	2	2	13	11
Information Services	103	301*	149	106
Procurement and Logistics	**695**	**674-749**	**1,123**	**1,660**
Equipment Procurement	54	54*	206	374
Defence Logistics Transformation	539	500-575*	714	951
Whole Fleet Management	56	54*	66	116
Estates Modernisation	37	31*	62	95
Other Procurement	9	35	75	124
Productive Time	**84**	**105***	**86**	**88**
Organisational changes	**0**	**0**	**2**	**14**
Relocation	**12**	**18**	**18**	**18**
Manpower	**88**	**86**	**285**	**449**
RN	15	15	32	32
Army	18	18	64	88
RAF	53	51	121	203
Civilian	2	2	68	126
Adjustment	**-9**	**-9**	**-41**	**-126**
TOTAL	**1,107**	**1,323-1,398**	**2,025**	**2,800**

Notes:
1. Planned Efficiencies and Achievement by 31 March 2006 include efficiencies during 2004-05 and 2005-06. Efficiency gains for 2005-06 are provisional, subject to final validation. Because of the size of the Defence Logistics Transformation Programme, the process of validation takes some time and this is the reason why a range is given in the table.
2. The planned efficiencies in the table reflect a number of changes agreed by the Office of Government Commerce and the Treasury since the most recent version of the Efficiency Technical Note was published in December 2005.
3. Adjustment to avoid double counting of manpower savings.
4. Efficiency gains marked with an asterisk include an element of non-cashable gains.
5. The Information Services total for 2005-06 includes a non-recurring £260M for the reduced in-year cost of sustaining legacy systems (see paragraph 128).
6. 'Force structure changes', 'Equipment Procurement', 'Manpower' and 'Adjustment' make up the efficiency savings of £1.2 billion announced in the *Future Capabilities* Command Paper (See paragraphs 107-113)

Purpose

CURRENT OPERATIONS

Objective: To succeed in Operations and Military Tasks today.

Public Service Agreement Target (SR2004 MoD Target 1)

Achieve the objectives established by Ministers for Operations and Military Tasks in which the United Kingdom's Armed Forces are involved, including those providing support to our civil communities.

Performance Measures and Assessment

Achieve the objectives established by Ministers for Operations and Military Tasks:

- **The Armed Forces continued to achieve a high degree of success against the policy and military objectives set for all Operations overseas, including in Iraq, Afghanistan and the Balkans, and in response to the South Asian earthquake;**
- **The Armed Forces contributed to six United Nations peacekeeping missions, in Cyprus, the Democratic Republic of Congo, Georgia, Liberia, Sierra Leone, and Sudan;**
- **A minimum nuclear deterrent capability was maintained throughout the year;**
- **The security of the UK's Overseas Territories, including the Falkland Islands, Gibraltar and the Sovereign Base Areas in Cyprus, was maintained;**
- **Continuing support was provided to the civil authorities at home, including in Northern Ireland, responding to civil emergencies, provision of Search and Rescue and Fisheries Protection services, and the investigation and disposal of suspected explosive devices.**

Monitor the proportion of the Armed Forces deployed in support of Operations and Military Tasks:

- **The proportion of regular forces deployed on operations and other military tasks increased from about 18% in the first quarter of the year (including about 21% of the Army) to just under 20% in the last quarter of the year (including about 25% of the Army);**
- **The Armed Forces continued to operate above the overall level of concurrent operations for which they are resourced and structured to deliver for the fourth successive year;**
- **An average of about 9,200 military personnel (including over 1,300 Reserves) were deployed on, or in support of, operations in Iraq throughout the year;**
- **UK military personnel deployed to Afghanistan increased from about 1,000 in April 2005 to about 3,000 in April 2006 (including Reserves);**
- **UK military personnel deployed to the Balkans reduced from about 1,100 in April 2005 to about 900 in April 2006 (including Reserves);**
- **About 350 civilians were deployed on, or in support of, operations outside the UK during the year including about 160 in support of Operation TELIC.**

Figure 1: Principal Deployments of the Armed Forces on 1 April 2006

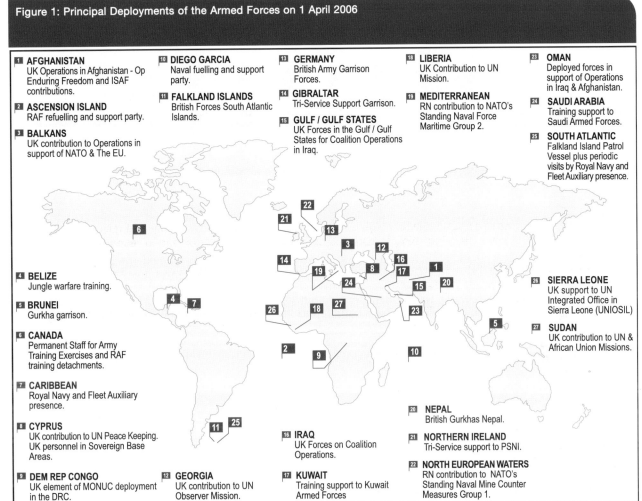

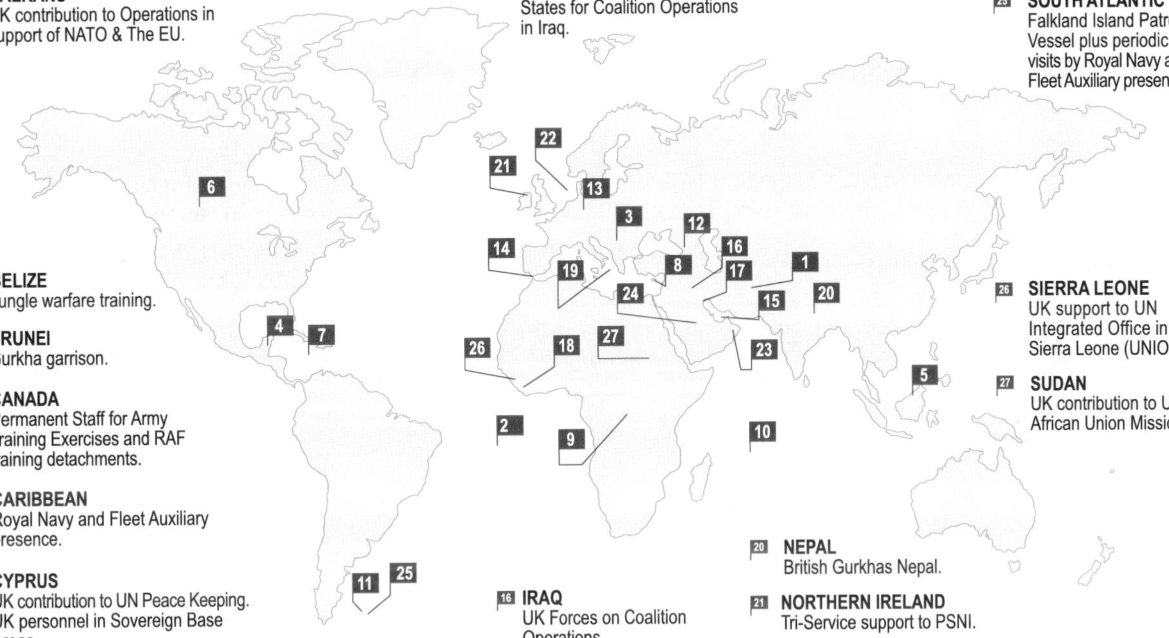

1. **AFGHANISTAN** UK Operations in Afghanistan - Op Enduring Freedom and ISAF contributions.
2. **ASCENSION ISLAND** RAF refuelling and support party.
3. **BALKANS** UK contribution to Operations in support of NATO & The EU.
4. **BELIZE** Jungle warfare training.
5. **BRUNEI** Gurkha garrison.
6. **CANADA** Permanent Staff for Army Training Exercises and RAF training detachments.
7. **CARIBBEAN** Royal Navy and Fleet Auxiliary presence.
8. **CYPRUS** UK contribution to UN Peace Keeping. UK personnel in Sovereign Base Areas.
9. **DEM REP CONGO** UK element of MONUC deployment in the DRC.
10. **DIEGO GARCIA** Naval fuelling and support party.
11. **FALKLAND ISLANDS** British Forces South Atlantic Islands.
12. **GEORGIA** UK contribution to UN Observer Mission.
13. **GERMANY** British Army Garrison Forces.
14. **GIBRALTAR** Tri-Service Support Garrison.
15. **GULF / GULF STATES** UK Forces in the Gulf / Gulf States for Coalition Operations in Iraq.
16. **IRAQ** UK Forces on Coalition Operations.
17. **KUWAIT** Training support to Kuwait Armed Forces
18. **LIBERIA** UK Contribution to UN Mission.
19. **MEDITERRANEAN** RN contribution to NATO's Standing Naval Force Maritime Group 2.
20. **NEPAL** British Gurkhas Nepal.
21. **NORTHERN IRELAND** Tri-Service support to PSNI.
22. **NORTH EUROPEAN WATERS** RN contribution to NATO's Standing Naval Mine Counter Measures Group 1.
23. **OMAN** Deployed forces in support of Operations in Iraq & Afghanistan.
24. **SAUDI ARABIA** Training support to Saudi Armed Forces.
25. **SOUTH ATLANTIC** Falkland Island Patrol Vessel plus periodic visits by Royal Navy and Fleet Auxiliary presence.
26. **SIERRA LEONE** UK support to UN Integrated Office in Sierra Leone (UNIOSIL)
27. **SUDAN** UK contribution to UN & African Union Missions.

1. The purpose of Defence is to defend the United Kingdom and its interests, strengthen international peace and stability, and thereby act as a force for good in the world. Throughout the year the Armed Forces, supported by their civilian colleagues, worked successfully for this goal at home and overseas, achieving a high degree of success against their policy and military objectives. In particular, in addition to meeting their standing tasks, the Armed Forces were deployed on operations in Iraq, Afghanistan, the Balkans, Africa and Southern Asia. Figure 1 shows the wide range of deployments of the UK Armed Forces on 1 April 2006. They also continued to provide wide-ranging support to the civil authorities at home.

IRAQ

2. Iraq remained the UK's largest foreign theatre of operations. UK military and civilian personnel have made a significant contribution to progress in Iraq, providing security, training the Iraqi Security Forces and creating the conditions for reconstruction and restoring the political process. During 2005 there was a successful referendum on a new constitution for Iraq in October, and national elections in December. Sectarian violence remained a concern, and the February 2006 attack on the Al Askariyah Shrine in Samara created a period of increased sectarian tension throughout Iraq.

3. The overwhelming majority of violence in Iraq remained concentrated in the four provinces of Baghdad, Al Anbar, Salah ad Din and Ninawa. Tackling this problem, with the Coalition's support, was and remains a high priority for the Iraqi authorities. Over the year the Iraqi Security Forces took on an increasing lead in delivering security as their capabilities developed. They provided all the immediate security for the referendum in October 2005 and for the December 2005 elections. They also demonstrated their growing capacity to lead counter-insurgency operations, such as in Tal Afar and the western Euphrates River Valley, and in clearing a suspected insurgent operating area north east of Samara. By 31 March 2006, with some 240,000 personnel trained and equipped, they had assumed responsibility for security in roughly 460 square miles of Baghdad and more than 11,600 square miles of other provinces in Iraq and were conducting more independent operations than the Coalition forces.

TURKEY
DAHŪK
Tall 'Afar
ARBĪL
NĪNAWĀ
AS SULAYMĀNĪYAH
AT TA'MĪM
SYRIA
ṢALĀḤ AD DĪN
Sāmarā'
IRAN
DIYĀLĀ
BAGHDAD
Ar Ruṭbah
WĀSIṬ
AL ANBĀR
BĀBIL
JORDAN
KARBALĀ'
MAYSAN
AL QĀDISĪYAH
Ash Shaṭrah
AN NAJAF
DHĪ QĀR
Al Başrah
MND (SE)
AL BAŞRAH
Umm Qaşr
SAUDI ARABIA
AL MUTHANNA
AL KUWAYT
THE GULF
KUWAIT

Maps are not to be taken as necessarily representing the views of the UK Government on boundaries or political status.

Iraq

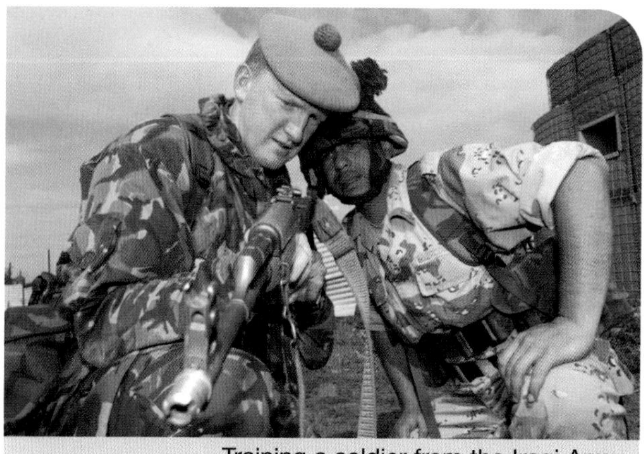
Training a soldier from the Iraqi Army

4. UK force levels were broadly stable throughout the year. On average about 9,200 UK military personnel were deployed to the region on or in support of Operation TELIC. Of these about 8,000 were based in Iraq itself, mainly in the four provinces of Al Basrah, Al Muthanna, Dhi Qar and Maysan in south-eastern Iraq covered by Multi-National Division (South East) (MND(SE)). The net additional cost of operations in Iraq during 2005-06 was £958M. UK forces continued to help the Iraqis deliver security where necessary, but the focus for Coalition forces in MND(SE) over the past year has been on security sector reform to building Iraq's national capacity to provide security on its own. Particular elements included:

- training and sustaining the 10th Division of the Iraqi Army;
- training the Iraqi Police Service in conjunction with over 120 civilian police advisers part-funded by Defence;
- training the Iraqi Department of Border Enforcement to protect Iraq's southern borders with Iran, Kuwait and Saudi Arabia;
- developing the Iraqi Navy, with a Naval Assistance and Training Team of almost 50 UK personnel at Umm Qasr Naval Base, and seaborne support to the Iraqi Navy and Marines; and,
- providing an additional £35M worth of equipment and infrastructure to assist the development of the Iraqi Security Forces.

Good progress was made and by the end of the year Iraqi Security Forces in MND(SE) were increasingly leading security operations and taking on greater responsibility for the security of the Iraqi people.

A soldier talking with local Iraqi children in Al Salman

5. UK military personnel worked closely with the Department for International Development to help the Iraqis rebuild their country. The key focus in MND(SE) remained improving the quality of life for ordinary Iraqis by helping to deliver essential services like water and power, and by supporting economic development. Building on the success of the Quick Impact Projects, the MoD contributed directly to this effort through the Civil Effects Fund. This is primarily designed for the purposes of force protection, consent-building and winning 'hearts and minds'. By the end of March 2006, MND(SE) had committed around £35M of UK money to projects such as road and bridge building and repair, providing clean water supplies for isolated villages, and refurbishing schools, markets and state-run industries. Over 800 projects have been undertaken, including education, law and order and public services.

6. The Reserve Forces continued to make an invaluable contribution to the UK's military operations and commanders in the field praised their adaptability and high skill levels, reflecting the diversity of the skills they brought with them from civilian life. During 2005-06, over 1,300 Reservists were mobilised to support operations in Iraq, consisting on average about 8% of the total number of UK forces deployed. This brought the total number of Reserves mobilised in support of Operation TELIC since the end of warfighting to some 13,000. In general the period of mobilised service for reservists has been increased this year to accommodate improved pre-deployment training and post-deployment leave, with those deploying on a full-length tocer now remaining in service for between seven and ten months. They provided formed units and sub-units, and reinforced regular units and formations of all the Services (such as the Royal Marines commando squadron that worked with the Iraqi authorities to provide security for the port of Umm Qasr). They also continued to provide essential specialists, such as medics, weather forecasters and air movements staff, where much of the UK Armed Forces' expertise is now concentrated in the Reserves.

7. Defence civilian personnel also continued to provide vital support to operations in Iraq, with some 160 deployed during the year (out of a total of about 350 deployed on operations outside the UK), normally for tours of up to 6 months. These personnel included policy and financial advisors to deployed UK forces and Coalition headquarters, and specialised support personnel from the Defence Science and Technology Laboratory, the Defence Fire Service and the Ministry of Defence Police. Defence civilians, working as advisors and mentors, also contributed to the development of the Iraqi Ministry of Defence. Defence contractors also continued to provide infrastructure, logistics and communication support across the whole of the UK's area of operation in southern Iraq. On 31 March 2006, there were approximately 330 Defence contractor personnel in theatre.

8. Although the MND(SE) area remained more peaceful than other parts of Iraq, UK forces continued to face risks during the conduct of their operations. Every effort is taken to minimise these risks and force protection is one of our top priorities. Nevertheless 17 UK soldiers, sailors and airmen were killed in the service of their country during the year, bringing to 103 the number killed from the start of Operation TELIC to 31 March 2006, of whom 79 were killed in action. Service personnel who died on operations overseas were brought home swiftly and with fitting ceremony. During the year a full review of the policy for repatriation of the dead confirmed that the procedures remained appropriate and dignified, and met the needs of both the bereaved families and the Services.

AFGHANISTAN

9. The UK has been a key contributor of international military support to Afghanistan, particularly through the successful NATO-led International Security Assistance Force (ISAF). ISAF has had a positive role in bringing security to Kabul and the north of the country, in helping the central government extend its influence in the provinces, and in helping the Afghan authorities provide security during the successful parliamentary election in September 2005. This was a crucial milestone in the democratic development and peaceful evolution of the country, consolidating the progress made in the 2004 presidential elections. The first democratically elected parliament in over 30 years was inaugurated in December 2005. The London Conference held on 31 January/1 February 2006 and jointly chaired by the UN, the UK and Afghanistan launched the 'Afghanistan Compact' marking the beginning of a new phase of international engagement with increased emphasis on Afghan ownership of the reform process. At the conference $10.5 billion was pledged over the next three financial years, including some £500M from the UK. The security situation remained fragile, and the number of suicide attacks rose around the turn of the year, but the presence of ISAF and coalition forces continued to prevent Taliban or other armed groups from presenting a credible threat to long-term stability and security in Afghanistan. Recorded opium production fell by 21% in 2005 (compared to 2004), although these levels are unlikely to be maintained into 2006.

Afghanistan

10. A number of military-civilian Provincial Reconstruction Teams (PRTs) are based in the Afghan provinces to extend the Afghan Government's presence and influence and to facilitate improved local stability and security, reconstruction and development. At the beginning of the year, the UK provided PRTs in Meymaneh (handed over to Norway in September 2005) and Mazar-e Sharif in the north of Afghanistan, and a Forward Support Base also in Mazar-e Sharif. In March 2006, UK troops in the PRT in Mazar-e Sharif reported the largest ever weapons cache found in the country. We provided an infantry company to help ISAF provide security in the capital, Kabul, a training team to help train Afghan National Army non-commissioned officers, and staff officers for ISAF HQ and Combined Forces Command Afghanistan. We also deployed six Harrier GR7 aircraft to Kandahar in the south-east of the country to support both ISAF and US-led coalition operations by providing close air support and reconnaissance capabilities. During the year we expanded our support to security sector reform, launching a new Officer Candidate School in Kabul, based on the Sandhurst model. Courses began on 3 April 2006, and the school will train up to 400 junior officers per year. We are also providing two Defence civil servants as advisors to help the Afghan Ministry of Defence reform, develop the Afghan National Army and develop civilian capacity in the Afghan Ministry of Defence.

11. During the year, preparations began for ISAF expansion into the south to bring stability and security to a volatile region of the country. A preliminary team started preparing the ground in late 2005 to build infrastructure, and was subsequently reinforced by 850 additional engineers and Royal Marines (for force protection). In January 2006, we announced that we would deploy 3,300 UK troops in Helmand Province, comprising a UK Taskforce and a UK-led Provincial Reconstruction Team. The US, Canada, The Netherlands, Denmark, Australia, Romania and Estonia are also contributing. The UK Taskforce comprises elements of the Headquarters of 16 Air Assault Brigade, an airborne infantry battlegroup, eight Apache Attack Helicopters (on their first operational deployment), four Lynx Light Utility Helicopters, six Chinook Support Helicopters, armoured reconnaissance vehicles, a battery of 105mm Light Guns, a battery of Unmanned Aerial Vehicles, and supporting specialist logistics, engineering and medical assets. We are also deploying four additional C-130 Hercules transport aircraft. In light of this increasing commitment we handed over our remaining northern activities to ISAF partners in March 2006. In April 2006 we announced that we were extending our deployment of six Harrier GR7 aircraft to Kandahar until March 2007. We assumed command of ISAF for a nine month period in May 2006, using HQ Allied Rapid Reaction Corps (ARRC), supported by elements of 1 Signal Brigade, thus committing a further 1,000 personnel.

Royal Marines providing security in Helmand Province

12. Reflecting this growing contribution to Afghan security and stability, the number of UK military personnel deployed to Afghanistan increased from about 500 in April 2004 to about 1,000 in April 2005, and over 3,000 in April 2006. This will continue to increase steadily to a peak of around 5,700 in the summer of 2006, and then drop to below 5,000 by the autumn, when the infrastructure is completed. The Reserve Forces continue to contribute across the full range of our operations in Afghanistan, across all three Services and about 50 Defence civilian personnel were deployed. The total net additional cost of operations in Afghanistan during the year was £199M.

THE BALKANS

13. The UK continued to contribute to peace support operations in Bosnia-Herzegovina and Kosovo. The UK commanded the EU military mission in Bosnia (EUFOR) throughout 2005, handing over to Italy in December. The structure of EUFOR remained largely unaltered with 33 contributing nations, 11 of which are non-EU members, and force levels of around 6,300 personnel. Our contribution reduced from 850 to 690 personnel following a force level review. During 2005-06 the NATO Kosovo Force (KFOR) transformed from Multinational Brigades to Multinational Task Forces, providing a more flexible and intelligence-led capability. The UK contribution remained small, falling from around 200 to 180 personnel, but provided a valuable specialist capability able to deploy across the province. We also provided one third of the Operational Reserve Force capability able to deploy to Bosnia and Kosovo. The total net additional cost of operations in the Balkans during the year was £63M.

The Balkans

14. Bosnia's reform programme made significant progress. This included the establishment of a single Ministry of Defence and a single multi-ethnic armed force, and a growing confidence and capacity of the local authorities, assisted by EUFOR when necessary, to recover illegally held weapons, ammunition and explosives and to combat organised crime. Agreement of the principles of police reform enabled the European Union formally to open Stabilisation and Association Agreement negotiations. The international community continued its pursuit of persons indicted for war crimes. Nine fugitives were apprehended, including Ante Gotovina, a former Croation general, but Radovan Karadzic, a former Bosnian Serb leader, and Ratko Mladic, former chief of the Bosnian Serb army, remained at large. We provided some £1M Global Conflict Prevention Pool funds for post-conflict reconstruction through the UK-led Peace Support Operations Training Centre in Bosnia. This provides professional military education for junior officers to encourage common bonds between entities and strengthens the state structure. We also provided training and advice to former soldiers returning to civilian life through the Transitional Assistance to Demobilised Soldiers project.

15. Following the report on the UN Comprehensive Review of Standards, Martti Ahtisaari, a former president of Finland, was appointed to lead the process of talks to determine the future status of Kosovo in November 2005. We continued to support UN work to transform and professionalise the Kosovo Protection Corps, appointing a senior military officer and continuing the successful Train the Trainer demining programme. The MoD Police continued to support the UN Police mission in Kosovo, but the number of officers deployed reduced from around 70 to 55 reflecting the reducing size of the UN police force.

CRISIS RESPONSE OPERATIONS

16. During the year the MoD made significant and wide-ranging contributions to two overseas humanitarian relief operations. In September 2005 we provided 475,000 ration packs for the Hurricane Katrina disaster relief effort (although US environmental regulations prevented their use at that time). Two UK Royal Navy Hydrographic specialists also supplemented the US Coastal Survey Team and we provided aviation support to the NATO Response Force. In October 2005, following the devastating earthquake in South Asia, we provided assistance both bilaterally and through NATO. Three heavy-lift CH-47 Chinook helicopters successfully delivered nearly 1,700 tonnes of aid, flying over 330 hours. We also provided four C-130 Hercules to the NATO airbridge to transport aid into Pakistan (one of these C-130s was not in the event required), and one RAF C-17 aircraft transported two civilian helicopters from Seville to Pakistan. An 86-man party of Royal Engineers (supported by Royal Marines) constructed emergency shelters for villagers in remote areas above 5,500 ft. Further assistance included a two-person Mobile Air Operations Team, a four person Mobile Medical Team, an Operational Reconnaissance Team, four logistics planners deployed to the UN Joint Logistics Centre and various personnel to the Joint Force Air Component Command, and 23,000 vegetarian and Halal ration packs.

UN PEACEKEEPING OPERATIONS

17. The UK remains committed to supporting United Nations (UN) operations and during 2005-06 we contributed to six UN Peacekeeping Missions, in Cyprus, the Democratic Republic of Congo, Georgia, Liberia, Sierra Leone and Sudan. The number of personnel at the UN Mission in Cyprus remained static at about 860 including about 280 personnel from the UK. At 1 April 2006 the number of UK military personnel dedicated to UN Peacekeeping Operations was about 300. This included staff officers (whose specialist skills and experience is highly valued in a range of UN Mission HQ staff appointments) as well as troops, through NATO and the EU, in support of UN-mandated missions.

OTHER MILITARY TASKS

Independent Nuclear Deterrent

18. The UK's Trident submarine force continued to provide a constant and independent nuclear deterrent capability at sea, in support of NATO and as the ultimate guarantee of our national security. A major investment in new facilities and staff at the Atomic Weapons Establishment, Aldermaston, was announced in July 2005. This will ensure that our Trident warheads remain reliable and safe throughout their intended in-service life. Work has also now started to prepare for decisions on the future of the UK's nuclear deterrent beyond the planned life of the current system. These decisions are likely to be necessary during the current Parliament.

Royal Engineers constructing emergency shelters in South Asia

A Chinook delivering humanitarian aid in South Asia

Security of UK Overseas Territories

19. Some 3,900 UK military personnel, together with Defence civil servants and locally employed civilians, continued to be stationed or deployed in support of the security and defence of the UK's Overseas Territories. In Cyprus we maintained important military facilities within the Eastern and Western Sovereign Base Areas. UK Forces in the Falkland Islands continued to demonstrate the Government's commitment to the security of the UK Territories in the South Atlantic, including South Georgia and the South Sandwich Islands. HMS Endurance both maintained British interests in the South Atlantic and Antarctica and helped to police the Antarctic Treaty to preserve the pristine nature of Antarctica. Gibraltar continued to provide a Forward Mounting Base with Gibraltar-based UK Armed Forces providing valuable security, logistics, communications and training facilities in support of operations.

MILITARY AID TO THE CIVIL AUTHORITIES

20. The response to disruptive challenges in the UK will always be a civil one, with the civil authorities taking the lead in dealing with the consequences of emergencies as well as the maintenance of the security of the citizen in the UK. The MoD fully supports enhanced resilience amongst responders, including the statutory duties placed upon them, by the Civil Contingencies Act 2004. Civil capabilities are improving all the time, reflecting investment in new capabilities and the development of more resilient and effective emergency services and local responders. At the same time, the Armed Forces regularly provide a limited number of niche capabilities and, if it proves essential, can augment the civil response, drawing on specialist military skills. The number of requests for support declined markedly in 2005-06, although they tended to increase in complexity. Provision of Explosive Ordnance Disposal support to the police outside London is regular and routine. Specialist capabilities are also deployed in support of criminal investigations and in support of police security operations protecting high profile events. Fairly extensive logistics support was provided to the police security operation protecting the G8 Summit at Gleneagles in July, and in the same month we met in full the requests for logistic and technical support to the Metropolitan Police response to the London bombings. Towards the end of the year, the Armed Forces were deployed to provide emergency fire cover during local fire strikes in Suffolk and the West Midlands. We welcomed the enhancement to resilience within the Fire and Rescue Service: alternative arrangements put in place by the Chief Fire Officer for Suffolk meant that Armed Forces were not actually used during that dispute. In close cooperation with other Government departments, agencies, and air traffic control authorities, the Royal Air Force also continuously provide a continuous immediate air reaction capability ensuring the integrity of UK Airspace at all times.

Northern Ireland

21. 2005-06 was a momentous year for operations in Northern Ireland. The military played a key role, in support of the Police Service of Northern Ireland, in establishing a security situation in which significant progress was made towards achieving an enduring political solution. Following the cessation of the Provisional IRA's armed campaign, the process of Armed Forces Normalisation commenced on 1 August 2005. This will mean the end of Operation BANNER, under which the Armed Forces have provided support to the police in Northern Ireland for over 30 years. The normalisation programme will result in a reduction in troop levels to a standing garrison of no more than 5,000, accommodated in no more than 11 core sites, by 1 August 2007. A further element of the programme, also announced on 1 August 2005, was the disbandment of the three battalions of the Royal Irish (Home Service), who played a critical role throughout the Troubles. In March 2006 the Government announced the terms of a settlement that treats them fairly and with the dignity and respect they deserve. Normalisation progress is being scrutinised by the Independent Monitoring Commission, which reported in March 2006 that significant steps had already been taken towards meeting the required reductions in line with the timeframe laid down in the Joint Declaration. Despite the security improvements,

the threat from dissident Republicans continued; military supported operations focussed on disrupting their activity. The extreme Loyalist violence at Whiterock in Belfast in September 2005 also provided a reminder of the unpredictable nature of violence in Northern Ireland and demonstrated the Armed Forces' riot control capability and the essential support they provide to the Police. Further information on Northern Ireland is set out in the essay on page 67.

Fisheries Protection

22. In 2005-06 the Fishery Protection Squadron, part of the Royal Navy's Portsmouth Flotilla, delivered 855 Fishery Patrol Days to the Marine Fisheries Agency (880 in 2004-05), part of the Department for Environment, Food and Rural Affairs. Of these, 72% were delivered by the River Class Offshore Patrol Vessels, which are demonstrating extremely high levels of availability through the innovative Contractor Logistic Support arrangement provided by Vosper Thorneycroft. A total of 5,025 fishing vessels were identified (5,001 in 2004-05) of which 1,312 were boarded (1,748 in 2004-05), leading to discovery of 290 infringements (123 in 2004-05). Of the vessels boarded, 19 were detained at a UK port for further investigation and prosecution (15 in 2004-05). Although the total number of boardings was substantially down on last year (owing mainly to weather factors) the number of detected infringements more than doubled, demonstrating that the move towards more intelligence-led operations is beginning to be effective.

Search and Rescue

23. The military Search and Rescue service exists to help military personnel and civilian aircrew in difficulty. In practice, most of the work involves assisting shipping or individuals in distress on land and at sea, in and around the UK, in support of the Emergency Services and the Department for Transport's Maritime Coastguard Agency (MCA). RN and RAF helicopters continued to maintain constant Search and Rescue cover within the UK Search and Rescue Region throughout the year, together with the Royal Air Force's Mountain Rescue Service and Nimrod maritime patrol aircraft. The RAF also provided helicopters in Cyprus and the Falkland Islands. The Armed Forces' rescue services were called out on 1,833 occasions in 2005-06 (1,740 in 2004-05), recovering and assisting 1,466 people (1,494 in 2004-05). On 9 May 2006 we announced plans for the MoD and MCA to launch a joint Private Finance Initiative competition to replace the ageing RN and RAF Sea King and MCA civilian Search and Rescue helicopters. The single contract will retain a high proportion of military aircrew, maintain the same high quality service and bring benefits to UK Search and Rescue operations as a whole.

Counter-Drugs Operations

A boarding party from HMS Cumberland seizes 2 tonnes of cocaine in the Caribbean

24. The Armed Forces provided assistance to HM Revenue and Customs and to other anti-narcotics agencies around the world. In particular, RN ships deployed to the Caribbean undertook patrols and joint operations with the US Coast Guard and other international partners. British Forces were directly involved in the seizure of around 14 tonnes of cocaine, with a UK street value of nearly £840 million, and the arrest of 25 traffickers.

ACTIVITY AND CONCURRENCY LEVELS

25. The proportion of regular forces deployed on operations and other military tasks increased from about 18% in the first quarter of 2005-06 (including about 21% of the Army), to just under 20% in the last quarter of the year (including about 25% of the Army). Figure 2 sets out the annual average activity level by Service for the last five years.

Figure 2: Percentage of Regular Armed Forces Undertaking Operations and other Military Tasks

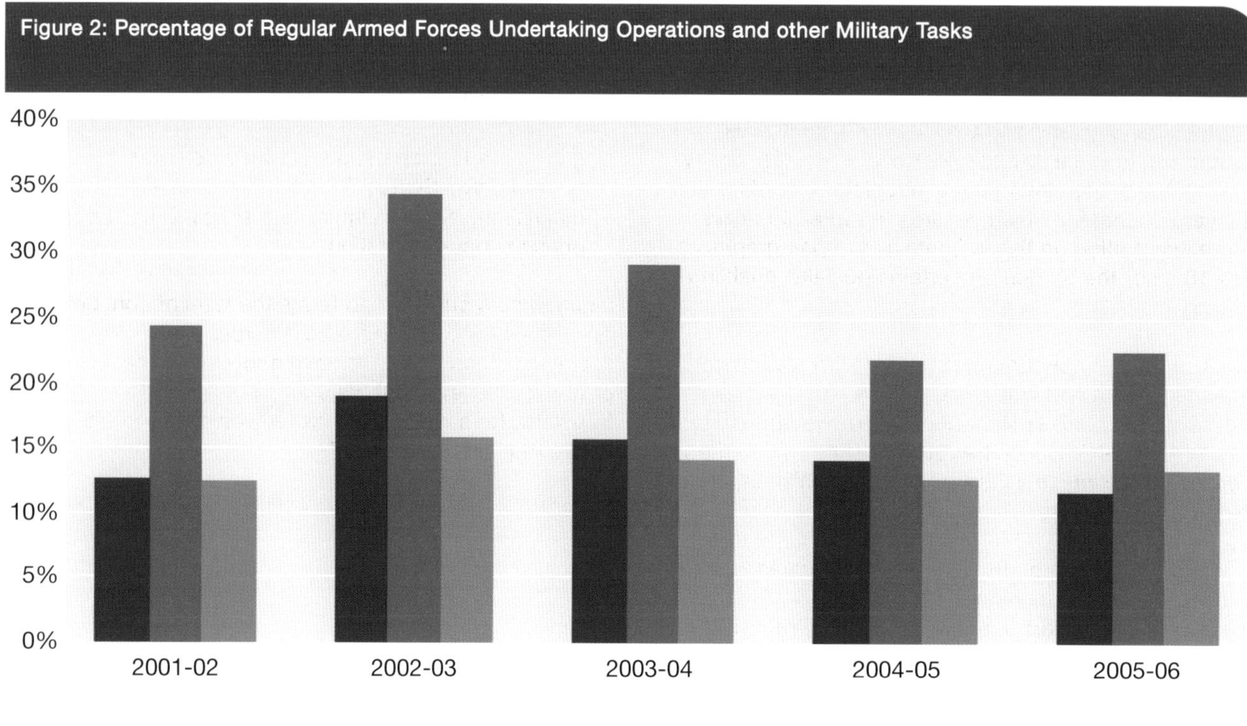

26. During the year, the Royal Navy maintained the Continuous at Sea Deterrent and a continuous presence in the Gulf and the South Atlantic, and carried out patrols in the Indian Ocean and the Caribbean. Royal Marines from 42 Commando deployed to Pakistan to provide humanitarian relief, and to Helmand province in Afghanistan. The Royal Navy also conducted a Five Powers Defence Arrangements deployment in South East Asia. At home, the Royal Navy helped to maintain the integrity of UK territorial waters and economic zones. The Royal Navy also provided a major contribution to the commemoration of the 200th anniversary of the Battle of Trafalgar. The overall percentage of Naval Service personnel deployed on operations throughout 2005-2006 ranged from 11.6% in Quarter 1 to 13.5% in Quarter 4.

27. The overall percentage of Army personnel committed to operations throughout 2005-2006 grew from 21.0% in Quarter 1 to 25.1% in Quarter 4, although some arms were much busier than others (see paragraph 181). The Army deployed troops on operations in Iraq, Afghanistan, Northern Ireland, Bosnia, Kosovo and Sierra Leone and supported a variety of worldwide UN operations (including Cyprus). In addition, the Army has been involved in several UK operations, including providing ongoing support to Global Counter Terrorism and provided earthquake relief in Pakistan.

28. The percentage of Royal Air Force personnel deployed on operations during 2005-06 ranged from 13.3% in the first quarter to 13.4% in the fourth quarter. The Royal Air Force's primary areas of overseas involvement continued to be the Gulf, Afghanistan and the Balkans. The Royal Air Force also contributed to the permanent British Forces commitments in Northern Ireland and the Falkland Islands, in addition to a range of other ongoing Military Tasks.

Table 1: Percentage of Regular Armed Forces undertaking Operations and other Military Tasks during 2005-06

	January 2006 to March 2006	October 2005 to December 2005	July 2005 to September 2005	April 2005 to June 2005
Navy/Marines	13.5%	12.1%	9.3%	11.6%
Army	25.1%	22.8%	22.0%	21.0%
RAF	13.4%	12.3%	11.9%	13.3%
Overall	**19.8%**	**18.7%**	**17.5%**	**18.0%**

Notes:
1. Percentages are quarterly averages and reflect the burden of activity imposed by the operations and military tasks undertaken by each service. Figures are based on man-day equivalents.
2. A list of Military Tasks can be found on the Department's website (www.mod.uk).

29. These activity level figures show, in percentage terms, the overall burden of the activity required to conduct the operations and military tasks undertaken by each service. They indicate a level of activity that can be compared to previous periods, and show how activity fluctuates throughout the year, but the figures themselves neither fully articulate the effect on our people of operating at a level above that for which we are structured to deliver (more information on this is contained in paragraphs 180-182) nor the burden on certain specialist enabling capabilities.

30. The level of concurrent operations we plan to be able to conduct and which we are resourced to have the capacity to deliver without creating overstretch, was set out in the December 2003 Defence White Paper *Delivering Security in a Changing World*. This stated that we should be able to:

- mount an enduring Medium Scale (MS) peace support operation simultaneously with an enduring Small Scale (SS) peace support operation and a one-off Small Scale intervention operation;
- reconfigure our forces rapidly to carry out the enduring Medium Scale peace support operation and a Small Scale peace support operation simultaneously with a limited Medium Scale intervention operation; and,
- given time to prepare, undertake a demanding one-off Large Scale (LS) operation while still maintaining a commitment to a simple Small Scale peace support operation.

Figure 3 sets out in broad terms the level of concurrent operations the MoD and Armed Forces have in fact sustained since 1999. We have operated at the limits of, or above, the level that we are resourced and structured to deliver, for six of the last seven years, and consistently above that level since 2002.

Figure 3: Concurrency 1999-2005

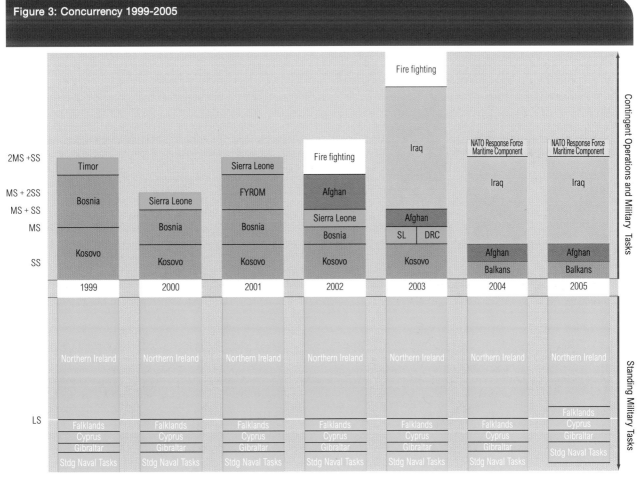

SS, MS and LS stand for Small, Medium and Large Scale Operations

FURTHER SOURCES OF INFORMATION

31. Additional information on Current Operations is available from the following sources:
- quarterly PSA reports to HM Treasury at www.mod.uk;
- *UK Defence Statistics 2006* available at www.dasa.mod.uk (from September 2006);
- detailed information on current operations at www.operations.mod.uk;
- NAO Report *Ministry of Defence Reserve Forces* HC 964 dated 28 March 06 available at www.nao.org.uk;
- Cost of Operations at paragraph 260 and the analysis of Conflict Prevention costs at Note 2 to the accounts on page 200.
- the Defence Committee Sixth Report of Session 2004–05 on *Iraq: An Initial Assessment of Post Conflict Operations* (HC 65-I on 24 March 2005) available at www.parliament.the-stationery-office.co.uk;
- *The Government's response to The Defence Committee Sixth Report of Session 2004–05 on Iraq: An Initial Assessment of Post Conflict Operations* (HC436 on 20 July 05) available at www.mod.uk;
- information on the Afghanistan Compact at www.fco.gov.uk;
- the Defence Committee Fourth Report of Session 2005-06 on *Costs of peace-keeping in Iraq and Afghanistan: Spring Supplementary Estimates 2005-06* (HC 980 on 16 March 2006) available at www.parliament.the-stationery-office.co.uk;
- *The Government's response to The Defence Committee Fourth Report of Session 2005-06 on Costs of peace-keeping in Iraq and Afghanistan: Spring Supplementary Estimates 2005-06* (HC1136);
- the Defence Committee Fifth Report of Session 2005-06 on *The UK Deployment to Afghanistan* (HC558 on 6 April 2006);
- Defence White Paper *Delivering Security in a Changing World,* (Cm 6041-I in December 2003) available at www.mod.uk.

Essay: Iraq – Reconstruction and Security Sector Reform

Under the terms of United Nations Security Council Resolution 1637, and as part of the coalition in Iraq, the United Kingdom is committed to helping the Iraqi people and their elected representatives establish a free, democratic and unified Iraq. As part of this commitment, the MoD is contributing to rebuilding the Iraqi Security Forces and delivering a security environment in support of wider economic and political progress. Iraq's infrastructure and public services have degraded over many years through mismanagement and neglect. Our Armed Forces provide the basic security that enables stabilisation, reconstruction and recovery. Their wider logistics, personnel, medical and project management support underpins all UK government activity in Iraq.

Within the UK's area of responsibility – which is known as Multi-National Division (South East), and covers 4 provinces in Southern Iraq – we have established strong and effective working relationships with the Department for International Development (DFID), the Foreign and Commonwealth Office (FCO), and Iraqi colleagues, to deliver Security Sector Reform and other development, reconstruction and capacity building efforts. We are strengthening our joined-up approach through the establishment of a Provincial Reconstruction Team located in Basra. Basra is Iraq's second largest city with a population of over 1.5 million and this joint civilian and military team will help the provincial authorities develop their capability and capacity in a range of areas including rule of law, governance and provincial administration. It will also play an important role in coordinating a framework of donors and agencies working in the province.

The main Defence contribution to security sector reform is the training and mentoring of the 10th (Southern) Division of the Iraqi Army. The Divisional Headquarters is established next to the UK's military headquarters in Basra to facilitate direct mentoring of the Divisional Headquarters Staff. We also provide mentors to all the Iraqi Army Brigade Headquarters in MND(SE). UK forces train the Iraqi Army, in barracks and on joint operations. By 31 March 2006, 8 out of 10 battalions of the 10th Division of the Iraqi Army had been formed and completed basic training. We aim to develop capability rather than just raw numbers, and are therefore also working to develop Iraqi leadership, command and control, intelligence and logistics capacities. These are essential for the Iraqi Armed Forces to operate independently and to provide security to their own people.

DFID is the lead department for UK reconstruction efforts in Iraq and building the capacity of the local government. We work closely with DFID to achieve greater effect and to benefit more Iraqis than would otherwise have been the case. UK military personnel, with their greater ability to move freely and quickly and their expertise in project management and logistics, complement DFID's technical expertise in governance. An example of this joined up working is the refurbishment of the Basra Provincial Council building. DFID received the request for the refurbishment project and provided the funding, and the Armed Forces provided project management and security expertise. This gave our Service personnel visibility within the local community and demonstrated their commitment to supporting Iraq's reconstruction and to improving security. MoD has also contributed funding to a number of quick impact reconstruction projects such as road and bridge building and repair, provision of clean water supplies for isolated villages, school refurbishment, provision of a centre for the disabled, and construction of children's play areas. These projects often involve the Iraqis themselves and are key to winning the hearts and minds of local people.

Stable society rests upon the rule of law, a crucial component of which is an effective police force. We work closely with the FCO on the UK programme to train over 25,000 Iraqi Police officers. Some 16,000 had been trained by 31 March 2006. The FCO has organised provision of over 120 civilian police advisors, including International Police Advisors and seconded UK civilian police officers, to train and mentor the Iraqi police. Defence is contributing significant resources to this programme. We have provided officers from the MoD Police Force and our Armed Forces work alongside the police advisors in theatre to provide basic skills training. We will continue providing this resource until the Iraqi authorities are able to take on responsibility for security themselves.

FUTURE OPERATIONS

Objective: Be ready for the tasks of tomorrow.

Public Service Agreement Target (SR2004 MoD Target 3)

Generate forces which can be deployed, sustained and recovered at the scales of effort required to meet the government's strategic objectives.

Performance Measures and Assessment

- **The National Audit Office found that the Department has a good system for reporting the readiness levels of the Armed Forces.**

Military Capability – by April 2008 achieve 73% in the numbers of Force Elements reporting no serious or critical weakness against peacetime readiness targets:

- **An average of 77% of Force Elements reported no critical or serious weaknesses in 2005-06;**
- **No Force Elements reported critical weaknesses from April to December 2005. 2% reported critical weaknesses from January to March 2006;**
- **The proportion of Force Elements reporting serious weaknesses increased from 25% in the first quarter to 26% in the last quarter of the year.**

Force Generation – by April 2008 achieve 71% of Force Elements reporting no serious or critical weakness against the assessed ability to move from peacetime to immediate readiness:

- **An average of 70% of Force Elements reported no critical or serious weaknesses in 2005-06;**
- **The proportion of Force Elements reporting critical weaknesses rose from 1% in the first quarter to 11% in the last quarter of the year;**
- **The proportion of Force Elements reporting serious weaknesses increased from 30% in the first quarter to 39% in the last quarter of the year.**

Force Sustainability – by April 2008 achieve 5% improvement in the ability to Deploy, Sustain and Recover forces for Contingent Military Tasks against the most demanding concurrency assumptions in Defence Planning Assumptions:

- **We are developing a system of assessment to report against this target. It is likely that performance will be lower than for the other two readiness measures.**

READINESS

32. We use a system of graduated readiness to ensure that the right Force Elements (such as an Aircraft Carrier, an Army Brigade or an aircraft) are ready to deploy as required. Measuring and aggregating readiness is complex. To achieve peacetime readiness requirements the three Services are each set specific parameters for manning levels, equipment support and collective training (that is the training units do together to ensure they can fight effectively as part of a larger force). Inevitably, however, while the operational tempo remains above the level which Defence is resourced to have the capacity to sustain, there is an impact on our ability to take on further commitments.

Performance against PSA Targets

33. Despite operating above our planning assumptions, by the end of the year we had achieved the Public Service Agreement target for readiness set out in the 2004 Spending Review. This is measured against peacetime readiness requirements, which require us to have our forces ready to respond to events in line with the levels envisaged in our planning assumptions. Between January 2005 and December 2005 no Force Elements reported critical weaknesses that would have made their deployment on operations in the required timescale almost impossible. However during the last quarter of the year 2% of Force Elements reported critical weaknesses relating to Royal Navy Readiness as detailed in paragraph 39. The proportion of Force Elements reporting serious weaknesses that would make deploying them within the required time difficult but not impossible increased from 25% in the first quarter to 26% in the fourth quarter. Over the year as a whole an average of 77% of Force Elements reported no critical or serious weaknesses in achieving their peacetime readiness – achieving our PSA target of 73% two years early. Despite this, the percentage of force elements still reporting serious weaknesses remains significant and it will be difficult to maintain this level of performance with our continuing high operational tempo.

Figure 4: Peacetime readiness

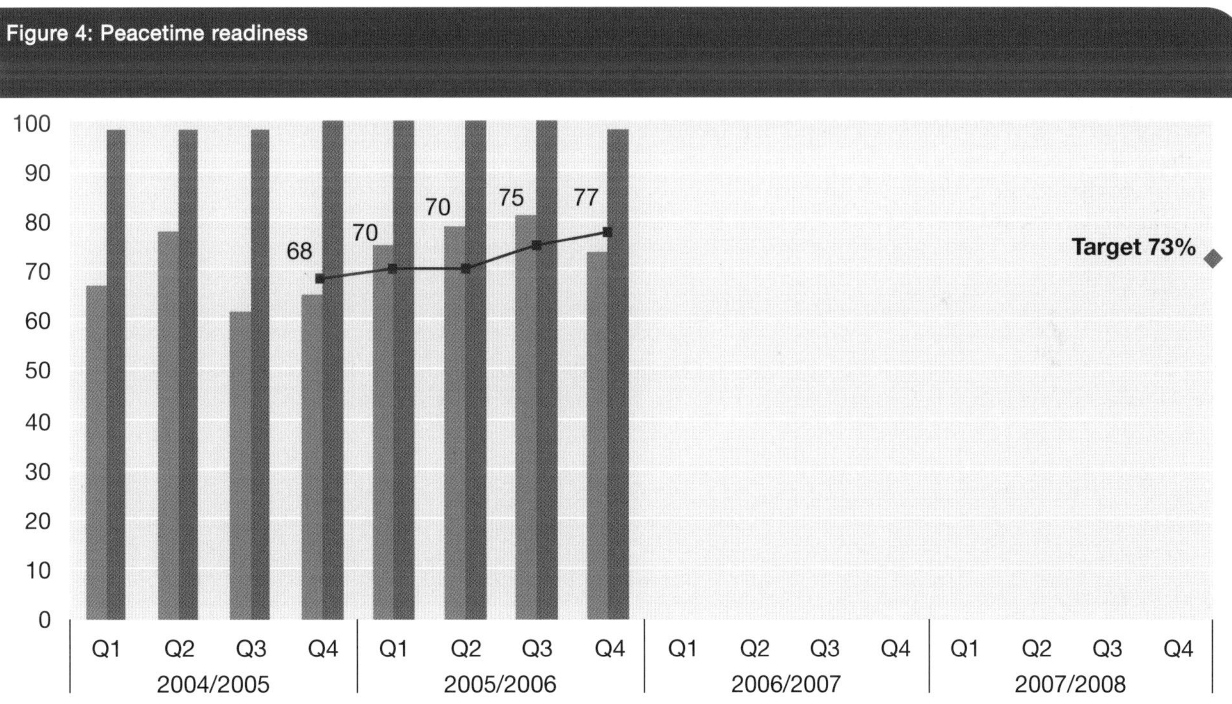

34. Under the PSA Readiness Target we also report on our ability to generate force elements from peacetime to immediate readiness, with a target of a 5% improvement to 71% reporting no serious or critical weaknesses by April 2008. Over 2005-06 an average of 70% of Force Elements reported no serious or critical weaknesses – slightly below the target. The slightly lower level of performance than that achieved for peacetime readiness reflects the pressure on the Armed Services resulting from operating above the Defence Planning Assumptions and concerns arising from our collective training (see paragraph 44-45).

35. Finally, the PSA Target requires us to report our ability to deploy the Armed Forces on operations at the most demanding level assumed by our planning assumptions (2 medium and a small scale concurrently), sustain them in theatre and thereafter recover them to their home bases. We have found that measuring this capability in the same way to the other readiness targets has proved significantly more complex than we had expected when negotiating this target in the 2004 Spending Review.

36. Although we are yet to articulate this capability in the same quantitative way as other measures of our readiness, we do make regular qualitative assessments. There have been some minor improvements this year, in terms of our assessed ability to support some Force Elements, in the Land environment and in terms of our assessed ability to deploy Force Elements, which we call strategic lift. This remains a particularly challenging area, reflecting the considerable calls made on the enabling assets that allow us to deploy, sustain and recover the full range of our force elements.

37. We are conducting ongoing work to develop a system of assessment that will allow us to report against this target in a way consistent with how the other elements of readiness are reported, including historical performance across the Spending Review period measured against consistent baseline information for 2004-05. To support this requirement the ongoing Logistic Sustainability and Deployability Audit has sought, explicitly, to articulate for the first time the Total Logistic Requirement and to reach judgements about what might be made available within the relevant warning times in order to support operations up to the most demanding level envisaged in Defence Planning Assumptions. This audit provided an updated assessment of sustainability and in so doing has provided the foundation for the articulation of the requirement in output terms. In future this will allow us to report our ability to deploy the Armed Forces on operations at the most demanding level assumed by Defence Planning assumptions in a way which is analogous to Force Elements at Readiness.

38. In June 2005 the National Audit Office (NAO) published a report on *Assessing and Reporting Military Readiness*. The NAO found that the Department has a good system for reporting the readiness levels of the Armed Forces, that this system is continuously improving,

Figure 5: Assessed ability to generate force elements from peacetime to immediate readiness

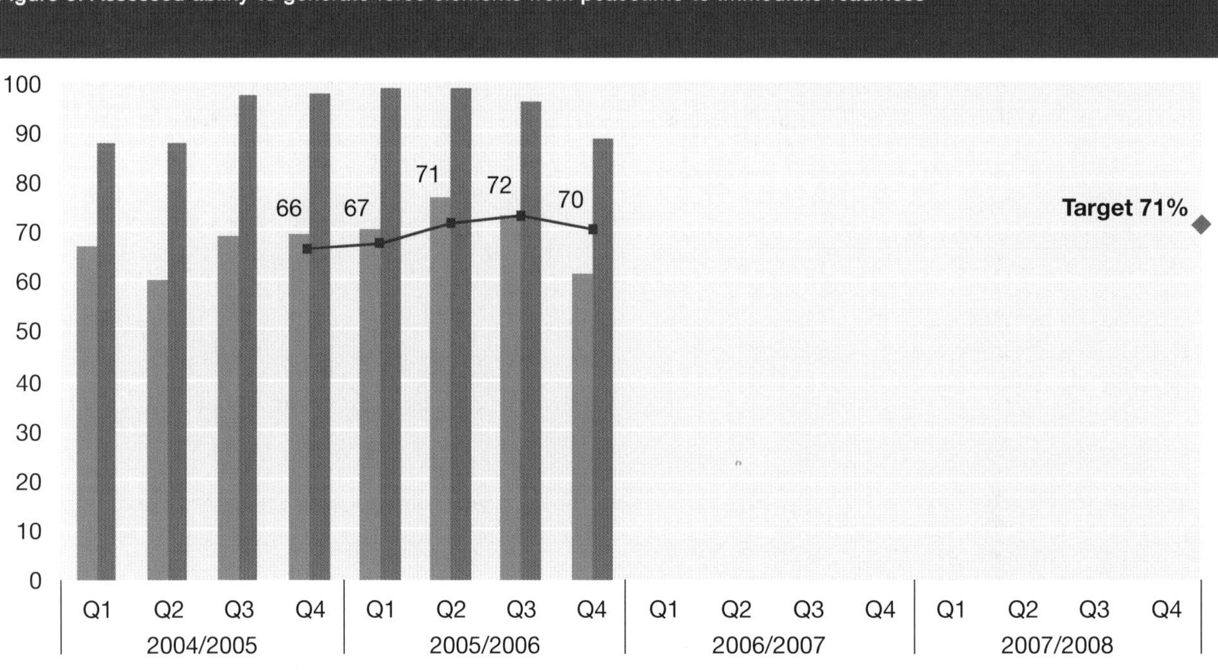

that it is used by commanders who have expressed confidence in it, that it has been validated by recent operations, and that it compares well with the systems used by other countries. The Public Accounts Committee then conducted a further enquiry into military readiness, publishing its report in January 2006. It also concluded that Department has developed a sophisticated system for defining, measuring, and reporting the readiness of the Armed Forces and made a few specific recommendations, which the Government acknowledged in its formal response in April.

Royal Navy Readiness

39. The Royal Navy met all its operational commitments within Home waters and overseas during 2005-06, maintaining a permanent presence in the Gulf, the Atlantic and within NATO's standing forces as well as sustaining the national strategic deterrent. However, while the Royal Navy broadly continued to meet mandated readiness targets, the combination of a few critical specialist manpower shortages, difficulties with logistic support and industrial challenges did impact, in some areas, on overall readiness states. These were manifested towards the end of the year in Merlin Mk1 Helicopter Fleet readiness and availability of amphibious support shipping. Work is in hand to address these and other support issues to ensure the Royal Navy is ready in all respects to respond to the operational demands placed upon it.

Army Readiness

40. The Army remained heavily committed to operations throughout the year. It successfully delivered trained and prepared Force Elements for all UK and overseas operations, but this high level of commitment meant that it could only maintain the Spearhead Land Element of the Joint Rapid Reaction Forces at very high readiness for all of the year, and the Airborne Task Force for only 75% of the year. The continued high level of operational commitment in Iraq and Afghanistan and the simultaneous programme to bring the Bowman communications system into service in the Field Army would have very substantially limited the Army's ability to provide a further High Readiness Brigade sized grouping to the Joint Rapid Reaction Forces second echelon for any additional contingent operation had this been required.

Soldiers storming a beach on exercise

Royal Air Force Readiness

41. The Royal Air Force continued to meet its out of area commitments and enduring Military Tasks in 2005-06, contributing forces to a number of theatres around the world including the Gulf, Northern Ireland, South Atlantic, Afghanistan and the Balkans. However, the readiness levels of some Force Elements (such as Hercules and Nimrod MR2) were slightly lower than required owing to modification and maintenance programmes, spells of poor serviceability and specific manning imbalances.

JOINT RAPID REACTION FORCES

42. The Joint Rapid Reaction Forces (JRRF) provide a pool of capable and rapidly deployable Force Elements, trained and available for short notice deployments in support of Britain's foreign and security policy objectives. The JRRF planning requirement is to meet the concurrency levels set out in paragraph 30. It operated above these levels throughout the year, and the expansion of operations in Afghanistan whilst maintaining a high level of commitment in Iraq was particularly stretching. The Land component has been under particular pressure, with personnel deployed in Afghanistan, Iraq and the Balkans. This would have severely constrained its ability to support any further short notice deployments had these been required. Other JRRF force elements, such as the Spearhead air assets, have also been heavily committed to current operations and therefore been unavailable to the JRRF pool.

16 Air Assault Brigade on exercise

43. The Joint Force Headquarters (JFHQ), which provides the standing operational headquarters to form the nucleus of a UK response to emerging crises, also maintained a high tempo of operational and training activity over the year. Operational activity included assistance to UK Embassies in the preparation of evacuation plans, and assistance to an EU Headquarters in Indonesia. Elements from the JFHQ deployed to Afghanistan to commence early UK shaping operations within Helmand province. There have been varying degrees of engagement in Africa, with staff assisting in the United Nations / African Union transition planning in Sudan and a full JFHQ Exercise in Malawi. The training programme included

several larger force projection and planning exercises, such as a combined exercise with the Norwegian Armed Forces and a Peace Enforcement exercise drawing on wider expertise from other Government Departments and the newly-created Post Conflict Reconstruction Unit. The Joint Force Logistics Command HQ, the Permanent Joint Operating Bases in Gibraltar and the Falkland Islands, and the Joint Task Force HQ have also all been exercised in a variety of scenarios to hone their command and control skills, as well as to develop war-fighting doctrine.

COLLECTIVE TRAINING

44. The continued pressure of operational commitments, the impact of increased fuel prices and the prioritisation of operational requirements in the Department's financial planning limited the scope for joint and combined training for contingent tasks during the year. Although the number of exercises cancelled fell from 20% in 2004-05 to 14% in 2005-06, less collective training was conducted than was necessary to support maintenance of the full contingent capability called for by the planning assumptions underlying the Department's readiness targets. Forces received the specific training and preparation they required for current operations, but there was insufficient capacity, especially in the Army, to do much more. These constraints, and the focus on deployment specific training, mean that significant improvement will not be possible until commitments return to the levels within Defence planning assumptions. At that point there will then be a further period for the necessary training to take place before a full contingent capability is restored.

45. Despite these pressures, we continued to work to improve the efficiency and effectiveness of collective training. In order to coordinate better the training required to achieve more efficient delivery of Force Elements a Joint Training and Exercise Working Group was formed during the year. This also increased the effectiveness of lower-tier joint training. Improvements were also made to the arrangements for air integration in land operations. The Joint Warfare Development and Training Centre was established at PJHQ to train potential joint force commanders and their staffs on scheduled and bespoke courses. Greater involvement of other Government Departments, particularly at the planning stage of exercises, increases the realism of training for potential operations. Exercises during the year therefore also featured improved inter-agency interoperability and more cohesive arrangements with other Government Departments.

46. Work continued to develop a new Defence Training and Exercise Strategy, informed by the results of the Directorate of Operational Capability's audit of collective training during the year and the definition of the detailed requirement for UK Joint Collective Training in order to guide near term capability growth. This strategy will produce a fully coherent and synchronised exercise programme to restore a balanced contingent capability once the level of operational commitments reduces. The focus will be on joint, combined and fully integrated training for operations that involves all components of capability and synchronises military effect with the efforts of other Government Departments and other agencies.

SUSTAINABILITY AND DEPLOYABILITY

47. The Armed Forces were successfully deployed and sustained on a wide range of military and humanitarian relief operations during the year. The net additional costs incurred to deploy, sustain and subsequently recover forces on operations are met from the central Government reserve. We continue to look for ways to increase the effectiveness of our sustainability and deployability processes, including the development of how we prepare for specific operational deployments. Resources are focused on providing those assets most likely to be needed to sustain operations or that we judge could not be bought within assumed readiness times. Given the stretching range of operations being sustained the UK has joined several multinational strategic lift initiatives to improve our ability to prepare, mount and deploy appropriate personnel and equipment. This includes the Strategic Airlift Interim Solution from January 2006 (see paragraph 51).

FURTHER SOURCES OF INFORMATION

48. Additional Information on Future Operations is available from the following sources:
- Defence White Paper *Delivering Security in a Changing World,* December 2003;
- quarterly SR2004 Public Service Agreement reports; to HM Treasury at www.mod.uk;
- SR2004 PSA Technical Notes at www.mod.uk;
- NAO Report *Assessing and Reporting Military Readiness*; (HC 72 on 15 June 2005) available at www.nao.org.uk;
- The PAC twenty-sixth report of Session 2005-06: *Assessing and Reporting Military Readiness* (HC 667 on 30 January 2006) available at www.publications.parliament.uk;
- *The Government's response to the PAC twenty-sixth report of Session 2005-06: Assessing and Reporting Military Readiness* (Cm 6775 on 30 January 2006) available at www.publications.parliament.uk.

Essay: Delivering readiness at the Front Line

The delivery and reporting of readiness is a complex subject. To give this some context this essay sets out what this means in practice for a front line light infantry battalion. A light role infantry battalion fights on foot using light, man-portable weapons, and is supported by a small fleet of wheeled vehicles. On operations it might be used on any of a full range of tasks, from peace support to high intensity warfighting, including complex activities such as Security Sector Reform. Light battalions provide the Army's main quick-reaction, high-readiness unit, known as the Spearhead battalion.

What does it involve? When a Spearhead battalion is ordered to deploy, its headquarters, lead company and logistic enablers have to be able to deploy from their barracks within 24 hours of receiving the order. The rest of the battalion, and any attached assets such as artillery, engineer and signals units, must be able to follow within a further 24 hours. A deployment can be anything from a few days to six months. Experience shows that a battalion may sometimes deploy even quicker than this and engage in operations on arrival. For example, when the 1st Battalion of the Royal Gloucestershire, Berkshire and Wiltshire Regiment deployed to Kosovo in March 2005, the majority of the Battalion arrived in theatre within 48 hours of being ordered to go.

How is it achieved? Most light role infantry battalions rightly claim they maintain a routinely high state of readiness; their ethos demands it. But more is required to reach the level of readiness required of the Spearhead battalion. In particular, it must be fully equipped, including specialist equipment, and hold three days worth of combat supplies to hand. Further supplies and theatre specific equipment will be issued when it is ordered to deploy. At the moment one of the biggest difficulties to be overcome is, in fact, driver training: light role infantry battalions are likely to deploy with specialist armoured Land Rovers; these require a Heavy Goods Vehicle licence, and it takes time and resources to train and qualify enough drivers. The full force with its supporting elements (such as artillery and engineers) must also be exercised as a whole by an external organisation or higher headquarters. For example, in 2004-05, HQ 52 Infantry Brigade controlled Exercise GRAND PRIX in Belize to prepare the Spearhead Battalion's main force by exercising the full battlegroup (at that time the 2nd Battalion the Light Infantry, together with attached Royal Artillery, Royal Engineer and Army Air Corps assets) across a range of operational scenarios from peace support to high intensity conflict, from planning through to execution.

How is it measured? The Army's operational headquarters has a well developed methodology linking resources to activity and output, which it uses to design, validate and measure training. In preparation for a Spearhead battalion commitment, the battalion's commanding officer uses this methodology to validate the battalion's performance and readiness, and then uses it to assess and report the level of readiness he is achieving and to identify any shortfalls at least every three months.

How is it maintained? Maintaining the highest readiness levels required of a Spearhead battalion is not easy. Equipment and supplies can be kept up to the necessary establishment relatively simply but the readiness of the soldiers, individually and collectively, inevitably declines unless active measures are taken to maintain it. The value of collective training diminishes over time, individual skills fade rapidly if not practised continually and administrative matters, such as passports, vaccinations and Next of Kin documentation, require constant refreshment (including keeping up with the constant inflow and outflow of personnel). A number of measures are taken to mitigate this potential 'readiness-fade', as battalions are unlikely to participate in a high-value overseas training exercise more often than once every 2 – 2½ years. Sub-unit exercises are run throughout the period of the Spearhead commitment, a Combined Arms Staff Trainer exercise is conducted to train and test the battalion headquarters staff and weekly company training programmes are scrutinised by the Battalion Headquarters to ensure meaningful, focussed training is undertaken on a regular basis. Finally, the Lead Company role is rotated between companies every month. This enables the Battalion Headquarters to 'call-out' the Lead Company, thus regularly auditing the companies' (and the battalion headquarters') abilities to deploy in the required timelines and with the correct equipment and documentation.

POLICY

Objective: Work with Allies, other governments and multilateral institutions to provide a security framework that matches new threats and instabilities.

Public Service Agreement Targets (SR2004 MoD Targets 2 and 5):

By 2007-08, deliver improved effectiveness of UK and international support for conflict prevention, through addressing long-term structural causes of conflict, managing regional and national tension and violence, and supporting post-conflict reconstruction, where the UK can make a significant contribution, in particular Africa, Asia, the Balkans and the Middle East. (Joint target with DFID and FCO);

Play a leading role in the development of the European Security agenda, and enhance capabilities to undertake timely and effective security operations, by successfully encouraging a more efficient and effective NATO, a more coherent and effective European Security and Defence Policy operating in strategic partnership with NATO, and enhanced European defence capabilities. (Joint Target with FCO)

Performance Measures and Assessment

A more efficient and effective NATO:

- **Expanded NATO commitment to Afghanistan;**
- **NATO training mission for Iraq;**
- **Progress towards achievement of NATO Response Force full operational capability and deployment of NATO Response Force elements to Pakistan for earthquake relief;**
- **NATO Agreement of Comprehensive Political Guidance for planning staffs.**

A more coherent and effective ESDP operating in strategic partnership with NATO:

- **Achievement of UK EU Presidency ESDP goals;**
- **EUFOR mission to Bosnia under UK command;**
- **Expansion of ESDP operations.**

Enhanced European defence capabilities:

- **Further development of European Defence Agency;**
- **Implementation of EU Battlegroups complementary to NATO Response Force.**

Implement Global Counter Terrorism strategy:

- **Provision of training to build the counter terrorist capacity of other nations.**

Counter the threat from Weapons of Mass Destruction:

- **Continued contribution to UK arms and export control policy and implementation, including work on verification of nuclear disarmament and assistance to destruction of Russian chemical weapons;**
- **Comprehensive programme of CBRN defence with a strong emphasis on force protection measures;**
- **Continued work with US and NATO on missile defence.**

Effective international and UK conflict prevention initiatives:

- **Security sector reform assistance in areas where UK forces are engaged, including training Iraqi Security Forces and the Afghan National Army;**
- **Support to development of deployable international peacekeeping capabilities.**

Effective international and UK conflict management initiatives:

- **Continued support of UN peacekeeping operations and capabilities;**
- **Work to develop operational capability of Post Conflict Reconstruction Unit.**

49. The maintenance of the transatlantic relationship and the security and stability of Europe are fundamental to our security and Defence policy, and we are a leading contributor to NATO and European Union security and Defence arrangements. But our security and prosperity depend also on wider international stability, freedom and stable economic development. As a permanent member of the UN Security Council, the United Kingdom strives internationally to support the rule of law and act as a force for good. We are working to address the threat posed by international terrorism and to counter the threat from weapons of mass destruction. We are also committed to tackling international conflict and its causes, to mitigate the effects of conflict when it breaks out, and to assist in the task of post-conflict reconstruction.

British soldiers and a German helicopter contributing to NATO relief efforts in Pakistan

NATO AND EUROPEAN SECURITY

North Atlantic Treaty Organisation (NATO): more efficient and effective

50. Throughout 2005-06 the UK continued to support NATO operations and missions. We assigned forces to Operation ACTIVE ENDEAVOUR (a maritime counter-terrorism operation in the Mediterranean) and to NATO's Training Mission in Iraq (training and mentoring Iraqi security personnel at NATO colleges and the Iraqi Staff College). We were also fully committed to the NATO mission in Afghanistan (see paragraphs 8-12). The year saw progress on NATO's transformation agenda, working towards the goal of Full Operational Capability of the NATO Response Force (NRF) by October 2006. We took forward a number of supporting policies during the year, including: aspects of Common Funding for strategic lift; for training; logistics command and control; development of three Deployable Joint Task Force Headquarters implementation of an Operational Preparation Directorate at Lisbon; establishment of an Intelligence Fusion Centre at RAF Molesworth; and Deployable Communications and Information Systems. The UK was a leading force contributor to the NRF. We commanded the Maritime Component in the first half of 2005, made a major contribution to the Air Component Command in the second half of 2005 (during which NATO deployed elements of the NRF, including RAF aircraft and personnel, to support international humanitarian relief work in Pakistan following the South Asian earthquake), and commanded both the Land and Air Components in the first half of 2006. However, engagement on all NATO Response Force rotations has been limited. Further work to build consensus on the way ahead may be needed, which could lead to a review of aspects of the underpinning concept.

51. There were improvements in the management of the Alliance. NATO Ministers agreed Comprehensive Political Guidance for planning staffs and follow-on work continues to articulate Military Committee guidance. We supported the Secretary-General's efforts to make NATO more efficient and effective, for example through better management of resources and reform of the NATO HQ. In August 2005, NATO agreed transition arrangements for introduction of a more equitable cost-share of NATO's common funding, even though Ministers were not able to agree a cost-sharing mechanism. Problems remain with force generation and the provision of key enablers for both NATO and EU missions. However, as a pragmatic interim approach we supported the Strategic Airlift Interim Solution. Under this arrangement 16 NATO and EU nations, including the UK, can call upon a number of large Russian and Ukrainian transport aircraft pending entry into service of Airbus A400M. We continued to support NATO's Usability Initiative, to increase the deployable and usable forces for international operations. Against NATO targets of 40% of Land Forces structured, prepared and equipped for deployed operations and 8% undertaking or planning for such operations, the UK has declared 56% and 17.3% respectively. But reluctance by some Allies to provide consistent data is limiting the Initiative's value.

European Security and Defence Policy: more coherent and effective

52. The UK continued to take a leading role in the development of European Security and Defence Policy (ESDP), and a key objective of our Presidency of the EU was to make ESDP more active, more capable, and more coherent. All our key delivery objectives were achieved. Further detail on the UK Presidency is contained in the essay on page 51. Work continued under the Austrian Presidency on the effective management of operations, using a collaborative approach to civil-military co-ordination, and on developing a long-term vision that sets out the context and conduct of military operations in 2020 and beyond, in order to identify the capabilities that Europe might need within the existing policy framework.

53. Increasingly the EU works with other organisations, such as NATO, the UN and the African Union, to improve global security. Substantial progress was made in developing European operational capabilities across the military, civilian and joint civilian-military spectrum. The largest EU operation is the 6,300-strong Operation ALTHEA (EUFOR) in Bosnia (see paragraph 13). This has proved the practical effectiveness of Berlin Plus arrangements, through a constructive relationship with the residual NATO presence, although NATO/EU cooperation remains a challenge at the political level. Other EU operations included a monitoring mission in Aceh in Indonesia, assistance to opening the Gaza-Egypt border at Rafah, missions to support the rule of law in Iraq and Palestine, support to the African Union in Darfur and Security Sector Reform in the Democratic Republic of Congo. The diversity of these operations underlined the EU's unique ability to deploy a range of military and civilian instruments to undertake tasks from security and stabilisation, to monitoring and mentoring of indigenous police forces, to training judiciary, border monitoring and tackling organised crime. The UK contributed to all but one of these missions.

Enhanced European Defence capabilities

54. ESDP has acted as a catalyst for many of our European partners to improve their rapidly deployable capability, through reform of their Armed Forces and political changes. The UK is committed to developing more rapidly deployable, sustainable and interoperable European capabilities. We recently launched a coherent strategic EU/NATO airlift initiative to identify European airlift shortfalls and preferred options in the short to medium term. We supported the European Defence Agency in its remit to identify common capability gaps and facilitate co-operation by groups of member-states in identifying and pursuing solutions. The Agency has a key role in elaboration of the Headline Goal 2010 and other continuing capability improvement initiatives, and we supported proposals for it to take forward the assessment and evaluation of member states' EU defence contributions. Agreement was reached on a UK-inspired Code of Conduct to open up the European defence equipment market.

55. Work to implement EU Battlegroups continued. EU member states have now committed a total of 19 Battlegroups to the EU rapid response capability, and 26 countries (including Norway and Turkey) contribute to the EU's battlegroup roster. The UK provides one national Battlegroup and one joint Battlegroup with the Netherlands. Together with a French Battlegroup we provided the EU's rapid reaction capability from January to June 2005. We worked to ensure mutual reinforcement and transparency between EU Battlegroups and the NRF (for example, by using NRF standards and criteria for the Battlegroups and harmonising planning timelines).

European Confidence and Security Building: Conventional Arms Control

56. Conventional arms control activities such as inspections, evaluations and confidence and security building measures continued to contribute to conflict prevention and stability across the Organisation for Security and Co-operation in Europe (OSCE) area. Under the terms of three key treaties (Conventional Armed Forces in Europe (CFE), Vienna Document 1999, and Open Skies), the UK received 15 inbound inspections or evaluations (including five on British Forces Germany) and conducted 33 outbound inspections or evaluations on non-NATO signatories. In October 2005, we hosted representatives of 40 states and international organizations from across the OSCE at the Land Warfare Centre, as a confidence and security building measure under the Vienna Document. We also brought back into service the Open Skies Andover C Mk1 observation aircraft, which was deployed over Russia, Ukraine and Georgia. Details of UK military equipment holdings declared under the CFE Treaty will be published in *Defence Statistics 2006*.

HMS Nottingham and Russian cruiser Moskva on combined exercises

COUNTERING TERRORISM

57. Defence continued to make an important contribution to the UK's counter terrorism strategy over the year. While there is no specific military solution to countering terrorism, the Armed Forces make a significant contribution, particularly overseas. They have a unique capability to perform a variety of specialised tasks as part of the Government's overall efforts and can play an important role in pursuing terrorists and those who support them in threatening the UK, our allies and our interests. We have continued to take forward the crucial task of building the counter terrorist capacity of other nations. Military training is only part of what the UK can offer but it encompasses a wide range of activities including combat skills, VIP protection, bomb disposal and coastguard operations.

COUNTERING THE THREAT FROM WEAPONS OF MASS DESTRUCTION

58. The need to reduce the risk that state and non-state actors acquire and use Chemical, Biological, Radiological or Nuclear (CBRN) weapons against the UK, our forces and our interests drives the work of both the MoD and the other Government departments involved. We need to constrain the intent and ability to acquire or increase illicit CBRN capabilities worldwide. This is most effectively dealt with through international treaties and diplomatic efforts. In parallel, we must also address the threat brought about by the transfer of CBRN know-how, material and weapons, as well as deterring potential proliferating states by diminishing their expected gains and raising expected costs. During 2005-06 the MoD continued to make a major contribution to the policy and implementation of counter proliferation and arms control activities. We also continued to maintain a nuclear deterrent capability as the ultimate guarantor of our national security. We improved the protection of our Armed Forces against CBRN weapons, to ensure that the UK can maintain its political and military freedom of action despite the CBRN threat, thereby minimising the incentive for any potential proliferators to acquire such weapons, or should they do so, to use them against us.

Nuclear Arms Control

59. We continued to press for multilateral negotiations towards mutual, balanced and verifiable reductions in nuclear weapons. The Nuclear Non Proliferation Treaty (NPT) remains the cornerstone of the international nuclear non-proliferation and disarmament regime. As a Nuclear Weapon State under the Treaty the UK is, and will remain, fully compliant with our own disarmament obligations under the NPT. During the 2005 NPT Review Conference, the MoD worked very closely with the FCO and DTI to make progress on nuclear disarmament and non-proliferation, and the Atomic Weapons Establishment delivered a well received presentation on the verification aspects of disarmament. We also became an active member of the Norwegian 7 Country Initiative; set up by the Norwegian Foreign Minister at the behest of the UN Secretary General, its purpose is to develop and promote viable and novel initiatives on disarmament, non-proliferation and access to the peaceful uses of nuclear technology. We developed and promoted proposals to strengthen the nuclear non-proliferation regime, particularly by tightening the controls against possible illicit use of civilian nuclear technology to develop military programmes and against the spread of sensitive nuclear technology to those who are not compliant with their non-proliferation obligations. We remain concerned about Iran's non-compliance with its nuclear safeguards obligations, as reported by the International Atomic Energy Agency (IAEA), and the possibility it is pursuing a covert military nuclear programme. The UK, along with France and Germany, has been negotiating with Iran in an attempt to produce a diplomatic solution, and Iran's activities have now been reported to the UN Security Council, in line with IAEA statutes. This clearly shows the breadth of international concern at Iran's lack of cooperation and transparency with the IAEA. North Korea's claim that it has nuclear weapons is also a concern and we continued to support the six party talks between North Korea, its neighbours and the US, as the best way forward.

Biological Arms Control

60. The MoD continued to support the 3-year programme of work to strengthen the Biological and Toxin Weapons Convention, with Defence personnel, particularly non-profileration experts from the Defence Science and Technology Laboratory (Dstl), making a key contribution. During 2005, the Convention was chaired by the UK and work focused on the content, promulgation and adoption of Codes of Conduct for scientists. The MoD is also contributing to preparations for the Sixth Review Conference in November 2006.

Chemical Arms Control

The metal parts furnace that will help destroy chemical weapons at Shchuch'ye, Russia.

61. We also continued to take a leading role in the UK's contribution to the implementation of the Chemical Weapons Convention, again drawing on Dstl's expertise. As part of the UK's contribution to the 'The Global Partnership against the spread of weapons and materials of mass destruction' the MoD supports Russia's programme to destroy its stockpiles of chemical weapons. There was substantial progress in planning and starting to implement a number of major equipment and infrastructure projects through the UK managed-programme at the Shchuch'ye Chemical Weapons Destruction Facility. Work began to build an 18km railway to transport 1.9 million nerve-agent munitions from the storage site to the destruction facility, to upgrade an electrical supply station, and to procure key destruction equipment. During 2005-06, Belgium, the Czech Republic, Ireland, The Netherlands, New Zealand, Norway and Sweden agreed new funding contributions. The UK has contributed some £14M to the Global Partnership, Canada over £45M, and other donors about

£6M. Detailed information is published on www.dti.gov.uk. We also made progress with the redirection of former WMD scientists. Potential new projects were identified in Georgia, Russia and Kazakhstan, we took part in workshops for Iraqi scientists in Jordan and the UK, and supported workshops held for Libyan scientists.

Export Controls

62. Defence experts supported implementation and development of international export control regimes and arrangements for equipment, materials and technology related to CBRN threats, missile and UAV systems, conventional weapons, and dual use equipment, materials and technology. We made a significant contribution to the UN Programme of Action on Small Arms and Light Weapons and supported an arms trade treaty process. We continue to work with other states on safe stockpile and security management practices and destruction work. The MoD also assesses UK export licence applications on behalf of the Department of Trade and Industry to consider the potential effect of proposed exports on our and our allies' defence and security and to assess the risk of diversion of the goods concerned to an undesirable end-user. Details of performance achieved in processing licence applications are published in the *Annual Report on United Kingdom Strategic Export Controls.*

Proliferation Security Initiative

63. The 2003 Proliferation Security Initiative strives to establish more coordinated and effective ways to impede and stop states and non-state actors from illicit trafficking in Weapons of Mass Destruction and associated delivery systems. We continued to take a leading role in its operational development, in particular driving forward elements of the exercise programme. We have hosted and chaired two of the nine Operational Expert Meetings and a Command Post Exercise in the air environment. In autumn 2005, we led a major maritime exercise and we are hosting a major maritime industry workshop in autumn 2006.

Deterrence

64. Deterrence aims to convince a potential adversary that the consequences of a particular course of action outweigh the potential gains. There is no doubt that deterrence is rather more complex now than during the Cold War and that it will not be straightforward to predict accurately in the decades ahead what threats may emerge and where they may come from. Our deterrence posture therefore seeks to anticipate potential threats and be flexible enough to deter both state and non-state actors from behaving in ways that would be harmful to the interests of the UK and our allies. All our military capabilities, conventional and nuclear, have a role to play in deterrence. Our nuclear weapons have a continuing role as the ultimate guarantee of the security of the UK. We have made it clear that our nuclear capability is a political tool aimed at deterring acts of aggression, and is not a war-fighting capability. Its use would only be contemplated in extreme circumstances of self defence, in order to achieve a strategic effect. Any use of nuclear weapons would be proportionate and in accordance with our international legal obligations.

Chemical, Biological, Radiological and Nuclear Defence

65. Our Armed Forces face a diverse range of potential CBRN threats and hazards on operations. We are taking forward a comprehensive programme, with a strong emphasis on force protection measures, to ensure that we maintain our political and military freedom of action. Internationally, we worked to improve interoperability with close allies (particularly the United States) and within NATO and the EU. We continued to play a leading role in NATO's Senior Defence Group on Proliferation, driving forward Alliance-wide CBRN policy and defensive capability improvements. During the year, we also took command of the fully operable NATO Multinational CBRN Defence Battalion.

Missile Defence

66. The United States continues to work towards an operational ballistic missile defence system to protect their country from missile attack. We maintained a close relationship with the US in this field, and continued technical co-operation with the US Missile Defence Agency through the UK Missile Defence Centre, to increase our knowledge of how a national missile defence system might work for us. No decision has been made on whether to acquire such a capability for the UK but we supported the upgrade of RAF Fylingdales to provide missile defence capabilities for the US system. NATO completed a feasibility study into missile defence for NATO territory and population centres and we are working closely with NATO bodies to examine the political and strategic implications. NATO is also planning to invest in the command infrastructure for an Active Layered Theatre Ballistic Missile Defence capability against shorter-range ballistic missiles which could threaten deployed forces. We remained closely engaged on the command arrangements, but the weapons systems for this capability will be provided by nations and we have no plans to acquire such systems ourselves.

UK AND INTERNATIONAL CONFLICT PREVENTION

67. While the primary focus of the Ministry of Defence remains providing the capability to conduct military operations, it is clearly better to prevent the need for them arising. We therefore continued to support the Foreign and Commonwealth Office and the Department for International Development in work to tackle the underlying causes of conflict and thus minimise the likelihood of a need for UK military intervention arising. This work is primarily taken forward through the Africa and Global Conflict Prevention Pools. These form a tri-departmental programme that ensures a coherent and consistent approach is taken across Government to deliver joined-up UK policy-making, action planning and activity to prevent conflict and dispel hostility. In Iraq and Afghanistan, in particular, the Armed Forces provide the security on the ground that enables such work to be

taken forward but we also contribute to the work of the Pools through our Defence Relations tools. In particular, we provided Security Sector Reform assistance in areas where UK forces were engaged on peace building tasks and supported the development of deployable African, Balkans and Central and Eastern European peacekeeping capabilities for regional and international security intervention operations. Further information on conflict prevention activities and performance against the joint Public Service Agreement targets can be found at Annex C.

Africa Conflict Prevention Pool

68. With around £30M to deploy via the Africa Conflict Prevention Pool, we devoted most of our resources to developing African capacity for planning and executing peace support operations and assisting selected Security Sector Reform programmes. During the year, we supported the African Union's planning for the development of an African Standby Force for peace support operations, and helped build up the conflict management capacity of key regional institutions such as the Economic Community of West African States. We also helped improve the capability of the armed forces of several African states to participate in peace support operations. UK support has been vital to establishing a number of regional training centres such as the Kofi Annan International Peacekeeping Training Centre in Ghana, the Karen Peace Support Training Centre and the UK-funded International Mine Action Training Centre in Kenya, which builds on previous mine clearance training provided to Kenya by the British Peace Support Team (East Africa). Since this Centre opened in February 2005, it has delivered de-mining and mine awareness training to 2,500 African personnel.

Figure 6: Global and Africa Conflict Prevention Pools

Global Conflict Prevention Pool

69. The Defence focus in the Global Pool is Security Sector Reform. In particular, through "train the trainer" schemes, we transfer our military skills within an accountable and democratic framework to help other countries become self-sufficient and responsible for their own security. During the year, we trained members of the new Iraqi army in professional leadership and military skills as part of the overall campaign to develop capacity and capability in the Iraqi Security Forces. We have also supported the development and training of the new Afghan National Army. The Peace Support Operations Training Centre in Sarajevo was opened in 2005 and was part-funded from the Global Conflict Prevention Pool. This delivers internationally-approved education and training in multinational peace support and humanitarian operations.

An Army Combat Medical Technician tends to a Masai Warrior

UK AND INTERNATIONAL CONFLICT MANAGEMENT AND RECONSTRUCTION

70. It is not always possible to prevent conflicts. We therefore also worked to improve the international community's capability to manage and confine them when they break out, in particular through the United Nations; to develop international humanitarian norms and obligations to minimise the impact of such conflicts on the innocent; and to assist in reconstruction and recovery once conflicts are over.

The United Nations

71. Demand for UN peacekeeping continued to grow. The UK is working closely with other nations in the UN Special Committee on Peacekeeping on ways to enhance peacekeeping capacity and capability. We are also developing a national action plan in response to the Zeid Report, which made recommendations on the responsibility of member states to ensure criminal liability for the actions of their nationals while engaged on peacekeeping missions. This will complement the National Action Plan to implement UN Security Council Resolution 1325 on Women, Peace and Security, announced on International Women's Day 2006.

International Humanitarian Law

72. We contributed to international consideration of a number of conflict-related humanitarian concerns. Although there was insufficient Parliamentary time in 2005 to

conclude the process of ratifying the legally binding Protocol V (Certain Conventional Weapons Convention) on Explosive Remnants of War (ERW) agreed in 2003, we intend to do so by the end of 2006. The Protocol contains new provisions offering significant humanitarian benefit to those in areas affected by ERW, making clearance of unexploded ordnance quicker and more effective. We also continued to work with Argentina, through the Joint Working Party, to address mine clearance issues in the Falkland Islands, including development of the Feasibility Study and the Statement of Requirement for the field survey by an explosive ordnance disposal contractor or Non-Government Organisation.

Post-Conflict Reconstruction

73. The Post Conflict Reconstruction Unit (PCRU) is an interdepartmental (FCO, MoD and DFID) organisation set up to enhance our national ability to plan, develop and deliver effective and co-ordinated post conflict stabilisation activity. During 2005-06, the PCRU focused on building an effective post-conflict operational capability. It conducted a number of assessments, including a review of the Global Conflict Prevention Pool Balkans strategy. It also provided a team to work alongside the Permanent Joint Headquarters in Helmand province in Afghanistan. It continued to develop an assessment methodology and a stabilisation planning tool. It also worked with the stabilisation units of other nations, in particular Canada and the US, and with international organisations. In addition, the MoD, in collaboration with volunteers from the Fire Service, led a Global Conflict Prevention Pool funded project to establish an amalgamated fire and emergency response service for the ethnically divided communities of East and West Mostar in Bosnia Herzegovina. Through retraining demobilised soldiers from the Bosnian armed forces, the new Fire Brigade not only provided a much needed enhanced service to the community but also engaged representatives of all ethnicities in the city, thus helping the process of local reconciliation and reconstruction.

Tito Bridge, Mostar built by the Royal Engineers

FURTHER SOURCES OF INFORMATION

74. Additional Information on Defence Policy is available from the following sources:

- Defence White Paper *Delivering Security in a Changing World,* December 2003;
- Command Paper *Delivering Security in a Changing World: Future Capabilities* (Cm6269, July 2004) available at www.mod.uk;
- quarterly PSA reports to HM Treasury at www.mod.uk;
- House of Commons Defence Committee Report 'Future Capabilities' Fourth Report HC 45-i & ii published 17 March 2005;
- House of Lords EU Committee Report 'Preventing Proliferation of Weapons of Mass Destruction: The EU Contribution' Thirteenth Report HL 96 published 5 April 2005;
- House of Commons Defence Committee Report 'Strategic Export Controls: HMG's Annual Report for 2003, Licensing Policy and Parliamentary Scrutiny' HC 145 published 24 March 2005;
- information on Global and African Conflict Prevention Pools, and Proliferation Security Initiative at www.fco.gov.uk;
- *Annual Report on United Kingdom Strategic Export Controls* published in July 2005 available at www.fco.gov.uk;
- Analysis of Conflict Prevention costs at Note 2 to the accounts on page 200;
- United Nations Security Council at www.un.org;
- ESDP at ue.eu.int;
- information on EU Battlegroups, EU Civilian Military Cell, Headline Goal 2010, EU Military Operations in Bosnia and Herzegovina, the European Defence Agency and the Berlin+ arrangements at ue.eu.int;
- background on NATO Response Force at www.arrc.nato.int/brochure/nrf.htm;
- Zeid Report at www.un.org;
- NATO reference publications and ministerial communiqués, including Comprehensive Political Guidance at www.nato.int;
- NAO Report *Joint Targets* (HC 453 on 10 October 2005) available at www.nao.org.uk;
- NPT/CONF.2005/WP.1. Verification of nuclear disarmament: final report on studies into the verification of nuclear warheads and their components: Working paper submitted by the United Kingdom of Great Britain and Northern Ireland at www.un.org.

Essay: European Security and Defence Policy: the UK Presidency of the European Union

At the beginning of the UK's six-month Presidency of the EU on 1 July 2005, we stated that we would be working to develop a European Security and Defence Policy (ESDP) that was more capable, more coherent and more active, underpinned by effective multilateralism. This essay sets out the progress made towards these goals. Work to improve crisis management structures, Defence capabilities, research and technology and financing was launched at the Hampton Court Summit in October 2005.

More Capable

ESDP has acted as a catalyst for several Member States to modernise their Armed Forces, both by procuring equipment and undergoing the training required in today's operational environment, and by taking forward national constitutional amendments to enable the rapid deployment of their Armed Forces when necessary. As part of the Headline Goal 2010 process, the final version of the Requirements Catalogue was delivered, setting out the military capabilities that the EU requires in order to achieve its identified level of ambition. The Catalogue was validated by operational analysis provided by NATO and work has begun to develop the Force Catalogue that represents the next stage of the Headline Goal process.

There was further progress on the Battlegroup initiative, including a strategic-level seminar in October and a tactical-level seminar in December. By the end of the UK Presidency, 26 Member States had pledged contributions to 19 Battlegroups, intended to achieve full operational capability in 2007. Each Battlegroup consists of about 1,500 troops held at very high readiness and available for deployment on ESDP missions on a rotational basis (two Battlegroups every six months). The UK provided a Battlegroup in 2005, and will provide the next in 2008, and then a joint Battlegroup with the Netherlands in 2010.

During the UK Presidency, the European Defence Agency (EDA) launched a Code of Conduct to prevent protectionism and open up European defence markets to increased competition. The EDA has only a relatively small budget, and we believe that its primary role should be as a “dating agency” to facilitate Member States' identification of common capability shortfalls and to benefit from economies of scale by adopting joint procurement programs. We demonstrated our commitment to the EDA by launching a joint project with France on Lightweight Radar under its auspices. The EDA has also initiated work to address the identified European Air Refuelling shortfall.

More Coherent

The UK worked hard to lay the foundations for a structured, professional approach to Civil-Military Co-ordination, agreed jointly with Austria and Finland to be taken forward during their Presidencies. This work included developing concepts for Security Sector Reform and for comprehensive planning to improve the EU's ability to bring its full range of military, diplomatic, economic, policing and judicial tools to bear in the most cost-effective manner. It was helped by the creation of a civil-military cell within the EU Military Staff. The cell's capacity to generate the EU Operations Centre is due to reach Full Operational Capability later in 2006. When activated, this Centre will be capable of fulfilling a command and control function for civilian, civil-military and low-intensity military missions. We played a leading role in the introduction of periodic comprehensive reviews for all continuing EU missions in order to ensure that, in a fluid international environment, the resources available continue to be used and prioritised in a way likely to deliver the desired goal.

More Active

During the UK Presidency, seven missions and other activities were launched, covering the Republic of Macedonia, Gaza, Indonesia, the Democratic Republic of Congo, Sudan and Iraq. ESDP is now undertaking a variety of tasks across three continents including security and stabilisation, monitoring and mentoring of indigenous police forces, judiciary training, border monitoring and tackling organised crime.

Effectively Multilateral

The need for an effective, multilateral approach is recognised by all Member States. The EU will never operate in isolation and to achieve maximum effect in any given scenario it will need to engage with a range of third states, global and regional institutions, Non Government Organisations and other actors. At the heart of achieving this is an ESDP that complements and reinforces NATO. Differences remain among Member States over this relationship. But the need to gain maximum capability from the 19 States belonging to both the EU and NATO, with their individual forces and defence budgets, supports the case for close cooperation and co-ordination between both organisations. During the UK Presidency, arrangements for EU-NATO liaison cells within the headquarters of both organisations were finalised and are now operational. On the ground, the EU and NATO continue to work closely together on the largest ESDP mission to date, Operation ALTHEA in Bosnia, and have cooperated in supporting the African Union in Darfur. The EU is also working through ESDP to support the UN in the Democratic Republic of Congo and the Association of South East Asian Nations in Indonesia.

WIDER GOVERNMENT

Objective: Contribute to the Government's wider domestic reform agenda, and achieve our Public Service Agreement and Performance Partnership Agreement[1] targets.

Performance Measures and Assessment

Implementation of sustainable development across Defence:

- **Strategies in place for travel, water, waste non-operational energy, estate procurement, heritage, timber, construction, biodiversity, social impacts, refrigerents and ozone depleting substances, estates disposals, estate adaption to climate change, land remediation, access and recreation and the Environmental Management System;**
- **150 sustainability and environmental appraisals and assessments conducted;**
- **Carbon emissions from Defence buildings reduced by 2% between 1999-2000 and 2004-05;**
- **7% of energy from renewable sources (target 10%).**

Raised expectations and achievements of disaffected young people:

- **Strengthened links with Learning and Skills Council to improve support for Service Apprenticeships and develop personnel with poor basic skills;**
- **Working with Government Skills to reflect needs of Armed Forces and develop Professional Skills for Government initiative;**
- **MoD Youth Council approved plan to introduce nationwide network of MoD Regional Youth Coordinators;**
- **Participation in wide range of social inclusion partnerships;**
- **4,108 Cadets registered for BTEC in Public Services;**
- **Government announcement of pilot expansion of cadet forces;**
- **Provision of support for London 2012 Olympic Games.**

Improved clinical support to the Armed Forces and the public:

- **Development of programme to increase awareness of the military operational environment among NHS personnel.**

Support to ex-Service personnel:

- **Revised Strategy for Veterans published March 2006;**
- **Some 17,000 personnel (85% of those entitled) drew on resettlement support in 2005-06. 96% of those who wished to continue to work secured employment within six months of discharge;**
- **Introduced specialist assessment of what disabled Service leavers can do and tailored assistance to find suitable employment;**
- **Set up new 10-year resettlement service contract to provide Service leavers with civilian career preparation and training and job-seeking services;**
- **Major commemorative events, including introduction of annual Veterans Day;**
- **Range of projects to tackle homelessness and associated problems;**
- **Review of veterans' mental health programmes and services;**
- **Continuing research into specialist veterans health issues;**
- **Faster processing of claims for war pensions and war widows;**
- **Review of operation of Far East Prisoners of War payment scheme and extended eligibility.**

[1] Performance Partnership Agreements were a central initiative to oversee Departmental management and coordinate Government business. During 2005 they were replaced by other systems including Departmental Capability Reviews.

DEFENCE IN THE WIDER COMMUNITY

75. The purpose of the Ministry of Defence and the Armed Forces is to defend the United Kingdom and its interests. We want to live in a strong, healthy, just and sustainable society nationally and internationally. Defence underpins this by providing security and helping sustain the rule of law, without which this would not be possible. Defence is an integral part of the national community and makes a significant further contribution to that community and to the Government's wider objectives in a number of ways. In all of this we work to implement the Government's sustainable development strategy set out in March 2005 in *Securing the Future*. We routinely support most other departments through the work of Defence personnel, military and civilian, and the provision of specialist military capabilities to the civil authorities. We own, or have access to, land across the country from the Outer Hebrides to the centre of London, covering about 1% of the UK land mass, making a substantial contribution to the protection of the environment and preservation of our heritage. We provide employment, much of it highly skilled, for around 600,000 people directly or indirectly. We place contracts and conduct complex scientific and technological research and development worth many billions each year. We recruit and train about 18,000 new Service personnel and over 4,500 civilians every year, and return a slightly larger number to the civilian economy with a wide range of acquired skills and qualifications. In addition, some 180,000 people have some form of Reserve commitment. The Cadet Forces provide challenging and enjoyable activities for about 130,000 young people in the UK and abroad that help raise their expectations and achievements and prepare them for their role in the community. Members of the Armed Forces make a strong contribution to sport in the UK, including representing their country in international competitions. There are over 10 million Service veterans and their dependents. Some 223,000 veterans and their dependants receive war pensions of over £1 billion every year in addition to substantial payments from the occupational scheme for injury or death due to service. We continue to work with other departments to improve the provision of support to veterans who need it. We also maintain a continuing programme of research into a number of specialist veterans health issues.

76. The MoD is responsible for over 8,000 archaeological and 1,000 scheduled monuments and 767 listed buildings, makes grants-in-aid of over £14M a year to the national museums for all three Services, and owns a wide range of historically significant assets. These include such unique items as HMS Victory, recently declared a national treasure and one of 100 'Icons of England', and the Battle of Britain Memorial Flight, as well as over 1,500 items of fine art and antiques in the MoD Art Collection. The collection provided the basis for the exhibition *Warriors For the Working Day* held in London in the summer of 2005 as part of the commemoration of the 60th anniversary of the end of the Second World War. This concentrated on the people working out of the front line and displayed works of art showing the effects of the war on the physical environment. There are also over 100 independent Regimental and Corps museums and collections across the country. Overall this represents a significant contribution to the Government's broader goals for heritage, education, and veterans.

SUSTAINABLE DEVELOPMENT

77. The core task of the MoD is to produce battle winning people and equipment. In doing this we seek to ensure that we act responsibly and sustainably, neither squandering resources, human or physical, nor degrading the environment, and that we treat our people and the wider community with respect. This is both right in itself and makes the most of every pound provided for Defence. It also supports the four sustainable development priorities of sustainable consumption and production; climate change and energy; natural resource protection and environmental enhancement; and sustainable communities, set out in the Government's sustainable development strategy *Securing the Future* in March 2005. We continue to work to minimise and reduce the inevitable impact that Defence activity has on the environment, manage this sustainably, and mitigate it where possible. We are developing our performance measurement, management and reporting systems to ensure that we understand and take into account the impact of our activity. Detailed reporting is contained in the MoD *Sustainable Development Annual Report 2005*, the key elements of which are set out below. Other aspects are brought out in the chapters on 'operations', 'policy', 'future capabilities and infrastructure', 'science, innovation and technology', 'personnel management' and 'health and safety'.

Waste segregation in action

Sustainable Consumption and Production

78. Detailed Defence-wide sustainable development strategies are in place for waste, timber, construction and sustainable procurement on the Estate. An example of sustainable production in practice in Defence is set out in the essay on Project Allenby/Connaught on page 154, we

have introduced the Project Orientated Environmental Management Systems for Integrated Project Teams to use in the equipment acquisition process. Some 30 equipment projects are applying this so far against a target of full implementation by April 2007. Our new timber strategy requires demonstration that all timber and timber products are procured from legal sources, that these should be acquired from a sustainable source, and consideration given to the use of reclaimed, re-used or recycled items. All paper used for Defence publications comes from sustainable forests. We are working to improve waste reduction, recovery and recycling rates across Defence and the *Sustainable Waste Management Strategy* published in May 2005 set a target of reducing the waste we produce by at least 1% each year. There are examples of good practice (for instance, Bicester Garrison in Oxfordshire has saved 20% of the cost of waste management and tripled its recycling rate). But we do not yet have data systems in place to measure performance across the entire estate. These are being progressively introduced as waste management contracts come up for renegotiation.

Climate Change and Energy

79. Detailed Defence-wide sustainable development strategies are in place for travel, energy, adaptation to climate change and refrigerants and ozone depleting substances. HMS Endurance helped the British Antarctic Survey to visit remote areas in their work in monitoring environmental change.

HMS Endurance in Antarctica

80. Defence accounts for about two thirds of the carbon used on the Government Built Estate. Carbon emissions from Defence buildings reduced by 2% from 1999-2000 to 2004-05. We are increasing the proportion of energy we buy from renewable sources. This has now reached 7% against a target of 10%.

Natural Resource Protection and Environmental Enhancement

81. Detailed Defence-wide sustainable development strategies are in place for Environmental Management Systems, water, land remediations, heritage and biodiversity. We are progressively developing and implementing Environmental Management Systems across Defence, and conducted 150 sustainability and environmental appraisals and assessments in 2005. We consume about 24 million cubic meters of water each year, which is about 80 cubic meters per person per year, which includes domestic (some sites operate 24 hours per day and every day in the year), commercial and industrial use and some distribution losses. We have set a target to reduce this to 51 cubic meters per person per year. Project Aquatrine (paragraph 313) will make a significant contribution to improving this performance. A small proportion of Defence land is contaminated. We are conducting assessments and developing decontamination plans over the whole estate with the aim of beginning a co-ordinated programme of work by the end of 2007. Further information on environmental enhancement is set out in paragraphs 315-318 and in the Annual *Stewardship Report on the Defence Estate*.

Sustainable Communities

82. A Defence-wide sustainable development strategy is in place for social impacts and access and recreation. The main Defence contribution in this area is set out in detail in the paragraphs below on young people (paragraphs 83-89) and veterans (paragraphs 91-105) and in the essay on Defence youth policy on page 60. Environmental noise from military flying and tank and artillery ranges is a legitimate concern for communities living close to the places where this takes place. We are taking forward the recommendations of the 2004 Aircraft Environmental Noise Report, providing routine advice for the public on Military Low Flying and publishing an annual review of low flying activity. Since the end of the Cold War the total number of low flying sorties has reduced by a third. During 2005 we reviewed the military helicopter low flying requirements and procedures in response to the Coroner's recommendations following the Heather Bell inquest.

YOUNG PEOPLE: BUILDING SKILLS AND RAISING EXPECTATIONS

83. Defence works with other Departments and the wider community to take forward the Government's skills and social responsibility objectives. In particular the cadet forces provide challenging and enjoyable activities for over 130,000 young people in the UK and abroad that help raise their expectations and achievements and prepare them for their role in the community.

Improving Skills

84. As part of our core business we provide considerable basic, specialist and professional skills training to newly-recruited young military and civilian personnel. This also contributes directly to the Government's skills development goals. Details are set out in paragraphs 187 to 189 in the chapter on Personnel Management. During 2005-06 we further strengthened our links with the Learning and Skills Council to improve the support to young Service personnel, particularly over funding of apprenticeships

and developing those identified with poor basic skills. We are also taking an active role in developing the newly created Government Skills, the Sector Skills Council for Central Government, to improve public service delivery across central government by driving skills development. In particular, we are working with it to ensure that it reflects the needs of the Armed Forces, and to help develop the Professional Skills for Government initiative. We also continue to use the Defence Education and Skills Advisory Board (which contains senior figures from across the public and private sector education and skills community) to inform and advise us on educational, learning and skills developments and to advocate for the MoD in appropriate national arenas.

Social Inclusion and Personal Development

85. Defence continues to make a significant positive impact to the Government's youth agenda by supporting a range of projects focussed on the well-being of young people and contributing to the formulation of Government-wide youth policies and initiatives. 2005 saw the first meeting of the MoD Youth Council, chaired by the Under Secretary of State and attended by senior representatives of the Services, the Department for Education and Skills and the Home Office. Reflecting the fact that local needs vary, the Council approved a plan to introduce a nationwide network of MoD Regional Youth Co-ordinators to ensure that activities respond to local priorities.

86. The success of the MoD's youth programmes is based on the expertise, enthusiasm and distinctive ethos of serving and retired Service personnel and Cadet Adult Instructors to lead programmes that are both challenging and appealing to young people of all sorts, and our ability to deliver such activities through the widely dispersed regional network of service establishments and Cadet locations. We participate in a wide range of social inclusion partnerships such as Skill Force and Outreach, and contribute to several joint programmes with the voluntary sector, in addition to our flagship Cadet organisations. In particular, we are increasing, to 50 per year, the number of team leaders seconded from the Services to the Prince's Trust team for disaffected youth, and this is managed by a full time Army officer working at the Trust's headquarters. Further information is contained in the essay on *Sustainable Communities: Defence Youth Policy* on page 60.

Cadet Forces

87. There are over 130,000 Cadets in the four Cadet Forces, supported by over 20,000 adult volunteers. The Sea Cadets had a particularly prominent year as they played an important role in the celebrations of the 200th anniversary of Trafalgar. Each Cadet Force fosters intangible personal qualities such as responsibility, citizenship and leadership, but Cadets are increasingly achieving formal educational and vocational skills as well. In 2005-06 4,108 Cadets registered for the Business and Technology Education Council vocational qualification in Public Services delivered through the Cadet Vocational Office in partnership with the Learning and Skills Council. During the year the Directorate of Operational Capability conducted a study into the operation and effectiveness of the Cadet Forces. This made a number of detailed recommendations for their future development, highlighted the importance of having a well-defined service framework and conditions of service for Adult Volunteers, and endorsed the existing duty of care arrangements.

A cadet receiving instruction

88. To involve young people more in celebrating the contribution of our Armed Forces, the Chancellor of the Exchequer and Defence Secretary announced in February 2006 that they wished to pilot an expansion of the Cadet Forces, especially in state schools, capitalising on the strength of the MoD supported Combined Cadet Forces which mainly operate in private schools. They also asked Mr Ian Russell, (the head of the Russell Commission, established in 2004 by the Chancellor and Home Secretary, to develop a new National Framework for Youth Action and Engagement, to increase the level of community participation by young people of 16-25 across the UK) to fund raise with the private sector. Funds raised are matched by the Government. Work on this is now being taken forward. Subsequently, in June 2006 the Treasury made available £800,000 to run the pilot scheme fo six new combined Cadet Force Units in state schools.

Sport

89. Sport helps to develop attributes required in service personnel such as physical fitness, courage, resilience and esprit de corps. These also support the Government's wider personal development and social responsibility goals. All members of the Armed Forces are encouraged to participate in sport and a number represent their country at international level. For example, eight members of the 40-strong British squad for the 2006 Winter Olympics were members of the Armed Forces, and 19 members of the Armed Forces represented the home countries at the 2006 Commonwealth Games. The MoD is supporting the London 2012 Olympic Games. We have agreed to provide a site at Woolwich Station for shooting events, and Horse Guards Parade for beach volleyball. An internal co-ordinating structure has been set up which supports the Inter-Departmental Olympic Steering Group headed by the Department for Culture, Media and Sports.

Royal Navy backing the London 2012 Olympic bid

HEALTH: IMPROVING CLINICAL SUPPORT

90. The key outputs of the Defence Medical Services are the ability to deploy the right medical capabilities to support military operations worldwide, and the delivery of healthcare services to all Armed Forces personnel (regulars and mobilised reservists) and entitled dependants and civilian staff. This is supported to mutual benefit by an effective working relationship with the National Health Service (NHS), and the MoD/Department of Health Partnership Board continued to provide strategic oversight of the relationship. The Defence Medical Services contribute to the NHS Improvement Plan, and this relationship will be further enhanced by the introduction of the new Managed Military Health System. Valuable liaison work routinely takes place at the local level. In particular, the Defence Medical Education and Training Agency has developed a programme to increase awareness of the military operational environment among NHS personnel working in the trusts that host sick or injured Service personnel.

VETERANS: SUPPORT FOR EX-SERVICE PERSONNEL

Strategy for Veterans

91. The MoD has a particular responsibility for supporting Service veterans, especially those whose physical or mental health has been damaged in the service of their country. The veterans' community in the United Kingdom is estimated to comprise over 10 million veterans and their dependants. In 2003 the MoD set out its approach to veterans' issues and what it aims to achieve, in partnership with other key stakeholders, in the *Strategy for Veterans*. During the year we reviewed the strategy in consultation with other Government Departments, the Devolved Administrations and ex-Service organisations. This highlighted the importance of improving the effectiveness of communications and the delivery of services, identified some areas that needed updating, but confirmed that our broad approach to veterans' issues held good. A revised *Strategy for Veterans* was published in March 2006. Its three key pillars remain to provide excellent preparation for the transition from Service to civilian life, to ensure that the nation recognises veterans' contribution to society; and to provide support to veterans who need it.

Transition from Service to civilian life

92. All Service personnel leaving the Armed Forces are provided with structured assistance on making the transition from military to civilian life. The level of support provided depends on their length of service and the circumstances of their discharge. Those who have served at least four years are entitled to finance and housing briefings and a job finding service for two years after discharge. Those who have served at least six years[2] are also entitled to resettlement training, coaching in job interview technique and CV writing, and dedicated career consultancy support. Some 17,000 personnel (about 85% of those entitled) drew on this support in 2005-06. Over half of those who wished to continue to work secured employment within a month of discharge, and 96% within six months. A further 8,400 personnel leave annually as Early Service Leavers who do not qualify for this resettlement support. However they receive a mandatory resettlement brief and interview prior to discharge that includes assessment of their vulnerability to social exclusion, discussion on accommodation post-discharge, and direction to agencies and organisations that provide support for employment, accommodation and welfare needs. We are working with the Department of Work and Pensions and HM Revenue and Customs to produce by April 2007 meaningful employment statistics for these individuals six months after discharge. Exceptional arrangements for additional support are made for those assessed as vulnerable to social exclusion. We have worked with ex-Service charities with niche capabilities to ease the transition of Service personnel to veteran status, particularly for specialist assessment of what disabled Service leavers can do and tailored assistance to find suitable employment. A new 10-year Public Private Partnership contract with a leading outplacement company has been signed to deliver career transition and job-finding services to entitled Service leavers as part of their resettlement preparation.

Recognition and status of veterans in society

93. An important part of raising awareness is the message that veterans' contributions, both past and present, continue to be valued:

- The national commemoration of the 60th anniversary of the end of the Second World War took place in London on 10 July 2005. The Department also helped organise commemoration of the British military presence in the Suez Canal Zone from 1939 to 1956 at the National Memorial Arboretum in Staffordshire in May 2006. A service to mark the 150th anniversary of the institution of the Victoria Cross and the 50th anniversary of the formation of the Victoria Cross and George Cross Association took place at Westminster Abbey in June 2006. Detailed planning began for national commemoration of the 25th anniversary of the South Atlantic conflict to be held in June 2007;

[2] Five years if enlistment before 1 September 2002

- We will build on the success of the 2005 Veteran Awareness Week by mounting annual events to raise public awareness about the veterans' community. The first Veterans Day took place on 27th June 2006. Key events were held in London, Cardiff, Dundee, Liverpool, Torquay, Hull and Blackpool. We provided around £130,000 to support Veterans Day events throughout the UK;
- Currently, all those who served in the Armed Forces at any time from the start of the First World War to 31 December 1959, and widows and widowers of those who died of illness or injury attributable to their Service and in receipt of a war widow(er)'s pension are eligible for the HM Armed Forces Veterans Badge. A modified version is being produced for members of the Merchant Navy who served in vessels facilitating military operations. Some 200,000 badges had been issued by 31 March 2006;
- In March 2005 the Prime Minister announced the introduction of an Arctic Emblem, available from the summer of 2006, as an additional form of recognition for those who served north of the Arctic Circle during World War II;
- Public fundraising for the Armed Forces Memorial to members of the Armed Forces (Regular and Reserve) killed on duty or as a result of terrorist action since the Second World War, was launched in April 2005. The Government announced on 13 February 2006 that it would make £1.5M available for the Memorial from the sale of coins to commemorate the Battle of Trafalgar.

94. Young people featured heavily in the 2005 awareness-raising events and a national art competition aimed at 9-11 year old children was run to coincide with the first Veterans Day. Work continues with the Department for Education and Skills and ex-Service organisations, capitalising on the national curriculum, to involve young people and schools in recognition and commemoration events and teach the younger generation about veterans' contribution and role in society.

Provision of support to veterans who need it

95. The MoD continued to work to ensure that help and advice is available to all veterans who may need it, including through improving communication and information services available to veterans and increasing awareness of their needs and of the organisations available to provide support to them. The Veterans Agency launched a new periodical, *Veterans WORLD*, that aims to educate and inform advisors in the public and voluntary sectors who come into regular contact with veterans. Conferences have been held in London, Edinburgh, Cardiff, Liverpool and Newcastle to increase understanding of veterans' issues and familiarise delegates with the help and support available. The Agency has also started a programme of regional publicity campaigns to raise awareness of the Agency and the services provided, with the first taking place in Newcastle in March 2006.

96. We have continued to work closely with the Office of the Deputy Prime Minister and subsequently the Department for Communities and Local Government, ex-Service organisations and the voluntary and corporate sector to prevent and tackle homelessness and associated problems. Work is underway to build supported accommodation in Aldershot for Service leavers at risk of homelessness. A new 25-bed hostel run by the English Churches Housing Group is due to open in Summer 2007, providing both accommodation and training facilities offering Service leavers the opportunity to develop marketable job skills.

97. As part of Project Compass, which seeks to help homeless veterans return to employment in London, plans are being developed to assist Service leavers from the Military Corrective Training Centre in Colchester, and to provide job coaching and back to work training for Service leavers in the Catterick area. We are also supporting research into the effectiveness of recent homeless support initiatives in London. This is expected to identify services that could be extended to other parts of the UK.

Veterans beside the memorial to Women in World War II

Plans of new hostel to be built on former MoD land in Aldershot

Veterans Health Issues

98. The MoD has a continuing duty of care to veterans suffering ill health caused by their military service and we support a wide range of research programmes into specialist veterans health issues. Since 1948 Government policy has been that health care for veterans and war pensioners should be delivered by the National Health Service, and we are working with Chief Medical Officers and the Royal Colleges to raise the awareness of civilian health professionals about military and veterans' matters and to provide information for ex-Service personnel on what to expect and where to go for assistance from civilian health services. But war pensions legislation retains a discretion which allows funding of treatment of war pensioners' accepted disablements, subject to certain conditions. Under this provision war pensioners, whose pensioned condition is a mental health problem and where it is clinically appropriate, have been able to access remedial treatment programmes at the homes run by the Ex-Services Mental Welfare Society (Combat Stress). In February 2005, in light of developing clinical practice and treatment for mental health problems and with the agreement and full co-operation of the Society, the Department commissioned the Health and Social Care Advisory Service to review the Society's programmes to ensure that they reflected wider good practice, taking into account special factors relating to military service. The review's recommendations went beyond the current war pensioner programmes and considered mental health services for veterans more generally. It concluded that some veterans with mental health problems can be treated in the community at large, some are best dealt with by Community Mental Health teams, some may need hospital referral and inpatient care, and that there may be a sub-group with complex needs who meet the criteria for specialist NHS treatment. It also determined that the perceived stigma and discrimination arising from mental health problems and a belief that they should be able to overcome them makes young men in particular, including those in the veterans' population, reluctant to seek help. We are working with UK Health Departments and Combat Stress to implement the review's recommendations.

99. We continued where appropriate to provide medical assessments for veterans through the Medical Assessment Programme, based at St Thomas' Hospital in London. In 2005-06, five former Porton Down Volunteers, 19 veterans of the 1990-1991 Gulf Conflict, and eight veterans of Operations in Iraq since 2003 (Operation TELIC) were assessed. Due to falling demand, the retrospective depleted uranium testing programme for Gulf (1990/1991) and Balkans veterans closed to new applications at the end of January 2006. All results have so far been negative.

100. While we acknowledge that the phrase "Gulf War Syndrome" has become quite widespread in popular usage, the overwhelming consensus of the scientific and medical community is that Gulf War Syndrome does not exist as a discrete pathological entity. This was supported by a Pensions Appeal Tribunal decision in October 2005, which stated that it was nevertheless a "useful umbrella term" to cover accepted conditions causally linked to the 1990-91 Gulf conflict. The Department agrees with this and we hope that use of the umbrella term will address the belief of some Gulf veterans that we do not recognise a link between their ill-health and the conflict. The MoD has continued to sponsor research into the ill-health reported by some veterans of the Conflict into the possible adverse health effects of the combination of vaccines and Nerve Agent Pre-treatment tablets offered to UK personnel. Regular publication of mortality data continues to show that Gulf veterans do not suffer an excess mortality compared with a group of similar Service personnel that did not deploy.

101. Research also continued into the physical health of those involved in Operation TELIC since 2003. A study by The King's Centre for Military Health Research published in May 2006 showed that to date there has been no repeat of the variety of symptoms reported by Regular personnel who served in the 1990-91 Gulf War, and that there is no substantial increase in ill health between those members of the Armed Forces who did deploy and those who did not. Other aspects of this research are covered at paragraph 215. Further results, including those on the level of uranium in the urine of personnel deployed to Iraq and of the UK military population in general, will follow.

102. The MoD is working on a comprehensive historical survey of the Service Volunteer Programme at Porton Down. We continued to fund and provide practical support to the independent epidemiological study into mortality and cancer incidence among veterans who took part in this Programme. Findings are expected in 2007. The Department had been seeking Judicial Review of the verdict of unlawful killing in November 2004 at the inquest into the death of a volunteer taking part in a trial in 1953. Although we accepted there was sufficient evidence for the Jury to consider whether the Serviceman was unlawfully killed as a result of gross negligence in the conduct and planning of the experiment, we did not agree that there was sufficient evidence for it to consider a verdict on issues of consent. In February 2006 the family of the deceased stated that they would not challenge this view and on that basis the MoD agreed not to proceed. This agreement left undisturbed the verdict of unlawful killing, while making clear the basis for that verdict. We are currently engaged in talks on appropriate compensation.

War Pensions and Armed Forces Compensation Scheme

103. The Veterans Agency provides financial compensation via the War Pensions Scheme and since April 2005, the Armed Forces Compensation Scheme, to some 183,000 veterans and 40,000 widows for death and disablement arising out of service in the Armed Forces. The number of war pensions paid each year continues to decline by some 12,000 a year. Direct welfare support is also provided to war pensioners and war widows by the

War Pensioners Welfare Service, operating from locations across the UK and the Irish Republic. £1.069 billion was paid on some 223,000 war pensions during 2005-06. Average clearance times for war pension claims reduced by 10% to 52 days and for war widow claims by 6.4% to 21 days during the year. The War Pensions Scheme received some 43,000 claims and appeals during 2005-06, a decrease from 45,000 in 2004-05. The Armed Forces Compensation Scheme, introduced in April 2005, has considered some 3,000 cases in its first year, this is expected to rise year on year. Further information on this can be found at paragraph 157.

104. In the course of work to identify and correct errors in the payment of Armed Forces pensions we have discovered that a number of invalidity awards to Service personnel, arising from causes due to their service, may not have been consistently up-rated over the years, in line with the War Pension Scheme deterioration claims which had been accepted by the Veterans Agency. Early estimates are that this might apply to about 1,800 (less than 1% of) pensions in payment. As announced by the Minister for Veterans on 3 July 2006, we have a programme of work, Project Collins, to identity and correct any such errors. We are considering what if any further recompense may be appropriate.

Far East Prisoners of War and Civilian Internees

105. The Far East Prisoners of War payment scheme awarded a payment of £10,000 to certain individuals held captive by the Japanese during World War II or the surviving spouses of those who died. In December 2005, following the emergence of inconsistencies in application of the qualifying criteria, the Minister for Veterans ordered a review of all 30,000 claims. In March 2006 the review concluded that the scheme should be extended to individuals who lived in the UK for 20 years since the Second World War and up until the introduction of the scheme in November 2000. Some 25,000 payments have already been made, and we estimate that a further 500 individuals will receive ex-gratia payments of £10,000 as a result of the revised criteria.

FURTHER SOURCES OF INFORMATION

106. Additional Information on Wider Government is available from the following sources:

- quarterly PSA reports to HM Treasury at www.mod.uk;
- information on Government Skills at www.government-skills.gov.uk;
- *Strategy for Veterans* available at www.veteransagency.mod.uk;
- *Veterans WORLD* available at www.veteransagency.mod.uk;
- UK Gulf Veterans Mortality Data at www.dasa.mod.uk;
- Depleted Uranium Oversight Board at www.duob.org.uk;
- National Radiological Protection Board at www.nrpb.org.
- Armed Forces Youth Policy *Armed Forces Overarching Personnel Strategy* at www.mod.uk;
- Veterans Agency Annual Report and Accounts 2005-06 at www.veteransagency.mod.uk (from July 2006);
- Commemorative Booklets at www.veteransagency.mod.uk;
- Homelessness research *Improving the Delivery of Cross Departmental Support and Services for Veterans* at www.mod.uk;
- *The 1990/1991 Gulf Conflict: Health and Personnel Related Lessons Identified* at www.mod.uk;
- Kings College research papers published in The Lancet '*The Health Of UK Military Personnel Who Deployed To The 2003 Iraq War*' and *'Is there an Iraq syndrome?'* available at www.thelancet.com;
- MoD *Sustainable Development Annual Report 2005* available at www.mod.uk;
- *Defence Estates Stewardship Report 2005* available at www.mod.uk;
- *The Pattern of Military Low Flying across the United Kingdom 2005-06* at www.mod.uk (available from August 2006);
- *Review of UK Military Helicopter Low Flying in Response to a Rule 43 Letter from the Louth and Spilsby Coroner* available at www.mod.uk;
- *Bequests to the Nation: An introduction to the MoD Art Collection* available at www.art.mod.uk;
- *Sustainable Waste Management Strategy* available at www.mod.uk;
- *Securing the Future* available at www.sustainable-development.gov.uk.

Sustainable Communities: Defence Youth Policy

Defence Youth Policy aims to increase knowledge and understanding of the Armed Forces among young people. It also makes a major contribution to the wider Government goal of improving the well-being and future prospects of young people, particularly those on the fringes of society.

The Cadet Forces are at the heart of MoD's youth systems. They are a nationwide military themed youth organisation, comprising the Sea Cadet Corps, Army Cadet Force, Air Training Corps, and the Combined Cadet Force units that operate within secondary schools. They offer a wide variety of activities (ranging from outdoor adventurous training to learning to play a musical instrument) many of which can lead to achieving formal qualifications. Their contribution is such that in February 2006, the Government announced that it wished to pilot an expansion of the Cadet Forces, especially in state schools, capitalising on the strength of Combined Cadet Forces. The Cadets attract some 130,000 youngsters across the UK from all walks of life. This number is steadily growing, but a shortage of adult volunteers has required serious examination of how much more growth can be sustained. We are therefore looking at how the Cadet Forces will operate in the long term. This will include the parameters that we think should govern their operations, and ensuring we retain and attract the right calibre of adult volunteer that will enable the Cadet movement to prosper. This is crucial if we are to continue offering youngsters the best opportunities that we can to help grow them into their fullest potential.

We support a range of curricular activities in schools and colleges that offer unique and positive ways to enhance understanding of the Armed Forces within society, and particularly the values, culture, traditions and ethos which underpin military effectiveness. We offer vocational training comprising professional and accredited educational and citizenship activities to enhance young people's skills and potentially lead to practical work-related qualifications. Examples include the Cadet First Diploma, work experience and e-mentoring schemes with schools and colleges. Our five School Presentation Teams contribute to the Government's Citizenship Curriculum and the 'We Were There' Exhibition to educate children about the contribution ethnic minorities have made to Britain's defence. A new e-based teaching resource for GCSE students on Defence issues is being developed.

We work in partnership with other public sector authorities, youth organisations and charities. This enhances our ability to reach sectors of the population where youth provision is lacking and allows us to contribute in a focused way to specific aspects of Government youth policy such as social inclusion and the drive to reduce certain types of anti-social behaviour. Over the last couple of years a number of community related initiatives have come to fruition, including national-level partnership agreements with The Youth Justice Board and The Prince's Trust (which attracts over 40 volunteers a year from the Services). We also support Outreach, an Army Cadet Force Association Project aimed at turning around disaffected 14 to 16 year olds through an intensive programme of outdoor based confidence training and leadership/team building activities, and the Skill Force, which is based in schools, to turn around disaffected youngsters and help them develop useful skills. The RAF has also established a network of Youth Activity Liaison Officers nationwide who engage with local communities to assist with the needs of young people and families, and to help public authorities within those communities.

Overall, by contributing to the development of the country's young people we aim to affirm the good reputation of the Armed Forces and nourish the values which contribute to a healthy and stable society.

Future Capabilities

FUTURE EFFECTS

Objective: More flexible Armed Forces to deliver greater effect.

Performance Measures and Assessment

Implementation of Force Structure Changes, in particular the Future Army Structure:

- Three Type 23 Frigates and one submarine withdrawn from service. Launch of first Type 45 Destroyer;
- Entry into service of Sonar 2087 system;
- Conversion of 19 Mechanised Brigade to 19 Light Brigade;
- Progressive conversion of 4 Armoured Brigade to 4 Mechanised Brigade;
- Provision of key enablers and enhancements to brigade capability;
- Enhanced supporting intelligence, signals, planning, medical and logistic capabilities;
- Progressive introduction into service of the Bowman communications system;
- Javelin medium-range anti-armour missile accepted into service;
- New Territorial Army structure announced to deliver a more operationally effective and fully manned Territorial Army better integrated with the Regular Army;
- Nine Expeditionary Air Wings established;
- Formation of Typhoon Operational Conversion Unit (29 Sqn), Operational Evaluation Unit (17 Sqn) and first operational squadron (3 Sqn);
- Full operational capability of Brimstone anti-armour weapon achieved.

Enhanced command, control and communications, in particular through Network Enabled Capability:

- Guidance on information management processes completed;
- NEC Competency Framework introduced;
- Research into military capabilities enabled by networking completed;
- Work to develop the Recognised Theatre Logistics Picture and produce the user requirement for an end-to-end Joint Logistics Picture;
- Progressive delivery and roll-out of Defence Information Infrastructure, Bowman, the Cormorant Joint Rapid Reaction Force command system and the Joint Operational Command System;
- Defence Information Infrastructure (Future) first used in January 2006;
- Development of Defence Intelligence Modernisation Programme.

FORCE CAPABILITY CHANGES

107. The programme of modernisation set out in the *Future Capabilities* Command Paper of July 2004 continues to be implemented across Defence. In order to meet the likely operational challenges of the future, we must transform Defence to provide more versatile and flexible Armed Forces with a supporting Defence organisation that is as efficient as possible. To this end the programme of transformation is underpinned by three main themes: improving military effectiveness (concentrating on the effect our Armed Forces and military systems deliver rather than the number of systems involved); delivering efficiency improvements (in order to resource front line capabilities better); and investing in new equipment (to exploit technological advances in communications and enhance our strike capability on land, in the air and at sea).

108. We remain on track to deliver efficiency savings of £1.2 billion from the modernisation of our force structure announced in the July 2004 *Future Capabilities* Command Paper. These are part of our wider 2004 Spending Review efficiency target of £2.8 billion. Most of these savings will be delivered in 2006-07 and 2007-08 reflecting the progressive implementation of the major force structure changes and consequential reductions to service and civilian manpower. Following detailed scrutiny and analysis we have reduced the estimated 2004-05 saving of £88M we declared in the *Annual Report and Accounts 2004-05* to £64M, including £41M specifically arising from force structure changes. This reduction reflects clarification on efficiency measurement with the Office of Government Commerce and the introduction of more robust governance and reporting arrangements for 'one-off' savings. Following verification a further £182M was achieved by 1 April 2006 and reported to the Office of Government Commerce, bringing the cumulative total delivered to £246M of the £1.2 billion required.

Viking All Terrain Vehicle used by Royal Marines

Royal Navy Force Structure and Capabilities

109. The Royal Navy has implemented many of the force structure changes detailed in the *Annual Report and Accounts 2004-05*. These were aimed at delivering a versatile maritime force, structured and equipped for rapid deployment anywhere around the world. The changing global threat, together with the benefits of new technology and improved efficiency, means the Royal Navy no longer requires the same number of some types of ship as before. We have reduced the number of Type 23 frigates by three ships, with HMS Norfolk, HMS Marlborough and HMS Grafton being withdrawn from service. We have made progress towards our objective of reducing the number of attack submarines to eight by 2008, with the withdrawal from service of HMS Spartan. HMS Sovereign is expected to leave the Fleet by the end of 2006. Progress towards the delivery of the future Royal Navy took a major step forward in February 2006 with the successful launch of HMS Daring, the first of the new and highly capable Type 45 air-defence Destroyers. The year also saw the landing ship HMS Mounts Bay start sea trials and the launch of its sister ships HMS Cardigan Bay and HMS Lyme Bay; the early acceptance into service of the Sonar 2087 submarine hunting system; deliveries of air-defence missiles and ship and submarine torpedo defence systems, and Viking protected vehicles to the Royal Marines. Contracts were awarded for upgrading the Merlin anti-submarine helicopter force, for advanced computerised training systems to improve the combat effectiveness of major surface warships, and for advanced small-calibre gun systems for Type 23 Frigates.

Future Army Structure and Capabilities

110. In December 2004 we set out detailed plans for a more balanced Army structure of light, medium and heavy forces. Work to implement this during 2005-06 included:

- successful conversion of 19 Mechanised Brigade to 19 Light Brigade in October 2005, enabling it to take on the NATO Reaction Force commitment in 2006. Re-roling to a fully light structure will be completed by August 2007, and the Brigade will have completed its move from Catterick to Northern Ireland and Scotland by December 2008;

- progressive conversion of 4 Armoured Brigade to 4 Mechanised Brigade, which will be complete by December 2006. The Brigade will return from Germany to Catterick in 2008;

- provision of key enablers and enhancements to brigade capability, including creation of four new Royal Artillery sub-units, the formation of four Logistic Support regiments to support the Armoured and Mechanised Brigades, enhancements to brigade signals capabilities and the formation of additional Critical Care Squadrons in the Close Support Medical Regiments;

- formation of an Operational Intelligence Support Group that will deploy to Afghanistan in support of the NATO Allied Command Europe Rapid Reaction Corps Headquarters;
- enhancements to divisional and operational level signals capabilities;
- creation of an Air Manoeuvre Planning Team to work alongside Headquarters 16 Air Assault Brigade;
- improvements to Special Forces medical support;
- the capability of 17 Port and Maritime Regiment has been enhanced by an extra squadron, making it more deployable, and additional Postal and Courier detachments have enhanced Medical Support and Postal and Courier capabilities and centralised that capability into two regiments.

We have also given particular emphasis during the year to measures to enhance force protection for personnel deployed on operations, including Saxon ambulances, improved protection for Warrior, Saxon and CVR(T) and new body armour.

111. Over the next decade there will be a substantial increase in equipment capability across the Army. The Bowman communications system is being progressively rolled out, with more than 9,000 radio units delivered during the year to equip 7 Armoured, 1 Mechanised and 12 Mechanised Brigades and a contract was placed for the Falcon battlefield communications network. Medium forces will increasingly be based on the Future Rapid Effect System (see paragraph 145). Modernisation of Warrior and Scimitar armoured vehicles continued with further deliveries of the Battlegroup Thermal Imaging System, and the Javelin medium-range anti-armour missile was accepted into service in July 2005, four months early. A prototype of Terrier, the combat engineer vehicle being developed for the Army, was rolled out and trials were conducted of Titan and Trojan, the new Engineer Tank Systems vehicles. The combination of the Intelligence, Surveillance, Target Acquisition and Reconnaissance (ISTAR) systems such as Watchkeeper (for which a £700M contract was placed during the year) and the ASTOR airborne ground surveillance system with long range precision attack capabilities, such as the Guided Missile-Launch Rocket System and the network-enabled ability to call upon Joint precision fires, such as Precision Guided Bomb, will enhance the Army's ability to prosecute targets faster and at greater range. Many of the equipments to support air manoeuvre, such as Future Lynx and replacements for Puma and Sea King, will also be fielded. Light force lethality will have been improved by Next Generation Light Anti-armour Weapon and Light Forces Anti-Tank Guided Weapon System.

Prototype Terrier combat engineer vehicle

Future Army Structures (Reserves)

112. We took forward work on a new Territorial Army (TA) structure to deliver a more operationally effective and fully manned TA better integrated with the Regular Army. This included comprehensive consultation with a wide range of stakeholders, particularly the TA itself. We announced our conclusions on 23 March 2006. Within a continuing overall establishment of 42,000 (including some 3,500 Officer Training Corps personnel) the TA will be rebalanced with some units re-roled, some expanded and others reduced. In particular, TA infantry and medical capabilities will be reduced and a number of new capabilities delivered, including a new Military Intelligence battalion; a new Army Air Corps Regiment to support Apache; enhancement to the Royal Engineers; and the formation of two new logistic regiments. Only three TA centres will close, and the TA's national footprint will be retained. TA units will be paired with the Regular counterparts they are to support, which will provide enhanced and more varied training opportunities. Transition to the new structure will be complete by 2012.

RAF Force Structure and Capabilities

113. The year saw further progress on development of the Royal Air Force to ensure that it can adapt to new threats and environments and is able to deploy forces worldwide and maintain air superiority. In particular, nine Expeditionary Air Wings were established on 1 April 2006. These create a clear focus for the combinations of formed units and supporting elements, thus developing a common ethos and identity that will enhance their collective effectiveness. We continued to drive forward RAF modernisation to ensure we maintain a flexible and agile Air Force with highly capable multi-role aircraft equipped with a range of advanced stand-off precision weapons and increasingly able to exploit networked capabilities. During the year the Typhoon Operational Conversion Unit (29 Sqn), the Operational Evaluation Unit (17 Sqn) and the first operational squadron (3 Sqn) were formed, the RAF took delivery of several hundred more ASRAAM and Stormshadow missiles, and the Brimstone anti-

armour weapon reached full operational capability. Network Enabled Capability will link combat assets, such as Typhoon and Joint Combat Aircraft, with commanders and surveillance assets, such as ASTOR and Nimrod MRA4, to enhance accuracy and speed of response.

Two Tornado GR4s carrying Brimstone

INFORMATION SUPERIORITY

114. Getting the right information to the right people at the right time in the right form while denying an adversary the ability to do the same gives us a relative advantage. There are a number of strands to this work which are described in the following paragraphs.

Network Enabled Capability

115. Network Enabled Capability (NEC) is not simply about acquiring the right equipment and technology, but about how we initially connect then integrate these together and about the way we operate to make use of the information to deliver an effects-based approach to operations. It is as much about culture as it is about equipment. The current phase of work to quantify the benefits that NEC will provide will be completed in 2006. Effective networks allow the Armed Forces, other Government Departments and agencies, and allies and coalition partners to operate in a timely and co-ordinated manner, and their importance is supported by lessons from operational deployments in Iraq and Afghanistan. We are working to achieve an initial NEC capability in 2009. This involves connecting sensors, decision-makers, weapon systems and support capabilities more effectively. Our ability to collect, process, disseminate and use information and intelligence better is also being taken forward within the Defence Intelligence Modernisation Programme (see paragraph 119).

Information Management and Exploitation

116. During the year we completed guidance on information management processes and introduced a new NEC Competency Framework. Together these provide a coherent approach to information management and will guide work on the requirement for information management training more generally. Work is also being done to produce the key reference information that provides the foundation for shared situational understanding. This includes developing the Recognised Theatre Logistics Picture, and producing the user requirement for an end-to-end Joint Logistics Picture. Progress was made in a number of equipment related areas. In particular the progressive delivery and roll-out of the Defence Information Infrastructure (see paragraph 118), Bowman (a secure tactical communications system for the Army), Cormorant (theatre communications system), the Joint Operational Command System which links UK forces and headquarters worldwide, and the Skynet 5 (satellite communications) programmes are starting to deliver information management benefits. The first phase of the research into military capabilities enabled by networking was successfully completed. This is now contributing to the development of a number of capability areas and we intend to trial these developments in NEC on some operational deployments in 2006-07. Information assurance, including an initial computer network defence capability, was reviewed to improve its governance and coherence.

Command and Battlespace Management

117. The Development, Concepts and Doctrine Centre is working to develop a number of concepts underpinning the concept of agility. This includes studies of how we will conduct command and control and joint battlespace management in the future. The Command and Battlespace Management programme, established in March 2001, aims to achieve a winning tempo in the conduct of operations by the development of decision superiority. It is an integral component of our efforts to enhance military capability and is a key tool for driving forward and managing the changes necessary to develop more integrated command, control and management on operations of joint military capabilities. Elements of the programme will only mature over 15 to 20 years.

Defence Information Infrastructure

118. The Defence Information Infrastructure (DII) will provide a modern information infrastructure across Defence, replacing some 300 diverse information systems across 2,000 locations worldwide. The programme will reduce costs through rationalisation and coherence of legacy infrastructures and the delivery of a new MoD wide infrastructure (DII (Future)). This new infrastructure will provide improved value for money, allow additional users to access applications such as the Joint Personnel Administration and is a key enabler for the Defence Change Programme (see paragraphs 121-134). Valuable experience was gained through the delivery of DII (Convergence), an interim system which was developed to meet business needs in advance of the delivery of the new Infrastructure, which currently has about 25,000 users across Defence. The DII (Future) programme has progressed well since contract award in March 2005 and

the system was first used on 31 January 2006. The DII(F) early sites migration programme is now underway and we plan to deliver 70,000 terminals and have 180,000 users on the system by mid 2007. Over £40M in recurring efficiencies were delivered during 2005-06.

Defence Intelligence Modernisation Programme

119. The Defence Intelligence Modernisation Programme is a 'programme of programmes' to modernise and transform Defence Intelligence over the next ten years. It aims to provide a state-of-the-art capability to collect, produce, analyse and disseminate intelligence information by 2016. It encompasses IS-enabled business change, an integrated information environment for Defence Geospatial Intelligence, and a rationalised Defence Intelligence estate embracing new working practices that will better support the Defence vision for network enabled, intelligence-led and effects-based operations.

An RAF controller

FURTHER SOURCES OF INFORMATION

120. Additional Information on Future Effects is available from the following sources:

- *2004 Spending Review: Stability, security and opportunity for all: investing for Britain's long-term future: New Public Spending Plans 2005-2008* (Cm 6237) at www.hm-treasury.gov.uk;
- The Defence Committee Fourth Report of Session 2004-05 *Future Capabilities* (HC 45-i & ii on 17 March 2005) available on www.parliament.the-stationery-office.co.uk;
- *The Government's Response to the Defence Committee Fourth Report of Session 2004-05 Future Capabilities* (Cm6616, July 2005) available at www.mod.uk;
- *Releasing resources to the front line: Independent Review of Public Sector Efficiency* at www.hm-treasury.gov.uk;
- *MoD Annual Report and Accounts 2004-05* available at www.mod.uk.

Essay: Military Drawdown in Northern Ireland

In August 1969, long running tensions in Northern Ireland erupted in a series of pitched battles between police and rioters in Londonderry. The riots stretched the police, the Royal Ulster Constabulary (RUC), to breaking point. The unrest worsened and spread and there were particularly violent outbreaks in North and West Belfast. Firearms were used, makeshift roadblocks were established and buildings were set on fire. The continued violence ultimately exhausted the 3,000 strong police force and many individual officers were injured. As a result, James Chichester-Clark, Prime Minister of Northern Ireland, asked the Government to send troops to restore order. The request was approved and troops were deployed on the streets of Londonderry almost immediately. Thus began, on 14 August 1969 military support to the police (originally the RUC and from November 2001 the Police Service of Northern Ireland (PSNI)) which continues today. The Armed Forces provide support to maintain public order and combat the challenges of terrorism and sectarian violence in Northern Ireland. This is the Armed Forces' longest running operation.

The first serving soldier was killed in Northern Ireland in 1971 and over 700 members of the Armed Forces have lost their lives since the deployment began. In 1972, at the height of the Troubles, there were approximately 25,000 troops deployed and over a hundred military deaths in the year. As the security situation has improved in recent years, the PSNI have increasingly been able to carry out their duties with less routine military support. This has enabled a steady reduction in the number of troops deployed to about 10,800 on 1 April 2005, comprising four resident general service infantry battalions, one roulement infantry battalion, 3 Royal Irish (Home Service) battalions and support structures.

Following the Provisional IRA's statement on 28 July 2005, formally ordering an end to their armed campaign, on 1 August 2005 the Government announced a two year normalisation programme, with details set out in an Annex to the UK and Irish Governments' Joint Declaration[1]. The military operation will end on 31 July 2007, when the Northern Ireland garrison will consist of no more than 5,000 troops in no more than 11 sites, which were identified by Minister (Armed Forces) in a written statement on 10 May 2006. The remaining troops based in Northern Ireland will then be available for worldwide operations just like those based anywhere else in the UK.

Since 1 August 2005 we have made considerable progress towards meeting our commitments under the Joint Declaration. A network of infrastructure was built over the past three decades to underpin the provision of military support to the police. The majority of this is now being dismantled or disposed of. As of 1 April 2006, 28 military sites were in use, down from 106 in 1994 when the Provisional IRA declared their first ceasefire. The numerous observation towers, visible across the skyline of South Armagh and a constant source of controversy for local residents, are being pulled down. The last three are scheduled to be cleared by 31 March 2007. The last roulement battalion, the 1st Battalion, the Royal Welch Fusiliers, left Northern Ireland on 16 January 2006.

As part of normalisation, the three Royal Irish (Home Service) battalions are also being disbanded. The Home Service battalions were established specifically to support the police. They and their predecessors in the Ulster Defence Regiment have provided invaluable support to the police and contributed much to creating the current environment. However, as they have no role outside Northern Ireland there is no military requirement for them with the end of the military operation. Over 3,000 Home Service personnel will consequently be discharged. We are keen not to lose the expertise they possess and are encouraging those who so wish to apply to transfer into the general service Army. A settlement package for Royal Irish personnel, including access to resettlement services, was announced on 9 March 2006[2]. Work continues to develop details of a bespoke aftercare service for all current members of the Royal Irish (Home Service), their predecessors and their dependents.

The removal of infrastructure, the disbandment of the Home Service battalions and the reduction to a garrison of no more than 5,000 has significant consequences for the Defence civilians who worked alongside their military counterparts throughout. As a result around 1,500 individuals are likely to be declared surplus (although 340 new jobs are being created at the remaining Defence sites). We are trying to avoid any compulsory redundancies and are discussing a possible additional package of support measures tailored to the particular circumstances with the Trades Unions.

After the Operation ends on 31 July 2007, military personnel in Northern Ireland will continue to provide specialist support to the police, such as bomb disposal, as they do elsewhere in the UK. They will also retain the ability to provide public order support to the Police in Northern Ireland[3] if needed in the event of substantial public order demands, as set out in Lord Patten's 1999 review of policing in Northern Ireland. This will focus on support during periods when contentious parades are held. We continue to work to create the conditions where even that role is no longer needed.

British Troops in Northern Ireland

[1] See www.nio.gov.uk/joint_declaration_between_the_british_and_irish_governments.pdf\
[2] See www.publications.parliament.uk/pa/cm200506/cmhansrd/cm060309/debtext/60309-10.htm#60309-10_spmin2.
[3] See www.nio.gov.uk/a_new_beginning_in_policing_in_northern_ireland.pdf

EFFICIENCY AND CHANGE

Objective: More flexible and efficient organisations and processes to support the Armed Forces.

SR2004 Efficiency Target

Realise total annual efficiency gains of at least £2.8 billion by 2007-08, of which three quarters will be cash-releasing

- **Reduce civilian staff numbers by at least 10,000;**
- **Reduce the number of military posts in administrative and support roles by at least 5,000;**
- **Be on course to have relocated 3,900 posts out of London and the South East by 2010.**

Performance Measures and Assessment

By 31 March 2006 between £1,323M and £1,398M of efficiencies had been delivered, including £200M of sustainable efficiencies realised in 2004-05.

Force Structure Changes:

- **Reductions to Type 42 Destroyer and Type 23 Frigate fleets;**
- **Reduction of Mine Hunter force level to 16 vessels and removal of 3 Northern Ireland patrol vessels;**
- **Re-roling and reduction of Challenger 2 armoured squadrons and AS90 artillery batteries;**
- **Reductions to Tornado F3 and Jaguar units;**
- **Operating and support cost savings from a reduced Nimrod fleet.**

Corporate Services:

- **Roll-out of Joint Personnel Administration system to the RAF in March 2006;**
- **Progressive roll-out of Human Resource Management System;**
- **Progressive roll-out of Defence Information Infrastructure.**

Procurement and Logistics:

- **Equipment procurement expenditure reductions of £54M;**
- **Improved logistic support to front line and between £500M and £575M of efficiencies through Defence Logistics Transformation Programme on the basis of the latest available evidence;**
- **First stage of Whole Fleet Management programme achieved Initial Operating Capability in October 2005;**
- **£31M efficiencies through Estates Modernisation programme;**
- **£35M efficiencies from other areas of procurement.**

Productive Time:

Productive Time:

- **Reduction in time taken to restore personnel to full fitness.**

Organisational Change:

- **Continuing rationalisation of TLB headquarters and organisation.**

Relocation:

- **1,229 posts relocated by 31 March 2006.**

Personnel Reductions:

- **Over 950 military and support posts disestablished and over 6,000 civilian reductions achieved by 1 April 2006.**

EFFICIENCY AND CHANGE PROGRAMMES

121. The Department has comprehensive efficiency and change programmes that extend right across the Department and affect every employee. They affirm the importance we attach to delivering the greatest possible military capability from the resources available for Defence. Improvements in areas such as logistics and medical services are already contributing directly to an increase in our military capability. Efficiencies in process and back-office functions are being reinvested in further enhancements. This chapter explains the relationships between the Change and Efficiency programmes and details our performance and progress against our efficiency targets.

Defence Change Programme

122. The purpose of the Defence Change Programme is to modernise departmental business processes to improve efficiency and effectiveness, thus maximising our investment in front-line operational capability. Launched in 2002, it now joins up the major change programmes across Defence under strong central direction, to produce a single, coherent programme. It ensures that each change initiative is worthwhile and delivers the expected benefits through robust governance and plans. In prioritising between the various change initiatives underway across the Department, the Change Programme ensures that scarce resources of people, money and skills are devoted to the most important and productive areas. It is a long term commitment to improved delivery, and therefore includes programmes that are now beginning to deliver benefits and new initiatives. There are 17 pan-Defence change programmes in all, covering almost every business process. As well as improving the way we do business, 12 of the programmes will deliver about £1.4 billion of benefits in the 2004 Spending Review period, corresponding to around 50% of our efficiency target. The Programme has been supported by investment of some £315M drawn down during 2005-06 from the Defence Modernisation Fund, which is a ring-fenced sum of £1 billion secured from HM Treasury over the three years of the 2004 Spending Review period.

Efficiency Programme

123. As part of the 2004 Spending Review, we agreed to realise total annual efficiency gains of at least £2.8 billion by 31 March 2008, of which three quarters will be cash releasing. Within that target, we aim to:

- Reduce the number of our civilian staff by at least 10,000;
- Reduce the number of military posts in administrative and support functions by at least 5,000;
- Be on course to have relocated 3,900 posts out of London and the South East by 2010.

124. Around half of the target will be achieved by programmes that were already within the Defence Change Programme, and a further 40% from implementation of the force capability changes set out in *Delivering Security in a Changing World: Future Capabilities*, published in July 2004 (see paragraphs 107-113). The remaining 10% will come from various other programmes, including TLB commodity procurement, relocations in response to the Lyons review and work to simplify and improve the finance function. The relationship between the Efficiency Programme and the Defence Change Programme is shown at Figure 7, together with the location of further details on specific projects. As this shows, the Change and Efficiency programmes are deeply embedded across Defence.

RAF training: preparing the next day's missions.'

Figure 7: Relationship of Change and Efficiency Programmes

Efficiency Programme

Defence Change Programme		Force Capability changes	Other
Defence Training Review Transformation (para. 192)	Defence Logistics Transformation (paras. 129, 233-234)	Force structure changes, including related estate rationalisation (paras. 107-113, 128)	Lyons (paras. 132, 305)
UK Military Flying Training System (para. 193)	Whole Fleet Management (para. 129)	Other manpower reductions (para. 133)	Finance (paras. 128, 275-276)
Command and Battlespace Management (para. 117)	Defence Information Infrastructure (paras. 118, 128)	Equipment procurement (para. 129)	Commodity procurement (para. 129)
Business Management System (paras. 246-254)	Estate Modernisation (paras. 129, 300-313)		
Defence Intelligence Modernisation Programme (para. 119)	People Programme (paras. 128, 162-165)		
	Joint Personnel Administration (paras. 128, 155-156)		
	Defence Health Change Programme (paras. 130, 211-213)		
	Defence e-Commerce (para. 129)		
	Defence Travel Modernisation (para. 129)		
	TLB HQ Collocations (paras. 131, 304)		

Governance

125. Rigorous governance structures are in place, with a particular emphasis on risks and benefits. Overall leadership of the Change Programme is provided by the Defence Change Programme Board, which is responsible to the Defence Council and Defence Management Board for managing cross-cutting issues such as common risks and interdependencies, and loading and capacity issues. It is chaired, when Ministers attend, by the Secretary of State, or by the 2nd Permanent Under Secretary in his absence. Each programme within the Change Programme has a Senior Responsible Owner who is personally accountable for maximising the delivery of benefits and reports regularly to the programme's sponsoring Minister. They are individually supported and challenged in this by the Change Delivery Group, routinely chaired by the 2nd Permanent Under Secretary, as the Senior Responsible Owner of the overall Defence Change Programme. The 2nd Permanent Under Secretary also has overall responsibility for delivery of the Efficiency Programme. He chairs the Efficiency Delivery Board, which oversees this on behalf of the Defence Management Board. The Defence Management Board receives regular progress reports on both the Efficiency and the Defence Change Programmes.

Performance against SR04 Efficiency Target

126. The MoD's Efficiency Technical Note describes the Efficiency Programme in detail and explains how we will deliver and measure the efficiency gains. Additionally, extensive work has been undertaken to embed efficiency targets within Top Level Budget Holders' financial control totals, and to develop robust methods to track delivery. Progress continues to be made in meeting the Department's efficiency targets. By 31 March 2006, between £1,323M and £1,398M of efficiencies had been delivered, including £200M of sustainable efficiencies realised in 2004-05. Details are set out in Table 2.

Table 2: Performance against SR04 Efficiency Target Programme	Planned Efficiencies by 31 March 2006 £M	Achievement by 31 March 2006 £M	Future Planned Efficiency gains 2006-07 £M	2007-08 £M
Force Structure changes	**106**	**106**	**298**	**388**
Corporate Services	**131**	**343**	**254**	**309**
Military Personnel Management	5	16	43	85
Civilian Personnel Management	21	24*	49	107
Finance Function	2	2	13	11
Information Services	103	301*	149	106
Procurement and Logistics	**695**	**674-749**	**1,123**	**1,660**
Equipment Procurement	54	54*	206	374
Defence Logistics Transformation	539	500-575	714	951
Whole Fleet Management	56	54*	66	116
Estates Modernisation	37	31*	62	95
Other Procurement	9	35	75	124
Productive Time	**84**	**105***	**86**	**88**
Organisational changes	**0**	**0**	**2**	**14**
Relocation	**12**	**18**	**18**	**18**
Manpower	**88**	**86**	**285**	**449**
RN	15	15	32	32
Army	18	18	64	88
RAF	53	51	121	203
Civilian	2	2	68	126
Adjustment	**-9**	**-9**	**-41**	**-126**
TOTAL	**1,107**	**1,323-1,398**	**2,025**	**2,800**

Notes:
1. Planned Efficiencies and Achievement by 31 March 2006 include efficiencies during 2004-05 and 2005-06. Efficiency gains for 2005-06 are provisional, subject to final validation. Because of the size of the Defence Logistics Transformation Programme, the process of validation takes some time and this is the reason why a range is given in the Table.
2. The planned efficiencies in this table reflect a number of changes agreed by the Office of Government Commerce and the Treasury since the most recent version of the Efficiency Technical Note was published in December 2005.
3. Adjustment to avoid double counting of manpower savings.
4. Efficiency gains marked with an asterisk include an element of non-cashable gains.
5. The Information Services total for 2005-06 includes a non-recuring £260M for the reduced in-year cost of sustaining legacy systems (see paragraphy 128)
6. 'Force structure changes', 'Equipment Procurement', 'Manpower' and 'Adjustment' make up the efficiency savings of £1.2 billion announced in the Future Capabilities Command Paper (See paragraphs 107-113)

Force Structure Changes

127. Following the 2003 Defence White Paper, the Department undertook a detailed study of force structures and the equipment programme and determined that extensive restructuring would allow us to achieve better policy outcomes with smaller, lighter and more capable forces. These changes were set out in *Delivering Security in a Changing World: Future Capabilities*, published in July 2004. In 2004-05, we delivered £41M of efficiency savings through changes to our force structures. By 31 March 2006, we had delivered a further £65M through:

- reductions to our Type 42 Destroyer and Type 23 Frigate fleets, enabled by revised assumptions about concurrent operations;
- reducing the Mine Hunter force level to 16, enabled by changed operational requirements, and removing the three Northern Ireland patrol vessels as a result of improving security;

- the continued re-roling and reduction of Challenger 2 armoured squadrons and AS90 artillery batteries to reflect a shift in emphasis from heavy to light and medium weight forces;

- reductions to Tornado F3 and Jaguar units in line with the introduction into service of Typhoon; and

- operating and support cost savings from a reduced Nimrod fleet.

Further information on force structure changes is at paragraphs 107-113

Corporate Services

128. The Department is undertaking a range of programmes to modernise and improve the effectiveness and efficiency of its corporate services:

- The Joint Personnel Administration will modernise the personnel management and administration of the Armed Forces by harmonising and simplifying a range of personnel policies and processes and by introducing a new commercial off-the-shelf information systems. The system was rolled-out to the RAF in March 2006. It has delivered £16M of benefits during 2005-06. See paragraphs 155-156 for further information;

- The People Programme will enable MoD civilians to make the best contribution to the UK's defence capability through a civilian workforce that is appropriately skilled, managed and motivated. Efficiency gains will be achieved through a reduction of civilian Human Resources (HR) staff, lower maintenance costs of the HR information system, implementation of a modern, simple pay, policy and processes and a reduction in administration tasks. Five new work-streams were endorsed in November 2005, including Performance Management and Diversity. The People Programme has delivered £24M of benefits during 2005-06. See paragraphs 162-165 for further information;

- The Defence Resource Management Programme aims to simplify and improve current financial processes, structures and systems to reduce costs and improve decision-making. Efficiency gains will be achieved from a reduction in the number of staff in the finance function and reduction in expenditure on external assistance. Just over £2M of efficiencies had been delivered by 31 March 2006. Further information is at paragraphs 275-276;

- The Defence Information Infrastructure (DII) is delivering a modern management information infrastructure across Defence. In addition to some £40M of recurring efficiencies delivered by 31 March 2006, the programme had delivered an additional non-recurring in-year benefit for 2005-06 of £260M reflecting the lower cost of sustaining legacy systems, for a total of some £301M. Further information on DII is at paragraph 118.

Procurement and Logistics

129. As set out in detail elsewhere in the Annual Report and Accounts, the Department is undertaking a range of programmes to build on Smart Acquisition, improve value for money from expenditure on the future equipment programme, increase the effectiveness, efficiency and flexibility of Defence logistics activity, and modernise management of the Defence estate. We are also working to improve the efficiency of commodity procurement across Defence. These programmes comprise the Procurement and Logistics element of our overall efficiency programme. In particular:

- *Future Capabilities* identified opportunities to improve value for money from equipment procurement expenditure. Revised procurement strategies for the future helicopter fleet and the Future Rapid Effects System, a more efficient way to provide the offensive air capability, and reprofiled acquisition increments for indirect fire precision attack produced a total of £54M efficiencies during 2005-06;

- The purpose of the Defence Logistics Transformation Programme is to transform the means by which all logistics support is delivered to the three Services. On the basis of the available information, the programme delivered between £500M and £575M of efficiencies by 31 March 2006 against a target of £539M. Further information is at paragraphs 233-234 and in the essay on page 119;

- Whole Fleet Management will provide better management of the Defence land vehicle fleet and facilitate the training of force elements to the required standard on future reduced fleets. Savings are achieved through reduced spares consumption and battery use, improved management of the vehicle fleet and productive time efficiencies. The first stage of the programme achieved initial operating capability in October 2005. Efficiencies of £54M had been delivered by 31 March 2006;

- The Estate Modernisation programme is rationalising and improving the condition of the Defence estate and obtaining better value for money from estate expenditure through the introduction of Prime Contracting, the modernisation of single living accommodation and the provision of water and waste water services. Efficiency gains are achieved through personnel reductions, lower management overheads for Service families' accommodation and reduced operating costs. £31M of efficiencies had been delivered by 31 March 2006. Further information is at paragraphs 300-313;

- The 'Other Procurement' Initiative extends the Defence Logistics Organisation's Procurement Reform programme across other areas of Defence. This aims to maximise the Department's buying power using reverse auctions, electronic purchasing, incentives and rationalisation of contracts, and had delivered a further £35M of efficiencies by 31 March 2006. This includes £12M from the Defence Travel Modernisation

programme to deliver a modern and coherent travel e-booking capability. We are working closely with the Office of Government Commerce and other Government Departments in travel and a number of other areas to maximise the potential benefits of procurement reform for the MoD and across Government.

Productive Time

130. The objective of the Defence Health Change Programme is to increase the proportion of military personnel who are fit-for-task by improving the quality of healthcare using regional rehabilitation units and other methods. By 31 March 2006, we have delivered £105M of non-cashable annual efficiency gains from reducing the time taken to restore personnel to full fitness. Further information is at paragraphs 211-215.

Organisational Changes

131. A number of initiatives are in hand to slim down the Department's management overhead, both in the Head Office in London and elsewhere across the Top Level Budget organisations:

- Following the completion of the successful modernisation programme to refurbish the MoD Main Building, introduce new technology and improved working practices, and reduce Head Office numbers, we have disposed of five central London headquarters buildings (Northumberland House, Metropole Building, St Giles' Court, Great Scotland Yard and St Christopher House); and in early 2006 we announced our intention to develop detailed proposals to vacate the Old War Office in Whitehall. By March 2005, we had achieved a reduction in management costs in Head Office and other top-level headquarters of 12% towards our 2002 Spending Review PSA target of a 13% reduction. As explained below, substantial further reductions in management costs are in prospect from 2006-07 onwards, but as these benefits do not fall in the SR02 period the final achievement against the PSA target remains at 12%;

- Rationalisation of a number of TLB Headquarters and organisation continued throughout the year. In particular work to merge the Royal Navy's Fleet and 2nd Sea Lord Top Level Budget organisations was completed and a single Naval Top Level Budget organisation with a unified Headquarters in Portsmouth stood up on 1 April 2006. This will save 125 military and 325 civilian posts and will generate around £17M of efficiencies by 31 March 2010. Project Hyperion is taking forward the reorganisation of Land Command and the Adjutant General's Department and the establishment of a new collocated Headquarters. This is expected to save about 110 military and 240 civilian posts and generate £15M of efficiencies by 31 March 2011. Collocation of the headquarters of the Royal Air Force Strike Command and Personnel and Training Command Top Level Budget organisations at RAF High Wycombe progressed, with completion planned for October 2006. This is expected to save around 475 military and 525 civilian posts and generate £30M efficiencies by 31 March 2010. Further information is at paragraphs 304-307.

The new Fleet Headquarters – Sir Henry Leach Building

Relocations

132. We remain on track to deliver a net reduction of 3,900 posts in London and the South East by 2010. 1,229 posts had been relocated and some £18M efficiencies delivered by 31 March 2006, as a result of the restructuring of the Army Technical College, which moved from Arborfield to Harrogate and other sites. Further information is at paragraph 305.

Personnel Reductions

133. The changes to force capabilities and the departmental Change and Efficiency Programmes will produce further personnel reductions:

- The number of military personnel will reduce by over 10,000 by April 2008. This will enable over 5,000 military administrative and support posts to be abolished. Over 950 of these posts had been disestablished by 1 April 2006. Further information is at paragraphs 155-156 and 207.

- We are planning to reduce civilian personnel numbers by over 11,500 by 1 April 2008. This will be achieved by a combination of natural wastage (normal retirements and resignations), moves to private contractors on Transfer of Undertaking and Protection of Employment terms, reduced recruitment and a voluntary early release scheme. A reduction of over 6,000[1] had been achieved by 31 March 2006, and the total number of civilians employed by the MoD reduced from 108,470 Full Time Equivalents on 1 April 2005 to 103,930 on 1 April 2006. See paragraphs 292-293 for further information.

[1] This is based on agreement with the Treasury and includes Tranding Fund reductions but excludes operational Locally Engaged Civilians.

FURTHER SOURCES OF INFORMATION

134. Additional Information on Efficiency and Change is available from the following sources:
- quarterly PSA reports to HM Treasury available at www.mod.uk;
- MoD Autumn Performance Report 2005 available at www.mod.uk;
- *Delivering Security in a Changing World: Future Capabilities* available at www.mod.uk;
- *SR2004 Efficiency Technical Note* available at www.mod.uk;
- *2004 Spending Review: Stability, security and opportunity for all: investing for Britain's long-term future* (CM 6237 on 12 July 2004) available at www.hm-treasury.gov.uk;
- *The independent review of Public Service Relocations – Well Placed to Deliver? – Shaping the Pattern of Government Service' by Sir Michael Lyons* available at www.hm-treasury.gov.uk;
- *The Gershon Review: Releasing Resources for the Frontline: Independent Review of Public Sector Efficiency* (July 2004) available at www.hm-treasury.gov.uk.

Essay: The Changing Defence Footprint in the United Kingdom

In 1990, just after the end of the Cold War, there were about 315,000 Service personnel, of whom about 17,000 were women and only a few thousand came from ethnic minority backgrounds. They were supported by about 141,000 UK based civilians. The Armed Forces were spread throughout the UK and a disproportionately large number of civilian staff were based in London. By around 2010, there will be about 191,000 Service personnel, of whom about 17,000-18,000 will be women and 10,000 will come from ethnic minority backgrounds, supported by about 90,000 civilians, a much smaller proportion of whom will be based in London and the South East of England. We are also bringing home some of the Forces from Germany. Operations in the Balkans, Iraq, Afghanistan and elsewhere have demonstrated that the Armed Forces must be able to conduct short-notice expeditionary operations and be highly flexible. Housing, training, deploying and maintaining this type of force is a very different challenge from that of the past. And the transition to this more demanding environment has to be delivered and sustained within a broadly constant level of resources. We are therefore taking forward a wide ranging programme to deliver the supporting infrastructure we will need and that makes the most effective use of Defence resources to deliver as much Defence capability as possible. This will involve greater functional and geographic focus around clusters of fewer but better used and supported sites, with a streamlined management superstructure. Wider Government policy initiatives, including Sustainable Development and the Lyons Review, are being embraced in our planning. We are achieving this in an evolutionary manner and have been moving in this direction for a number of years.

While many details are unresolved, the broad geographical picture is fairly clear. In future the Armed Forces will increasingly be concentrated in larger, denser, clusters:

- **The Royal Navy** has already established an integrated single Headquarters in Portsmouth and is concentrating around sites in Portsmouth, Plymouth and on the Clyde. Portsmouth will be home to over half the surface fleet, including the aircraft carriers, Type 42 destroyers, Type 23 frigates and training units. Devonport in Plymouth, the largest Naval Base in Western Europe and the only site in the UK equipped to conduct nuclear submarine refits, will be home to Type 22 and Type 23 frigates, the amphibious assault ships, Trafalgar class submarines and the Royal Naval Surveying squadron. The Fleet Air Arm and the Royal Marines will also be mainly concentrated in the South West of England. On the Clyde, Faslane and the linked Royal Naval Armaments Depot at Coulport are home to the strategic nuclear deterrent and responsible for the storage, processing, maintenance and issue of the Trident Weapon System and ammunitioning for all submarine embarked weapons;

- **The Army** is creating a single integrated Headquarters probably at Andover in Hampshire. It is moving towards a more balanced deployable force organised around two armoured brigades, three mechanised brigades, a light brigade and an air assault brigade, supported by appropriate, deployable specialist units. To house these coherently it is working to develop over time a number of multi-Battalion 'supergarrisons' around the country to replace many existing, mostly single-battalion garrisons. Some of these will be large single-site, multi-unit locations (such as the 16 Air Assault Brigade in Colchester). Others will probably comprise a related and geographically coherent group of separate facilities (such as the garrisons around Salisbury Plain). Infrastructure and training requirements make it likely the heaviest forces will be concentrated in the south around Salisbury Plain and Aldershot (where Project Allenby/Connaught is providing a modern living and working environment) and in Germany. 4th Armoured Brigade, currently based in Germany, is converting to a mechanised brigade and will relocate to Catterick in 2008-09. 19 Mechanised Brigade, currently based in Catterick, started conversion to a light brigade in January. The Northern Ireland garrison will in the long term comprise no more than 5,000 troops, based coherently at a smaller number of locations. The Army is also working to deliver improved geographic cohesion over time for non-deployable functional supporting units. As well as improving deployability and administrative efficiency, this strategy should deliver greater long-term stability for the personnel involved and their families;

- **The Royal Air Force** is establishing a single integrated Headquarters at RAF High Wycombe in Buckinghamshire. It is also setting up nine Expeditionary Air Wings, to provide a clear focus for combinations of formed units and supporting elements when deployed on operations. The coming reduction in the number of types of aircraft in service will enable a parallel reduction in the number of airfields it needs, and this is being taken forward incrementally through the Defence Airfield Review. Typhoon squadrons will be based at RAF Leuchars in Scotland and RAF Coningsby in Lincolnshire; Tornado squadrons at RAF Lossiemouth in Scotland and RAF Marham in Norfolk; Harrier squadrons at RAF Cottesmore in Rutland; Nimrod Maritime Reconnaissance aircraft at RAF Kinloss in Scotland, deployed to RAF St Mawgan in Cornwall; the communications fleet at RAF Northolt in Middlesex; the air transport and refuelling fleet at RAF Lyneham in Wiltshire and RAF Brize Norton in Oxfordshire; helicopters at RAF Aldergrove in Northern Ireland, RAF Benson in Oxfordshire and RAF Odiham in Hampshire; the surveillance fleet at RAF Waddington in Lincolnshire; the RAF Regiment at RAF Honington in Suffolk and RAF Leeming in Yorkshire; and flying training units at RAF Valley in North Wales, RAF Linton-on-Ouse in Yorkshire and RAF Cranwell in Lincolnshire. Non-flying units are predominantly based at a number of locations across central southern England, the east Midlands, Lincolnshire and Yorkshire;

- **Joint Forces.** The increasingly integrated nature of Defence has been reflected in various joint structures established to ensure effective coordination of related capabilities and to command operations. The Permanent Joint Headquarters is based at Northwood in north London, the Joint Helicopter Command is collocated with the Army Headquarters at Wilton in Wiltshire, and Joint Force Harrier is based at RAF Cottesmore.

These capabilities are supported by a substantial enabling infrastructure. Following the successful relocation of the Defence Procurement Agency to Bristol in the mid 1990s there has been a steady trend towards creation of coherent regionally focused supporting specialisms:

- **London Head Office:** We have reduced from more than 20 MoD headquarters buildings in London in 1990 to three today, and are also looking to dispose of the Old War Office Building in Whitehall. We are taking forward further rationalisation of the Greater London estate, which will eventually be concentrated mainly on facilities at Woolwich and RAF Northolt;

- **Acquisition and Logistics:** The Defence Procurement Agency (then the Procurement Executive) relocated from London to Abbey Wood near Bristol in the early 1990s. We have announced our intention to create an acquisition hub with improved decision-making and better through-life management of Defence equipment in the Bath and Bristol area where the Defence Procurement Agency and Defence Logistics Organisation already work closely together. In the longer term this is likely to include relocation of the logistic land and air environment Integrated Project Teams from their current sites, mainly at Andover in Hampshire and RAF Wyton in Huntingdonshire, and collocation of supply chain staff in Andover, though no final decisions have yet been made;

- **Training and Education:** The Defence Academy at Shrivenham in Oxfordshire provides advanced training and education, including the Joint Service Command and Staff College. The Defence Training Review rationalisation programme will provide modern, cost-effective specialist training, improved accommodation and facilities and by harmonising training currently delivered by individual Services will enable more efficient use of a smaller training estate;

- **Personnel Administration:** Service personnel administration, including pensions and benefits, will mainly be delivered by the Armed Forces Personnel Administration Agency at RAF Innsworth in Gloucestershire, Portsmouth in Hampshire, and Glasgow and civilian personnel administration mainly by the People, Pay and Pensions Agency in Bath in Somerset;

- **Corporate Finance:** We are creating a Financial Accounting Shared Service Centre to provide specialised financial transaction services for the entire Department. This will be based in Bath (for financial accounting business) and Liverpool (for bill processing and paying);

- **Scientific Support:** The Defence Science and Technology Laboratory is rationalising scientific support to core sites at Porton Down in Wiltshire, Portsdown West near Portsmouth and Fort Halstead near Sevenoaks in Kent. Specialist hydrographic and meteorological services are provided by the UK Hydrographic Office in Plymouth and the Met Office in Exeter.

Conclusion

We have come a long way from the situation at the end of the Cold War. But we have some way further to go. We are working both to reduce further the number of sites we use and to consolidate significant blocks of Defence business in geographically coherent areas mainly located away from London and the South East of England. In 1993 nearly 50,000 MoD civilians were employed in and around London. This has shrunk to some 24,000 and will reduce further. The Head Office and Permanent Joint Headquarters will remain in London. The Royal Navy is already concentrated in Portsmouth, Plymouth and on the Clyde. The Army will remain widely spread across the United Kingdom, although over time we aim to create a smaller number of regional centres of gravity for deployable forces comparable to the current major garrisons in central southern England, Essex, and Yorkshire. The Royal Air Force centres of gravity will remain central southern England, the east Midlands and East Anglia, Lincolnshire and Yorkshire, and eastern Scotland. The primary focus of acquisition, logistics, personnel administration and corporate finance business will be in the west of England around Bristol, Bath and Gloucester leading to an increase in the number of civilian personnel, currently some 24,000, employed in this area.

FUTURE CAPABILITIES AND INFRASTRUCTURE

Objective: Progress future equipment and capital infrastructure projects to time, quality and cost estimates.

Public Service Agreement Targets (SR2004 MoD Target 6 and SR2002 MoD Target 7

Deliver the Equipment Programme to cost and time by achieving:

- **At least 97% of Key User Requirements, for all Category A to C Projects that have passed Main Gate Approval, to be achieved throughout the PSA period.**
- **An average in-year variation of forecast In Service Dates, for all Category A to C Projects that have passed Main Gate Approval, to be no more than 0.7 months in FY05/06, 0.5 months in FY06/07 and 0.4 months in FY07/08.**
- **An average in-year variation of forecast costs for Design and Manufacture phase, for all Category A to C projects that have passed Main Gate approval, of less than 0.4% in FY05/06, 0.3% in FY06/07 and 0.2% in FY07/08.**

Increase value for money by making improvements in the efficiency and effectiveness of the key processes for delivering military capability:

- **Achieve 0% average annual cost growth (or better) against the major equipment procurement projects (measured against estimated project costs at the beginning of the year).**

Performance Measures and Assessment

At least 97% of Key User Requirements, for all Category A to C Projects that have passed Main Gate Approval, to be achieved:

- **97% of Key User Requirements predicted to be achieved (99% 2004-05).**

On average, less than 0.4% in-year variation of forecast costs for Design and Manufacture phase of projects over £20M:

- **0.2% average increase in costs measured against estimated cost at beginning of year (2.2% average decrease 2004-05).**

On average, no increase in costs of 20 largest Major Projects:

- **0.1% average annual cost decrease of 20 Major Projects measured against estimated cost at beginning of the year (4.6% average increase 2004-05).**

No more than 0.7 months in-year slippage of forecast In-Service Dates for projects over £20M:

- **0.7 months average slippage (0.9 months 2004-05).**

DPA delivery of at least 90% of planned in-year asset deliveries, by value:

- **107% of planned in-year assets delivered (100% 2004-05).**

Other Measures:

- **90 Urgent Operational Requirements to support operations in Iraq and Afghanistan approved during 2005-06;**
- **Continuing progress with equipment-led capability change programmes headed by Senior Responsible Owners;**
- **Defence Industrial Strategy White Paper issued;**
- **Office of Government Commerce Peer Review of DPA Forward programme;**
- **UK Defence export contracts worth over £4 billion, and agreement on sale of Typhoon aircraft to Saudi Arabia.**

EQUIPMENT PROCUREMENT

135. The Equipment Programme delivers battle-winning equipment to the Armed Forces, harnessing new technologies and concepts. It is rigorously reviewed every two years, as part of the MoD's overall planning and programming process, to ensure that we make the best possible use of available resources and provide the UK Armed Forces with the affordable capabilities they need for operations today and in the future. Table 3 sets out the Department's performance against the 2004 Spending Review Public Service Agreement targets, and the Defence Procurement Agency's performance against its complementary Key Targets. This performance has been certified by the National Audit Office. In 2005-06, for the first time, the Department and the Defence Procurement Agency met all the acquisition targets.

2004 Spending Review Public Service Agreement Targets

136. In the 2004 Spending Review, the Defence Public Service Agreement target for equipment acquisition was amended to cover a much broader range of projects than had been the case in previous Public Service Agreements, in order to provide a better and more comprehensive picture of the performance of the Equipment Programme overall. Previously it had only included the twenty largest projects in development and manufacture that were covered by the annual Major Projects Report. It now includes all projects with a capital value greater than £20M, that have passed their main investment decision point but not yet achieved their In-Service Dates at the start of the financial year; this equates to 46 projects in all in 2005-06. This is also the target set used to measure the performance of the Defence Procurement Agency. In 2005-06 the equipment delivered showed minimal increase in costs or project slippage levels overall. The twenty projects covered by the Major Projects Report showed a 0.1% average annual cost decrease against their estimated cost at beginning of the year, which met the value for money target set in the 2002 Spending Review.

Defence Procurement Agency Key Targets

137. Although the Defence Procurement Agency's performance is measured against the same target set of projects used to measure the Department's acquisition performance, the Department recognised the degree of challenge involved by setting slightly less demanding targets on the Agency, for cost and time, in its Key Targets and treating the Public Service Agreement targets for variation of project In-Service Dates and project Costs as stretch targets The Defence Procurement Agency (DPA) was also set targets for asset delivery and a range of efficiency measures. It met all its Key Targets in 2005-06 for the first year since its establishment. Further details on the DPA's performance can be found in the *DPA Annual Report and Accounts*. Summary information on the performance of major equipment projects by capability area is contained in Annex G and detailed information on these projects is continued in the annual *Major Projects Report* published by the National Audit Office.

European Space Agency Ariane 5 rocket that will be used to launch Skynet 5 satellites (photo: ESA)

Table 3: PSA and Defence Procurement Agency Targets and Achievements	2005-06	2004-05	2003-04
Predicted achievement of Key User Requirements[1]	**97%**	**N/A**	**N/A**
Met	**97%**	**N/A**	**N/A**
Equivalent DPA Key Target	*97%*	*97%*	*98%*
Met	*97%*	*99%*	*99%*
Average In-Year slippage of In-Service Dates not to exceed[1]	**0.7 months**	**N/A**	**N/A**
Met	**0.7 months**	**N/A**	**N/A**
Equivalent DPA Key Target	*1.0 months*	*0.9 months*	*0.5 months*
Met	*0.7 months*	*0.9 months*	*2.4 months*
Average In-Year variation of costs not to exceed[1]	**0.4%**	**N/A**	**N/A**
Met	**0.2%**	**N/A**	**N/A**
Equivalent DPA Key Target	*0.6%*	*0%*	*0%*
Met	*0.2%*	*-2.2%*	*2.7%*
Asset delivery achievement (percentage by value of planned asset deliveries)[2]	*>90%*	*85%*	*N/A*
Met	*107%*	*100%*	*N/A*
i) Asset Turnover Ratio (months)[3]	*<83 months*	*<70 months*	*N/A*
Met	*72 months*	*59 months*	
ii) Assets delivered per £ of Operating Costs[4]	*>£13.20*	*>£10.72*	*N/A*
Met	*£15.23*	*£14.36*	
iii) Assets produced per £ of Operating Costs[5]	*>£23.16*	*>£16.23*	*N/A*
Met	*£23.83*	*£19.13*	

Notes:
1. PSA Target set changed from 2005-06 to covered all equipment over £20M that have passed their main investment decision point, but not yet achieved ISD at the start of the financial year, in line with DPA Key Targets. Performance against the SR2002 PSA Targets for 2003-04 and 2004-05 was measured on a different and not fully comparable basis.
2. Key Target introduced from 2004-05.
3. This is an approximation of how many months assets/equipment sit on the DPA balance sheet before they are finished and delivered. A decreasing number indicates improving efficiency.
4. This measures the assets / equipment delivered to the DPA's customers against the DPA's operating costs. An increasing number indicates improving efficiency.
5. This measures the assets added to the Balance Sheet over DPA's operating cost. An increasing number indicates improving efficiency.

Deliveries and key contacts placed

138. The Defence Procurement Agency delivered new equipment valued at £3.3 billion (£8.3 billion[1] in 2004-05), representing 107% of the asset value planned for delivery in-year against a target of 90%. Nine projects were formally accepted into service. Key milestones included:

- delivery of twelve Typhoon combat aircraft to the RAF;
- delivery to the RAF of over 200 combat-proven Storm Shadow cruise missiles and completion of delivery of ASRAAM air to air missiles;
- delivery of several hundred Brimstone anti-armour weapons to the RAF and achievement of Brimstone full operational capability;

A Typhoon two seat trainer

[1] This includes work relating to Typhoon development. See paragraph 222 of *Annual Report and Accounts 2004-05*.

Soldiers using Bowman

HMS Daring being launched in Glasgow

- acceptance into Army service of the Javelin medium-range anti-tank missile, four months ahead of schedule, and delivery of missiles and launcher units;
- acceptance into service by the Royal Navy of the Sonar 2087 submarine hunting system, five months ahead of schedule;
- delivery to the Armed Services of more than 190 wheeled fuel and water tankers;
- deliveries of the air mobile Cormorant Joint Rapid Reaction Force command system and the Joint Operational Command System;
- delivery of Seawolf air defence missiles to the Royal Navy, and High Velocity and Rapier air defence missiles to the Army;
- delivery of over 9,000 Bowman radio units;
- launch of HMS Daring, the first Type 45 Destroyer;
- launch of the landing ships HMS Cardigan Bay and HMS Lyme Bay;
- award of a £750M contract to upgrade the Royal Navy's Merlin anti-submarine helicopter force;
- award of a £700M contract for demonstration and manufacture of the Watchkeeper advanced battlefield surveillance system;
- award of a £700M, 15-year, Private Finance Initiative contract to provide plant equipment for the Armed Forces;
- award of contracts for the Falcon battlefield communications network, improved target acquisition and night vision equipment for Apache helicopters, new advanced naval training systems, self defence guns for warships, and the long range, precision strike Guided Multiple Launch Rocket System;
- award of a series of risk-reduction contracts on advanced technologies that may be used in Future Rapid Effects System armoured fighting vehicles;
- announcement of a £1 billion programme at the Atomic Weapons Establishment, to ensure the safety and reliability of Trident warheads for the remainder of their service life;
- announcement of planned investment of £300M on developing the design of two new aircraft carriers to the point at which manufacturing can begin, the expansion of the aircraft carrier Alliance that will deliver them to MoD, and the agreement of the French Ministry of Defence to co-operate on the project; and,
- announcement of the decision to add a third satellite to the successful Skynet 5 satellite communications programme, to provide a longer service life.

Urgent Operational Requirements

139. The Urgent Operational Requirement (UOR) process is used to procure additional equipment capability urgently needed for specific operations. It aims to provide speedy and flexible procurement using a streamlined version of the Department's normal procurement procedures. As such it makes a significant contribution to today's operations. Over 90 UORs in support of operations in Iraq and Afghanistan were approved during 2005-06; further requirements continue to be progressed. Additional capital expenditure to support operations in Iraq in 2005-06 was £160M, and in Afghanistan was £51M. This mainly represents expenditure on UORs. The process has been very successful and 98% of UORs delivered to Iraq during the warfighting phase of the operation, and reported upon, have been found to be either effective or highly effective. Notable UOR successes include the provision of High Frequency communication systems in just four months, ensuring that British troops could safely oversee the Iraqi elections, and the rapid procurement of enhancedbody armour to protect our troops on the ground.

140. In June 2005 the House of Commons Public Accounts Committee 26th Report *Ministry of Defence: the rapid procurement of capability to support operations* complimented the MoD on the flexibility, speed and ingenuity shown in its approach to Urgent Operational Requirements. The Report concluded with recommendations on how to improve the smooth and effective procurement of UORs, the majority of which have been accepted and

implemented across the Department as appropriate. The most significant include the appointment of a Senior Responsible Owner for UORs and the implementation of a single UOR register that tracks every requirement from initial submission through to delivery and assessment of effectiveness. This tool has ensured that all UORs can now be tracked, managed and audited with ease.

CAPITAL INFRASTRUCTURE

141. The Department invests heavily in strategic infrastructure to support Defence outputs. In order to improve the decision making process regarding priorities for investment in infrastructure, the Department is brigading funding for major infrastructure within the Non Equipment Investment Plan (NEIP). In future planning rounds, the Department will be able to plan and prioritise investment in infrastructure against competing infrastructure proposals. The NEIP covers some 75 projects with a cost of around £2.5 billion of annual expenditure. This includes major Information System (IS) projects such as the Defence Information Infrastructure which will provide a coherent IS network across Defence; estate maintenance projects such as the Regional Prime Contracts, which cover the maintenance of the Department's estate; and estate modernisation programmes such as Project SLAM, which will improve the standard of single living accommodation.

PRIVATE FINANCE INITIATIVE

142. The Private Finance Initiative (PFI) has become a well-established delivery tool in the provision of innovative and efficient services for Defence. We remain committed to involving the private sector where appropriate, and using PFI where the requirement is for long-term services based around the provision or refurbishment of a capital asset that can be funded by third-party finance. During 2005-06, we published new guidance on the PFI procurement process and consulted industry in developing the new MoD project agreement based upon Standardisation of PFI Contracts version 3. Standardisation and improvements made to the procurement process will lead to better value for money and drive down the length of the bidding process and bid costs. We signed three more deals in 2005-06, with a capital value of £1,398M (see Table 4), bringing total private sector capital investment, in Defence, through PFI to over £5.5 billion. Further details on signed PFI transactions are provided in note 27 to the Departmental Resource Accounts on page 230.

143. We also initiated a review of all PFI projects in construction and the early years of operation, with total contract costs in excess of £19 billion, to assess how PFI has performed to date for the MoD. The structure of the review was developed with the National Audit Office and Partnerships UK. It concluded that:

- PFI in the MoD substantially delivers projects on time and within budget. All projects were delivered on budget. All except three were delivered within two months of the agreed date;
- PFI projects in MoD are performing well and are delivering the services required. All of the project teams surveyed reported that the performance of their PFI project was satisfactory or better. Three quarters of project teams rated the performance of their PFI project as good or very good; and
- Long term PFI contracts in MoD are flexible enough to accommodate future change and to deliver on a sustained basis. The review identified that 85% of projects reported that their PFI contracts were suitably flexible to accommodate change and had effective change management mechanisms.

144. In June 2006 we won four major awards at the Public Private Finance Awards, including the Grand Prix prize for the best PFI project in operation from across all sections which was awarded to the Heavy Equipment Transports project. These awards provide independent recognition that PFI is working well in the Defence sector. We have a robust and diverse forward PFI programme (see Table 5) with an estimated capital value of approximately £6 billion.

Table 4: PFI Deals Signed in 2005-06

Project Name	Estimated Capital Value[1] (£M)
'C' Vehicles[2]	114
Portsmouth 2 Housing PFI	27
Allenby Connaught[3]	1,257

Notes
1 Based on private sector's capital investment where known (or otherwise the capital value of the Public Sector Comparator).
2 Earthmoving and Specialist Plant, Engineer Contractors and Materials Handling services.
3 Redevelopment of barracks in Aldershot and Salisbury Plain areas, and long-term provision of associated support services.

Table 5: Major PFI Projects in Procurement as at 31 March 2006
Project Name
Combined Aerial Target System
Corsham Development Project
Future Provision of Marine services
Future Strategic Tanker Aircraft
Northwood Public Private Partnership
RAF Brize Norton Service Families Accommodation
Royal School of Military Engineering
Defence Training Review
UK Military Flying Training System

INTEGRATING FUTURE CAPABILITIES

145. The introduction of new and enhanced military capability does not simply mean the purchase of new equipment. It also involves the integration of equipment with all the other components that contribute to Defence capabilities: Training, Concepts and Doctrine, Organisation, Personnel, Infrastructure, Information and Logistics. These components are known as the Defence Lines of Development and the Interoperability is also considered when any of them is being addressed. Directors of Equipment Capability are accountable for the coherent delivery of all components of new or enhanced military capability in the programmes for which they are responsible. Five major, equipment-led capability change programmes (UK Military Flying Training System, Medium Weight Capability, Rotorcraft Capability, Combat ID and Carrier Strike), which have individual projects of significant complexity at their core and/or requiring integration have Senior Responsible Owners responsible to the Defence Managment Board for the coherent through-life development and management:

- The UK Military Flying Training System programme issued an Invitation to Negotiate in March 2005 and received industry bids in August 2005. (See paragraph 193);
- Several Rotorcraft Capability improvement projects were approved. We placed contracts to upgrade Merlin Mk1 helicopters to ensure continuity of capability and introduce an open-systems architecture, and to establish a single configuration baseline for the Chinook fleet to reduce its overall support cost, as well as contracts to support the Chinook and Merlin fleets;
- Four Future Rapid Effects System contracts were awarded for Technical Demonstration Programmes in January 2006, to look at Chassis Concepts, Light Bridging Concepts, Integrated Survivability, and Electric Armour. These will inform decisions on which technologies will be used for the Army's next generation of armoured fighting vehicles. We also awarded contracts to upgrade the existing fleet of FV430 vehicles and entered a Partnering Agreement to improve the reliability, availability and effectiveness through life of our existing Armoured Fighting Vehicles fleets;
- A key Combat ID demonstration was completed providing clear direction to the programme and helping ensure interoperability with US forces. The March 2006 NAO report on *Progress in Combat Identification* highlighted the good progress we have made on major equipment systems, including the ASTOR surveillance system, the Friend or Foe air identification system and other systems to improve situational awareness at sea, on land and in the air;
- The Carrier Strike programme (which comprises Joint Combat Aircraft, Future Carrier, Maritime Airborne Surveillance and Control and other enabling projects) remains on track. Both Joint Combat Aircraft and the new aircraft carriers are approaching Main Gate decision points in 2006-07. Access to the data necessary to support and operate the Joint Strike Fighter independently is fundamental, as the Minister for Defence Procurement has emphasised to the US Administration and the Senate Armed Services Committee. In December 2005, we announced that we have committed £300M to develop the design of the ships to the point at which manufacturing can begin and that the Aircraft Carrier Alliance team would be expanded. Plans for construction and assembly of the carriers at Alliance members' yards have also been agreed.

ACQUISITION REFORM

Defence Industrial Strategy

146. The *Defence Industrial Strategy* White Paper in December 2005 set out a significant acquisition reform agenda, which is now being implemented. The strategy recognises that acquisition is evolving, and that the acquisition environment is becoming more complex and demanding. It provides greater visibility of our forward plans to inform industry's own planning, explains how we will take into account broader industrial issues in our acquisition decisions and sets out how we, and industry, need to change. This change programme is built around improving: through-life relationships with industry; the

delivery of integrated solutions; innovation, agility and flexibility; consistency in our approach; and professional delivery skills. Further information on the Defence Industrial Strategy is provided in the essay on page 85. We are conducting a high level review into the extent to which Defence processes, structures, and organisations impede our ability to deliver lasting and transformational change and how they may need to be adjusted.

147. The change programme is being driven by the Acquisition Policy Board chaired by the Minister for Defence Procurement. It is building on the significant progress already achieved by Smart Acquisition, the Defence Logistics Transformation Programme and DPA Forward. We published *Defence Values for Acquisition* in the revised *Acquisition Handbook* in October 2005, setting out the behaviours needed to deliver and maintain improvements in acquisition. We are working to ensure that these are reflected in our approach to project and programme management, and embedded throughout Defence, including in our decision-making and performance assessment. To help establish best practice in through-life capability management, we are taking forward two 'Pathfinder' programmes for Sustained Armoured Vehicle Capability and Surface Combatant Capability. As part of the Office for Government Commerce's wider cross-Government initiative, we have established the Programme and Project Delivery Centre of Excellence, to provide a strong lead and driving force for improving programme and project delivery across Defence.

DPA Forward

148. DPA Forward provided much of the foundation from which Department-wide changes under the Defence Industrial Strategy are being taken forward. It was launched in October 2004 to help the Defence Procurement Agency deliver projects more consistently in accordance with Smart Acquisition principles and ensure that equipment is routinely delivered to performance, cost and time targets. It is focused on re-invigorating application of Smart Acquisition principles by improving processes and developing new ones. In November 2005, the Office of Government Commerce conducted a formal Peer Review of the programme, which confirmed significant achievements in joint working between the Defence Procurement Agency and the Defence Logistics Organisation, Project Review and Assurance, Key Supplier Management, More Effective Contracting, and Performance Management. The review also recommended that more needed to be done in areas such as individual project governance, benefits measurement and programme communications, and that the programme should be restructured to increase focus on what remains to be achieved. DPA Forward's priorities have now been realigned in line with these recommendations and the conclusions of the Defence Industrial Strategy, to ensure it complements and supports the wider change programme.

Key Supplier Management

149. Key Supplier Management has improved the coherence of our strategic engagement with our most important suppliers. It also provides a structured way to measure and promote improvements in project performance and enhances our capability as an intelligent customer to produce better informed major investment decisions. We are working to increase our knowledge of the full Defence industrial supply chain, and in particular to understand better where important capabilities may be at risk. We also expect our top suppliers to demonstrate a more strategic and inclusive approach to their respective supply networks that recognises their contribution to the overall Defence effort and to cost-effective through-life capability delivery.

DEFENCE EXPORTS

150. The Defence Industrial Strategy confirmed the Government's continuing strong support for legitimate Defence exports and outlined the benefits to Defence from such sales. UK Defence exports contracts worth £4 billion were signed in 2005. With the support of the Defence Export Services Organisation, UK companies won several major orders. In particular, Augusta Westland, in partnership with Lockheed Martin, won the contract to supply the US101 helicopter, a variant of the EH101, for the US Presidential Flight, against competition from Sikorsky, which had provided the aircraft for this flight for some forty years. Agreement was reached to begin full-rate US production of M777 Howitzers, developed by BAE Systems and assembled under licence in the US by BAE Systems North America from parts manufactured in the UK and US. In December 2005 we signed an understanding with Saudi Arabia that will lead to a greater partnership in modernising its Armed Forces and sustain the Defence equipment relationship for many years to come, including the supply of Typhoon aircraft to replace the Tornado aircraft in service with the Royal Saudi Air Force. Orders were also secured for twelve A400M aircraft from South Africa and Malaysia. Three Type 23 frigates recently withdrawn from Royal Navy service were sold to Chile.

EH101 variant to be supplied for the US Presidential flight

FURTHER SOURCES OF INFORMATION

151. Additional Information on Future Capabilities and Infrastructure is available from the following sources:

- quarterly PSA reports to HM Treasury at www.mod.uk;
- *UK Defence Statistics 2006* available at www.dasa.mod.uk (from September 2006);
- *Defence Procurement Agency Corporate Business Plan 2005* available at www.mod.uk;
- *DPA Annual Report and Accounts 2005-06* available at www.mod.uk (from July 2006);
- the Public Accounts Committee 26th Report *Ministry of Defence: The rapid procurement of capability to support operations* (HC 70 on 30 June 2005) available at www.publications.parliament.uk;
- *Annual Report on United Kingdom Strategic Export Controls* published in July 2005 available at www.fco.gov.uk;
- NAO Report: *Driving the Successful Delivery of Major Defence Projects: Effective Project Control is a Key Factor in Successful Projects* (HC 30 on 19 May 2005) available at www.nao.org.uk;
- NAO *Major Projects Report 2006* (HC 595-I on 25 November 2005) available at www.nao.org.uk;
- NAO Report *Progress in Combat ID* (HC 936 on 3 March 2006) available at www.nao.org.uk;
- NAO Report *Using the contract to maximise the likelihood of successful project outcomes* (HC 1047 on 7 June 2006) available at www.nao.org.uk;
- *Defence Industrial Strategy* White Paper (Cm 6697 on 15 December 2005) available at www.mod.uk;
- *Defence Departmental Investment Strategy* available at www.mod.uk;
- *Enabling Acquisition Change: An examination of the Ministry of Defence's ability to undertake Through Life Capability Management* available at www.mod.uk;
- *The Acquisition Handbook* (Edition 6, October 2006) available at www.mod.uk;
- Delivering Security in a Change World: Future Capabilities available at www.mod.uk.

Essay: The Defence Industrial Strategy

The UK Armed Forces' requirements have changed substantially over the past 15 years, shifting from the provision of platforms for relatively discrete tasks, to flexible systems that can operate in a networked environment. As the pace of technological change has accelerated, particularly in information and communication systems, the need to ensure these systems remain able to fulfil their tasks and meet changing threats throughout often very long service lives, puts a premium on the ability to upgrade equipment through-life. In parallel, industrial consolidation has continued, and sustaining competition to meet domestic requirements has become increasingly difficult in some sectors. Despite this, in several sectors, there will be substantial overcapacity in production facilities in the UK Defence industry following the entry into service of major projects. While we can source significant elements of our equipment from overseas, we nevertheless need to recognise the extent to which overseas supply can constrain the choices we make about how we use our Armed Forces. All this means that the size, shape, and skills of the UK Defence industry (especially the systems engineering skills, at all levels of the supply chain, to maintain and upgrade equipment in-service) also need to change to meet the new demands and sustain the key industrial capabilities we need to keep, in the interests of national security, in the absence of regular, new, platform-based programmes.

The Defence Industrial Strategy (DIS) White Paper (Cm6697) in December 2005 outlined how, based on a clearer exposition of our potential requirements and planning assumptions, the UK Defence industrial base needed to respond to meet the challenges of the next decades and ensure that the capability needs of the Armed Forces can be met, now and in the future. The DIS is a demanding framework for action. For example, for industry it advocates substantial changes in the maritime sector to remove duplication and to nurture the high-end skills this country needs to maintain; in aerospace, to respond to the challenges and potential of new technology, including that relating to Uninhabited Air Vehicles, and the likely downturn in new manned aircraft design and production programmes; in the complex weapons sector, to maintain key skills in an era when we will have completed much of our shift towards precision-guided weapons; and to achieve real improvements in support to our armoured fighting vehicles fleet. The DIS promotes action now, to address these issues in good time, and plan for an effective transition, rather than facing crises in a few years time.

We are asking industry to change its way of working; to plan more effectively and jointly for the long term, and to commit to the real changes in business models, behaviours and cultures required. But in asking industry to change, we have to recognise that Defence needs to change as well. Real commitment on both sides will be necessary to make DIS a success, and we are already working to put it into action. Since the publication of the DIS we have appointed the Enabling Acquisition Change Team Leader, reporting to the Permanent Under Secretary, to conduct a review from first principles of the wider acquisition construct. This was completed in June, and the conclusions were announced on 3 July 2006, of which the most significant was that the Defence Procurement Agency and Defence Logistics Organisation will be merged into a single integrated procurement and support organisation. The Directorate of Defence Acquisition, reporting to the Acquisition Policy Board chaired by Lord Drayson, Minister for Defence Procurement, is coordinating all of the various urgent improvements to which we have, as well as the sectoral work, and is reporting good progress to date. A Complex Weapons Team has been set up and is engaging well with industry to tackle the challenging situation in that sector. Two working groups are conducting the further analysis on technology which we recognised would be needed, including one jointly chaired by industry to understand better the innovation process in the Defence industry; and work is well underway on the two Pathfinder projects described in Chapter C1 of the DIS White Paper. More information on internal change work undertaken as part of DIS implementation can be found at paragraphs 146-149 and at www.mod.uk

These examples demonstrate our commitment to the implementation of the DIS. We are working hard with industry to meet all of the specific milestones that we set out in Chapter C2 of the DIS White Paper, many of them in the second or third quarter of 2006, recognising that it is for companies themselves to deliver on the industrial changes we believe are required. Having delivered the DIS in 2005, we are now looking to apply it to transform Defence procurement in 2006, and for industry to respond to the information the DIS offers, at all levels of the supply chain. If we succeed, we will see the results in our improved performance from 2007 onwards and real benefits for those parts of industry which have engaged actively.

FUTURE PERSONNEL PLANS

Objective: Develop the skills and professional expertise we need for tomorrow.

Performance Measures and Assessment

Deliver the Service Personnel Plan – More holisitic and flexible military personnel administration systems:

- Joint Personnel Administration (JPA) rolled out to RAF in March 2006 on time and on budget;
- Risk reduction decision taken to delay JPA roll-out to Royal Navy until October 2006 and Army until March 2007 to integrate better with roll-out of Defence Information Infrastructure.

Deliver the Service Personnel Plan – Develop the military personnel package:

- New Armed Forces Pension Scheme 2005, Reserve Forces Pension Scheme 2005 and Armed Forces Compensation Scheme introduced April 2005;
- Armed Forces Redundancy Scheme 2006 introduced April 2006;
- Criteria broadened for Long Service Advance of Pay to help Service personnel buy their own homes;
- Increase in the basic salary of 3.0% for military personnel, and 3.3% for Privates, Lance Corporals and their equivalents, as recommended by Armed Forces Pay Review Body;
- Introduction of Armed Forces Bill to Parliament in November 2005 to create single system of Service law.

Deliver the Service Personnel Plan – Better Understanding of People:

- Research programme continues.

Deliver the People Programme:

- Production of first Civilian Workforce Plan in October 2005;
- Online new Human Resource Management System achieved initial operating capability in April 2006, on time and on budget;
- New redeployment pool created July 2005;
- New internal recruitment service launched December 2005-June 2006;
- New People, Pay and Pensions Agency launched in April 2006;
- New Corporate Human Resources and Human Resources Business Partner groups launched April 2006.

SERVICE PERSONNEL PLAN

152. The Service Personnel Plan provides a framework for the coherent delivery, now and in the future, of the different elements of Service personnel policy needed to support Armed Forces personnel in their delivery of operational capability over the next 15 years. Its main objectives, many of which are reported elsewhere in the *Annual Report and Accounts,* are to:

- develop a more holistic and flexible manpower accounting and planning administration system; this is being taken forward in particular through the Joint Personnel Administration programmes;
- exploit all sources of personnel provision; this includes work to increase harmony in using Regular and Reserve personnel (see paragraph 180-182), and activities to stimulate and encourage young people to join the Armed Forces (see paragraph 83-90);
- deliver the Training and Education change programme (see paragraphs 187-193);
- deliver the Defence Health Change Programme (see paragraphs 211-215);
- develop the overall military personnel package appropriate for the future context (for instance, through improvements to pay and conditions of service);
- develop a more coherent Defence Estate (see paragraphs 299-312); and
- develop a better understanding of people to inform future policies and resource decisions.

153. During the year, the Service Personnel Plan was reviewed to ensure that it remained consistent with Defence Strategic Guidance and continued to reflect the challenges and opportunities that changing demographics, cultural and societal norms and peoples' expectations and aspirations present to our aim of delivering and sustaining sufficient, capable and motivated personnel across the three Services. The main focus of work was to support individual choice for Service personnel through the development of innovative, flexible, imaginative and affordable benefit packages for individual and family mobility and stability throughout a Service career. In particular we made progress with strategies for future living accommodation requirements and future personnel career packages for both Reserves and Regular personnel, and in developing Health and Training and Education strategies. The Service Personnel Plan 2006 will be published later this year, along with revised Personnel Policy Guidelines articulating the policy baseline from which the plan is developed.

154. The Service Personnel Balanced Scorecard was reviewed in parallel, to track and reflect better progress against the Plan's objectives. This feeds directly into the Defence Balanced Scorecard used by the Defence Management Board. Within the Department's new Business Management System we also worked with the Services, the Armed Forces Pay and Administration Agency and the Veterans Agency to improve the effectiveness and efficiency of the key personnel processes that Top Level Budget Holders use to deliver their outputs.

Royal Marines personnel

Joint Personnel Administration

155. Joint Personnel Administration (JPA) is a major change programme to revolutionise the way the Armed Forces are administered by harmonising and modernising military personnel information systems. The programme is being delivered by the Armed Forces Personnel Administration Agency and EDS Defence Ltd. By simplifying administrative regulations and processes, automating much of the work and replacing many of the old computer systems with a single, modern Information Technology package, over 1,400 jobs have been removed from the administrative organisations of the Armed Forces. Together with associated business improvements, this will generate savings of approximately £100m per year in steady state.

156. In February 2006 we took a conscious de-risking decision to delay slightly the JPA launches for the Royal Navy and the Army from June and November 2006, to integrate them better with roll-out of the Defence Information Infrastructure. We now plan to roll-out JPA to the Royal Navy in October 2006, and to the Army in March 2007. However, JPA was successfully rolled to over 48,000 RAF Service personnel throughout the world in March 2006, on time and on budget, and the first RAF pay roll using JPA was successfully achieved on 28th April as planned. As with any project of this complexity, there were invariably a small number of technical issues to overcome when the system went live. Although the system performed within satisfactory parameters on initial roll-out to RAF personnel administrators, when self-service users were granted access the volume of early transactions caused system performance to slow to unacceptable levels. A number of fine-tuning fixes were

made that allowed the progressive introduction of additional functionality, whilst providing core processes and maintaining acceptable system performance levels. By mid-May, personnel staff and self-service users had full access to the system with no degradation to the on-line service. There were also a small number of start up issues on the first pay run, all of which were resolved by the end of May. We worked hard to ensure that the small number of individuals affected were not financially disadvantaged.

Military Personnel Package

157. Two new pension schemes for Regulars (Armed Forces Pension Scheme 2005) and Reserves (Reserve Forces Pension Scheme) were introduced for new entrants from 6 April 2005. Personnel in service at that date were given an Offer To Transfer to the new schemes from 6 April 2006. By 31 March 2006, over 85% of personnel had engaged actively in this exercise, which is significantly higher than comparable pensions exercises elsewhere. The new Armed Forces Compensation Scheme was also introduced from 6 April 2005 for injuries, illnesses or deaths caused by Service from that date. The new Scheme covers all Regular (including Gurkhas) and reserve personnel and for the first time allows claims from in-service personnel to be considered. New redundancy terms for members of the regular Armed Forces were announced in June 2005. The terms as set out in the Armed Forces Pension Scheme 1975 will remain unchanged until 31 March 2008, but will change for those leaving after that date. A new scheme, known as the Armed Forces Redundancy Scheme 2006, will come into force on 6 April 2006 for those who joined the Armed Forces after 5 April 2005 and those in service on that day who transferred to AFPS 05.

158. We aim to provide personnel with a choice of suitable accommodation through both private and Service accommodation, and from 1 December 2005 we broadened the eligibility criteria for Long Service Advance of Pay to help those Service personnel who wish to buy their own houses.

159. In February 2006, the Armed Forces' Pay Review Body (AFPRB) recommended an increase in the basic military salary of 3.0% for military personnel up to the rank of Brigadier or equivalent, with an increase of 3.3% for Privates, Lance Corporals and their equivalents on the lower pay range. This was based on broad comparability with similarly-weighted civilian jobs and took into account a number of considerations, including recruitment, retention and motivation of the Armed Forces. The AFPRB also recommended an increase of 3% in the rates of specialist pay (such as Flying Pay, Submarine Pay and Diving Pay) and compensatory allowances (such as separation allowances) and an increase in accommodation and food charges. These recommendations were accepted by the Government and came into effect from 1 April 2006. In March 2006, the Senior Salaries Review Body recommended that the basic pay of senior officers in the Armed Forces should also rise by 3%.

160. For the first time in over fifty years the legislation that underpins Service law is being completely re-written. The intention is to support operational effectiveness by harmonising and modernising the military justice system under a single system of service law, applicable across the Royal Navy, the Army and the Royal Air Force. The Armed Forces Bill was introduced to Parliament on 30 November 2005. Further details are contained in the essay on page 90.

Better Understanding of People

161. We are undertaking a focused programme of research projects to gain a better understanding of behaviour and how changes, both internal and external to the Armed Forces, are likely to affect issues such as recruitment, morale and retention. This includes research to identify how the aspirations and expectations of personnel with regard to issues such as pay, allowances, housing and family support change as they progress through their careers, which informs policy development in these areas. We are also undertaking research, in partnership with the Equal Opportunities Commission, on the nature and extent of sexual harassment in the Armed Forces (see paragraphs 285-287).

CIVILIAN PERSONNEL DEVELOPMENTS

People Programme

162. The People Programme is a major change programme which is implementing the new strategy for civilian personnel that was launched in 2002. It has four themes:

- developing the skill and behaviours that individuals will need in the future (set out in paragraphs 194-200);
- developing managers' ability to deliver through their teams (paragraph 197);
- modernising the delivery of personnel services; and
- modernising Human Resources to move from policing and processing to strategic planning and support.

163. The purpose of the civilian personnel process is to deliver sufficient numbers of capable and motivated civilian employees, taking account of relevant legislation and trends in the national labour market and recognising the value of a diverse workforce. The first annual Civilian Workforce Plan was produced in October 2005. This aims to define and direct the overall programme to develop the civilian contribution to Defence. It analysed the changing context in which the civilian workforce will make its contribution to Defence, made a number of deductions about this context, and reviewed the fitness of the People Programme to deliver the workforce that the Department needs now and in the future.

164. The programme to deliver modernised personnel services through the online Human Resource Management System achieved its first year targets for time, cost and performance as set out in the Human Resource Service Delivery Main Gate Business Case. Initial Operating Capability was achieved in April 2006, providing services such as resourcing, development support, performance management and time/absence reporting) on time and on budget. The take-up of online services continues to rise, with nearly 70,000 employees having now registered their emergency contact details. For those without online access, telephone, fax or mail provide an equivalent service. Information Systems infrastructure issues affected system performance and adjustments to the service roll-out schedule were made to stop further degradation of system performance and allow time for these to be addressed. The programme remains on track to provide Full Operating Capability by April 2008.

165. In July 2005 a new re-deployment pool was created to handle those displaced by reduction of 11,000 civilian posts across Defence. In December 2005 a modernised internal recruitment service was launched, phased in up to June 2006, making use of on-line self service wherever possible. This is the first of three main phases in the build up of the new People, Pay and Pensions Agency launched on 3 April 2006. Work to establish the complementary new Corporate Human Resources and Human Resources Business Partner groups continued during the year. This included finalising roles and numbers, and resourcing the new posts ahead of the formal launch in April 2006. A range of initial training has been provided to help prepare business partners for these new roles.

FURTHER SOURCES OF INFORMATION

166. Additional Information on Future Personnel Plans is available from the following sources:

- quarterly PSA reports to HM Treasury at www.mod.uk;
- *UK Defence Statistics 2006* available at www.dasa.mod.uk (from September 2006);
- information on the Armed Forces Pension Scheme 2005, the Reserve Forces Pension Scheme 2005 and the Armed Forces Compensation Scheme at www. veteransagency.mod.uk.

Essay: Armed Forces Bill

The Armed Forces Bill, now before Parliament, will replace the current Service Discipline Acts (the Naval Discipline Act 1957, the Army Act 1955 and the Air Force Act 1955) with a single system of service law that will apply to the personnel of all three services. Although a more modern piece of legislation, the Bill does not set out to make radical changes for the sake of it. From the start of work in 2001, our intention has been to support operational effectiveness by moving to a single system of Service law. This covers the full range of disciplinary work from the internal disciplinary process, which is normally the responsibility of unit commanding officers, right through to courts martial. The Bill covers some other important areas such as the right of personnel to complain to the Service Boards; Service Inquiries; and a range of miscellaneous matters such as recruitment, enlistment and terms and conditions of service. Details can be found at www.armedforcesbill.mod.uk.

From the beginning we worked with stakeholders to develop the policy providing the foundations of the Bill. As part of this work we examined the current Service Discipline Acts, and in particular the differences between them, so they could be harmonised. We also looked at all of the sections in other pieces of legislation that relate to the Armed Forces, to see where these needed to be updated or repealed. And we spoke to members of each of the Services at all levels, Defence ministries of other nations, and interested parties such as Ministry of Defence lawyers.

Some issues were straightforward, either because the three Services operated in much the same way or because the provisions were so clearly out of date that agreeing modernised provisions, where appropriate using civilian law comparators, was reasonably simple. There were also areas of significant difference which required careful consideration to reach solutions that jointly met the different needs of all three Services and yet still recognised the individual ethos of each. One example was that, for historical reasons relating to ships being at sea for months at a time and unable to communicate with the Admiralty, Royal Navy commanding officers have powers to deal with a very wide range of criminal offences and may award periods of detention up to 90 days. In the Army and the Royal Air Force, commanding officers have powers to deal with a more limited number of criminal offences and to award a maximum of 60 days detention (and then only with the agreement of higher authority). Providing the Armed Forces with a single system that meets the all their needs took detailed analysis of their different summary justice systems. In achieving this, we have reduced the powers of Royal Navy commanding officers and slightly increased those of their counterparts in the Army and the Royal Air Force.

The Bill is a much more significant piece of legislation than the normal five-yearly Armed Forces Bills. It is the largest and most complex piece of legislation that the Department has ever sent to Parliament: with 378 clauses and 17 schedules on introduction, it took almost four years to prepare and two years to draft. It was introduced to the House of Commons in November 2005, and committed to a Select Committee the following month after its second reading debate. The Select Committee took evidence from witnesses; visited units in Cyprus, Oman and Iraq, as well as at home in Colchester and Windsor; and examined the Bill's proposals in detail. Its report, published on 9 May, endorsed all the key discipline proposals. The Bill had its remaining stages in the Commons on 22 May and has now moved to the House of Lords. All being well, Royal Assent should be received by November 2006.

Once the Bill is approved (as the Armed Forces Act 2006) we will move on to its implementation. The target date for full implementation is December 2008. Preparation began in 2005 with the first steps to quantify the secondary legislation, regulations, manuals and guidance needed before we can get to grips with training the Armed Forces in the full range of new provisions and procedures. All of this will be crucial to ensure that the legislation will work effectively in practice.

SCIENCE INNOVATION AND TECHNOLOGY

Objective: Exploit new technologies.

Performance Measures and Assessment

Support to Operations:

- **Establishment of MoD Counter Terrorism Science and Technology Centre;**
- **Provision of Science Advisers to commanders in the field and operational headquarters;**
- **Delivery of innovative technological solutions through the equipment programme.**

Effective support to current and future Equipment Programmes:

- **Customers' critical success factors met;**
- **Timely and high quality advice provided to business managers;**
- **Research and Technology reflected in the Defence Industrial Strategy;**
- **Research collaboration with allies work was cost effective, coherent with Defence objectives, and complemented UK operational requirements;**
- **Improved investment scrutiny.**

Research:

- **Wide ranging review of Defence research addressing quality and alignment to Defence needs;**
- **Introduction of greater peer review of the research programme;**
- **Some £480M of research contracts awarded (£470M in 2004-05);**
- **Continued broadening of research supplier base. 25% of the relevant portion of the programme was competed (17% in 2004-05);**
- **Continued development of Defence Technology Centres and Towers of Excellence in partnership with industry and academia.**

SCIENCE INNOVATION TECHNOLOGY TLB

167. The Science Innovation Technology Top Level Budget organisation is the focus for science, innovation and technology throughout Defence. Its work underpins our Defence capability by providing world class scientific support to decision making, developing and implementing technical solutions, supporting operations and reducing risk. Operational analysis supports policy development, decision making, resource planning, investment decisions and current operations. World-wide military and commercial technological developments are monitored to identify upcoming threats and opportunities to enhance our own Defence capabilities. International research collaboration with allies facilitates cost and risk minimisation and expands our research capabilities. Defence Research enhances existing technologies, identifies and develops emerging technologies, and supports their cost effective implementation whilst minimising risk.

SUPPORT TO OPERATIONS

168. We have always provided science and technology support to military operations. With the Armed Forces facing an increasing threat from improvised weapons and explosive devices we have been drawing on our Science and Technology resources. There are scientific adviser branches in the Permanent Joint Headquarters and the Warfare Centres. Deployed Scientific Field Teams with links back to Defence laboratories provide operations commanders with in-theatre advice as well as protective measures. We have taken forward other operationally related work, particularly on the detection of chemical and biological agents and enhanced medical treatment. We recognise that further benefit can be supplied beyond these niche areas and work is in-hand to enhance our ability rapidly to identify and counter emerging operational issues, if possible before they have an operational impact. Defence science and technology capability has also supported the relevant UK civil authorities and agencies in responding to terrorist attacks. In April 2006 we opened the MoD Counter Terrorism Science and Technology Centre at Porton Down to help address the growing threat from terrorism (see the essay on page 95).

EFFECTIVE SUPPORT TO CURRENT AND FUTURE EQUIPMENT PROGRAMMES

169. Effective science and technology helps deliver cost-effective military capability and enable effective acquisition. Recent analysis suggests that Defence research investment is a key determinant of equipment quality 10 to 20 years downstream, underpinning tomorrow's Armed Forces. It also has a wider economic benefit through supporting national competitiveness. We aim to identify and increase the proportion of Defence research used effectively in Defence Equipment and wider civil uses. During the year science and technology advice contributed to the development of the Defence Industrial Strategy and helped inform equipment capability management decisions and develop and exploit emerging technologies. Examples included hydrodynamic work to optimise the hull design for the Type 23 Frigate for reduced fuel consumption without compromising capability; successful trials of the Zephyr high altitude long endurance Unmanned Aerial Vehicle (UAV) with the potential of flying continuously for months and performing surveillance and communications functions where satellites, manned and unmanned aircraft may not be available or suitable; and research into Defence networking performance to minimise the effects of congestion – particularly those deployed to operational theatres. Feedback from business and equipment programme managers suggests that the science and technology advice they receive meets their time, quality and focus needs.

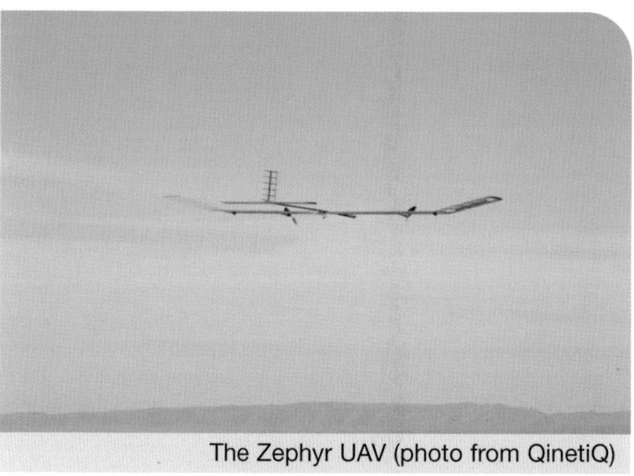
The Zephyr UAV (photo from QinetiQ)

170. International research co-operation is a long standing mechanism to gain access to wider science and technology, share risk, develop interoperability and carry out Defence research more cost effectively. It is coherent with our Defence objectives, and complements our operational requirements and the Defence equipment programme. Allies benefit similarly, as such co-operative efforts make best use of the technological strengths of each partner. During 2005-06 we continued to work with international partners on collaborative research programmes to broaden capability and share the costs of meeting shared policy objectives. In particular we built further on our broad and effective research collaboration with the United States and forged closer strategic links with France. We are actively engaged in developing the European Defence Agency model as a vehicle for identifying areas for European research collaboration, which nations are free to engage in if they wish.

171. We also continued to work to improve the scrutiny process and the quality of business cases to facilitate better investment decision making. Initiatives during the year included greater emphasis on maturity of investment analysis and spend on risk reduction measures prior to the main approval point and the inclusion of historic trend analysis. The number of business cases requiring resubmission and the overall time required to gain approval both fell, suggesting an improvement in business case quality. Further improvements are required and work continues into improving cost and time estimation and the way business cases cover risk.

RESEARCH

172. The Defence research programme is managed by outputs to ensure that work is aligned to Defence needs and meets critical success factors. In its report on *The Management of Defence Research and Technology* the National Audit Office found that the Department has made much progress in developing new approaches to the management of Research. Success is measured by the satisfaction of output customers and from external peer review of the programme. A thorough review of the range, quality and alignment of much of the research programme has been undertaken and early results are encouraging. Clear customer supply relationships in the provision of Defence Research have delivered increased efficiency. We are seeking to increase the early sharing of Defence needs with industry to facilitate joint planning and the development of research roadmaps for important Defence technologies and capabilities. This will help us both to plan our investment and work cooperatively to build UK Defence capability.

173. During the year we awarded research contracts worth some £480M (£470M in 2004-05). Research during the year included:

- Early identification of infection with Biological Warfare Agents, substantially increasing the chances of survival and recovery by allowing earlier treatment;
- Lightweight Chemical Agent Detection helping protect Service personnel by providing rapid and accurate detection of chemical warfare agents. Advances were made in effectiveness, through life costs and improved environmental performance;
- Recombinant Factor VIIa (rFVIIa), a blood clotting drug, potentially providing battlefield casualties with enhanced survival times to enable evacuation to surgical facilities. Experimental evidence shows its use prolongs survival time by up to six hours after the onset of uncontrolled haemorrhage. It may also be of use in civil health treatment of trauma patients;
- The Interactive Trauma Trainer, a proof-of-concept computer application using computer games technology, enhancing the decision-making skills of trauma surgeons.

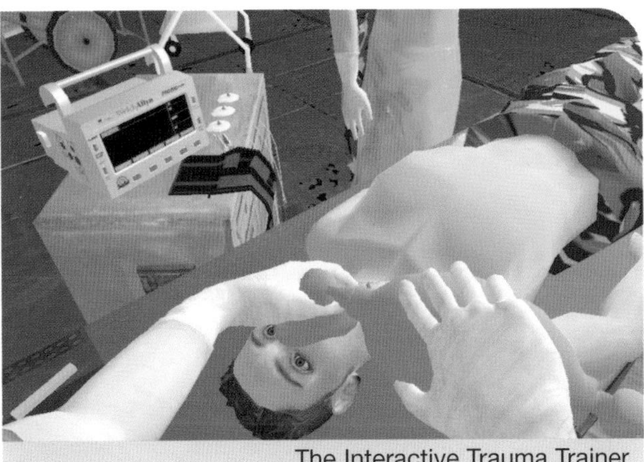
The Interactive Trauma Trainer

174. The delivery of high quality technology and technical advice requires access to world class suppliers. We seek to take advantage and extend our range of potential partners and suppliers by drawing on the excellence of the UK university research and technology base, the innovative sector of small and medium sized enterprises, as well as the established Defence industry. We are actively pursuing further competition in the supply of Defence Research to encourage innovation in the UK research supplier base and enhance value for money. In 2002-03 around 90% of MoD research was done in Dstl or QinetiQ. In 2004-05 17% of the relevant portion of the programme was competed, rising to 25% in 2005-06. By 2009-10 around 60% of the equivalent programme of research will be competed across industry and academia. We held a supplier day in June 2005, which attracted representatives of major Defence companies, small and medium sized enterprises, and academia. We also took forward measures to improve the management of Research suppliers. These include improved data and analysis on where research money is spent, monthly review of project performance, and the use of an external peer reviewer when assessing bids.

175. During the year we started a review cycle to look thoroughly and systematically at the quality of our research and development work. This will combine peer review, citations, assessment of objectives achieved and post project evaluations. External reviewers, sought through the Defence Scientific Advisory Council, assessed the quality of a large portion of our research projects. The early assessments are encouraging, and the broader understanding facilitates more effective and efficient management of the overall programme.

176. In its report on *The Management of Defence Research and Technology* the National Audit Office recognised that we have made progress in encouraging joint working with industry through the establishment of Towers of Excellence and Defence Technology Centres. Towers of Excellence are selective partnerships with industry and academia, directing resources into priority areas of technology research. The development of technology through to a final product and more general technology transfer to industry are a major benefit of operating Towers of Excellence. Defence Technology Centres are an alternative partnering approach jointly funded by MoD and industry (usually as consortia). The Centres are based around topics critical to Defence where investment is likely to produce significant returns. A range of suppliers, including small and medium sized enterprises and academia provide input to the Centres, which are managed to allow a flexible response to emerging needs and priorities. The MoD dominates Government investment in innovation based small and medium sized enterprises. The quality of advice and technology delivered continued to be very high.

177. The Defence Industrial Strategy highlighted the importance of Research and Technology as a vital enabler of our National Defence Capability. As such it was embedded throughout the Strategy. The chapter on 'technology priorities to enable defence capability' draws together the critical underpinning and cross cutting technologies that need to be sustained in the UK. It identifies as key tasks the need to maintain technological advantage to counter emerging threats, to develop knowledge management and systems integration skills, to recruit and retain skilled people and to enable technology insertion throughout equipment life. Implementation is overseen by the National Defence Industries Council's Research and Technology Sub Group. This is a mixed Government and industry forum with dedicated working groups on people (focussing on the recruitment and retention of the best scientists and engineers), innovation, and technology strategies. Further opinions are sometimes also sought from academia and small and medium sized enterprises.

The Lightweight Chemical Agent Detector

FURTHER SOURCES OF INFORMATION

178. Additional Information on Science Innovation and Technology is available from the following sources:

- *UK Defence Statistics 2006* available at www.dasa.mod.uk (from September 2006);
- information on Science Technology Innovation at www.science.mod.uk;
- *Defence Science and Technology Laboratory Annual Report and Accounts 2005-06* available at www.dstl.gov.uk;
- NAO Report *MoD: The Management of Defence Research and Technology* (HC 360 on 10 March 2004) available at www.nao.org.uk.
- *Defence Industrial Strategy* White Paper (Cm6697 on 15 December 2005) available at www.mod.uk.

Essay: The MoD Counter-Terrorism Science and Technology Centre

The Government is committed to using science and technology to counter terrorism. The events of 7 July 2005 demonstrated the seriousness of the threat at home. Overseas, the Armed Forces are facing increasing threats from asymmetric forces using improvised weapons and explosive devices. Such devices presently account for the greatest loss of coalition forces in Iraq. We have been making increasing use of our science and technology resources to counter such attacks, and this is now a larger part of the work of the MoD's Science and Technology staff.

In order to make the best use of the available resources, ensure that our existing programmes are coherent, and broaden the technical base on which we draw, we have now established a world-class Counter-Terrorism Science and Technology Centre. This will ensure that the best science and technology underpins our response to the threats posed by terrorism and serve as a unifying core for Defence laboratories, universities and industry to work together on counter-terrorism and national security projects. The Centre's governance structure is similar to those of the Defence Technology Centres which are designed to facilitate collaboration between the MoD, UK Defence industry, small and medium size enterprises and the universities, and have proved excellent vehicles for early exploitation of novel technology. This is of particular value in the context of countering evolving terrorist capabilities. The Director of the Defence Counter-Terrorism Science and Technology Centre is appointed by the MoD's Chief Scientific Adviser and reports to an Oversight Board including representatives from Defence, other Government Departments, industry and the universities.

The MoD Counter-Terrorism Science and Technology Centre achieved initial operating capability in April 2006, based in a new building at Porton Down. It is managed by the Defence Science and Technology Laboratory (Dstl), to take advantage of existing technical and business infrastructure, and is staffed by experts from Dstl and the Atomic Weapons Establishment. It is initially providing technical support on countering improvised explosive devices to counter-terrorism and security operations; on chemical, biological, radiological, and nuclear threat reduction; and on network analysis. Whilst it focuses on Defence requirements, it also supports other Government Departments engaged in counter-terrorism.

When fully operational in April 2007, the Centre will have the following roles:

- to help understand and define the science and technology contribution to solving problems arising from terrorism, supported by operational and scenario based analysis;
- to ensure coherence and focus in the scientific research underpinning our response to terrorism;
- to bring together existing capabilities from across Government, industry and academia to find science and technology-based solutions and draw in new contributors from the broader UK science and technology community;
- where required capabilities are not available, to provide facilities for teams of scientists from Government, industry and academia to develop new ones;
- to act as a focal point for potential science and technology suppliers;
- to facilitate access to and use of security-sensitive technologies and capabilities while protecting national security;
- to facilitate engagement with industry for transfer of technology and exploitation of UK intellectual property; and,
- to enable and focus international research collaboration within our extant multinational research framework.

Enabling Process

PERSONNEL MANAGEMENT

Objective: Manage and invest in our people to give their best.

Public Service Agreement Targets (SR2004 MoD Target 5)

Recruit, train, motivate and retain sufficient military personnel to provide the military capability necessary to meet the Government's strategic objectives and achieve manning balance in each of the three Services by 1 April 2008.

Performance Measures and Assessment

Harmony – No more than 660 days Separated Service for RN personnel over a rolling 3 year period; Fleet units to spend a maximum of 60% time deployed in a 3 year cycle:

- **Fewer than 1% of RN personnel breached separated service guideline. Only submarine fleet breaching unit tour interval guideline.**

Harmony – No more than 415 days separated service for Army personnel over a rolling 30 month period; 24 Month average interval between unit tours:

- **14.5% of Army personnel exceeded separated service guideline at 31 December 2005[1]. Continuing breaches of tour interval guidelines. Infantry averaging 20.6 months (21 months in 2004-05). Royal Armoured Corps, Royal Artillery and Royal Engineer units close to guideline.**

Harmony – No more than 2.5% of RAF personnel to exceed 140 days separated service over a rolling 12 month period; unit tour intervals to be no less than 16 months:

- **About 4.6% of personnel breached guideline (3.9% in 2004-05). RAF Regiment field squadrons tour interval of around 12 months.**

Individual Personnel Development – Basic Skills. New entrants below National Level 2 to be screened and assessed. 50% of new entrants to RN and RAF below Level 2 to improve by one level within one year of entry. All new Army entrants below Level 2 to achieve National Level 1 within 3 years of entry:

- **Assessment of new entrants from April 2006 using literacy and numeracy assessment tool developed with DfES. Majority of RN and RAF new entrants enter an apprenticeship scheme with literacy and numeracy qualifications at Levels 1 or 2. Work continues to meet Army target by March 2007.**

Individual Personnel Development – Information and Communication Technology Fundamental Skills: All new entrants and existing personnel without appropriate competence to be in training scheme:

- **Over 95% of RN/RAF recruits and 30% Army recruits undertook training.**

Individual Personnel Development – National Qualifications:

- **Across the Services 12,710 Level 2 or 3 qualifications, 5,718 Apprenticeships, 2,527 Advanced Apprenticeships, 544 Foundation Degrees, and 279 graduate or post-graduate qualifications gained during the year.**

Career Satisfaction – 5% improvement in overall satisfaction levels for Service personnel:

- **63% of RN personnel (59% 2004-05), 73% of Army Officers and 56% of Soldiers (58%/42% 2004-05), 65% of RAF Officers and 55% of Other Ranks (61%/48% 2004-05) satisfied/very satisfied with Service life.**

Career Satisfaction – 70% career satisfaction rate for civilians:

- **Average civilian satisfaction of 71% (70% 2004-05);**
- **77% (73% 2004-05) satisfied with MoD as an employer.**

[1] Position at 31 March 2006 not available at the time of publication due to missing information from individual units.

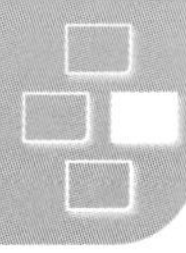

179. We ask a great deal of our people. Managing them well embraces a range of activities including recruitment, initial and career training, and career planning, particularly for Service personnel in relation to the time between operational tours. If they are to deliver what is required, we need to give them the necessary skills to do the job, provide a career path and listen to their views and act accordingly.

HARMONY GUIDELINES

180. In order to strike the best balance between operations and other activities such as recruitment and training, we set harmony guidelines for the amount of time service personnel spend away from their families (known as individual separated service), and the time that units should have between operational deployments (known as tour intervals). Each Service's guidelines differ to reflect the nature of service, skills sets and how they deploy on operations. For the first year, all three Services had mechanisms in place to monitor and report both unit and individual harmony in 2005-06, but in some cases the data is still immature and has not been available long enough to establish clear trends. The guidelines are based on our conducting operations at no more than the 'routine' level of concurrency that we are resourced to have the capacity to sustain of one Medium Scale and two Small Scale operations (see paragraph 30). The Armed Forces have been operating at or above this level for the last five years. This is inevitably limiting their ability to meet the harmony guidelines, particularly for personnel in certain pinch point specialist trades required for almost every operation (see paragraphs 279-280). We monitor these carefully.

Unit Harmony

181. All three Services breached their unit harmony guidelines during the year, with the Army most and the Royal Navy least affected:

- the Royal Navy was close to meeting its unit harmony guideline that fleet units should spend a maximum of 60% time deployed over three years. Only the submarine fleet breached this;
- Tour intervals for certain Army units continued to exceed the guideline of a 24 month average interval between tours. The average tour interval for Infantry units was 20.6 months (21 months in 2004-05) within a range from 12 to 37 months, with the Armoured Infantry most affected. This is improving with the return of the last reinforcement battalion from Northern Ireland in January 2006. Royal Armoured Corps, Royal Artillery and Royal Engineer units are all close to the 24-month guideline (respectively 24 months, 19 months and 31 months in 2004-05);
- In the RAF, Harrier and Nimrod squadrons are pushing the boundaries of the guideline of 16 months between tours and the interval for RAF Regiment field squadrons has remained around 12 months, exceeding the guidelines. Operational tasking for multi-engined aircraft squadrons remains heavy, but cannot be quantified in terms of Tour Intervals as they deploy in and out of theatre as required. Most Air Combat Support[2] and Service Support Units[3] also remain above individual harmony guidelines, some by as much as 250 days per annum.

Individual Separated Service

182. Individual separated service data is produced and managed by information systems in each of the Services. For the Naval Service and the Army this is immature and may be understated. The Joint Personnel Administration programme (see paragraph 155-156) is introducing a harmonised military personnel administration system that will produce separated service records for each individual, together with management reports and trend information. The picture on individual separated service for each Service was similar to that for unit tour intervals. All three breached their guidelines to some degree, again with the Army most and the Royal Navy least affected overall. All three Services faced particular shortfalls in identified pinch point trades (see paragraphs 279-280):

- Fewer than 1% of the Royal Navy personnel have breached the guideline of no more than 660 days over a three year period, although there were more serious shortfalls in pinch point trades;
- At 31 December 2005[4], 14.5% of Army personnel were exceeding the guideline of no more than 415 days separated service in any 30 month rolling period, with greater shortfalls in pinch point trades;
- Breaches in the RAF of the guideline of no more than 140 days detached duty in 12 months remained steady at about 4.6% of personnel (3.9% in 2004-05), again with greater shortfalls in pinch point trades.

Operational Welfare Package

183. In order to support the emotional and physical well-being of our personnel when they are deployed on operations and in remote locations around the world, we provide a well received Operational Welfare Package to all personnel. This varies between the Services and because of technical and logistic constraints. In general in the first month of a new deployment it includes welfare telephones, mail services, newspapers, books, and shop and laundry services. Later on it also includes email and internet access, television and radio programmes provided through the British Forces Broadcasting Service, televisions and DVDs, fitness equipment and return journeys back to the UK for rest and recuperation. We demonstrated the flexibility and adaptability of the operational welfare package, with early entry communications packs for the detachments providing aid for victims of the tsunami and famine relief following the earthquake in Pakistan. The package was improved further during the year with the introduction of a free postal packet scheme for a designated month prior

[2] Air Combat Support Units provide operations support and force protection to the primary Force Elements and include deployed fighter controllers, police, media operations and mobile meteorological units.
[3] Air Combat Service Support Units provide the support to primary Force Elements and Combat Forces, primarily administration, logistics and communications.
[4] Position at 31 March 2006 not available at the time of publication due to missing information from individual units.

to Christmas. This recognises both that it is particularly difficult to be separated from family and friends at this time and also the contribution made by all Service personnel throughout the year.

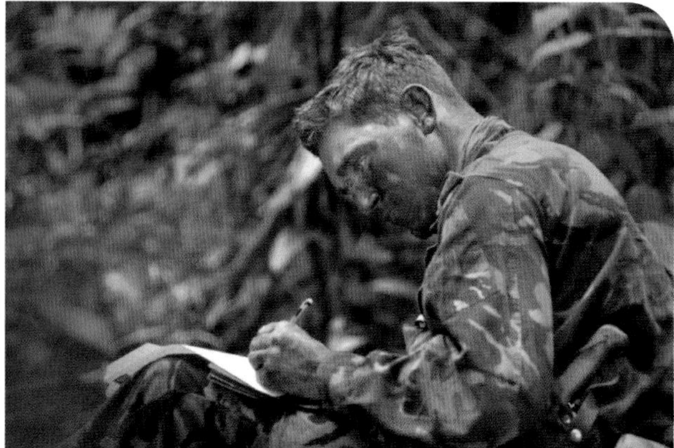

A soldier writing a 'bluey' (forces free mail)

SERVICE PERSONNEL DEVELOPMENT

Duty of Care and Welfare

184. We have a duty of care to all Service personnel. In recent years we have made considerable efforts to reinforce the policies and procedures to provide this and ensure the welfare of Service personnel. The deaths of four young soldiers under training at the Princess Royal Barracks at Deepcut in Surrey between 1995 and 2002 acted as a catalyst for many of the changes. The House of Commons Defence Committee report on Duty of Care and the Government's Response acknowledged the progress that had been made, but stressed that there was more to do. The Adult Learning Inspectorate was engaged to carry out rigorous inspections of the training organization. Nicholas Blake QC was appointed to carry out a review of the four deaths at Deepcut and the circumstances surrounding them, reporting in March 2006. The Government's Response to the Deepcut Review has been published in full and can be found on the MoD website. Further information is contained in the essay on page 107.

185. We are determined to improve further standards and systems of care in initial training. Changes already made include:

- much greater attention to risk of self-harm and preventative measures, including stricter controls over access to firearms;
- better supervision of recruits and trainees; more investment in facilities and accommodation; new guidance for commanding officers on care of under 18s;
- guidance to manning authorities and commanding officers about the management of alleged offenders;
- a new harassment complaints procedure that provides a swifter, fairer and more transparent complaints system applicable to all three Services and civilian staff; and,
- a review of welfare procedures leading to a new Joint Service Publication on welfare provision and standards, improvements to governance, sharing of best practice and money to recruit and train more civilian welfare officers.

Training Efficiency

186. Under the Defence Training Rationalistion Programme, we aim to modernise the delivery of specialist training, using best practice learning techniques through newly created national centres of excellence for each specialism and to rationalise and improve the quality of the remaining training estate. Other expected benefits include the transfer of risk for training demand and the increase of first time pass rates achieved by students. We expect the rationalistion process to be completed by 2012, and the overall programme to produce benefits in the order of £3 billion over a 25 year period. We are currently evaluating several bids. Additionally, all three Services continue to look at ways to improve the management of recruits and to reduce the numbers of recruits choosing to leave, sharing ideas and good practice. If successful, such measures will increase the efficiency of the initial training system. But in the light of the changes made to implement the House of Commons Defence Committee, Director of Operational Capability and Adult Learning Institute recommendations into initial training, we are no longer looking for training efficiency savings through changes to supervisory training ratios at training establishments as set out in our 2002 Spending Review value for money target (see paragraph 270).

Basic Skills – Literacy and Numeracy

187. In recent years we have developed Basic Skills Policy for the Armed Services, to provide clear priorities for improving training of Service personnel with weak literacy and numeracy skills. The Army have developed a new literacy and numeracy initial assessment tool with the Department for Education and Skills. This is now being used to assess all new entrants without a formal Level 2 qualification[5]. The assessment is conducted systematically in recruiting offices or early in initial training and will achieve standardisation in the assessment of Basic Skills abilities of new entrants across the Services. No-one will be allowed to start recruit training with an assessment below Entry Level 2[6] in literacy or numeracy, and all applicants will be screened for their speaking and listening ability in the recruiting process. This ensures that those whose ability levels put them most at risk are not taken into training until they achieve adequate improvement in these key areas.

188. All three Services are working coherently towards ensuring that the needs of those new entrants with

[5] Level 2 qualification – the normal educational standard expected to enter into skilled employment. Equivalent to: GCSE levels A-C, NVQ Level 2, Level 2 Diplomas/Certificates.
[6] Entry Level 2 is the normal educational standard expected of a 7 year old.

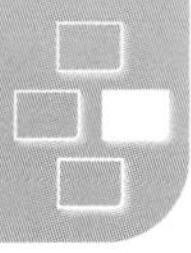

the weakest Basic Skills are addressed during training. Each Service has targets for new entrants that link formal achievement of Level 1[7] and Level 2 in literacy and numeracy to length of service or career progression, subject to availability of the necessary resources to address identified shortfalls. The RN and the RAF aim for 50% of new entrants below National Level 2 Basic Skills to improve by one level within one year of entry, and the majority of their new entrants enter an apprenticeship scheme that includes literacy and numeracy qualifications at Levels 1 or 2. The Army aims for all new entrants below National Level 2 Basic Skills to achieve National Level 1 within three years of entry (by March 2007 for the first group to whom this applies). We have significant internal capacity to deliver Basic Skills through internally-funded tutors and resources. We are also working closely with the Learning and Skills Council to augment our Basic Skills training capacity by drawing on the Basic Skills programmes and facilities it supports.

Basic Skills – Information and Communication Technology Fundamental Skills

189. Service personnel increasingly need basic information and communication technology skills to be effective in the modern networked battlespace. We therefore intend that all new entrants and existing personnel without the relevant competence should undertake an appropriate training scheme. As in 2004-05, in 2005-06 over 95% of Royal Navy, Royal Marine and Royal Air Force recruits and 30% of Army recruits undertook basic information and communications technology skills training. Training policy is being revised to provide a tiered approach with minimum and target levels for different parts of the Defence population. Higher qualification levels will be set for specialist and more senior staff in order to provide a better skills match and ensure they can operate the Defence Information Infrastructure and the new military and civilian personnel systems effectively. The European Computer Driving Licence will continue to be used as the core qualification and online testing is being introduced in parts of the Army to improve take-up.

Individual Training

190. In order to spread best practice and to ensure high quality and consistency across the Armed Services, we are developing new training policies for Common Military Skills subjects. These are common to at least two of the Services, and require initial and continuation training for the majority of personnel regardless of their career specialisation. Some, such as weapons handling, physical education and fitness, chemical biological radiological and nuclear defence, the law of armed conflict and First Aid are fundamental to collective training and are required before individuals deploy on operations. Service personnel also have mandatory training to counter identified security threats, promote equality and diversity and address problems posed by substance misuse. The priority has been to harmonise Common Military Skills training delivered in Defence Training Establishments. Following agreement of policies for health and safety, physical development and security by the end of 2004-05, six more were issued during 2005-06, covering chemical, biological, radiological and nuclear defence; First Aid; substance misuse; personal weapon handling and shooting; Equal Opportunities and law of armed conflict. We are also developing implementation plans for stress management training, validating and reviewing some of the policies already issued and extending the scope of work on embedding military ethos into tri-Service Defence Training Establishments. A revised Defence Language Training Policy was issued in February 2006 which included a trial three-year incentives package for trained linguists in three key operational languages, which are currently Arabic, Farsi/Dari and Pushtu. A Defence Individual Pre-Deployment Policy was published to standardise training better on operational theatre requirements.

National Qualifications

191. Training is essential to enable our Service people to do their jobs. It also supports their continuing development, encourages greater professionalism and provides an opportunity to acquire professional and vocational qualifications. Service personnel increasingly pursue a wide range of national qualifications through external accreditation of their Service education, training and experience. During the year such accreditation schemes provided for 12,710 Level 2 or 3[8] qualifications; 5,718 Apprenticeships; 2,527 Advanced Apprenticeships; and 544 Foundation Degrees. We also sponsor personnel on full-time courses, and 279 achieved graduate or post-graduate qualifications during the year. We have recently promulgated a revised Defence Accreditation Policy that seeks to improve the coherence and management of schemes across Defence and focus on supporting the key qualifications reflected in the Government's Skills Strategy. Service personnel are also financially supported through the Learning Credits Scheme to pursue learning opportunities on an individual basis. This financial support can be drawn down for up to 10 years after leaving the Services.

Rationalisation of Specialist Training

192. The Defence Training Review Rationalisation Programme will provide modern, cost-effective specialist training, improved accommodation and facilities. By harmonising training currently being delivered by individual Services it will also offer significant savings through the more efficient use of a smaller training estate. It comprises two packages:

- Package One – Aeronautical Engineering; Communications and Information Systems; and Electro-Mechanical Engineering;
- Package Two – Logistics; Joint Police and Personnel Administration; and Security, Languages, Intelligence and Photography.

[7] Level 1 qualifications equivalent to GCSE levels D-G.
[8] Level 3 qualifications equivalent to A level.

The Programme continued to make progress during the year. Bidders' proposals were received for both packages and are now being evaluated. We need to work extensively with the bidders to clarify their proposals and we do not expect to announce Preferred Bidders until the end of 2006.

UK Military Flying Training System

193. The UK Military Flying Training System programme is working to replace the present flying training arrangements for the Royal Air Force, Fleet Air Arm and Army Air Corps with a single tri-Service military flying training system. This will train fast jet, helicopter and multi-engine aircraft pilots, weapons system operators and rear crew disciplines, from the beginning of formal aircrew training up to the point of entry into Operational Conversion Units for frontline aircraft. The Programme is currently in assessment phase and we plan to take the investment decision to appoint a Training System Partner in late 2006, award a contract in 2007 and build the system incrementally to achieve full provision in 2012. We intend to make a significant investment to implement the MFTS programme over the next six years, generating substantial improvements in efficiency and effectiveness from the next decade onwards.

Hawk aircraft

CIVILIAN PERSONNEL DEVELOPMENT

Basic Skills – Literacy and Numeracy

194. As part of the Government's "Skills for Life" agenda, and in parallel with the work on Basic Skills for the Armed Services, we sampled Defence civilian literacy and numeracy skills in June 2005. About 200 people were tested and the results gave an indication of the literacy and numeracy skills gap in the Department while showing that our basic skills are nevertheless above the national average; 10% of staff were below Level 1 in literacy (DfES 2003 National Survey 16%) and 25% below Level 1 in numeracy (DfES 2003 47%). We expect that the release of the DfES basic skills assessment tool will raise the profile of basic skills self-assessment. We are reviewing how to support staff who want to improve their literacy and numeracy skills in the future.

Training Initiatives

195. During the year we pressed on with implementing the Professional Skills for Government (PSG) programme. The Single Skills Framework was launched in December 2005. It includes a revised set of core competences at Band B and below (the leadership framework for Senior Civil Servants is provided by the Cabinet Office) which place a stronger emphasis on delivery and programme and project management skills and in which PSG core skills and leadership qualities are embedded. Our core competence model has been cited as an example of good practice to other Government Departments. Work is also underway to develop a consistent approach to competences under a pan-Defence competence framework. The Single Skills Framework will embed PSG professional expertise requirements through functional competence frameworks. Advice on the application of the PSG requirement for "broader experience" was provided on the MoD's intranet and through more specific material targeted at senior managers and high fliers. Training provision was reviewed to make clear the links between specific development options and the PSG frameworks. Over 800 senior and middle managers took part in a PSG survey to establish a skills baseline for further work, and to identify those skills which staff needed or wanted to develop further. The Single Skills Framework now enables us to capture data on individuals' competences and skills, and those required for posts, to inform future skills planning. The data will be captured on the Human Resource Management System through the completion of post and personal skill profiles, which were launched in February 2006. Internal use of these profiles will be mandatory from September 2006, ensuring a natural build up of data.

196. Our skills network was strengthened by the formal appointment of 19 Skills Champions in June 2005. They head up groupings of Job Families covering all civilian posts and together with Heads of Profession own the functional competence frameworks. The groupings are broadly functional, and the Skills Champions will take a strategic overview across Defence to complement the business-area focused perspective of the Business Partners. They will be supported in this role by Heads of Profession and other skills stakeholders such as the PPA Business Partners.

197. There is a wealth of personal development information available on the Defence Intranet to help staff and their line managers identify development opportunities and plan their careers. This was developed and updated over the year and now includes guidance on developing leadership skills and core competences and a self-assessment tool to help individuals assess themselves against the new core competences. We have introduced voluntary 360° feedback for senior middle managers (Band Bs) to improve their people-management and leadership skills through confidential feedback from their

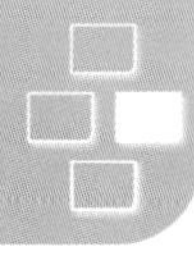

staff, peers and line managers. We also made progress towards the introduction of a Defence-wide civilian mentoring service and a career consultancy service.

Development Schemes

198. We continued to run a number of Departmental management development schemes (such as MIDIT – Means of Identifying and Developing Internal Talent) and support personal development schemes (such as Druidstone, a Prince's Trust community venture aimed at developing team working and communication skills; and New Horizons, a government personal development programme for junior ethnic minority staff designed to provide them with the skills, abilities and confidence to help them compete more effectively for opportunities). The Band B Development Scheme continued to develop talent to fill the majority of Senior Civil Service posts at 1* level in the future. All members are selected following short listing by the Senior Staff Assessment Board and independent assessment. Several were promoted during the year. Others are now ready for promotion as and when suitable vacancies arise (although we have been unable to promote more than 20 people a year to the Senior Civil Service within the Department for some years). The main challenge is to match supply and demand in terms of skills, readiness for promotion and the provision of tailored development opportunities to help scheme members meet their full potential. We aim to refine the assessment process and expand membership to about 75 members.

Civilian qualifications

199. We have a well qualified and diverse civilian work force committed to its work. In April 2005 we introduced a new service enabling them to record and maintain their academic, vocational and professional accomplishments as a step towards populating personal development records. Individuals record their level of qualification as they broadly equate to the National Qualifications Framework. In the interests of consistency we have developed a broad comparison table of equivalent English, Scottish, Welsh, Northern Irish and Irish qualifications. As this database is populated we will be able to capture a great deal more information on education and skills levels on the new Human Resource Management System. This will allow corporate personnel and senior business managers to understand better the range of skills and level of education within the Department and identify and address skills gaps in functional and professional areas.

200. We continued to encourage and sponsor professional development across a wide range of disciplines. We sponsor about 150 staff for Post graduate degrees, Diplomas and Higher degrees, and another 50 or so Honours degrees. We have some 1,500 staff registered for NVQs or equivalent qualifications at levels 2-4 (including some 20 apprenticeships and around 50 advanced apprenticeships). During the year around 640 staff completed qualifications at NVQ or equivalent levels 2-4, 10 Honours degrees and 30 postgraduate degrees. We also have nine students studying for the pathfinder foundation degree, Foundation for Government, and we are evaluating the course to ensure that it meets both the Department's and individuals' requirements.

COMBINED TRAINING

Defence Academy

201. The Defence Academy continued to take forward improved, integrated specialist Defence training and education. At the Royal College of Defence Studies, the new 4-term structure was effective and well received. The Defence College of Management and Technology was formed in April 2005, bringing together elements of the former Royal Military College of Science, the Defence Leadership and Management Centre, including the Defence School of Finance & Management, and Defence Business Learning (*dblearning*). The College has been working in particular to develop the education and training necessary for implementing the Defence Industrial Strategy. In September 2005 we opened the new Defence Sixth Form College at Loughborough. The new Academic Provider contract for the Defence Academy was signed with Cranfield University in November 2005. Staff training at the Joint Services Command and Staff College was increasingly joint in nature, and the number of students trained during the year increased significantly. The Advanced Research and Assessment Group continued to build its reputation for innovative thinking, reinforced by the Conflict Studies Research Centre, including among other government departments and NATO. It contributed to over 100 overseas seminars and symposia and provided high-level consultancy to capacity-building activity in Iraq, and security sector reform in Ukraine. The Armed Forces Chaplaincy Centre continued to develop the scope and variety of its courses and to increase its usage.

The Joint Services Staff and Command College

202. The Academy increased collaboration with other Government departments. Work continued to develop a pilot Defence/FCO/DFID political-military workshop to achieve a more comprehensive approach to the planning and conduct of operations. It also engaged with the

National School of Government, which expressed interest in the Academy's Defence Strategic Leadership Programme, in cooperative development of the Senior Responsible Owners programme, and in promoting greater non-Defence attendance on Academy courses and modules. The Academy took on responsibility for liaison with academia, particularly with universities, aimed at satisfying their wish to have a single initial point of contact for general enquiries and to act as a market place for Defence research and education business opportunities. The Single Service Directors of Defence Studies who also have important links with academia are now affiliated to and accommodated within the Academy.

Acquisition Leadership Development Scheme

203. The Acquisition Leadership Development Scheme continued to develop. Its membership expanded by 119 to 721 civilian, military and industry staff by the end of the year, of whom 403 were alumni members[9]. The Acquisition Leadership Development Scheme courses continue to be provided by the Defence Academy. From 2006 the underpinning development criteria for the scheme is based on the new Single Skills Framework.

Defence E-Learning Delivery

204. The Defence Centre of Training Support continues to develop the Defence-wide e-learning management and support capability. Access is now possible over the internet. Full Operating Capability was achieved in January 2006 and almost 50,000 extra users were added in February 2006 as part of roll-out of Joint Personnel Administration to the Royal Air Force. Further work was undertaken to support training for the Defence Information Infrastructure programme.

Investors in People

205. As at 31 March 2006, more than 99% of all Defence personnel, military and civilian were working in organisations recognised as Investors in People. We are now working to the 2004 Standard for all of our assessment activity. We are taking forward plans for corporate recognition of the Department as a whole. While large areas of the Department are currently undergoing major structural changes, the work to support people through those changes, such as the Breakthrough programmes, is consistent with the requirements of the Standard and will provide good evidence for the corporate assessment.

CAREER SATISFACTION

Service Personnel

206. Continuous Attitude Surveys are run by the three Services to assess and monitor the attitudes of serving personnel, who are subject to a combination of sources of positive and negative satisfaction. The most recent surveys were undertaken in the Royal Navy in September 2005, in the Army between September 2005 and December 2005, and in the RAF between May and November 2005. Satisfaction with Service life in all three Services has increased, in the Royal Navy by 4% overall, in the Army by 15% among Officers and 14% among Other Ranks, and in the Royal Air Force by 4% among Officers and 7% among Other Ranks.

207. The main sources of satisfaction and dissatisfaction are shown in Tables 7 and 8. These have changed little. Job security, challenge and responsibility dominate the Royal Navy and Army positive retention factors, and enjoyment of life the Royal Air Force's. Negative retention factors continue to reflect the high levels of operational commitment and, for the Royal Air Force, the very substantial drawdown and restructuring under way.

Table 6: Percentage of those reported to be satisfied or very satisfied with Service life.

	2005-06	2004-05
RN	63%	59%
Army	73% Officers, 56% Other Ranks	58% Officers, 42% Other Ranks
RAF	65% Officers, 55% Other Ranks	61% Officers, 48% Other Ranks

[9] Alumni members are those people that have graduated from an ALDS level and are not actively developing through the scheme.

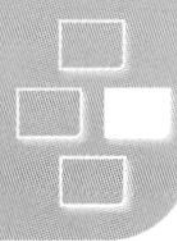

Table 7: Sources of Satisfaction Top indicators in 2005-06 surveys	Top indicators in 2004-05 surveys
RN (September 2005)	
Security of employment (86%)	Job security (86%)
Amount of responsibility (78%)	Amount of responsibility (78%)
Accuracy of assessment of appraisal report (73%)	Accuracy of assessment of appraisal report (73%)
Army (September to December 2005)	
Job security (Officers 73% and Other Ranks 71%)	Job security (Officers 77% and Other Ranks 69%)
Challenging job (Officers 71%)	Excitement (Officers 70%)
Pension entitlements (Other Ranks 61%)	Pension entitlement (Other Ranks 54%)
RAF (Aggregation of three surveys from May to November 2005)	
Enjoyment of life in the RAF (85%)	Enjoyment of life in the RAF (86%)
Adequacy of training (over 72%)	Opportunity to gain qualifications (59%)
Leave Allowance (68%)	Own line management (59%)

Table 8: Sources of Dissatisfaction Top indicators in 2005-06 surveys	Top indicators in 2004-05 surveys
RN (September 2005)	
Current X factor rate of 13% (RN 48%, RM 58%).	Current X factor rate of 13% (RM 64%)
Amount of fun in the Service (RN 46%)	Inability to plan life particularly in the long term (RN 50%)
Ability to plan their own long term life (RN 44%)	Quality of equipment (RN 47%)
Medical treatment in units (RM 63%)	Amount of fun in the service (RN 46%)
Army (September to December 2005)	
Impact of Army lifestyle on personal domestic life (Officers 62% and Other Ranks 47%)	Impact of Army lifestyle on personal/domestic life (Officers 62% and Other Ranks 47%)
Effect of operational commitment and overstretch (Officers 55% and Other Ranks 38%)	Effects of operational commitments and overstretch (Officers 58% and Other Ranks 42%)
RAF (Aggregation of three surveys from May to November 2005)	
Effects of overstretch (86%) and gapping of posts (72%)	Effects of overstretch (85%)
Effects of civilianisation and contractorisation (75%)	Effects of civilianisation and contractorisation (77%)
Impact of change on the RAF (56%)	Not feeling valued by the RAF (51%)

208. Reflecting the increasingly joint nature of the military environment, we are harmonising the three Service strands of feedback. This will enable joint and single Service personnel policy development be informed by objective and timely analysis of joint attitudinal data, and each Service to understand the specific concerns and needs of its own people. We are developing a Tri-Service Attitude Survey process, and plan to conduct the first such survey from April 2007.

Civilian Personnel

209. The continuous Civilian Staff Attitude Survey is now in its fourth year. Results continued to be encouraging despite uncertainty for staff, with an average positive response rate to career satisfaction survey of 71%, compared to 70% in the previous two years. Satisfaction with MoD as an employer remained high, staff continue to understand how their role contributed to the achievement of our overall objectives, and they judged that good use was made of their skills in their work and that they could get access to training that met both personal development and job needs. Line Managers continued to feel equipped with the right skills to develop individuals within their teams; most staff were satisfied with their immediate Manager's leadership and that they could express their ideas and views and have them taken seriously. However, while most staff supported the principle that those who made a greater contribution should receive a greater financial reward, fewer than a quarter thought that our current performance pay arrangements rewarded better performance and only just over half thought the more flexible arrangements for 2005-06 were an improvement. This is being reviewed in the context of Pay 2006 negotiations. Only a third of staff reported confidence in the Department's senior leadership (Military and civilian staff at 3* and above). We are researching what lies behind this.

Table 9: Extent of Civilian Career Satisfaction

Questions	Positive Reponses		
	2005-06	2004-05	2003-04
Considering everything, how satisfied are you with the MoD as an employer?	77%	73%	73%
Are you aware of the MoD's aims and objectives?	73%	80%	82%
How would you rate your understanding of how your job contributes to the MoD's aims and objectives?	94%	90%	90%
I have access to the kind of training that I need to carry out my job properly.	83%	85%	78%
My job makes good use of my skills and abilities.	70%	71%	70%
I can express my ideas and views and have them taken seriously by Managers.	72%	70%	67%
Do you regard the MoD as an equal opportunities employer?	90%	89%	88%
Individuals who make a greater relative contribution towards achieving business outputs should receive a greater financial reward.	73%	74%	N/A
The MoD's current performance pay arrangements reward better performance.[2]	22%	16%	14%
The move to introduce a more flexible percentage split for the reward of performance is the right thing to do.	54%	56%	N/A
Average positive response rates for each year.[3]	71%	70%	70%

Notes:
1. 2005-06 results originate from a survey undertaken in Autumn 2005.
2. Figures have been changed from those shown in 2004-05 to show positive responses (strongly agree, agree).
3. The average positive response rate is based upon questions shown in the table. As the questions have changed the average from the previous years have been restated.

FURTHER SOURCES OF INFORMATION

210. Additional Information on Personnel Management is available from the following sources:
- quarterly PSA reports to HM Treasury at www.mod.uk;
- *UK Defence Statistics 2006* available at www.dasa.mod.uk (from September 2006);
- *DGCP Civilian Continuous Attitude Survey Annual Report 2004-05* available at www.mod.uk;
- *Continuous Attitude Surveys (CAS): Results for Service Personnel* available at www.mod.uk;
- the Defence Committee Third Report of Session 2004-05: *Duty of Care* (HC 63 on 3 March 2005) available at www.publications.parliament.uk;
- *The Government's Response to the House of Commons Defence Committee's Third Report of Session 2004-05 on Duty of Care.* (Cm 6620 on July 05) available at www.mod.uk;
- *The Deepcut Review* by Nicholas Blake QC published on 29 March 2006 and available at www.deepcutreview.org.uk;
- *The Government's Response to the Deepcut Review* (Cm 6851 on 13 June 2006) available at www.mod.uk.

Essay: Duty of Care and Welfare

The Armed Forces' approach to their duty of care towards Service personnel, especially those under 18 and those under training, has been a key issue in the past year. The issue was stimulated by the deaths of four young soldiers under training at the Princess Royal Barracks, Deepcut, between 1995 and 2002; the consequent police investigations; the inquests; concerns about bullying and harassment; internal departmental inquiries and review; the House of Commons Defence Committee's report on Duty of Care; and the Final Report of the Surrey Police into the Deepcut deaths which looked at wider issues affecting care in the training organisations. In November 2004 the Minister of State for the Armed Forces appointed Nicholas Blake QC to review the circumstances surrounding these deaths. Mr Blake published his report on 29 March 2006 (HC795).

The Deepcut Review concluded that, although the Army did not cause the deaths of the four young soldiers, there were failures to identify and address potential sources of risk and to address them. Important questions have been raised about the nature of the training environment at the time. The Review also concluded that no new reliable evidence concerning how the four soldiers met their deaths is likely to be available, and that on this basis a Public Inquiry is not necessary. This is a view we share given the extensive investigations that have taken place, and we see no public or Service interest in pursuing a Public Inquiry.

The Government published its response to the Deepcut Review on 13 June 2006 (Cm6851) accepting the great majority of the recommendations made by Mr Blake. In a few cases this acceptance is with some qualification or modification.

The Government acknowledged that mistakes were made and that there were deficiencies in the systems of care for young and sometimes vulnerable trainees. The Services had, of course, already made significant changes and improvements before publication of the Deepcut review, as Mr Blake readily acknowledges in his report. For example, much greater attention is being paid to risk of self-harm and preventative measures; there are stricter controls over access to firearms; supervision of recruits and trainees has improved; appreciable new investment in facilities and accommodation has occurred and is ongoing; and a new harassment complaints procedure has been implemented. However, the Deepcut Review has highlighted that there is more that we can do, particularly in some key areas.

In particular, we accept the Review's objective to provide independent assurance that the procedures are working as effectively as they can and that systemic issues of concern are addressed. We propose independent, external inspection and review of the military justice system and the military complaints system, together with independent members on Service complaints panels dealing with complaints of bullying and harassment. In light of this, the Government proposed to bring forward amendments to the Armed Forces Bill to provide for a Service Complaints Commissioner.

Work to improve the care regime has included publication of a Guidance Note for Commanding Officers on the care of personnel under 18 years of age (July 2005). There are additional legal requirements associated with Service personnel aged under 18 and, whilst maturity and experience vary considerably between individuals, those under 18 may be more vulnerable than older personnel. Their care requires particular attention. This Guidance Note is to be amended and re-issued in light of the Deepcut Review.

The MoD Harassment Complaints Procedure was published on 1 April 2005. It is a guide for all Service and civilian personnel on making, responding to, advising on, investigating, and deciding on complaints of harassment and bullying. It is MoD policy that all military or civilian personnel, regardless of rank, grade or status, have a right to protection from harassment, and a responsibility to ensure that the working environment is free from harassment and that the dignity of others is respected. We will review this document during 2006.

We have completed a review into the way in which welfare is provided in the Services. The final report in March 2006 offered recommendations for the improvement of welfare provision including the publication of a Joint Service Publication on Welfare, improvements to governance and the sharing of best practice and establishing an assurance procedure to verify that professional standards are being achieved and maintained. These recommendations will be implemented during 2006.

Moving Forward

The work put in place to address the important duty of care issues raised has been progressed as a priority. A great deal has already been done to improve the training and welfare environment, and Mr Blake has clearly identified further areas where we can and should improve. His wide-ranging Review contains important and relevant recommendations which, whilst difficult and challenging in some cases, pay testament to its independence and thoroughness.

We will use the Deepcut Review as a blueprint for further action. Action is already in progress on many of the matters raised by the Review, we are committed to sustaining this momentum, and to allocating the investment necessary to deliver real, measurable improvements in duty of care.

HEALTH AND SAFETY

Objective: A safe environment for our staff, contractors and visitors.

Public Service Agreement Target (SR2004 MoD Target 5)

Recruit, train, motivate and retain sufficient military personnel to provide the military capability necessary to meet the Government's strategic objectives and achieve manning balance in each of the three Services by 1 April 2008.

Performance Measures and Assessment

Reduce number of Service Personnel medically downgraded and level of civilian absence:

- **Reduction from 89.0% to 87.9% in proportion of Service personnel reported fit for task during 2005-06;**
- **Reduction from 85.4% to 84.2% in proportion of Army personnel reported fit for task during 2005-06;**
- **Civilian sickness absence for Defence non-industrial staff 7.3 days per staff year against a target of 7.5 days;**
- **Improved civilian sickness absence reporting and management.**

No fatalities attributable to Health and Safety failures:

- **8 fatalities recorded attributable to Health and Safety failures;**
- **One Crown Censure on the MoD during the year;**
- **Publication of revised policy statement on Safety, Health and Environmental protection in Defence.**

Reduce the number of serious injuries by 10% against previous year:

- **904 serious injuries reported in 2005-06, providing baseline for future reductions.**

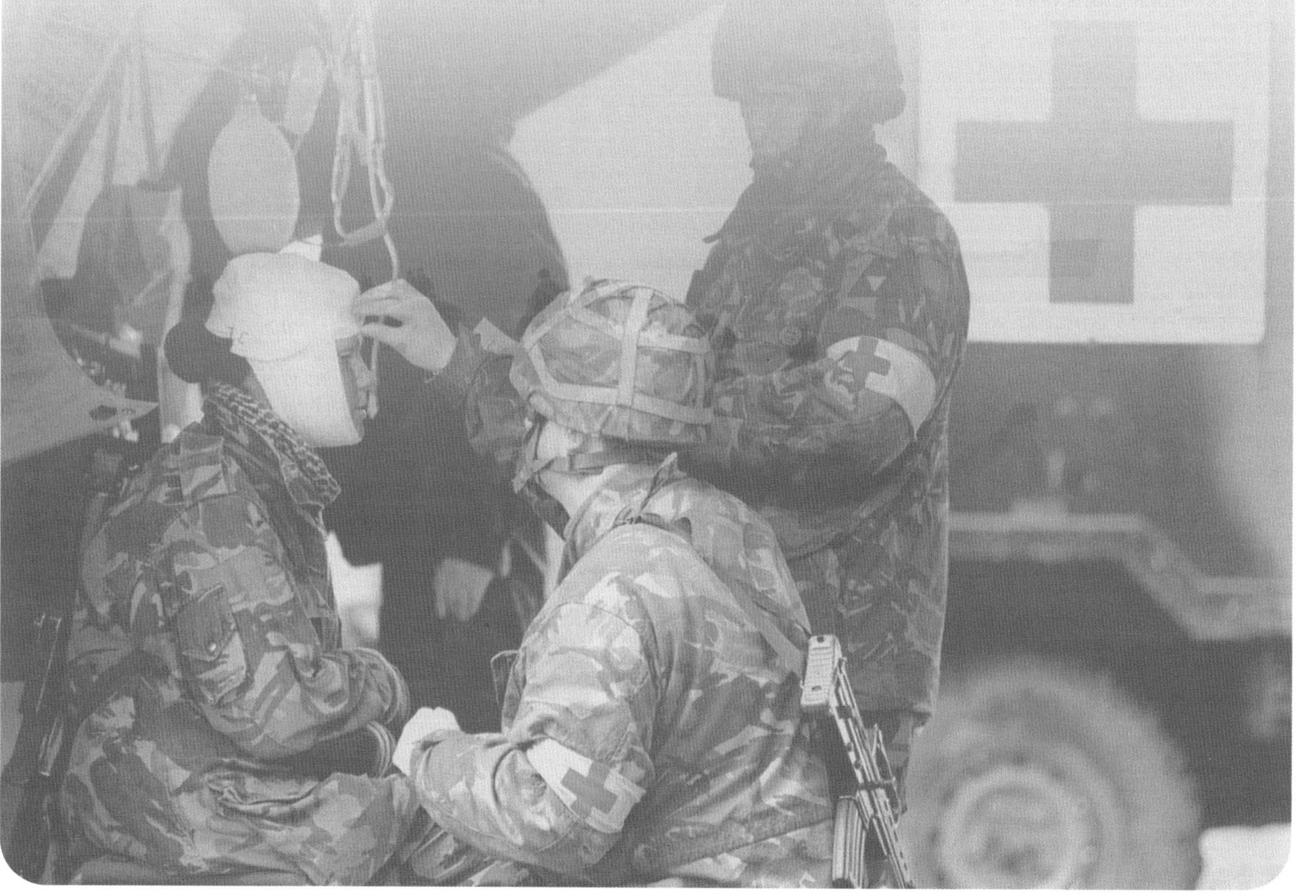

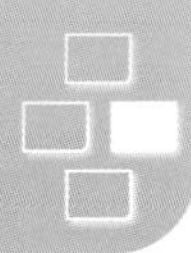

HEALTH OF SERVICE PERSONNEL

211. It is essential that the Armed Services have personnel who are fit and able to carry out their intended role. When people are not fit, it is important that the management information systems record this and that we provide the necessary care for their recovery. We must also ensure that we do not unduly endanger our personnel through our activities and have taken steps to ensure that the health and safety of our people is always considered.

212. At 31 March 2006, 87.9% of the overall Armed Services personnel were reported as 'fit for task', that they were posted to the unit/ship/establishment to perform. This is a deterioration of 1.1% over the year. (These figures are not comparable to rates of civilian sickness absence, as many military personnel not graded fit for task can and do work full time in less physically demanding posts). The enduring high operational tempo and more accurate reporting and downgrading procedures led to a steady reduction in the fitness rate over the year. This reflected the fact that ensuring unfit personnel do not deploy on operations drives stricter compliance with downgrading criteria than would apply in a less challenging operational context. The position in the Army is more marked, the number fully fit reducing from 85.4% on 31 March 05 to 84.2% on 31 March 06. However, only 1.4% are unfit for any task and the remaining 14.4% who are not fully fit for their primary task continue to make a contribution to operational effectiveness.

213. We took steps during the year to improve further the care we give to our personnel when they are injured. On 24 November 2005 His Royal Highness the Prince of Wales officially opened the new Limb Fitting and Amputee Rehabilitation Centre at the Defence Medical Rehabilitation Centre, Headley Court. This is a world-class rehabilitation facility run by the Defence Medical Services which has no equivalent in the NHS. It provides high quality, appropriate prosthetics and adaptations, manufactured on site and individually tailored as necessary to the specific patient, with the aim of enabling service personnel to return to duty wherever possible. But most injuries do not require these specialist services at Headley Court, and the Defence Medical Services continued to build on the scheme introduced in April 2003 to provide fast track access to routine surgery, cutting down on often lengthy waits for assessment, diagnosis and surgical treatment, and contributing to the numbers available for deployment. Between 1 April 2004 and 30 September 2005 6,558 patients were assessed at Regional Rehabilitation Units. Only 766 required onward referral to fast-track orthopaedic surgery. 85% were therefore successfully managed with rehabilitation alone, enabling priority referral for those requiring surgery. Of the 6,558 patients assessed and treated, 2,558 have returned to duty. Further information on the treatment of injured personnel is contained in the essay on page 112.

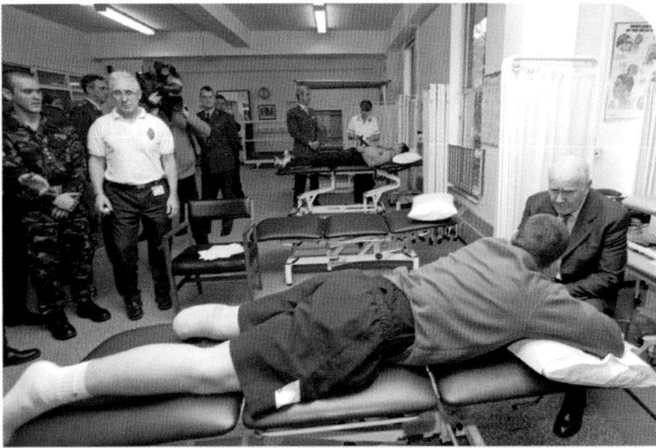

A VIP visit to Headley Court

214. The Defence Medical Service continued to provide mental health support through its 15 Departments of Community Mental Health in the UK (plus satellite centres overseas), ensuring better access to specialised mental health support within or close to an individual's unit or home. This also enables Defence mental health staff to work within their local Service community, which is more closely aligned with their operational role. In-patient care is provided regionally by the private Priory group of hospitals. Further information on liaison with the National Health Service and the provision of medical support for veterans is set out in paragraphs 98-102.

Reservists

215. In May 2006 a study by The Kings Centre for Military Health Research found higher percentages of Reservists displaying symptoms of common mental health problems and Post Traumatic Stress Disorder, as a result of service in Iraq in 2003, than either the Regulars who served or those Reservists who did not deploy. In this context, on 16 May 2006 we announced our intention to introduce enhanced mental healthcare support for reservists. In future any member of the Reserve Forces who has been demobilised since January 2003 following deployment overseas will be eligible for a dedicated mental health assessment programme offered by the Defence Medical Services. In the event that an individual is assessed as having Post Traumatic Stress Disorder, or a related mental health problem, they will be offered outpatient treatment by the Defence Medical Services who have particular expertise in this area. If a case is particularly complex or acute and requires in-patient care, the Defence Medical Services will assist access to NHS treatment.

CIVILIAN SICKNESS

216. In 2005-06 our sickness absence rate was 7.3 days per non-industrial employee, beating our target of 7.5 days. This compares with a 2004 rate (the most recent published) of 9.1 days for the civil service as a whole, within which the MoD had the lowest absence rate of the four 'large' Departments (defined as those with over 30,000 staff). It

also compares favourably with private sector performance, where the most recent annual CBI/AXA Absence Survey, published on 15 May 2006 reported an average sickness absence rate of 7.4 days per employee in large organisations with over 5,000 staff. We nevertheless continue to work to reduce the rate further and improve the management of sickness absence. Since April 2005 managers have reported sickness absence themselves, which is improving the quality of our data and reinforcing the link between staff and their managers. They are also expected to conduct return to work interviews ensuring appropriate discussion of absence and any necessary actions to follow it up. We are also encouraging earlier referral of cases to occupational health experts.

217. A complete review of our approach to Occupational Health is underway. This will further improve management of return to work, including adjustments to the affected individual's working environment where necessary. We will be designing our new Occupational Health contract, to be placed in 2007, specifically to bear down on sickness absence and we plan to trial a number of new concepts before then. Occupational Health support and advice is available to all Defence civilian staff. We are reviewing our stress management policy against revised Health and Safety Executive guidelines, and provide separate training for managers and individual members of staff on the management and control of stress.

HEALTH AND SAFETY

Policy

218. The MoD and the Armed Forces attach high importance to the Health and Safety of military and civilian Defence personnel, contractors and visitors to Defence establishments. In May 2005 we issued a revised policy making clear the high standards of safety, health and environmental performance that are required and are critical to the delivery of battle winning people and equipment. This explains to all personnel, Service and civilian, what is required of them in order to ensure that health and safety and environmental protection obligations are recognised, understood and properly discharged at all levels; and to make governance arrangements clearer. Recently the Sir George Earle Trophy for outstanding performance in health and safety by a company or organisation was awarded to the Naval Base Commander, Devonport by the Royal Society for the Prevention of Accidents. This top health and safety award shows that at our best, we do this as well as or better than anyone else.

The Sir George Earle Trophy, presented to the Naval Base Commander, Devonport

219. But military operations are inherently dangerous, and we would be failing in our duty of care to our military personnel if their training were not sufficiently robust to prepare them for the conditions they are likely to face on operations. We cannot therefore completely avoid the risk of injuries and fatalities. What we do expect and require is that these risks are properly considered and managed. This has not always been the case. There was one Crown Censure[1] on the MoD during the year, for severe injuries caused in September 2002 at Royal Marines Poole by a malfunctioning Safety Line Air Gun, resulting in non-life threatening injuries to two people. The Censure was for failure to ensure the health and safety of MoD personnel and its contractors and to make a suitable and sufficient risk assessment. New arrangements have been put in place for safety management of tests and trials.

Avoiding Fatalities

220. Our goal is that there be no fatalities in Defence attributable to health and safety failures (excluding combat-related deaths and training designed to simulate combat conditions, suicide, natural causes, and road traffic accidents). During 2005-06, eight fatalities were recorded that are likely to be attributable to health and safety failures. A full investigation was set in hand following each fatality and several investigations are still underway. In most cases the root causes are still being determined, but the circumstances ranged from sports and leisure activity to accidental weapon discharge.

Minimise Serious Injuries

221. We also aim to reduce the number of serious injuries (as defined by the Health and Safety Executive's Reporting of Injuries, Diseases and Dangerous Occurrences Regulations) by 10% year on year against a baseline of 904[2] serious injuries reported in 2005-06. Reporting of accidents, including serious injuries, has increased over the past two years as a result of the introduction of call centres as they make it easier and less bureaucratic to report accidents. This has produced a clearer understanding of the causes of accidents and allowed better management direction to be given to controlling risks.

[1] Crown censure is an administrative procedure, whereby HSE may summon a Crown employer to be censured for a breach of the Act or a subordinate regulation which, but for Crown Immunity, would have led to prosecution with a realistic prospect of conviction.
[2] This figure is obtained from reports from individual Top Level Budget and Trading Funds.

Management and Governance

222. The Defence Environment and Safety Board provides direction, sets objectives, monitors, reviews and reports to the Defence Management Board on safety and environmental performance. It is supported in this by Functional Safety Boards to develop policy, set standards, and ensure that suitable scrutiny and, where appropriate, regulation is applied to all Defence activities. A risk-based annual report on Safety and Environmental Protection is agreed by the Defence Environment and Safety Board and reviewed by the Defence Audit Committee, and provides evidence for MoD's Statement of Internal Control (see page 182). The key information from this report is incorporated into the *Sustainable Development Annual Report* and published on the MoD website. It concluded that health and safety performance was generally satisfactory, but that further improvements to safety culture could and should be made.

223. Key initiatives and achievements over the year were:

- Improved reporting of health and safety to the Defence Management Board;
- Development of a new audit strategy to focus on safety risks rather than safety systems in order to focus attention and resources on our most significant safety risks and how they are being managed;
- Further clarification and senior management direction on the responsibilities for managing health and safety on multi-occupier sites, and sites operating under Regional Prime Contracting, though application of MoD procedures on control of contractors remains patchy;
- Rationalisation of our extensive safety documentation, producing a simpler, less onerous, yet comprehensive safety management system;
- Work to update and improve the MoD accident reporting system to provide more accurate and relevant statistics for assessing performance;
- Work to benchmark the different business areas within MoD.

FURTHER SOURCES OF INFORMATION

224. Additional Information on Health and Safety is available from the following sources:
- Civil Service *Sickness Absence Report 2004 available at www.civilservice.gov.uk;*
- *Safety Health and Environmental Protection in the Ministry of Defence – A Policy Statement by the Secretary of State for Defence* available at www.mod.uk;
- *Sustainable Development Annual Report 2005* available at www.mod.uk;
- *UK Defence Statistics 2006* available at www.dasa.mod.uk (from September 2006).

Essay: Caring for the Injured

Our Armed Forces require a high level of fitness to be effective as a fighting force. Our Servicemen and women deserve a high standard of healthcare in recognition of the jobs they do. We aim to give all our injured personnel the best medical help we can at the right time and in the right place. The Defence Medical Services work to help our personnel lead fit and healthy lives in the first place, and if they become ill or injured, to return them to operational fitness whenever, and as soon as, possible. This is not just because it is right for the individual. Medical services can be a real force multiplier and this is increasingly important at a time of a high tempo of operations. The commonest cause of medical unfitness amongst Service personnel is through muscle, bone and joint injury – a 'musculo-skeletal injury' in medical terms. This essay describes how we treat and rehabilitate such patients, and casualties from military operations, and is indicative of our wider approach.

Medical Rehabilitation Programme

We have a three-tier approach to the treatment of musculo-skeletal injuries, matching the level of treatment to the severity of the problem and including fast-track access to orthopaedic surgery if necessary. The first stage is provided by Primary Care Rehabilitation Facilities to which the patient has access via his or her parent unit. These provide immediate care for injuries. Wherever possible, access to a detailed assessment by an experienced doctor and/or physiotherapist follows within two working days of presentation. For simple cases, the patient receives local treatment and rehabilitation. The decision on whether they need more intensive treatment will depend on the need for a firm diagnosis, the severity of the injury and the availability of local physiotherapy and rehabilitation facilities. As a rough guide, a patient is referred to such a facility if they can be expected to return to fitness within one month.

The second stage is assessment at one of our 12 UK Regional Rehabilitation Units, or similar facilities in Germany and Cyprus. These contain doctors, physiotherapists and Remedial Instructors – Physical Education instructors who have received additional training in-group rehabilitation. They provide diagnosis through access within 20 days to a Multi-disciplinary Injury Assessment Clinic. Here a team with enhanced skills in the diagnosis of musculo-skeletal disorders following injury has access to specialist diagnostic aids such as Magnetic Resonance Imaging. The team aims to establish a firm diagnosis so that the most appropriate care is given and, working with the individual's primary care unit and occupational medicine specialists, predict the time it will take for patients to be fit again to take up their duties. Our target for a scan is 10 days. Informed by the scan results, the team decide which patients need to be offered orthopaedic surgery and develop a post-operative rehabilitation plan before surgery takes place. The units also provide treatment, if needed, in carefully structured groups that follow a set programme of therapy.

The third stage is treatment at the Defence Medical Rehabilitation Centre at Headley Court in Surrey. This is a world-class facility, run by the Defence Medical Services, with no equivalent in the NHS. Patients with complex and/or multiple injuries, including amputees and those with brain injuries, are transferred to be looked after by multi-disciplinary teams. The aim is to achieve the best outcome for all patients by providing physiotherapy and group rehabilitation for complex musculo-skeletal injuries; high quality artificial limbs which are manufactured or assembled on site and individually tailored for each patient by the Centre's Limb Fitting and Amputee Rehabilitation Centre and rehabilitation for brain-injured patients. We are developing links with the Brain Injury Rehabilitation Trust to help with neuro-psychology and the onward care of those individuals unable to return to duty in the Armed Forces at centres across UK that provide in-patient and community support. We aim for seamless transition of these patients back into civilian life following medical discharge from the Service. Because of its unique facilities and capabilities, the Unit plays a critical role in the rehabilitation of severely injured casualties returning from operational theatres.

Medical care for those injured on operations

Our Armed Forces are deployed on operations around the world, some in environments that are challenging in terms of climate and local disease and where they face the risk of hostile action. Before our troops are sent overseas, we determine the level of medical support that they will need in-theatre. The aim is to match this to the size of deployment, the hazards to be faced, and the support available from the host country or other nations participating in the operation. We provide this care for mobilised reservists as well as regular Service personnel. In theatre, medical teams provide assessment and immediate treatment of all casualties. This is again delivered in a tiered approach. It includes training all our people in 'buddy-buddy' and first-aid care, and increasingly specialised unit medical support, field hospitals and a hospital ship if necessary, to provide the best possible care in the most difficult operational environments. On larger operations, the medical teams in theatre will comprise both regular and reservist doctors, dentists, nurses and other health professionals from all three Services covering a range of specialisms and backed up by a hospital administration support team and trained welfare staff. They have advanced medical equipment that can be transported and is able to operate worldwide, and access to telemedicine to enable complex cases to be discussed with specialists back in the UK. Not all injuries are life threatening, and when clinically and operationally appropriate, patients are treated and rehabilitated in-theatre.

Defence Medical Rehabilitation Teams

In some cases it is necessary to fly the patient back to the UK for further treatment. Specialist RAF medical teams accompany patients. Once in the UK, they will receive care according to the level of their injuries. The Defence Medical Rehabilitation Centre evaluates and coordinates these care pathways to ensure that injured personnel are looked after from the time of their return to the UK until they are fully recovered or medically discharged from the Armed Forces. Patients with complex musculo-skeletal or neurological needs, as a result of hostile action or other injury, who require hospital care are referred to the Royal Centre for Defence Medicine at University Hospital Birmingham for treatment; patients with moderate or minor injuries, who have been assessed, have a working diagnosis and a planned care pathway, are referred to the rehabilitation unit responsible for the patient's parent unit; patients who have a musculo-skeletal injury who do not fit into the first two categories and who have not had a rehabilitation assessment in theatre are referred to Headley Court for assessment. When hospital treatment is complete, injured personnel are transferred to the best place for their continuing rehabilitation. For those with severe injuries this is Headley Court.

Conclusion

The Defence Medical Services are dedicated to the well being of our people at all times: we are continually monitoring and improving our service to them. The rehabilitation programme is now in its third year and delivering remarkable results. Managed pathways for operational casualties have been in force since January 2006. Both provide timely return to full operational capability or seamless transfer back into civilian life as necessary. The care pathways put our service personnel at the centre of care, managed at every phase of therapy by dedicated healthcare teams, in a programme that has significantly improved morale by demonstrably providing a standard of healthcare that matches the operational demands placed on our Service personnel. We continue to work to improve the speed and quality of the care our medical staff and system offer – our Servicemen and women deserve nothing less.

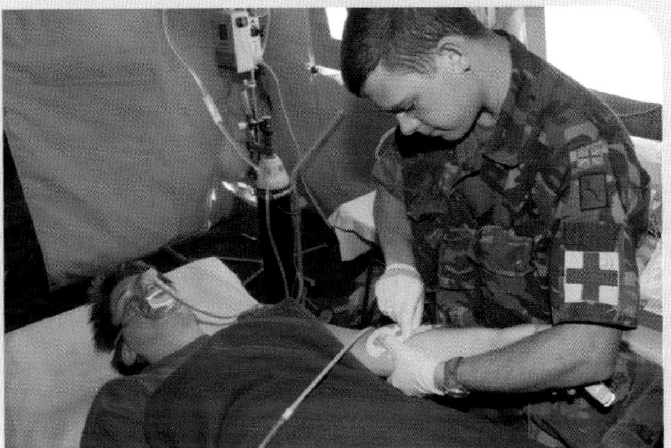

An army medic

LOGISTICS

Objective: Support and sustain our Armed Forces.

Public Service Agreement Target (SR2002 MoD Target 7)

Increase value for money by making improvements in the efficiency and effectiveness of the key processes for delivering military capability: Year-on-year output efficiency gains will be made each year from 2002-03 to 2005-06, including through a 20%[1] output efficiency gain (relative to April 2000) in the Defence Logistics Organisation:

- **Reduce by 14% (relative to planned expenditure in 2002-03) the output costs of the Defence Logistics Organisation by April 2006, while maintaining support to the Front Line.**

Performance Measures and Assessment

Deliver 98% of logistic support for funded levels of readiness and funded logistic support to enable force generation within planned readiness times, as set out in Customer Supplier Agreements with Top Level Budget Holders:

- **94.5% of logistic support outputs delivered (2004-05 95%, 2003-04 93.4%).**

Provide funded logistic sustainability for future contingent operations:

- **We are working to ensure we understand the full logistic recuperation requirements and cost to restore contingent forces' readiness to conduct a wide range of operations when the high tempo of current operations reduces;**
- **The Logistic Sustainability and Deployability Audit in 2005 provided an updated assessment of our sustainability capability.**

Deliver Logistics efficiency savings agreed in 2002 and 2004 Spending Reviews:

- **The Strategic Goal required the Defence Logistics Organisation to achieve a further 4.2% (£374M) reduction in its output costs during 2005-06. Subject to validation, we expect the amount achieved to fall between £350M and £400M. We will complete validation of performance against the Strategic Goal by the Autumn.**
- **The wider Defence Logistics Transformation Programme was to achieve £539M savings by 31 March 2006. We estimate that we achieved from £500M to £575M, including £350M to £400M under the Strategic Goal on the basis of the available information.**

Achieve a disposal sales gross cash receipt of £50M from the sales of surplus equipment and stores:

- **60.2M gross cash receipts achieved.**

[1] Relative to April 2000 (1999-2000 outturn). Performance thus includes efficiency achieved in 2000-01 and 2001-02.

DELIVERY OF LOGISTIC SUPPORT

225. The Defence Logistics Organisation (DLO) is responsible for providing front line support to the British Armed Forces. To achieve this it works closely with Front Line Commands, the Defence Procurement Agency, other parts of the MoD and industry.

Performance against Customer Supplier Agreements

226. The level of logistic support provided by the DLO to the Armed Forces is agreed through Customer Supplier Agreements with each of other Top Level Budget holders. These define, within the resources allocated, the logistic outputs to be provided by the Chief of Defence Logistics to support the Commanders-in-Chief and other Top Level Budget Holders in their delivery of military capability at the levels specified in their own Service Delivery Agreements with the MoD Head Office. In 2005-06 the DLO achieved the agreed service levels for delivery against funded levels of readiness of 94.5% of its logistic support outputs, against a target of 98%, a slight decrease from 95% in 2004-05. This was driven by shortfalls in a few areas, in particular:

- defects and spares availability difficulties across the surface fleet;
- difficulties supporting ageing Royal Fleet Auxiliary ships;
- shortfalls in the availability of spares for Apache attack helicopters; and,
- fragile spares delivery programmes for Typhoon and Hercules C-130J.

Supporting Operations

227. The DLO remained focussed on support to operations and demonstrated it's ability to respond to short notice surge requirements. The main logistic effort was in support of Operation TELIC in Iraq, where we continued to introduce incremental improvements to the management of Urgent Operational Requirements, Logistic Command and Control, asset tracking, air transport and the Coupling Bridge. We also planned and began support to expansion of Operation HERRICK in Afghanistan. A key lesson identified from Operation TELIC was the need for a permanent, single organisation to co-ordinate all logistics activity in-theatre. The Joint Force Logistics Component acts as the front end of the supply chain, providing a single channel for support from the DLO in the UK to the forces deployed in theatre. The Joint Force Logistics Component Headquarters was established in December 2005 and has deployed to Afghanistan to take command of logistic operations in Theatre. The DLO also provided immediate and effective logistic support to the humanitarian relief operations following the Pakistan earthquake, and supplied some 475,000 Operational Ration Packs worth over £3M to the US to assist the relief effort following Hurricane Katrina (see paragraph 16). Although the rations were impounded by the US Department of Agriculture for not meeting import regulations, they have been subsequently redistributed to the Organisation for Security and Cooperation in Europe and to non-governmental organisations for humanitarian purposes.

228. We are working to ensure we understand the full logistic recuperation requirements and cost to restore contingent forces' readiness to conduct a wide range of operations when the high tempo of current operations reduces. We also continue to look for ways to increase the effectiveness of our sustainability and deployability processes, including the development of how we prepare for specific operational deployments. The Logistic Sustainability and Deployability Audit carried out in 2005 sought to articulate both the Total Logistic Requirement and to reach judgements about what might be made available within the relevant warning times in order to support operations up to the most demanding level envisaged in Defence Planning Assumptions, thus providing an updated assessment of our sustainability capability. Resources are focused on providing the assets most likely to be needed to sustain operations and which we judge could not be bought within assumed readiness times. We continued to develop our ability to evaluate and articulate logistic risks within the wider resource programming process to ensure that affordability decisions take full cognisance of the implications for logistic capability requirements.

229. In its report into *Assessing and reporting military readiness*, published in February 2006, the House of Commons Committee of Public Accounts recommended that we should draw up contingency plans to accelerate our work to introduce a robust asset tracking system in the event that this were required for operational deployments in the shorter term. We currently have a consignment tracking capability that has been tested in Afghanistan. The trend over recent months has been one of steady improvement as the changes to regulations, training, and equipment made as a result of Lessons Identified begin to deliver improved visibility of materiel in transit. There has been no opportunity to test the improved consignment tracking system during the peak flow to a Large Scale operation and we do not yet have a full computer based Asset Tracking capability (defined as the means of providing timely and accurate information on the location, movement, status and identity of units, personnel, equipment and materiel). We plan to deliver a range of Logistic Information Systems between 2006 and 2012 that will provide the base data to support asset tracking for the future. In the light of the Committee's recommendation we are now drawing up contingency plans to accelerate the programme to track material in transit should increased capability for large scale operational deployments be required in the shorter term.

IMPROVING LOGISTIC EFFECTIVENESS AND EFFICIENCY

Management of Logistics

230. Logistics is one of the enabling processes within the Department's Business Management System (see paragraphs 248-254). As process owner the Chief of Defence Logistics has responsibility for the delivery of the logistics process across Defence including the Equipment Capability Customer, industry, Defence Procurement Agency, Front Line Commands and the Chief of Joint Operations, as well as in the Defence Logistics Organisation. The April 2006 Defence Logistics Programme provides the strategy and supporting delivery programme to take logistics forward. It draws together the most significant work currently underway in improving delivery of logistics across Defence, including the current Defence Logistics Transformation Programme activities, and provides the strategic direction for logistics to meet the current and future needs of the operational commander.

The Defence Logistics Organisation Strategic Goal

231. On its creation in 2000 the Defence Logistics Organisation was set a goal, known as the Strategic Goal, of reducing its output costs by 20% relative to April 2000 by the end of 2005-06. In the 2002 Spending Review this was rebaselined to a reduction of 14% relative to planned expenditure in 2002-03 (a reduction of £1,262 billion), and included within the Department's overall value for money Public Service Agreement target. A reduction of 6.6% was achieved by April 2004. In the *Annual Report and Accounts 2004-05*, we estimated that the Defence Logistics Organisation had achieved over a further £400M annual output efficiency savings during 2004-05. We made clear that this reflected the best information available to us at the time of publication and was subject to validation. Accounting for efficiency is a complex process that inevitably takes some time. It is validated through detailed scrutiny of a proportion of the efficiency claim by Defence internal auditors and extrapolated from that to reach an overall total. This arrangement is visible to the National Audit Office and the conclusions are shared with them. Our validation of the 2004-05 total concluded conservatively that there was evidence to substantiate at least £280M of benefits, producing a minimum cumulative reduction of 9.8% against the Strategic Goal target of 14% by April 2006. While the reduction from the initial estimate was disappointing, it demonstrated the rigour of the process to ensure that our efficiency claims are fully supported by evidence.

232. In the light of this exercise we improved the guidance on what can be claimed as efficiency and how to measure it, took steps to ensure that the Integrated Project Teams and others responsible for efficiency reporting maintained robust audit trails for efficiency achievements for 2005-06 and subsequent years, and set in hand an internal sampling of projects to review the evidence supporting reported benefits. Achieving the Strategic Goal required the Defence Logistics Organisation to achieve a further 4.2% (£374M) reduction in its output costs during 2005-06. We expect the final total to fall between £350M (discounting initial claims to the proportion validated for 2004-05) to £400M (based on some preliminary results reflecting the improvements taken forward in light of the results of the 2004-05 validation exercise). We expect to complete validation of the 2005-06 achievement in Autumn 2006.

The Defence Logistics Transformation Programme

233. The Defence Logistics Transformation Programme (DLTP) was launched on 1 April 2004. The Programme embraces all Defence logistics activity, not just in the Defence Logistics Organisation, whether it occurs in preparation for operations,deployed in-theatre, within Defence industry, during the early stages of equipment acquisition, or when planning for equipment disposal. Its aim is to transform the means by which logistics support is delivered to all three Services through improvements in effectiveness, efficiency and flexibility of logistic support, thereby improving logistic support to the front line and releasing substantial resources for investment elsewhere in Defence. It incorporates all previous logistics change and efficiency programmes, including the Defence Logistics Organisation Change Programme underpinning the Strategic Goal and the End-to-End Logistics Review. It is an extremely complex programme comprising over 1,000 separate projects. The emphasis of logistics transformation matured from early delivery of efficiency in 2004-05 to the enabling of improvements in operational effectiveness in 2005-06.

234. Although the programme predates the Gershon efficiency review conducted as part of the 2004 Spending Review, the Treasury agreed that it contributed effectively to the goals of that review. With an overall target of £951M efficiency savings it is the single largest element of the Department's £2.8 billion efficiency programme from 2005-06 to 2007-08. The programme's target was to achieve £539M savings by 31 March 2006 (including some efficiencies generated during 2004-05). We estimate, on the basis of the available information, that we achieved from £500M to £575M of efficiencies, including £350M to £400M under the Strategic Goal and including over £70M of efficiencies from the Procurement Reform programme to maximise the Department's buying power using reverse auctions, electronic purchasing, incentives and rationalisation of contracts. Some examples of savings and effectiveness are set out below.

Examples of improved logistics effectiveness and efficiency

235. The DLTP remains on track to deliver further improvements in efficiency and effectiveness. Figures are for in year 2005-06 benefits delivery, unless otherwise stated. They will form part of the overall 2005-06 achievement and are all subject to validation. The Attack

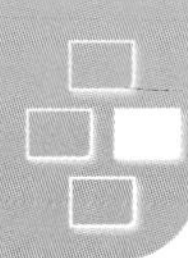

helicopter benefits have been reviewed in an internal audit and Tornado benefits were the subject of review by the House of Commons Defence Committee earlier this year. Key achievements during the year included:

- the application of Lean techniques particularly in the area of aircraft, ship and vehicle maintenance. In particular lean process were introduced for support of Harrier and Hunt Class Mine Counter Measures Vessels;
- improved support arrangements for the Harrier Pegasus engine delivered savings of £3.8M;
- improvements in the Avionics support chain delivered savings of £9M;
- the Land Guided Weapons IPT delivered £16M through the drawdown of Rapier;
- the Attack Helicopter IPT delivered savings of £36M through the reduction of capital spares holding;
- the Submarine IPT delivered further savings of £16M through their submarine upkeep improvement programme;

Pre-flight check at RAF Marham

- the creation of a single location for all major repair, maintenance and upgrade for Tornado GR4 aircraft at RAF Marham continued to deliver results. A new contract with BAE Systems that will release six aircraft from the repair cycle to the front-line by 2008, and that is expected to deliver savings of £321M over five years, delivered £13M in 2005-06. A similar contract with Rolls-Royce is expected to save £136M over five years while improving Tornado engine availability and reliability;
- The introduction of Priming Equipment Packs is improving the Army's ability to prepare and deploy on operations. These are operational packs of materiel based on prepared scales of equipment and spares, delivered to units 72 hours before deployment. They were trialled on a major exercise in November 2005 and reduced the value of unit equipment holdings from £9.1M to £2.8M while improving availability against demand from 38 to 78 per cent. They are now being rolled out across the Army and will be used to support deployments to Afghanistan;
- A combination of changes in the organisation and command and control arrangements in the Joint Supply Chain and the introduction of common Joint processes have improved delivery times in the UK and to deployed theatres. Delivery times in the UK have reduced from 28 days to 13 days, with a target of 7 day delivery anywhere in the UK and NW Europe. These changes will also facilitate the introduction of new logistics information systems.

236. A major activity has been the broadening of new partnering arrangements with industry. 'Contracting for Availability' moves the Department away from a spares, repair and overhaul buying organisation into one which rewards industry for agreed levels of availability at an agreed price. This principle has been applied successfully in Rotary wing where Integrated Operational Support solutions for Chinook and Merlin ensure an agreed level of aircraft availability, spares provision and overhaul at a fixed price. A five-year Contract for Availability replaces five Island Class Offshore Patrol Vessels with three modern River Class vessels (HMS Mersey, Tyne and Severn). The contractor owns and supports the ships and is incentivised for good performance. Between them they are available for 960 days per year or 98% of the time, compared with 82% for the Island Class (achieved with more ships). This benchmark support solution is on target to save MoD at least £12M.

Restructuring

237. The Defence Logistics Organisation is part way through a major restructuring programme to improve its efficiency and effectiveness. This also contributes to the Department's overall manpower efficiency savings. The first phase came into effect on 4 April 2005 and concentrated on making corporate support services more effective. The second phase is intended to embed the changes to date and improve effectiveness across the whole organisation. As part of the programme, the DLO has been formulating proposals to collocate further elements alongside the Defence Procurement Agency in the Bristol/Bath area to create an acquisition hub and foster improved decision-making and better through-life management of Defence equipment. These objectives are consistent with the establishment of the new integrated acquisition and support organisation from 1 April 2007, announced on 3 July 2006.

Merlin

Defence Aviation Repair Agency

238. In November 2005 the Minister for the Armed Forces announced the planned closure of the Defence Aviation Repair Agency's Fast Jet and Engine businesses by April 2007. The closure of the Fast Jet business at St Athan was largely determined by the decision to roll forward the Tornado GR4 aircraft to RAF Marham, which left insufficient work to sustain a viable business. The decision to close the Engine business at Fleetlands was a result of the lack of success in winning work in competition with Rolls Royce. The VC10 business at St Athan, Rotary repair and maintenance business at Fleetlands, and Components business at Almondbank in Perthshire are now being market-tested to determine if their sale would offer better long-term prospects for the workforce and greater value for Defence. The Electronics business at Sealand will be retained within MoD ownership while work is undertaken to determine the Department's future avionics support arrangements.

239. The First Minister for Wales formally opened the Agency's new superhangar at St Athan in April 2005. It is regarded as one of Europe's finest aircraft repair facilities and is a highly marketable facility for South Wales as the Agency's workload at St Athan draws down towards closure in April 2007. The superhangar has enabled the Agency to deliver significant efficiency improvements and costs savings and we expect to have fully recovered our investment in the project by then. We continue to work closely with the Welsh Assembly Government and others to explore commercial opportunities for the future long-term prospects of St Athan. Further information on DARA is set out on pages 263-264.

ABRO

240. In July 2005 the first phase of a rationalisation programme was announced reducing ABRO's workforce by up to 294 to reflect a downturn in its workload. Preliminary plans for a second phase were announced in November 2005, but in March 2006 we announced that there had been a number of developments with a potential impact on the proposed rationalisation, including a deeper understanding of the future threat environment on deployed operations. As a result the depth repair programme for the FV430 fleet will be extended, providing work for the armoured vehicle repair centre at Bovington, and repair work on Warrior and Combat Vehicle Reconnaissance (Tracked) will remain at Donnington in the medium term. Revised rationalisation proposals for the armoured vehicle and related business units in light of these changes will be announced later in 2006. Rationalisation of the 'one-stop shops' at Warminster and Colchester will proceed as planned with up to 339 further redundancies. Further information on ABRO is set out on page 263.

Equipment Disposals

241. The Disposal Services Agency had another successful year in which it achieved £60.2M in gross sales, including £12M of repayment sales, £8M worth of surplus vehicles and £5M sales on behalf of Other Government Departments. The year also saw an agreement signed for the sale of three surplus Type 23 frigates to Chile.

FURTHER SOURCES OF INFORMATION

242. Additional Information on Logistics is available from the following sources:
- quarterly PSA reports to HM Treasury at www.mod.uk;
- *UK Defence Statistics 2006* available at www.dasa.mod.uk (from September 2006);
- *SR2004 Efficiency Technical Note* available at www.mod.uk;
- The Defence Logistics Organisation Plan 2005 available at www.mod.uk;
- *Defence Logistics Programme 2006* available at www.mod.uk;
- *ABRO Annual Report and Accounts 2005-06* available at www.abrodev.co.uk (from July 2006);
- *Defence Aviation Repair Agency Annual Report and Accounts 2005-06* available at www.daranet.co.uk (from July 2006);
- *Disposal Services Agency Annual Report and Accounts 2005-06* available at www.mod.uk (from July 2006).

Essay: Transforming Logistics Support to the Armed Forces

The last eight years have seen a fundamental reshaping of Defence logistics following the formation of the tri-service Defence Logistics Organisation in 1998. Historically, logistics support was a series of separate tasks performed within different organisations with the front-line user at the end of the chain. However, the End-to-End principle at the heart of logistics transformation treats logistics as a continuous process across organisational boundaries, with the needs of the front-line customer as the start point. This is a departure from the traditional view, but is rapidly being adopted and embedded across Defence. This common, shared understanding of how logistics support contributes to the delivery of operations is a major step forward and has been the springboard for key transformational activities in 2005-06, with the emphasis firmly on the delivery of effectiveness.

The application of lean techniques has been successful in removing waste and wasteful processes; from vehicle maintenance in barracks to ships alongside. Applying lean techniques for the first time to refurbish AS90 self-propelled guns in Germany, Lance Corporal Dean John of 5 Battalion REME, said: "I think leaning is an excellent idea. It meant I could spend more time on the kit rather than having to demand spares and fill in paperwork. Now we only do spanner stuff – it's much better to be in the grease!"

Supporting this view is the introduction of the Joint Asset Management and Engineering System version 1 (JAMES 1) in the Army. For every piece of equipment, JAMES 1 tells the user what the item is, where it is and the current task it's being used for. It also says who owns it, its serviceability state, what its next task will be and when it needs maintaining. Lance Corporal Phillip Merrills of 102 Logistics Brigade said: "It's easy enough to use. Now that I'm used to it, I like it. I wasn't so sure at first."

Another major milestone was recognition of the need to provide coherent through-life support for major platforms and equipment. The introduction of new capabilities such as Typhoon, the Type 45 Destroyer, the Future Aircraft Carrier and Astute submarines means that we must have plans in place to provide the best support, at the right price, based on experience and innovation to deliver the intended capability. A major element of that innovation will come from implementation of the Defence Industrial Strategy. This has given even greater emphasis to through-life support by its concept of Through-Life Capability Management that includes progressive capability enhancement and technology insertion.

Transformation on the scale delivered in Defence logistics cannot be achieved without changes in our relationship with industry. Progress in this area has been rapid, particularly on RAF main operating bases where the support landscape is changing. At RAF Marham, BAE Systems and Rolls-Royce are on-base delivering support to the front-line managed by the DLO, mirroring arrangements already in place in the Maritime environment. Partnering with industry continues to increase, with some contracts for equipment and whole platform availability in place and others imminent.

Although much has been achieved in the last year, challenges remain. The first is to ensure that transformational activities are correctly prioritised and resourced to contribute to improved support to current and future operations. The second is to embed these organisational, process and behavioural changes throughout the logistics community and industry, to produce *'confidence in logistics'*, *'confidence in industry'* and to *'deliver logistics for operations'*.

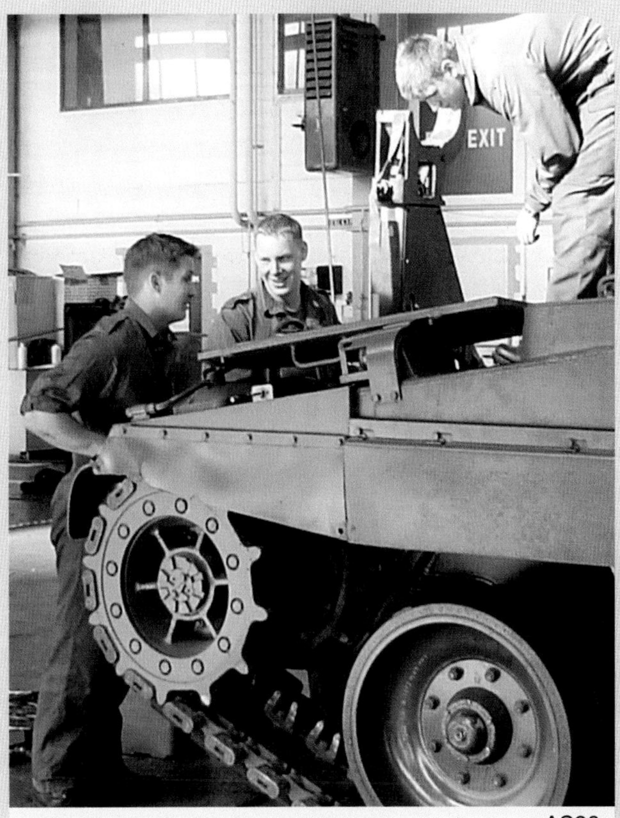

AS90

BUSINESS MANAGEMENT

Objective: Deliver improved ways of working.

Performance Measures and Assessment

Organisation and Governance:

- **Publication of Defence Framework document in January 2006;**
- **Continuing review of MoD top structure and corporate processes, including work on changes required to implement Defence Industrial Strategy;**
- **Publication of first Defence annual corporate governance report.**

Implementation of the Business Management System:

- **Business Management System introduced in April 2005, including enabling pan-Departmental processes and senior Process Owner accountable to the Defence Management Board for:**
  - **logistics;**
  - **civilian workforce;**
  - **Service personnel;**
  - **communications;**
  - **financial management;**
  - **commodity procurement.**
- **Development of coherent Defence Logistics Programme;**
- **Production of first Civilian Workforce Plan;**
- **Harmonisation and simplification of Service Personnel processes;**
- **Improvements to communications including improving planning and opinion research and an enhanced regional press officer network.**
- **Implementation of Financial 'Simplify and Improve' programme, including creation of the Financial Accounting Shared Service Centre in Bath and introduction of the Certificate in Resource Management;**
- **Introduction of central contracting arrangements for widely required commodities and expansion of e-procurement arrangements.**

TOP LEVEL ORGANISATION AND GOVERNANCE

243. We continue to work to improve the efficiency and effectiveness of the Department's management and governance arrangements, which drive the way we work to deliver military capability. The Ministry of Defence's *Departmental Framework* document, published in January 2006, sets out the framework within which the Ministry of Defence operates to deliver Defence outputs, the roles, responsibilities and governance framework that underpin the business of Defence, and explains how these integrate to support the delivery of the Defence Vision and Defence outputs. This is summarised in Annex B on the Organisation and Management of Defence.

244. A continuing strand of our change and efficiency programme has been work to ensure that the overarching top-level management structure of Defence remains fit for purpose and works in a coherent way consistent with good corporate governance practice to deliver strategic oversight and direction with the minimum overhead. This work has a number of elements. Our 2002 Spending Review PSA value for money targets included a reduction in the size of the Head Office enabled by improved Information Systems and working practices (see paragraphs 269-270). Our 2004 Spending Review efficiency targets built on this with a series of targets for further improvements in the delivery of corporate services and Head Office organisation (paragraph 128). In addition to those we have been considering the implications of the Defence Industrial Strategy for our central planning and programming systems (see the essay on page 85), and are reviewing our senior committee structure to ensure that its various elements provide clear oversight and direction in a mutually supportive way to take forward the policy set by Ministers and the Defence Management Board. There is also a programme of rationalisation among the Single Service Top Level Budget organisations, the Defence Procurement Agency and the Defence Logistics Organisation (paragraph 304).

Corporate Governance

245. We follow as closely as possible the Code of Good Practice on *Corporate Governance in Central Government Departments* published by the Treasury in July 2005. This was developed through a lengthy process of interdepartmental consultation, including with Ministers, which we fully supported. The Code is designed to provide an overview of corporate governance processes and responsibilities within departments, focusing in particular on the role of management boards. All departments are expected to apply its principles flexibly in light of their specific circumstances. It raised no fundamental issues of principle for Defence, which has long operated in accordance with its basic principles. It is not intended to cut across any legal obligations or constitutional requirements, which is an important provision for us given the constitutional role of the Defence Council and the integration of the Armed Forces in all aspects of the Department's activity up to and including the Defence Council and Defence Management Board. However, the role and structure of Defence, and in particular our fully integrated civilian-military organisation, mean that there are, and will continue to be, a few areas where our governance arrangements differ from the strict letter of its guidance. The Department's first Annual Report against the Code of Practice is published on www.mod.uk.

IMPLEMENTATION OF THE BUSINESS MANAGEMENT SYSTEM

246. A key element of this work has been the development and implementation of the Department's Business Management System. There are a number of departmental high level processes which define standards and requirements for key activities (such as personnel and financial management) which take place across the various business units, to ensure that they operate consistently and effectively across Defence. These enabling processes do not deliver specific outputs, but condition how that delivery is carried out. The Business Management System was introduced in April 2005 to enable better management of a range of these. In the first instance it identified six enabling pan-Departmental processes, for logistics; civilian workforce; Service personnel; communications; financial management; and commodity procurement. A further three Head Office enabling functions were also defined, for planning and resourcing, the strategic context, and the peace-conflict cycle. A senior Process Owner was appointed for each process, accountable to the Defence Management Board for ensuring that their process is efficient and effective, coherent with other processes and functions, and is implemented consistently across all Top Level Budget organisations. Little of this was new in itself, but it brought greater clarity, coherence and accountability to the way the Department is managed and underpinned work to take forward our efficiency goals by defining the interconnection between these processes, the roles and responsibilities of the senior military and civilian process owners responsible for them, and their relationship with Top Level Budget Holders and Senior Responsible Owners responsible for specific outputs.

247. During the year the Business Management System provided a useful framework for identifying and exploiting opportunities to improve the way we do business. Initial work focussed on understanding the various processes, how they operate across all parts of the Department and how they might be made to operate more efficiently and effectively. Process Owners have now established Terms of Reference for the management of their processes and functions, and for delivering improvements in the efficiency and effectiveness with which they operate. They also have the clear authority of the Defence Management Board to ensure that the process they specify is implemented across the Department.

Logistics

248. As the Logistics Process Owner the Chief of Defence Logistics is responsible for enabling the efficient and effective delivery of logistics across Defence, not just in the Defence Logistics Organisation. Working through a stakeholder board, which includes high-level representation from all involved Top Level Budget organisations, he has developed a Defence Logistics Programme providing the strategy and supporting delivery programme to take logistics forward. It draws together the most significant work currently underway in improving delivery of logistics across Defence, including the Defence Logistics Transformation Programme, and provides strategic direction for logistics to meet the current and future needs of the operational commander.

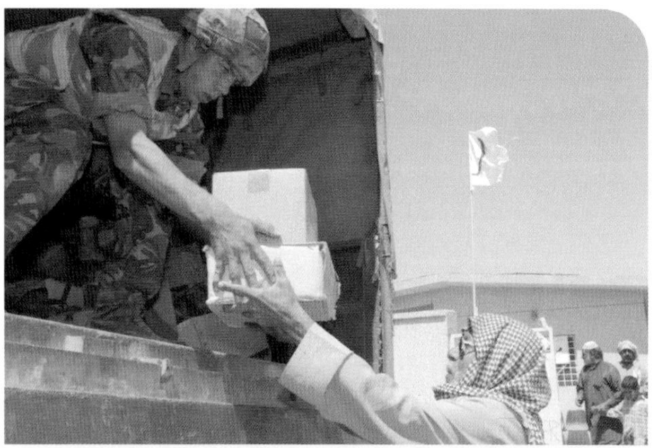

The Royal Logistic Corps delivers medical supplies

Civilian Workforce

249. The Civilian Workforce Process underpins the delivery of the People Programme and a number of associated changes. During the year the Personnel Director, as process owner, produced the first Civilian Workforce Plan (see paragraph 163) to develop the civilian contribution to Defence and to ensure that over the long term the Department has the workforce it needs.

Service Personnel

250. As process owner for Service Personnel, the Deputy Chief of the Defence Staff(Personnel) has developed the Service Personnel Plan to encompass process improvement as well as policy development (see paragraphs 152-153). This has incorporated work to drive forward harmonisation and simplification of the Service Personnel process (especially in the recruitment and training arena), and develop the requirement beyond 2009 for the services delivered by the Armed Forces Pay and Administration Agency. There has also been progress in scoping establishment of a process improvement capability within the Service Personnel community to identify and take forward coherently relevant lessons from Joint Personnel Administration, the Defence Training Review leverage and the administration of the Armed Forces Pay and Administration Agency.

Communications

251. Improvements to communications, both within Defence and between the Department and its many stakeholders, are being taken forward by the Director General of Media and Communications. We are working to improve communications planning and opinion research, and develop an enhanced regional press officer network.

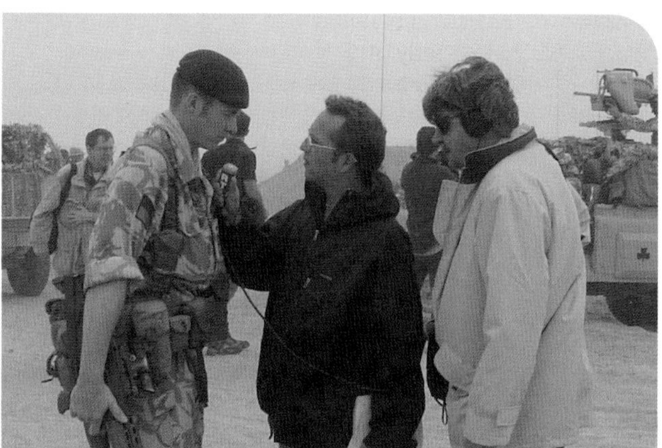

Press reporting on operations

Financial Management

252. Financial Management improvements have been taken forward by the Finance Director as process owner through the 'Simplify and Improve' programme endorsed by the Defence Management Board in February 2005. In particular the creation of the Financial Accounting Shared Service Centre in Bath and Liverpool is streamlining the financial accounting process by centralising transactional activity and allowing staff in the Head Office and TLBs to concentrate on value added management accounting activities to support decision-making. Together with the successful embedding of resource based accounting across the Department this is producing an evolving change towards a greater relative emphasis on management rather than financial accounting skills and expertise in our Top Level Budge organisation's financial staff. This is reflected in the Department's internal financial training programme, the Certificate in Resource Management, which is accredited by the Association of Accounting Technicians and cited by the Treasury as an example of best practice in Government.

Commodity Procurement

253. On commodity procurement, under the 2nd Permanent Under Secretary as process owner, work focused on introducing central contracting arrangements to replace ad hoc local procurement of widely required commodities. This was supported by a programme to introduce more widespread e-procurement arrangements, supported by e-catalogues. Work is now in hand to ensure that the new arrangements are fully embedded and working effectively across all Top Level Budget organisations.

254. The Business Management System will continue to develop as Process Owners become more familiar with the discipline of process management and with the requirements and authorities of their role. Work to embed this will concentrate on Maintaining the momentum of the Enabling Processes, and ensuring that Process Ownership becomes business as usual; ensuring good governance, so that we have clearly understood targets and good knowledge of what is being achieved; and defining the processes comprising Acquisition, for subsequent inclusion in the framework.

FURTHER SOURCES OF INFORMATION

255. Additional information on Business Management is available from the following sources:
- *Ministry of Defence Framework Document* available at www.mod.uk
- *Corporate governance code for central Government departments: Code of Good Practice* available at www.hm-treasury.gov.uk;
- Defence Annual Corporate Governance Report available at www.mod.uk;
- Defence Logistics Programme 2006 available at www.mod.uk;

Essay: The role and value of independent Non-Executive Directors in Defence

Over the past few years the role and responsibilities of independent non-executives in UK industry and government has been a key element of several reviews, all of which highlighted the importance of non-executives on management boards and audit committees. The Cabinet Office are producing guidelines on non-executive directors for central Government departments. In July 2005 the Treasury published the *Corporate Governance in Central Government Departments: Code of Good Practice*[1]. This provided an overview of corporate governance processes and responsibilities within departments particularly, focusing on the role of departmental management boards including non-executives. It is important that no individual or small group of individuals can dominate decision-making and that the board can draw upon a wide range of experience. The code therefore sets out that there should be at least two non-executive members on management boards to provide balance and to ensure that executive members are both supported and constructively challenged in their roles. One non-executive director should chair the board's audit committee with the others as members.

The MoD fully supports these principles, and for several years has engaged non-executives in its management boards and audit committees in all top-level areas of the Department including its Agencies. At the top of the Department the Defence Management Board has at least two non-executive members. They also sit on the Defence Audit Committee, which one of them chairs (currently Mrs Philippa Foster Back of the Institute of Business Ethics). The size and diversity of Defence are such that we do not take a 'one size fits all' approach, but we are reviewing our corporate governance arrangements to ensure that we consistently follow best practice tailored to the context. All those involved in appointing non-executives are required to follow procedures laid down in MoD guidance. Vacancies are filled through open and fair competition and selection is proportionate to the nature and accountabilities of the role. But ultimately, the selection and appointment of non-executives is the responsibility of the management board chair.

Dr Zenna Atkins is a non-executive member of the Royal Navy Fleet executive board and a good example of the benefits that non-executives bring to Defence. She is an executive consultant for a social sector consultancy company; chairs the Portsmouth NHS Teaching Primary Care Trust; is group chair of an organisation that provides a range of regeneration solutions across the UK; and voluntary chair of an innovative organisation for young persons. She is also a columnist for the *Guardian* and has extensive publications in health and housing press. Her skills and experience bring a wider perspective to Fleet's strategic management. Her capacity to deal with complex information and clear understanding of governance and accountability is a real benefit to a Department as diverse as the MoD.

Dr Zenna Atkins

It is important for non-executives to understand the priorities and concerns of the organisation. This enables them to fully carry out their roles on boards and committees by;

- participating in the formulation of strategic options and helping to set the "big picture" strategy;
- helping the board define policies;
- adding value to decision making by interrogating and challenging decisions;
- advising in the management of major change programmes;
- bringing commercial knowledge and experience to the validation of major investment decisions;
- acting as a sounding board to balance the executive management's enthusiasm; and,
- when specifically requested by the Chair, to act as an interface with outside stakeholders.

Non-executives are good for the successful management of non-operational Defence business. They help ensure the effectiveness and efficiency of our management boards, and widen the horizons within which strategy is determined by applying the benefits of their wider general experience and by bringing to discussions their different specialist skills, experience and perspective.

[1] www.hm-treasury.gov.uk./documents/financial_management/governance_government/pss_audit_corporategovernance.cfm

Resources

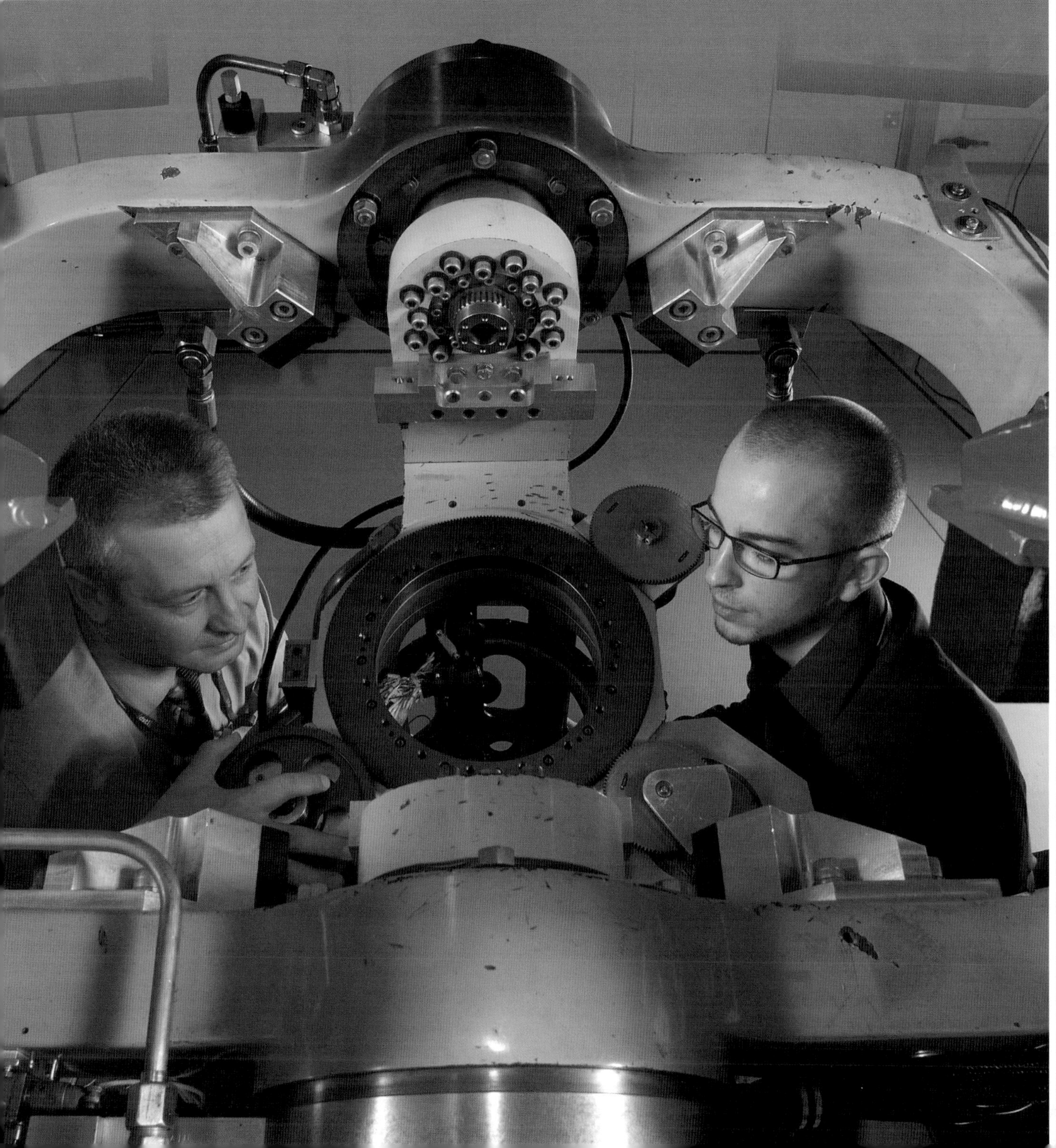

FINANCE

Objective: Control our expenditure within allocated financial resources, while maximising our outputs.

Public Service Agreement Target (SR2002 MoD Target 7)

Increase value for money by making improvements in the efficiency and effectiveness of the key processes for delivering military capability. Year-on-year output efficiency gains of 2.5% will be made each year from 2002-03 to 2005-06, including through a 20%[1] output efficiency gain in the Defence Logistics Organisation:

- **Reduce the per capita cost of successfully training a military recruit by an average of 6% by April 2006;**
- **Achieve 0% average annual cost growth (or better) against the Major Equipment Procurement Projects;**
- **Reduce by 14% (relative to April 2002) the output costs of the Defence Logistics Organisation, while maintaining support to the Front Line;**
- **Reduce MoD Head Office and other management costs by 13%;**
- **Identify for disposal land and buildings with a Net Book Value of over £300M.**

Performance Measures and Assessment

In-year Departmental financial management:

- **Net resource consumption of £32,738M for provision of Defence capability against resources voted by Parliament of £34,665M;**
- **Net additional Resource and Capital expenditure of £1,266M on operations against resources voted by Parliament of £1,431M;**
- **Expenditure against war pensions and allowances of £1,069M, against resources voted by Parliament of £1,073M;**
- **Outturn of £31,855M against Resource Departmental Expenditure Limit[2] of £32,626M;**
- **Outturn of £6,627M against Capital Departmental Expenditure Limit of £6,468M.**

Achieve 10% cumulative overall efficiency improvement compared to 2001-2002:

- **Subject to confirmation and validation, we believe we have met the overall target of 10%;**
  - **Following organisational changes it is no longer possible to measure the per capita training cost on the basis used in the PSA target;**
  - **0.1% in-year reduction on Major Equipment Projects (target 0% cost growth);**
  - **9.8% cumulative reduction in Logistics costs by 2004-05 compared to 2001-02 (target 10%); we expect the achievement for 2005-06 will lie in the range £350M-£400M, producing cumulative reduction of at least 13.7% (target 14%);**
  - **12.0% cumulative reduction in Head Office costs (target 13.0%);**
  - **Cumulative value of £456M land and buildings identified for disposal (target £300M).**

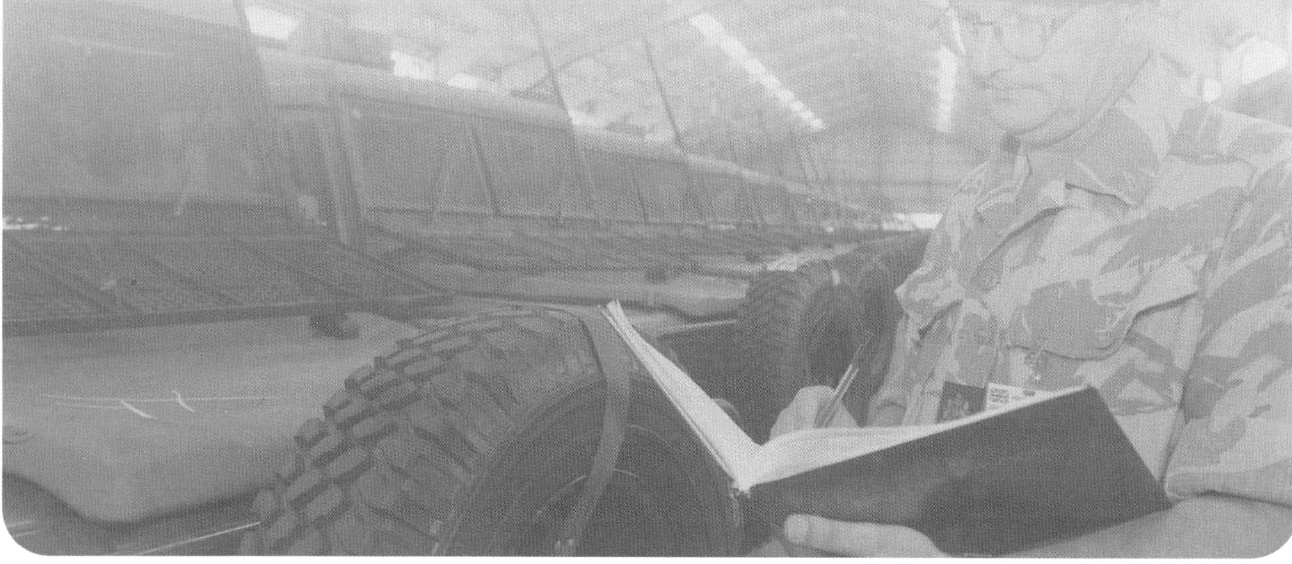

[1] Relative to April 2000 (1999/00 outturn). Performance thus includes efficiency achieved in 2000/01 and 2001/02.

[2] The Departmental Expenditure Limits (DELs) are budgetary figures. Resource DEL includes provision for cash release of nuclear provisions. Capital DEL includes estimated capital additions for the Royal Hospital Chelsea, neither of which are voted by Parliament.

DEFENCE BUDGET AND SPENDING

256. The Ministry of Defence again achieved an unqualified opinion from the Comptroller and Auditor General that the Departmental Resource Accounts in Section 2 of this report give a true and fair view of the state of affairs of the Department and of its net resource outturn, recognised gains and losses and cash flows for the year.

Departmental Outturn

257. Planned expenditure for the year was set out in the *Ministry of Defence: The Government's Expenditure Plans 2005/06 to 2007/08*, and in the Main, Winter, and Spring Supplementary Estimates voted by Parliament. Provisional outturn for the year was set out in the *Public Expenditure Outturn White Paper 2005-06* which was published in July 2006. Table 10 compares final performance against the final estimates approved by Parliament, as reported in the Statement of Parliamentary Supply on page 187 of the Accounts. It includes Resource Departmental Expenditure Limit (Resource DEL), Annually Managed Expenditure (AME)[3] and Non Budget[4], but does not include income payable to the Consolidated Fund, shown in Note 5 to the accounts. Total Defence expenditure in 2005/06 was contained within voted provision, with an overall Net Resource underspend, which includes both cash and non cash items and unallocated provisions, of £1,977M.

258. As set out in the explanation of variation between Estimate and Outturn in the Departmental Resource Accounts on page 188, the main elements in RFR1 were underspends of £375M against Resource DEL[5], £263M in AME, and £1,289M in Non Budget. The underspend in Resource DEL relates to lower than estimated depreciation costs following reviews of stocks and fixed assets. AME is showing an underspend due to the transfer of nuclear liabilities to the Nuclear Decommissioning Authority. The underspend on Non Budget is due to lower than expected charges when the discount rate was changed, and again the transfer of nuclear liabilities to the Nuclear Decommissioning Authority. Explanations of the differences between Outturn and the Departmental Expenditure Limit are shown at paragraph 263.

259. One of the principal pressures on the Defence budget in 2005-06 was the increase in fuel and utility costs, which showed increases from 2004-05 of 55% and 21% respectively. Due to actuarial changes to pension contribution rates, contribution rates for Service personnel were increased at a higher level than anticipated, and the overall increase in pension costs (known as SCAPE[6]) from 2004/05 to 2005/06 was 18%, compared with an increase in salaries and wages of 1.5%.

Table 10: 2005-06 Parliamentary Controls (£M)

	Final Voted Provision	Net Resource Outturn	Variation
Request for Resources 1 (Provision of Defence capability)	34,665	32,738	(1,927)
Request for Resources 2 (net additional cost of operations)	1,101	1,055	(46)
Request for Resources 3 (war pensions and allowances)	1,073	1,069	(4)
Net Resources	36,839	34,862	(1,977)
Net Cash Requirement	31,502	30,603	(899)

[3] Annually Managed Expenditure (AME) covers programmes that are demand-led, or exceptionally volatile in a way that could not be controlled by the Department.
[4] Non Budget costs, are items of expenditure subject to Parliamentary, but not Treasury, controls.
[5] Direct Resource DEL consists of items such as pay, equipment support costs, fuel and administrative expenses.
Indirect Resource DEL, also known as 'non cash' includes items such as depreciation, cost of capital and movements in the level of provisions;
[6] SCAPE: Superannuation Contributions Adjusted for Past Experience.

Cost of Operations

260. No formal budget is set for the cost of operations. The Department is voted additional resources in RfR 2 to cover the net additional costs of operations and Conflict Prevention Programmed Expenditure, and the request for resources is normally made in the Supplementary Estimates which is the first occasion when the Department can reach a reasonably firm forecast of costs. Total net expenditure is set out in Table 11 below. Overall expenditure in 2005-06 was £1,266M, including £957M for operations in Iraq, £63M for operations in the Balkans (Bosnia and Kosovo), and £199M for operations in Afghanistan. Additional detail is shown in Note 2 to the Departmental Resource Accounts (page 200).

Resources by Departmental Aims and Objectives

261. Details of the MoD's expenditure for 2005-06 broken down against our three primary Public Service Agreement objectives are summarised in Table 12 and set out in detail in the Statement of Operating Costs by Departmental Aims and Objectives (page 192) and Note 24 (pages 225 to 228) to the Departmental Resource Accounts. It is shown net of the £468M[7] for excess Appropriation-in-Aid and Consolidated Fund Extra Receipts included in total outturn of £34,862M in Table 10 (see Note 5 to the Defence Resource Accounts 2005-06 on page 203).

Outturn against Departmental Expenditure Limit

262. In addition to the Net Resource controls set out above, against which Departmental expenditure is presented in the Departmental Resource Accounts and audited by the National Audit Office, the Department works within two Departmental Expenditure Limits (DELs) covering both the majority of the Department's operating costs (excluding some non-cash costs specifically relating to nuclear provisions) and capital expenditure. Detailed outturns by Top Level Budget Holder against their RFR1 DEL control totals are set out in Table 13. The Estimates figures shown in Note 2 of the Departmental Resource Accounts were based on provision at the half year point, and there were budgetary movements between TLBs between then and the year end reflecting changing circumstances. The total outturn for FY 2005/06 was contained within the Resource DEL with an underspend of £771M. The apparent overspend of £159M in Capital DEL was a consequence of a technical

Table 11: Net Additional Costs of Operations 2005/06 (£M)

	Final Voted Provision	Outturn	Variation
Resource			
Iraq (Operation TELIC)	838	797	(41)
Afghanistan (Operation HERRICK)	150	148	(2)
Balkans (Operation OCULUS)	64	63	(1)
Programme Expenditure (African and Global pool)	49	47	(2)
Total Resource	**1,101**	**1,055**	**(46)**
Capital			
Iraq (Operation TELIC)	260	160	(100)
Afghanistan (Operation HERRICK)	70	51	(19)
Balkans (Operation OCULUS)	–	0	0
Total Capital	**330**	**211**	**(119)**
Total Net additional cost of Operations	**1,431**	**1,266**	**(165)**

Table 12: Resources By Departmental Objectives 2005-06 (£M)

	Net Operating Cost
Objective 1: Achieving success in the tasks we undertake	**3,564**
Objective 2: Being ready to respond to the tasks that might arise	**26,601**
Objective 3: Building for the future	**3,160**
(Total RfRs 1 & 2)	**33,325**
Paying war pensions benefits (RfR3)	1,069
Total Net Operating Cost	**34,394**

[7] This comprises the receipts from the flotation of QinetiQ, receipts in excess of Appropriations in Aid, and income that is not classified as Appropriations in Aid.

accounting change that arose from a review of the balance sheet value of the intangible assets associated with the Joint Combat Aircraft Programme. It does not lead to an increase in the overall programme costs or to any change in the planned profile of cash expenditure. Nor does it represent a breach of Parliamentary supply. The Resource DEL underspend mainly resulted from lower than expected depreciation costs.

Resource and Capital DEL Variances

263. Table 13 shows an underspend against the DEL of £612M. The variations on Direct Resource DEL relate to:

- Commander in Chief Fleet (£16M underspend) – the majority of the underspend was the consequence of changes in asset lives, notably the major refit and overhaul for *HMS Vanguard* which reduced spend against Indirect Resource DEL.

- General Officer Commanding (N Ireland) (£36M overspend) – the overspend relates to the provision for future civilian redundancy payments and write-offs for base closures in the Province as a result of the normalisation process.

- Commander-in-Chief Land Command (£97M overspend) – there was an over spend against Direct and Indirect Resource DEL. The reasons for the former included higher SCAPE charges and new arrangements for Ghurkha National Insurance Contributions. The reason for the latter was principally impairments relating to the Quinquennial revaluation.

- Chief of Joint Operations (£81M overspend) – this is predominantly because of asset write offs in preparation for the accounting re-organisation to single balance sheet owners.

- Chief of Defence Logistics (£346M under spend) – Indirect Resource DEL was underspent due to the review of stocks and fixed assets.

- 2nd Sea Lord/Commander-in-Chief Naval Home Command (£26M overspend) – the majority of the over spend was a consequence of the write off of an intangible asset balance.

Table 13: RFR1 Outturn against Departmental Expenditure Limits (DEL) 2005-06 (£M)

	DEL	Outturn	Variation
Resource DEL			
Allocated to TLBs:			
Commander-in-Chief Fleet	3,564	3,548	(16)
General Officer Commanding (Northern Ireland)	544	580	36
Commander-in-Chief Land Command	5,535	5,632	97
Commander-in-Chief Strike Command	4,042	4,043	1
Chief of Joint Operations	489	570	81
Chief of Defence Logistics	7,869	7,523	(346)
2nd Sea Lord/Commander-in-Chief Naval Home Command	752	778	26
Adjutant General	1,764	1,924	160
Commander-in-Chief Personnel and Training Command	934	904	(30)
Central	2,309	2,458	149
Defence Procurement Agency	2,303	2,272	(31)
Defence Estates	1,139	1,056	(83)
Corporate Science and Technology	501	502	1
Departmental Level Adjustments	881	65	(816)
Total Resource DEL	**32,626**	**31,855**	**(771)**
Capital DEL			
Allocated to TLBs:			
Commander-in-Chief Fleet	6	7	1
General Officer Commanding (Northern Ireland)	6	4	(2)
Commander-in-Chief Land Command	67	47	(20)
Commander-in-Chief Strike Command	19	10	(9)
Chief of Joint Operations	17	19	2
Chief of Defence Logistics	1,049	1,045	(4)
2nd Sea Lord/ Commander-in-Chief Naval Home Command	13	11	(2)
Adjutant General	14	17	3
Commander-in-Chief Personnel and Training Command	19	13	(6)
Central	(7)	(44)	(37)
Defence Procurement Agency	5,051	5,228	177
Defence Estates	222	274	52
Corporate Science and Technology	0	0	0
Departmental Level Adjustments	(8)	(4)	4
Total Capital DEL	**6,468**	**6,627**	**159**

- Adjutant General (£160M overspend) – the overspend relates to the provision for future redundancy payments.
- Air Officer Commanding-in-Chief RAF Personnel & Training Command (£30M underspend) – this indirect Resource DEL underspend was due to a revaluation of training aircraft and a reduction in depreciation for land and buildings.
- Central (£149M overspend) – the Indirect Resource DEL overspend was primarily due to the write off of fixed assets and redundancy provisions.
- Defence Procurement Agency (£31M underspend) – there was an underspend in Direct Resource DEL, where cash release of provisions was lower then expected, due to the transfer of nuclear liabilities to the newly formed Nuclear Decommissioning Authority.
- Defence Estates (£83M underspend) – there was an underspend in Indirect Resource DEL mainly on lower than originally estimated provision costs for contamination relating to the disposal of firing ranges held by the former Defence Evaluation Research Agency (DERA).
- The Departmental Level Adjustments line shows the Indirect Resource DEL that was held centrally (the Departmental Unallocated Provision), which was not allocated to specific TLBs. The Departmental Unallocated Provision was drawn down at Spring Supplementary Estimates to ensure that sufficient resources were available to cover forecasts of Indirect Resource spend from Top Level Budget Holders (TLB), including provisions for redundancy payments.

264. Land Command TLB underspent against Capital DEL allocation by £20M principally through a slippage in capital payments to contractors. Within the Central TLB the redemption of QinetiQ preference shares prior to the flotation of QinetiQ contributed additional receipts which, combined with lower than expected expenditure on capital assets, gave a total underspend of £37M. The overspend of £177M in the Defence Procurement Agency reflects the technical accounting change in the Joint Combat Aircraft programme (see paragraph 262). The overspend in Defence Estates of £52M relates principally to a slippage in the disposals programme which will be recovered in 2006/07.

Reconciliation between Estimate and DEL

265. Table 14 provides a reconciliation between the outturn shown in the DEL Table 13 with the Estimate, to assist in understanding the differences between the tables presented here in the annual report, and those shown in the Departmental Resource Accounts. The totals shown for Resource and Capital DEL are for RFR1 only. Non voted items in this table relate to the cash release of nuclear provisions which is not a Parliamentary control, but which makes up part of the Department's net cash requirement. There is a small element of non voted funding within Capital DEL.

Reconciliation between Estimates, Accounts and Budgets

266. The Department is required to use different frameworks to plan, control and account for income and expenditure. The planning framework uses resource and capital budgets broken down into DEL and AME and these budgets are referred to throughout the Spending Review, Budget Red Book, Pre-budget Report and individual Departmental Annual Reports. Control is exercised through the Parliamentary approval of Supply in the Main and Supplementary Estimates. Some elements of DEL and AME are outside the Supply process. Equally, some expenditure is voted but outside the scope of the budgets. Audited outturn figures are reported within the Departmental Resource Accounts, prepared under the conventions of UK GAAP, adapted for the public sector, with adjustments necessary to reconcile to either the planning or control totals. Table 15 provides the reconciliation between these three bases.

Table 14: Reconciliation between Estimate and DEL £M

	Provision	Outturn
Resource Estimate (RfR 1)	**34,665**	**32,738**
Less: Annually Managed Expenditure	(87)	177
Less: Non Budget	(2,349)	(1,060)
Add: Non Voted	397	0
Resource DEL (Table 13)	**32,626**	**31,855**
Capital Estimate	**6,782**	**6,793**
Less: RfR 2	(330)	(211)
Less: AME	16	46
Less: Capital Spending by Non Departmental Bodies		(1)
Capital DEL (Table 13)	**6,468**	**6,627**

Table 15: Reconciliation of Resource Expenditure between Estimates, Accounts and Budgets £M

	Provision	Outturn
Net Resource in Estimates	**36,839**	**34,862**
Adjustments to include:		
Consolidated Fund Extra Receipts in the OCS		(468)
Other adjustments		
Net Operating Costs in DRAc	**36,839**	**34,394**
Adjustments to remove:		
Voted expenditure outside the budget	(2,349)	(1,060)
Adjustments to include:		
Other Consolidated Fund Extra Receipts		468
Resource consumption of non departmental public bodies	24	24
Resource in Treasury Budget	**34,514**	**33,826**
Of which		
Departmental Expenditure Limit	33,727	32,937
Annually Managed Expenditure	787	889

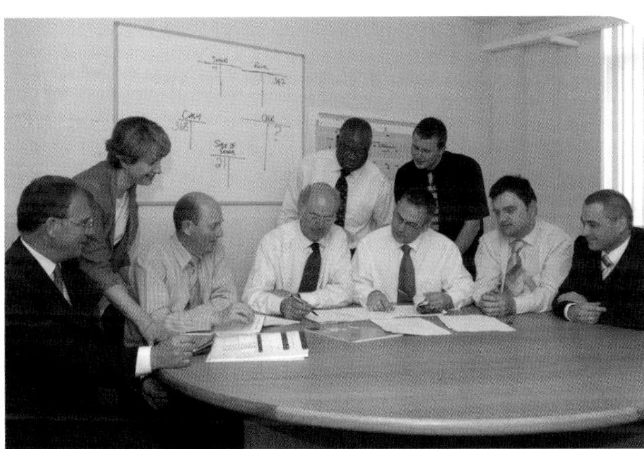

A meeting to review the Accounts

Losses and Write-Offs

267. Details of losses, gifts and special payments are set out in Note 31 to the Departmental Resource Accounts (pages 236 to 240). The total value of new and potential losses and special payments arising in year (both closed cases and advance notifications) fell by a further 36%, from £222M in 2004-05 to £143M in 2005-06. We continue to work to minimise the number of new cases that arise. Excluding, gifts and payments made by the Veterans Agency the value of cases closed during the year amounted to £394M, a decrease of 6% from 2004-05. 88% of this was from final closure of cases previously notified. £252M was from two cases over five years old: £105M from the UK's decision not to proceed with the medium range anti-tank guided weapons system (MR TRIGAT) in 2000; and £147M from the failure of the project to construct a Radioactive Liquid Effluent Treatment Plant at the Atomic Weapons Establishment Aldermaston.

268. The losses statement also identifies potential losses that have not yet been brought to completion and have therefore been identified for formal incorporation in a future year's accounts (known as advance notifications). The costs identified are estimates, so the final loss declared may therefore be either larger or smaller. The estimated value of our advance notifications of losses and special payments reduced by about 25% over the year, from about £817M to about £607M. This reflected the closure of several substantial historic cases (see previous paragraph) and the limited number of new cases identified. 84% by value of the advance notifications comes from cases identified before 1 April 2005. This includes two cases, each of £205M, for the UK's withdrawal from the multinational long range anti armour missile programme (LR TRIGAT) in 1995 and for writing-down of the value of Chinook Mark 3 helicopters. We cannot close the former case until all related transactions by all the original partners have been completed. Pending final agreement of the way forward on the latter project we have deliberately taken a very prudent accounting approach that maximises the size of the potential write-off.

2002 SPENDING REVIEW EFFICIENCY PROGRAMME

269. The Department's Public Service Agreement following the 2002 Spending Review (SR2002) included a target of year-on-year output efficiency gains of 2.5% from 2002-03 to 2005-06, to be achieved by making improvements in the efficiency and effectiveness of the key processes for delivering military capability. This is measured as the weighted average of performance against a set of process-related supported targets, the weighting being determined by the relative resources covered by each supporting target. Overall results are set out in Table 16. As explained at paragraph 231, the scrutiny of the Defence Logistics Organisation's efficiency achievement for 2004-05 has concluded that there is evidence to substantiate at least £280M of the efficiency savings of over £400M reported in the Annual Report and Accounts 2004-05. Consequently, we have revised the achievement of 11.1% against the SR2002 logistics target reported last year to 9.8%, and the overall achievement

from 8.2% to 7.3%. As explained at paragraph 232, work (which should be completed by autumn 2006) is in hand to confirm the SR2002 logistics efficiency achievement for 2005-06. On the basis of work to mid-June 2006, we expect the achievement for 2005-06 will lie in the range £350M-£400M. We have assessed performance against the PSA target in Table 16 using the lower end of this range.

270. The measurement of performance against the Training supporting target was discontinued from 2004-05, and the contribution against this target towards the overall target has been taken as zero. This is explained further at paragraph 186. In year, the Procurement supporting target has been achieved; further details on performance against procurement targets are at paragraphs 136-137. As explained at paragraph 131, we have assessed the final achievement against the management costs target as remaining at 12%, as the benefits from the new organisational initiatives included in the SR2004 efficiency programme do not fall within the SR2002 period. The final achievement on the Estates disposals target was £456M against a target of £300M. Subject to confirmation and validation, we believe we have met the overall target of 10%, as collectively the supporting targets included a contingency margin that has allowed the overall target to be achieved although several of the supporting targets have been missed.

Table 16: SR02 Efficiency Improvements

Target	Weighting	Cumulative Trajectory			
		2002-03	2003-04	2004-05	2005-06
Reduce by an average of 6% the per capita cost of training a successful military recruit to the agreed standard.	9	2%	4%	5%	6%
Achievement		1.7%	4.2%	Discontinued	Discontinued
Achieve 0% average annual cost growth (or better) against the equipment procurement projects included in the Major Projects Report, while meeting customer requirements.	6	0%	0%	0%	0%
Actual in-year cost growth		5.7%	3.1%	-4.6%	-0.1%
Reduce by 20% the output costs of the Defence Logistics Organisation, while maintaining support to the Front Line	68	2%	6%	10%	14%
Achievement		3.1%	6.6%	9.8%[1]	13.7%[2]
Reduce MoD Head Office and other management costs by 13%	5	5%	9%	12%	13%
Achievement		6.3%	10.6%	12%	12%
Identify for disposal land and buildings with a net book value of over £300M	12	£84M	£134M	£258M	£300M
Achievement		£135M	£230M	£395M	£456M
Overall Target	**100**	**2%**	**5%**	**8%**	**10%**
Overall Achievement		2.3%	5.0%	7.3%[1]	10.0%

Notes:
1. The 2004-05 achievement against the Logistics target and the overall achievement have been amended from that reported in the *Annual Report and Accounts 2004-05* to reflect subsequent checking and validation. See paragraph 231 for further information.
2. Logistics performance is subject to validation by Defence Internal Audit.
3. The net book value of land and buildings reflects their valuation in accordance with the Department's accounting polices. The actual income from the sales could vary significantly from this value and will be dependant upon the market conditions at the time of sale.

2004 SPENDING REVIEW EFFICIENCY PROGRAMME

271. The Government is committed to funding the Armed Forces as they modernise and adapt to meet evolving threats and promote international stability in the changing global security environment. The 2004 Spending Review announced in July 2004 increased planned spending on Defence by an average of 1.4% per year in real terms over the three years to 2007-08, with total planned Defence spending £3.7 billion higher in 2007-08 than in 2004-05. In cash terms, the equivalent increase is £3.5 billion, an average real growth of 1.5% per year. Further modernisation of Defence will be supported through the continued provision of the Defence Modernisation Fund, amounting to £1 billion over the three years to 2007-08, which represented an increase in both its size and scope. Building on our existing change programme, we also undertook to realise total annual efficiency gains of at least £2.8 billion by 2007-08, of which three-quarters will be cash releasing, to be re-invested in Defence capability and further modernisation initiatives. Further detail about the current performance against this target and the wider Defence Change Programme is set out in paragraphs 121-133.

SALE OF QINETIQ

272. Under the public private partnership for Defence research which began in 1998, QinetiQ has been transformed from an in-house research and development organisation into an international Defence technology and security company that develops cutting-edge technology for our Armed Forces and provides technological advice and services to MoD, other Government Departments, the US Department of Defense, and non-government customers. QinetiQ was jointly owned by its employees (13%), the MoD (56.5%) and The Carlyle Group (30.5%). On 10 February 2006 the company was successfully floated on the London Stock Exchange in the next stage of the its transition to the private sector. This raised £347M net for the taxpayer of which £250M is being reinvested in the Defence programme. The MoD retained a 19.3% stake and a Special Share to safeguard Defence and security interests of the UK. We also nominate a non-executive director to the QinetiQ Board.

273. The results highlighted in QinetiQ's audited preliminary accounts for 2005/06 reflect the company's success in delivering its growth strategy including through the commercialisation of Defence technology and expansion of its US presence, while continuing to deliver value to its primary customer the MoD. Group turnover for the year grew 22.9% to £1,051M and operating margin increased to 8.6%, contributing to an operating profit of £90.7M.

WIDER MARKETS INITIATIVE

274. The aim of the Treasury's Wider Markets Initiative is the commercial exploitation of departments' assets which need to be retained but are not fully used. Defence activities under the initiative have grown steadily since its launch in 1998. These include the Defence Communication Services Agency's contract with Arqiva to exploit the Boxer Communication Towers, the Services' efforts to protect and exploit the military 'brands', exploitation of our intellectual property, sale of surplus training capacity, letting of land, making available sites and facilities for filming purposes and renting out surplus storage capacity. We have worked to improve our management processes. In 2005-06 we trained about 100 people as Wider Markets Practitioners and began to provide training for Commercial Officers in contracting for sale. In a recent Government-wide report on the Initiative the National Audit Office concluded that we had been particularly pro-active in improving the overall quality of the management of our commercial activities.

Wider Markets Initiative: Filming Top Gear.

FINANCE PROCESS IMPROVEMENT

275. The Finance Director initiated a review of the Finance Function in 2004, in part as a response to the Gershon Initiative, to review our internal performance and plans for simplifying and improving financial processes, structures and systems. As a result of this review the "Simplify and Improve" Programme was created, which is being delivered through the Defence Resource Management Programme. The two main recommendations were:

- creation of a Financial Accounting Shared Service Centre, which will save some posts by removing transactional processing from TLBs, and allow skilled professional staff to concentrate on value added activities to support decision-making; and,

- centralisation of fixed assets onto Single Balance Sheets to place assets with those parts of the Department which make the real decisions concerning their purchase and support. The Defence Logisitcs Organisation will own Single Use Military Equipment and Plant Machinery and Transport, the Defence Procurement Agency will own Equipment related Assets Under Construction, Defence Estates will own Land and Buildings, and the Defence Communications Services Agency will own IT and Communications. This went live on 3 April 2006.

The Shared Service Centre is being created incrementally and will be based in Liverpool and Bath.

276. A Treasury team reporting to the Head of the Government Accountancy Service conducted a review of the MoD's financial management processes and presented its findings in July 2005. This concluded that the overall picture was of positive progress and that the Department had or was putting in place the processes, systems and standards to deliver an effective strategic financial management function. As well as finding much to commend in our current arrangements, the review supported our plans for the future, including our strategic determination to shift the focus of the finance function from transactional processing to improved support for decision-making at all levels. Specific recommendations in the report included implementation of the 'Simplify and Improve' programme, the introduction of Biennial Financial Planning to bring greater stability and discipline to the forward Defence Programme and allow for a more measured timetable and approach to the planning round, and the introduction of a new finance information system – the Planning, Budgeting and Forecasting tool – to improve financial planning and forecasting across the Department. This is being rolled out for in-year management in 2006-07 and the 2007 planning rounds.

FURTHER SOURCES OF INFORMATION

277. Detailed Information on the Department's financial performance is contained in the Departmental Resource Accounts in Section 2 of this report. Further information is also available from the following sources:

- *2004 Spending Review: Stability, security and opportunity for all: investing for Britain's long-term future: New Public Spending Plans 2005-2008* (Cm 6237) at www.hm-treasury.gov.uk;
- SR2004 Public Service Agreement and technical note at www.mod.uk;
- SR2004 Efficiency technical note at www.mod.uk;
- *Ministry of Defence: The Government's Expenditure Plans 2005/06 to 2007/08 (Cm 6532)* at www.mod.uk;
- *Central Government Supply Estimates 2005-06: Main Estimates (HC 2)* available at www.hm-treasury.gov.uk;
- *Central Government Supply Estimates 2005-06: Main Estimates 2005-06 Supplementary Budgetary Information (Cm 6489)* available at www.hm-treasury.gov.uk;
- *Central Government Supply Estimates 2005-06: Winter Supplementary Estimates (HC 672)* available at www.hm-treasury.gov.uk;
- *Central Government Supply Estimates 2005-06: Spring Supplementary Estimates (HC 827)* available at www.hm-treasury.gov.uk;
- *Public Expenditure Outturn White Paper 2005-06* available at www.hm-treasury.gov.uk (July 2006);
- Veterans Agency *Annual Report and Accounts 2005-06* available at www.veteransagency.mod.uk (August 2006);
- NAO Report *Ministry of Defence Wider Markets Initiative* available at www.nao.org.uk.

Essay: Understanding Losses and Special Payments

In common with any large Government Department or company with a significant capital investment programme and a sizable asset base, the Ministry of Defence will always have write offs to report. This is particularly true in a period of strategic change as assets that are no longer needed are disposed of. When write off action is taken we have formal processes to ensure that lessons are identified and learned. Major write offs are brought to the attention of departmental Audit Committees chaired by non-executive directors from outside the MoD.

In line with standard accounting practice the losses and special payments, shown at Note 31 of the Departmental Resource Accounts, are split into two sections:

- Closed cases – where the losses and special payments have been formally signed off;
- Advance Notifications – where the losses and special payments arose during 2005-06 and prior years but where the cases have not yet been formally signed off and the amounts are our best estimates. Once they are formally signed off they will appear in future accounts as closed cases.

The losses statement provides a level of visibility and transparency not matched by commercial accounts, as private sector organisations are not required to disclose similar information. The size of the MoD and of its capital assets under active management, together with the range and complexity of Defence business, means that we face a scale of challenge unique in the public sector.

Reported losses are not necessarily indicative of a failure of control, although we obviously seek to identify those that are and learn appropriate lessons. But losses also result from sensible management decisions (such as the decision to withdraw from the Medium Range TRIGAT project to procure a more advanced solution more quickly at a lower through-life cost). The changes envisaged in the December 2003 Defence White Paper *Delivering Security in a Changing World*, in the July 2004 *Future Capabilities* paper, and the significant organisational efficiencies and rationalisations contained in the Department's 2004 Spending Review Efficiency programme following the Lyons and Gershon reviews, will inevitably generate further write-offs in future years as force structures and our organisation are adjusted to meet changing circumstances.

We are working to improve processes for losses and special payments in three areas:

- greater consistency in recording and reporting, based on a clearer understanding of the purpose of the losses statement in public sector accounting;
- improvements in the identification and dissemination of lessons learned; and
- more systematic review of the information and actions relating to losses by MoD management boards and audit committees, with due regard to materiality and proportionality.

We are also working to ensure that identified losses are assessed and closed as early as possible in order to ensure that any lessons arising are learned in a timely fashion. In this respect it is worth noting that the value of our advance notifications of losses and special payments reduced by about 19% since last year, and of that value only 14% relates to cases identified during 2005-06 as opposed to a number of long-standing historic cases (see paragraphs 267-268). It can take some time to complete write off from the time of advance notification. This can be for a variety of reasons, including legal issues and the valuation of complex cases. The same losses can therefore appear over a number of years until the case is finally closed, and this needs to be taken into account when reading the accounts.

The existing MoD guidance on losses and special payments is under review and revised guidance will be issued later in 2006. The Treasury has also undertaken to review the rules on losses and special payments in Government Accounting. The Defence Audit Committee is pursuing improvements in identifying and disseminating lessons learned. Further information on this is contained in the Committee's Annual Report, published on the MoD website. Top Level Budget (TLB) Audit Committees review losses and special payments, and TLB Holders are required to draw any significant concerns to the attention of the Permanent Under Secretary, as Accounting Officer. They do so in their annual submissions to him which underpin the Statement on Internal Control in the Departmental Resource Accounts. The Defence Audit Committee also reviews losses at the Departmental level as part of the year-end process. Individual TLBs have developed specific approaches tailored to their own circumstances, for example requiring cases over a certain value to be addressed personally by the TLB Holder. Others are identifying trends and involving their audit committee in commissioning remedial action. Whilst the Defence Audit Committee addresses the spreading of best practice we do not believe it would be right to adopt a "one size fits all" approach as the issues are distinct in different TLBs.

With such a large capital investment programme (£13.7 billion of assets under construction at 31st March 2006) there will inevitably be cases where we decide not to proceed with programmes when priorities or requirements change to reflect an evolving wider Defence need, or we conclude that the technical challenge is too demanding. As part of the Smart Acquisition initiative, we have sought to increase the level of investment in the concept and assessment phases of programmes to bound risk more carefully prior to major investment decisions. In this way, we should limit losses arising from a subsequent project failure – but this will not impact on major changes in requirement or procurement strategy.

MANPOWER

Objective: Achieve overall Service manning balance and a smaller civilian workforce.

Public Service Agreement Target (SR2004 MoD Target 5)

Recruit, train, motivate and retain sufficient military personnel to provide the military capability necessary to meet the Government's strategic objectives to achieve manning balance in each of the three Services by 1 April 2008.

Performance Measures and Assessment

Trained strength of Forces between +1% and -2% of the overall requirement 1 April 2008. As at 1 April 2006:

- **RN/RM trained strength of 35,470, or 96.3% of overall requirement (95.1% on 1 April 2005);**
- **Army trained strength of 100,620[1], or 98.8[1]% of overall requirement (98.3% on 1 April 2005);**
- **RAF trained strength of 46,900[2], or 99.2%[2] of overall requirement (101% on 1 April 2005);**
- **RN/RM Volunteer Reserve strength of 3,170, or 81% of overall requirement (69% on 1 April 2005);**
- **Army Volunteer Reserve strength of 32,150, or 84% of overall requirement (82% on 1 April 2005);**
- **RAF Volunteer Reserve strength of 1,450, or 65% of overall requirement (67% on 1 April 2005).**
- **Critical shortage groups remained in all three Services**

Achieve stable Voluntary Outflow rates for each Service:

- **Slight increase in Voluntary Outflow rates across all three Services, but Army and RAF continue to remain within stable long term goal rate.**

Civilian Workforce:

- **103,930 Full Time Equivalent civilian staff employed on 1 April 2006 (108,470 at 1 April 2005) including 15,100 Locally Engaged Civilians outside the UK.**

Civilian Progression:

- **Limited scope for progression, reflecting current drawdown programme.**

Diversity:

- **Overall Service ethnic minority strength (including Commonwealth recruits) increased to 5.5% at 1 April 2006 (5.3% at 1 April 2005) against target of 6% by 2006. UK ethnic minority intake:**
  - **RN 2.0% (target 3.5%, 2004-05 intake 2.3%);**
  - **Army 3.6% (target 3.9%, 2004-05 intake 3.7%);**
  - **RAF 1.5% (target 3.6%, 2004-05 intake 1.7%).**
- **As at 1 April 2006, women comprised 9.1% of UK Regular Forces, and 9.6% of the total 2005-06 intake;**
- **Proportion of women and disabled increased at all levels of Defence civil service. Proportion of ethnic minorities stable or slightly reduced. Civilian diversity targets exceeded for disabled personnel in MoD Senior Civil Service and women in Band B, and just missed for women in Band D. Significantly below target for women and ethnic minority personnel in Senior Civil Service, ethnic minority and disabled personnel in Band B and Band D.**

[1] Figures for Army Office Intake and Strength are provisional pending ongoing investigation of possible late reporting of intake data
[2] Due to the introduction of a new personnel administration system all RAF data is provisional.

SERVICE MANPOWER

Trained Strength

278. On 1 April 2006, the total trained strength of the Royal Navy and Royal Marines was 35,470. This was a shortfall of some 1,370 personnel or 3.7% against the requirement of 36,830, but represents a recovery of 1.2% against the position a year earlier. This improvement was achieved using standard manpower levers such as extensions of service, acting high rank, use of Full Time Reserve Service and firm requirement control. The Army's total trained strength was 100,620[3] on 1 April 2006, a shortfall of some 1,180[3] personnel or 1.2%[3] against the requirement target of 101,800, again a slight improvement on the shortfall of 1.7% on 1 April 2005. The total trained strength of the Royal Air Force was 46,900[4] on 1 April 2006 against a requirement of 47,290[4], a shortfall of some 390[4] personnel or 0.8%[4] compared to an excess of 1% on 1 April 2005. Although this represents the formal figure at 1 April, the deficit has varied throughout the year by as much as -2.3%. RAF personnel numbers will fall further during the year as the Service continues reducing towards a size of around 41,000 by 1 April 2008. There is therefore likely to be a growing shortfall in RAF personnel against requirement throughout 2006-07 until the next formal requirement reduction takes effect on 1 April 2007. Overall at 1 April 2006 the Army and Royal Air Force were therefore within the Public Service Agreement Manning Balance target range of +1% to –2%, but the Royal Navy, while making progress, remained below the range.

Sandhurst Cadets passing out

Table 17: Strength and Requirements of Full Time UK Regular Forces, Full Time Reserve Service & Gurkhas

	Royal Navy/Royal Marines			Army			Royal Air Force		
	2006	2005	2004	2006	2005	2004	2006	2005	2004
Trained Requirement	36,830	38,190	38,720	101,800	104,170	106,730	47,290	48,730	49,890
Trained Strength	35,470	36,320	37,470	100,620 P	102,440	103,560	46,900 P	49,210	49,120
Variation	-1,370	-1,870	-1,250	-1,180 P	-1,730	-3,170	-390 P	+480	-770
Untrained Strength	4,650	4,520	4,500	11,260 P	10,970	13,650	2,180 P	3,020	4,650
Total UK Regular Forces	40,110	40,840	41,970	111,880 P	113,420	117,210	49,070 P	52,230	53,770

Notes:
1. Data from DASA.
2. Figures are rounded to the nearest ten and may not sum precisely to the totals shown. Figures at 1 April include Full Time Trained UK Regular Forces, Trained Gurkhas and Full Time Reserve Service personnel. Untrained figures includes Full Time Untrained UK Regular Forces and Untrained Gurkhas.
3. 'P' denotes provisional. Army Officer figures are provisional pending investigation. RAF figures are provisional due to the introduction of the new Joint Personnel Administration system.

[3] Figures for Army are provisional pending investigation of possible late reporting of intake data.
[4] Due to the introduction of a new personnel administration system all RAF data is provisional.

Figure 8: Service Manning Surplus/Deficit[5] over the last year

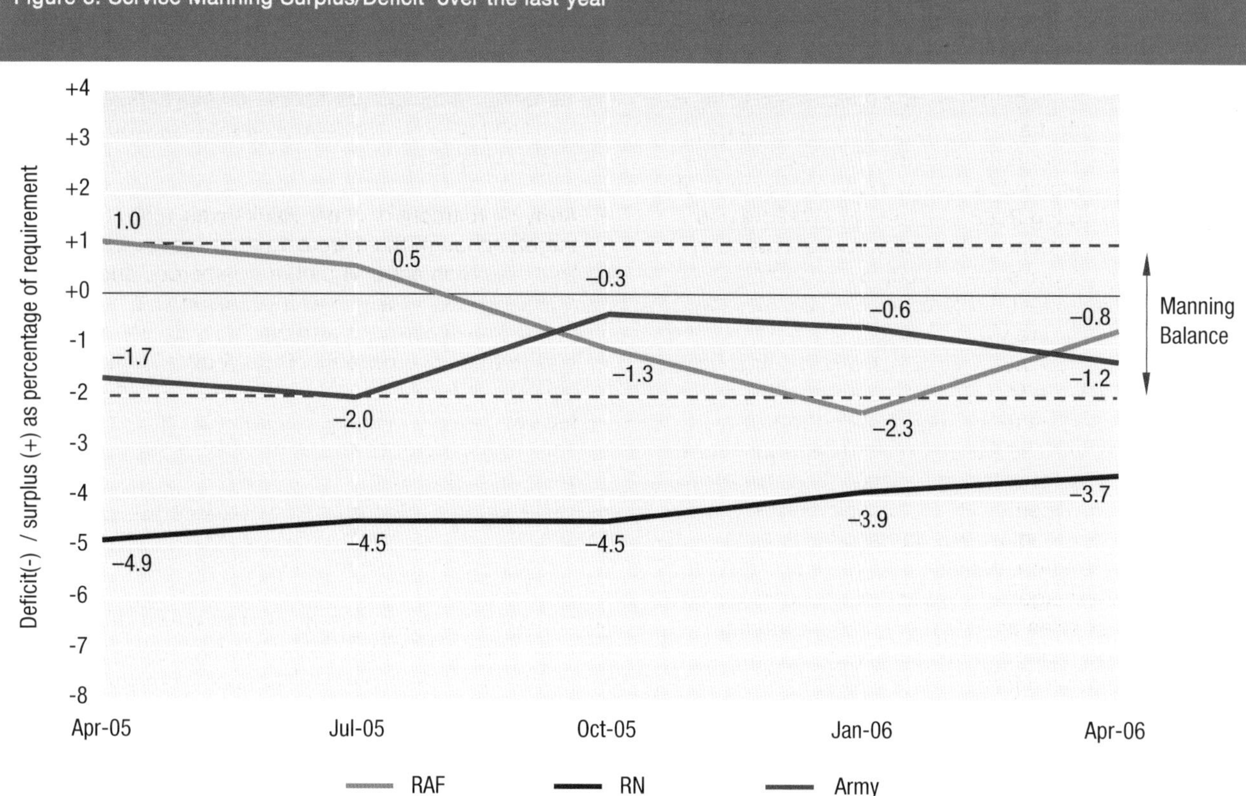

Manning Pinch Points

279. Within these broad totals, there are a number of specific skill groups where there are not enough personnel to meet requirements. These are known as Manning Pinch Points and are defined as a trade or area of expertise with insufficient trained strength (Officers or Other Ranks) to perform directed tasks. This can result from a shortage of people, an increased operational requirement to deploy personnel, or a combination of the two. Manning Pinch Points are managed by the individual Services, with a central working group maintaining an overview to identify trends and ensure best practice. Each Service maintains a dynamic list reflecting operational commitments and manning levels within branches and trades as they vary over time:

- In the Royal Navy, shortages in Petty Officer Mine Warfare, Nuclear Marine Engineering watchkeepers, Warfare Leading Hands, Royal Marine Other Ranks and Air Engineering Technicians remain a concern. Their impact on operational capability continues to be mitigated through a combination of micro-management of the pinch point communities and prioritisation of manning according to task;

- The Army had 24 Manning Pinch Points trades in 2005-06, including Intelligence Operators and Vehicle Mechanics. Each pinch point has a mitigation plan which is reviewed regularly and systematically. Manning of the Royal Artillery and Infantry are also major foci of effort, where sustained operational requirements are creating the greatest shortfalls against harmony guidelines;

- The Royal Air Force is facing a period of deficit manning as the drawdown programme proceeds. During this year there were deficits in a number of specialisations including Junior Officer Pilots, Fighter Controllers, Medical Officers, Weapons Systems Operator (Linguist), Weapons Systems Operator (Air Load Master), Provost/Security, Medical Support and Nurses, causing breaches of Individual Harmony Guidelines in some cases.

[5] These figures are calculated using total trained strength versus total trained requirement. Data from DASA.

280. During 2005-06, work continued to refine the Deployable Medical Capability we need to meet planning assumptions. Preliminary conclusions suggest that there may be potential to reduce the overall personnel requirement, which would have the effect of reducing medical officer shortfalls from 22.1% to 7%, and dental officer shortfalls from 8.4% to 5.2%. Medical recruitment and retention continued to improve with an increase of 342 personnel during 2005 to a total of 7,712 trained personnel in the Defence Medical Services in January 2006. Medical Officer shortfalls continued to be concentrated in anaesthetics, psychiatry, and Accident and Emergency. There were nursing shortfalls in Accident and Emergency and Intensive Therapy Units. The Defence Medical Services are trying to improve recruitment and retention by selective re-skilling, adapting the training input and outflow to address particular shortage areas, and increasing direct entry recruitment. The new Armed Forces Pension Scheme with its specific bonus arrangements for medical and dental officers should also improve retention. We also mitigate shortfalls by employing civilian agency contractors and working closely with our allies and partners on operations. Despite the continuing shortfalls, at no point have the Defence Medical Services been unable to meet operational commitments.

Recruitment and Trained Inflow

281. 2005-06 was a difficult year for recruitment, especially for the Naval Service and the Army. The Armed Services continue to face stiff recruiting competition in the face of high levels of employment. Specifically:

- Naval Service Officer recruitment levels remained at 370, but this was against a higher target than the previous year. However application levels for Royal Navy ratings and Royal Marine other ranks showed a significant improvement, mainly as a result of a sustained and coordinated focus on Royal Marine recruiting. Additional resources for Royal Marine recruiting (£1.2M) made available in year also had a positive impact;

- Army recruitment of Other Ranks was 1,200 below target, although there were 1,000 more recruits than last year. High employment, a prosperous and strong economy and attractive alternatives in further education all compete with the Army for young men and women. The majority of the shortfall reflected low application levels and enlistments in the first half of the year, which then picked up in the second half. The Army is addressing the shortfall in several different ways. In particular it is trying to attract more high quality recruits, to reduce wastage during training, and working to keep retention levels steady. Infantry recruiting was a primary focus for effort;

- The Royal Air Force broadly met its recruiting targets during 2005-06, but this mainly reflected the reduced target during the drawdown period. The Service therefore concentrated much of its outreach effort on those not yet of recruitment age, to ensure that interest in a career in the Royal Air Force is maintained for when the recruiting requirement rises again. Lower than expected recruitment figures for officers in previous years and a disruption in the officer training pipeline in 2004-05 had a negative effect on our Gains to Trained Strength figures. For non-commissioned aircrew, lower than expected recruitment figures in previous years significantly reduced the Gains to Trained Strength figures.

Table 18: Intake to UK Regular Forces from civilian life

	Royal Navy/Royal Marines			Army			Royal Air Force		
	2005-06	2004-05	2003-04	2005-06	2004-05	2003-04	2005-06	2004-05	2003-04
Officer intake	370	370	340	770 P	760	880	320 P	290	520
Other Rank intake	3,570	3,320	3,780	11,910	10,940	14,310	1,110 P	1,880	3,640
Total intake	3,940	3,690	4,120	12,690 P	11,690	15,190	1,430 P	2,180	4,160

Notes:
1. Data from DASA.
2. UK Regular Forces includes Nursing Services and excludes Full Time Reserve Service Personnel, Gurkhas, the Home Service battalions of the Royal Irish Regiment and mobilised reservists. It includes trained and untrained personnel.
3. All intake to UK Regular Forces includes re-enlistments and rejoined reservists.
4. 'P' denotes provisional. Army Officer figures are provisional pending investigation of possible late reporting of intake data. RAF figures are provisional due to the introduction of the new Joint Personnel Administration system.
5. Figures are rounded to ten and may not sum precisely to the totals shown.

Table 19: Gains to Trained Strength	Numbers achieved in 2005-06	Target (and % achieved)
Naval Service Officers	370	410 (90%)
Naval Service Other Ranks	2,330	2,700 (86%)
Army Officers[2]	750	810 (93%)
Army Other Ranks[2]	7,770	9,230 (84%)
Royal Air Force Officers	360 P	370 (98%) P
Royal Air Force Other Ranks	1,770 P	1,800 (98%) P

Notes:
1. Naval Service and RAF figures come from DASA. The Army figures come from the Adjutant General TLB.
2. The Army numbers and target show officers completing the Royal Military Academy Sandhurst and soldiers completing Phase 2 training. This metric is used for internal manning management and does not match the figures produced by DASA and published in Tri Service Publication 4.
3. 'P' represents that figures are provisional due to the introduction of the new Joint Personnel Administration system in the RAF.

Retention and Voluntary Outflow

282. Rates of retention and voluntary outflow (previously known as premature voluntary release) also contribute to the achievement of manning balance. The Armed Forces have set thresholds, based upon historical averages, against which they manage the potential impact of early exits in order to achieve a desirable balance between retaining skills and experience and new recruitment. We therefore track the number of Service men and Service women voluntarily leaving the Forces before the end of their agreed term, against of stable long-term voluntary outflow rates of 2% and 5% for RN officer and ratings respectively, 4.1% and 6.2% for Army Officers and soldiers, and 2.5% and 4% for RAF officers and Other Ranks. Figures for the last three years are set out below. There was a significant increase in Voluntary Outflow exits rates for RAF Other Ranks during 2005-06 which put the RAF above its long term target range. This was caused by faster processing of applications for redundancy from staff during the drawdown period; Voluntary Outflow application rates did not change significantly. Whilst some of the Voluntary Outflow figures are above the stable long term goals this is partly a reflection of employment opportunities outside the Services. We have a number of initiatives to improve retention and morale in general, including improving living accommodation (see paragraphs 301-302), better travel allowances to allow people home more readily, better work-life balance and improved working conditions at the front-line.

Table 20: Voluntary Outflow Exit Rates	Stable long term Voluntary Outflow goals	12 months ending 31 March 2006	12 months ending 31 March 2005	12 months ending 31 March 2004
RN/RM Officers	2.0%	2.8%	2.5%	2.5%[2]
RN/RM Ratings	5.0%	6.0%	6.4%	5.7%
Army Officers	4.1%	4.3%	3.9%	3.7%
Army Soldiers	6.2%	5.5%	5.7%	5.3%
RAF Officers	2.5%	2.5% P	2.4%	2.1%
RAF Other Ranks	4.0%	4.8% P	3.8%	3.7%

Notes:
1. Data from DASA and Voluntary Outflow goals from the Departmental Plan 2005-2009.
2. This figure is different to that published in the Annual Report and Account 2003-04 due to the introduction of a new exit code which was not correctly classified.
3. 'P' denotes provisional. RAF figures are provisional due to the intoduction of the new Joint Personnel Administration system.

Table 21: Outflow of UK Regular Forces	Royal Navy/Royal Marines			Army			Royal Air Force		
	2005-06	2004-05	2003-04	2005-06	2004-05	2003-04	2005-06	2004-05	2003-04
Officer outflow	520	510	470	1,070	1,100	950	690 P	700	620
Other Rank outflow	3,960	4,130	4,300	13,120	13,970	13,640	3,870 P	3,020	3,410
Total outflow	4,490	4,630	4,770	14,190	15,070	14,600	4,570 P	3,730	4,040

Notes:
1. Data from DASA.
2. UK Regular Forces includes Nursing Services and excludes Full Time Reserve Service Personnel, Gurkhas, the Home Service battalions of the Royal Irish Regiment and mobilised reservists. It includes trained and untrained personnel.
3. All intake to UK Regular Forces includes re-enlistments and rejoined reservists.
4. 'P' denotes provisional. RAF figures are provisional due to the intoduction of the new Joint Personnel Administration system.
5. Figures are rounded to ten and may not sum precisely to the totals shown.

Diversity of the Armed Forces

283. Despite continuing efforts, we continue to find recruiting proportionately from UK ethnic minority groups to the Armed Services difficult. Performance against in-year recruiting goals is set out in Table 22. While the Army nearly met its target, limited recruitment opportunities were a significant constraint on the Royal Navy and the Royal Air Force. Overall ethnic minority representation within the Armed Forces continued to increase, reaching 5.5% by 1 April 2006 (see Table 23), reflecting continuing recruitment from a number of Commonwealth countries to, in particular the Army.

284. The Armed Forces regularly review their recruiting policies in consultation with the Commission for Racial Equality and other experts in the field, with a view to engaging ethnic minority groups, raising awareness and promoting careers in the Services. They remain committed to becoming more representative of the society they serve, with a goal of 8% ethnic minority representation by 2013. The Army has topped the public sector performers list for the sixth consecutive year in the 'Race for Opportunity's annual benchmarking report on race in the workplace. The RAF and Navy also finished in the top ten public sector performers. Of the top ten overall performers (comprising both private and public

Table 22: Armed Forces UK Ethnic recruitment	2005-06		2004-05		2003-04	
	Target	Actual	Target	Actual	Target	Actual
Navy	3.5%	2.0%	3.0%	2.3%	2.5%	2.1%
Army	3.9%	3.6%	3.4%	3.7%	2.9%	2.8%
RAF	3.6%	1.5%	3.1%	1.7%	2.6%	1.8%

Notes:
1. These figures are unaudited single Service estimates of UK ethnic minority intake.
2. The Army officer intakes is measured by intake into Sandhurst.

Table 23: Armed Forces ethnic minority representation	1 Apr 2006	1 Apr 2005	1 Apr 2004	1 Apr 2003	1 Apr 2002
Royal Navy	2.6%	2.5%	2.4%	2.3%	1.8%
Army	8.0%	7.6%	6.9%	5.9%	4.5%
RAF	2.4% P	2.5%	2.5%	2.6%	2.6%
Armed Forces	5.5% P	5.3%	4.9%	4.3%	3.5%

Notes:
1. Data from DASA.
2. Includes UK and Commonwealth nationals.
3. 'P' denotes provisional. RAF figures are provisional due to the intoduction of the new Joint Personnel Administration system.

organisations), the Army finished fifth nationally and the RAF in tenth. Further information on diversity in the Armed Forces is contained in the essay on page 147.

Soldiers take time out

Sexual Harassment

285. On 23 June 2005, the Secretary of State for Defence and the Chief of the Defence Staff signed an agreement with the Equal Opportunities Commission on *Preventing and Dealing Effectively with Sexual Harassment in the Armed Forces*. This aims to create a working environment in which sexual harassment is not tolerated; to ensure that Service personnel who experience sexual harassment feel able to complain and have confidence in the complaints process, including a robust investigation process, high quality support, the use of effective sanctions, a focus on resolving the problem, and protection from future harassment or victimisation; and to monitor the nature and extent of harassment in the Armed Forces in order to correct deficiencies and build upon the strengths of our policies and processes.

286. As part of the first phase of the agreement, we conducted extensive research during the year to clarify the nature and extent of sexual harassment, including a survey of all Service women. There was a high response rate (52%) and the responses were broadly consistent across the three Services. The research found that sexualised behaviours (jokes, stories, language and material) were widespread in all three Services. Almost all (99%) Service women who responded had been in situations where such sexualised behaviours had taken place in the previous year. Of those who responded, 15% reported having had a "particularly upsetting" experience and 67% reported having had such behaviours directed at them personally.

287. With women comprising over 9%[6] of UK Regular Forces and over 9.5%[6] of the total intake, it is clear from this research that we have a serious problem with which we must deal urgently. This is about operational effectiveness. The success of the Armed Forces depends fundamentally on respect, trust and mutual dependence. Anything that weakens those bonds of trust and respect weakens the Armed Forces as a fighting force. Harassment does just that, so it is crucial that we deal with it. Acknowledging the problem was an important first step. In light of these findings on 26 May 2006, we agreed a new action plan with the Equal Opportunities Commission to prevent and deal with sexual harassment in the Armed Forces, with a clear undertaking to create an environment, through strong leadership, in which harassment is recognised as inappropriate and preventable. It commits the MoD to deliver real improvements for Service personnel, including increased confidence in the complaints system and a reduction in the number of women reporting unwanted behaviour of a sexual nature being targeted at them. The Equal Opportunities Commission will work with us to monitor progress until the current phase ends in June 2008. At the end of this period, the Commission will decide whether we have complied fully with the agreement, or whether it will need to take further action.

RESERVES MANPOWER

Type and Structure

288. It is Government policy to have more capable, usable, integrated and relevant Reserve Forces supporting their Regular counterparts on operations overseas. The operational utility of the Reserve Forces has again been borne out in the past year through their contribution to operations worldwide, under the five call-out orders currently in force. These cover operations in Iraq, Afghanistan, the Balkans, Sierra Leone and in support of the Government's counter-terrorist objectives. The Reserves are now an integral part of Defence capability, to be drawn upon for use on enduring operations where necessary. A National Audit Office report on the Reserve Forces, published in March 2006, concluded that we have been successful in using the Reserves and that we have successfully developed a culture where the Reserves now expect to be used on operations. In a major survey of Reservists conducted for the study, over 60% of recent entrants to the Reserves stated the desire to serve on operations as an important reason for their joining. Integration into the overall Defence framework is also evident in steps taken to reform the structure and management of the Reserves. The Territorial Army restructuring exercise, announced in March 2006, was complementary to previous work on Future Army Structures for the Regulars (see paragraph 112). On 1 April 2006, the management of the Royal Naval Reserve and the Royal Marines Reserve was brought together under a 1-star Commander Maritime Reserves based in Portsmouth.

[6] Figure from DASA and are at 1 April 2006.

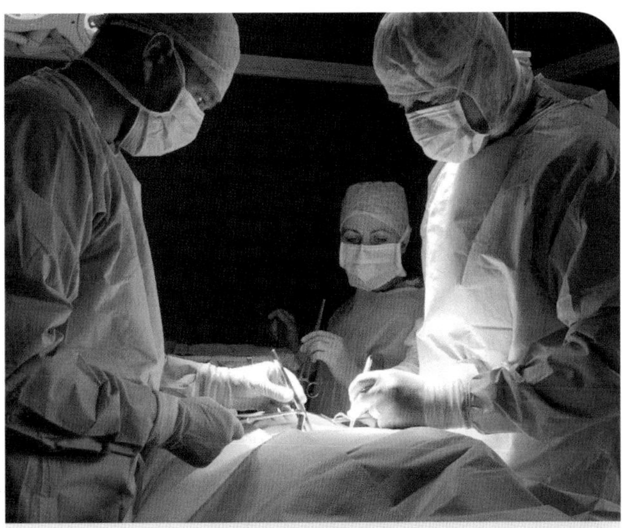

Royal Naval Reserve nurses at work

289. The continuing use of Reserves to augment the Regular Forces requires a sufficient supply of Reservists to be available to undertake these tasks. We are therefore undertaking major efforts to increase levels of recruitment and retention in the Reserve Forces. A breakdown of the current strengths of the Volunteer and Regular Reserve Forces is shown in tables 24 and 25. Although all the Volunteer Reserve forces failed to meet their manning balance target of 95%, the downward trend in manning levels has slowed across each of those forces, and 2005-06 saw an increase in overall strength of both the Royal Marines Reserve and Territorial Army. This is the first such increase in Territorial Army strength since major changes to its size and structure were introduced following the 1998 Strategic Defence Review. In order to improve manning levels, both the Army and the Navy are combining their Regular and Reserves recruiting operations under a single professional organisation, to ensure high quality and consistent branding. The Army has also initiated a wide-ranging manning action plan, covering a range of issue from training to welfare and recruitment to estate infrastructure.

Table 24: Trained Strength and Requirements of Volunteer Reserves at 1 April

	Royal Navy / Royal Marines			Territorial Army			Royal Auxiliary Air Force		
	2006	2005	2004	2006	2005	2004	2006	2005	2004
Requirement	3,930	4,840	4,840	38,430	38,430	38,430	2,220	2,220	2,220
Strength	3,170	3,320[2]	3,780[2]	32,150	31,410	32,240	1,450	1,480	1,550
Of which mobilised	N/A	10	60	1,110	1,460	2,890	80	20	20
Manning Balance	81%	69%	78%	84%	82%	84%	65%	67%	70%

Notes:
1. TA and R(Aux)AF strength and mobilised data from DASA. RN/RM and all requirement from single service sources.
2. Figures will differ from that shown in previous reports.
3. Figures are rounded to the nearest ten.
4. RN/RM strength and requirement excludes University RN Units. TA strength and requirement excludes non-regular permanent staff, Officer Training Corps and Full Time Reserve Service personnel. R(Aux)AF strength and requirement excludes University Air Squadrons.
5. Volunteer Reserve Manning Balance is calculated from overall requirement against overall strength.

Table 25: Strength of the Regular Reserve Forces at 1 April

	Royal Navy / Royal Marines			Army			Royal Air Force		
	2006	2005	2004	2006	2005	2004	2006	2005	2004
Strength	10,400	10,530	10,700	32,060	31,420	31,220	8,100	8,440	9,520
of which mobilised	–	–	–	260	170	150	10	10	10
Individuals liable to recall	10,060	11,650	12,000	95,520	102,760	110,720	26,570	26,720	27,120
Total	20,460	22,180	22,700	127,580	134,190	141,940	34,670	35,160	36,610

Notes:
1. Army and RAF data from DASA, RN/RM data from single service source.
2. Figures exclude Full-Time Reserve Service personnel.
3. '–' denotes zero or rounded to zero.4. Figures are rounded to the nearest ten, and due to rounding the totals may not always equal the sum of the parts.

290. A number of other initiatives are aimed at making staying in the Reserves a more attractive proposition for those currently serving. In April 2005, we introduced a new Reserve Forces Pension Scheme and Armed Forces Compensation Scheme. The latter significantly enhances Reservist's conditions of service because it also takes into account a reservist's civilian as well as his military earnings, even when training. A number of Reserves welfare initiatives have improved communication with Reservists and their families, improved access to welfare facilities for families (special requirements are necessary because, unlike regulars, Reservists do not live within close-knit communities typical of Regular forces) and better management of the sick and injured. This included our undertaking in November 2005 to provide injured Reservists with improved access to diagnosis and treatment at the Reserves Training and Mobilisation Centre at Chilwell, and, where appropriate, at Ministry of Defence Hospital Units. In May 2006 we also announced mental healthcare support for Reservists (see paragraph 215).

CIVILIAN MANPOWER

Civilian Contribution to Operations

291. About 350 UK-based civilian staff deployed to operational theatres alongside their uniformed colleagues during 2005-06. They worked with military commanders as policy advisers as well as providing local contractual, secretariat and financial advice to deployed forces. Personnel from the Defence Science and Technology Laboratory, the Defence Fire Service and the Ministry of Defence Police have also made a valuable contribution to operations over the last year. On 1 April 2006, we also employed about 15,100 Locally Engaged Civilians, of whom some 3,280 were employed in operational areas. The 2,340 personnel of the Royal Fleet Auxiliary Service regularly deploy to operational theatres alongside their uniformed colleagues, operating a range of Royal Fleet Auxiliary ships to support the front line.

RFA Bayleaf supporting operations in the Gulf.

Staff Numbers

292. We remain on course to meet or exceed our efficiency target to reduce the number of civilian posts in administrative and support roles by 11,000 (including 1,000 Locally Engaged Civilians) by the end of March 2008. We currently plan to reduce around 11,570 posts, of which around 3,250 had been achieved by 31 March 2006, 3,030 in 2006-07 and 5,290 in 2007-08. The total number of civilians employed by the Department (including its Trading Funds and Locally Engaged Civilians) reduced from 108,470[7] Full Time Equivalents on 1 April 2005 to 103,930 on 1 April 2006. This comprised some 3,640 UK based staff with the balance being Locally Engaged Civilians.

293. We are making every effort to minimise and, where possible, avoid compulsory redundancies. Natural wastage (mainly normal retirements and resignations) and moves to private contractors, on Transfer of Undertaking and Protection of Employment terms, are expected to produce the majority of the planned reductions. Others will be achieved by reduced recruitment and a voluntary Early Release Scheme. Individuals whose posts are cut are being managed through a Department-wide Redeployment Pool, which gives those in the Pool priority consideration when filling new or vacant posts. Staff leaving through the Early Release Scheme receive assistance including access to a MoD-funded Outplacement Service. Staff leaving on early or normal retirement terms attend a workshop on 'Planning for Retirement'.

Civilian Diversity

294. Details of our diversity performance against our targets are set out in Table 26. The MoD's Unified Diversity Strategy continues to provide the overarching strategic guidance for actions taken to improve the diversity of the Department's civilian staff. This challenge will be significantly more difficult to meet when, in order to deliver our contribution to the Government's efficiency and relocation objectives, we are further reducing the size of our workforce, relocating elements from more to less ethnically diverse parts of the country and limiting recruitment. We refocused our diversity programme following the release in November 2005 of the Civil Service's ten-point plan to increase the pace of diversity reform at senior levels in the Civil Service, drawing together into a single delivery plan our continuing diversity initiatives and those required under the Civil Service plan. This provides our blueprint for diversity reform and sets out the actions the MoD will pursue to support the achievement of diversity targets. A new Equality and Diversity Scheme, taking account of existing, new and likely future legislation to promote equality and diversity, was developed during the year and was launched in May 2006. The Scheme, which will be in force until 2009, sets out our strategy for meeting the statutory general and specific duties for Race, Disability and Gender and our approach to other diversity strands.

[7] These figures are those normally published in UK Defence Statistics and other DASA publications. They differ from those on page 205 which are in accordance with HM Treasury Financial Reporting Manual and shows the average over the year. A detailed explanation is provided on page 205.

Table 26: Percentage of Women, Ethnic Minority and Disabled Non-Industrial Civilian MoD Staff	2007	2006		2005		2004	
	Target	Target	Achieved	Target	Achieved	Target	Achieved
Total Senior Civil Servants in the MoD[3]							
Women	15.0	15.0	10.1	15.0	9.2	13.0	8.8
Ethnic Minorities	3.2	3.2	2.6	3.2	2.2	3.0	2.2
Disabled	2.0	2.0	2.9	2.0	3.3	1.9	3.0
Band B							
Women	18.0	18.0	19.1	16.0	18.5	15.0	16.6
Ethnic Minorities	3.5	3.5	2.3	3.0	2.4	2.7	2.5
Disabled	4.0	4.0	2.7	4.0	2.4	3.6	2.0
Band D							
Women	40.0	40.0	38.5	40.0	37.6	38.0	36.1
Ethnic Minorities	4.0	4.0	3.2	4.0	2.9	3.5	2.9
Disabled	6.0	6.0	4.3	6.0	4.2	5.8	4.2

Notes:
1. Data from DASA. Figures at 1 April.
2. Percentages of Ethnic Minority Staff calculated as percentages of staff with known ethnicity status.
3. Percentages of Disabled staff have been calculated as percentages of total staff (ie including those who have declared or not declared their status), to be comparable with set targets. This differs from the methodology used in all external publications and in the recruitment table where percentages of Disabled staff are calculated from staff with known disability status.
4. Senior Civil Service data covers SCS and equivalent grades e.g. medical consultants.

295. These initiatives reinforce our commitment to inculcating Diversity into how the MoD goes about achieving its business, and to build on our achievements to date. These were recognised through external benchmarking during the year. We maintained our silver 'Race For Opportunity' standard (an independent organisation working on race and diversity) and achieved a gold award in the 'Opportunity Now' benchmarking exercise. We improved from 59th to 35th in Stonewall's Corporate Equality Index this year. An independent benchmarking exercise conducted during the year concluded that our diversity policy framework compares very favourably with other public and private sector organisations assessed to date. However, while the benchmarking report also indicates that we have an appropriate policy framework in place, it also showed that there are gaps between our policy and practice in the workplace. We are therefore now focusing on how best to ensure the appropriate policy framework is implemented.

Civilian Recruitment

296. The 2004 Spending Review committed the Department to substantial civilian manpower reductions. Recruitment in 2005-06 was consequently lower than in the previous two financial years and is expected to fall further (see Table 27). However, despite this reduction in recruitment, diversity figures have remained constant and in some cases have improved. The number of women as a percentage of the total industrial and non industrial staff recruited has remained stable (38.9% in 2003-04, 40.5% in 2004-05, 38.8% in 2005-06). We intend to maintain targeted recruitment in certain specialist functions and to ensure an adequate supply of future senior managers. The recruitment information shown in Table 27 includes figures for recruitment of all permanent and temporary (casual) civilian personnel including Trading Fund staff. Additional recruitment information, in accordance with the Civil Service Commissioners' Recruitment Code, can be found at Annex F.

Table 27: Civilian Recruitment

	2005-06		2004-05		2003-04	
	Non Industrial	Industrial	Non Industrial	Industrial	Non Industrial	Industrial
Total Number recruited	3,510	1,130	5,480	1,700	6,530	2,710
Number and percentage of women	1,510 43.1%	290 25.6%	2,440 44.5%	470 27.5%	3,020 46.2%	580 21.3%
Number of people with declared minority ethnicity[3]	170 7.2%	20 3.0%	130 4.2%	20 2.3%	160 4.6%	20 2.7%
Number of people with declared disabilities[4]	10 ~	~ ~	40 0.7%	20 1.2%	40 0.7%	10 ~

Notes:
1. Data from DASA.
2. The recruitment statistics shown are for all permanent and casual civilian personnel including Trading Fund staff and do not include other methods of entry. No recruitment information is available for Royal Fleet Auxiliary or Locally Engaged Civilian personnel. Further civilian recruitment information required by the Office of the Civil Service Commissioner can be found in Annex F.
3. Percentage of staff recruitment is based on known declarations of ethnicity and excludes staff with unknown or undeclared ethnicity.
4. Percentage of staff recruitment is based on known declarations of disability status and excludes staff with unknown or undeclared disability status.
5. ~ indicated strength of less than ten or percentage based on strength of less than ten.
6. All figures are on a Full Time Equivalent basis.
7. All figures have been rounded to meet Freedom of Information requirements and protect confidentiality.

Civilian Progression

297. The Department also set itself a number of targets on civilian progression, covering promotion to the Senior Civil Service (SCS), Management Development Programme pass-rates at the Assessment Centre for promotion to Band B, and success rates for 'In Service Nominations' to the Civil Service Fast Stream. The relatively small size of the Defence SCS (about 0.3 % of the Defence civil service are Senior Civil Servants, compared to a rate of about 0.9% across the Civil Service as a whole), combined with an unfavourable demographic profile and low rate of turnover that reflect a department that has been shrinking for over 15 years mean that promotion opportunities to and within the SCS remain limited. Although 93 staff applied for promotion to the SCS, we were only able to make 16 substantive promotions to the Defence SCS in 2005-06 against a target of 18. Similar constraints apply at Band B level. 641 staff applied to the 2006 Band B Assessment Centre. Following a sift exercise, only 17% of staff were invited to attend, compared to 34% in 2005 and only 11% of staff who had applied for promotion were successfully awarded a Band B promotion passport, compared to 24% in 2005. Within that total members of development schemes performed well. Of those invited to the Centre 100% of Fast Stream applicants succeeded against a target of 85%, and 79% of applications from our internal scheme to identify and develop internal talent. The In Service Nomination success rate for the Fast Stream in 2005 was 45% against a target of 50% (5 passes from 11 people sitting).

FURTHER SOURCES OF INFORMATION

298. Additional Information on Manpower is available from the following sources:
- quarterly PSA reports to HM Treasury at www.mod.uk;
- *UK Defence Statistics 2006* available at www.dasa.mod.uk (from September 2006);
- NAO Report *Ministry of Defence Reserve Forces* (HC964 on 31 March 2006) available at www.nao.org.uk;
- *Race Equality Scheme* at www.mod.uk;
- *Preventing and Dealing Effectively with Sexual Harassment in the Armed Forces* available at www.mod.uk;
- Agreement between MoD and Equal Opportunities Commission *Progress Report and Phase Three Action Plan* available at www.mod.uk;
- *Delivering a Diverse Civil Service – A 10-Point Plan* available at www.civilservice.gov.uk;
- *Equality and Diversity Scheme 2006-2009* available at www.mod.uk.

Essay: Diversity in the Armed Forces

For the Armed Forces, diversity is not a matter of political correctness. There is both a clear moral imperative and a compelling business case. The moral imperative stems from the fact that it is right that the Armed Forces be seen to be equally open to and drawn from across the society they serve. Women have as much a part to play in the Defence of the realm as in anything else, and an increasing proportion of our society, while British, come from a wide variety of ethnic and cultural backgrounds. If the Armed Forces are to command the confidence and support of the whole of British society, then they must actively encourage participation from all sections of society. Looked at in business terms, the Armed Forces compete with other employers for the best recruits, particularly as they become more technologically advanced. And drawing on the talents and skills of recruits from different backgrounds will increase flexibility and innovation and help the Armed Forces to understand and respond better to different types of situations and people by bringing different perspectives to their work. Moreover, demographic factors mean that the Armed Forces will have to look beyond their traditional recruiting grounds to find enough recruits of the right calibre. In short, rational self-interest would impel the Armed Forces to look to other sources of talent even if there were no moral case.

However, there are constraints: service in the Armed Forces is a difficult, sometimes dangerous, round-the-clock commitment. Their policies have to take this into account and the Armed Forces are therefore exempt from some aspects of diversity legislation, in particular on disability and age. Because of the need for all military personnel, whatever their trade, to be combat-effective in order to meet a world-wide liability to deploy, they must pass strict medical and physical fitness tests, and the Armed Forces therefore cannot admit people with certain disabilities (although they do recruit people with some disabilities covered by the Disability Discrimination Act, such as dyslexia). With regard to age, the delivery of military fighting power predominantly calls for the physical capacities of youth, and Service personnel need to be young enough when recruited to give a good return of service since their training is expensive. The Armed Forces also need to attract young people into the Services and progress the best of them through to command positions at non-commissioned and officer level in order to 'grow' people with the right experience to fill senior positions, since acquiring military knowledge and experience is a cumulative process and cannot be bought-in. Accordingly, the Armed Forces recruit almost entirely into the Junior Ranks and Junior Officer levels. A corollary of this is that the Services also need policies to encourage personnel to leave after a certain number of years to ensure there is constant movement through the promotion pyramid, otherwise career advancement would become static. This would be unacceptable since Service personnel are unable to move freely in and out of the labour market. Maintaining the balance of age and experience is therefore fundamental to delivering operational capability and the terms of employment for Service personnel are structured accordingly.

Some restrictions are also still imposed on the employment of women. Drawing on advice from the Chiefs of Staff and the conclusions of a detailed study into *Women in the Armed Forces*, the Secretary of State for Defence decided in May 2002 that the case for lifting the restrictions on women serving in ground close-combat roles where they could be required to close with and kill the enemy in hand-to-hand fighting had not been made. Accordingly posts in the Royal Marines General Service, the Household Cavalry and Royal Armoured Corps, the Infantry and the Royal Air Force Regiment remain closed to women. Health and safety considerations mean that submarine and mine clearance diving service also remain closed to women. But 71% of posts in the Royal Navy, 71% of posts in the Army and 96% of posts in the Royal Air Force are open to them.

There has, at times, been a good deal of sensationalist media coverage about 'gays in the Armed Forces'. In practice, the Services now treat sexual orientation as a private matter not relevant to an individual's suitability for a career in the Armed Forces. Personnel are free to choose whether or not to disclose their sexual orientation. The important thing is that if they wish to do so, they must be confident that they will not suffer abuse or intimidation. All members of the Armed Forces are expected to challenge homophobic behaviour, attitudes and all other forms of prejudice.

Encouraging diversity has led the Armed Forces to make a range of practical changes. Like any employer, their personnel planning now has to take account of maternity and paternity leave. Childcare considerations have led to the provision of crèches at many units. Career breaks are available to all at the discretion of the Service, in particular to help with caring responsibilities and domestic problems. In line with the terms of the Civil Partnerships Act, the Services also give parity of treatment, for example in the allocation of accommodation, to gay and lesbian couples who have formally registered their partnerships.

Reasonable adjustments have also been made to accommodate the needs of those from different cultural and religious backgrounds. Sikh men are allowed to wear their religious symbols (the 5Ks); Muslim and Sikh men are permitted to wear short, neatly-cut beards; Muslim women are allowed to wear uniform trousers rather than a skirt and may wear a hijab; male members of the Jewish faith may wear dark plain or patterned yarmulkes whenever they remove other headdress; vegetarian, Halal and Kosher meals can be provided in Service messes and in operational ration packs; and time-off for prayer and religious observance is normally allowed and suitable facilities provided. Reflecting their increasing presence in the Forces, we recently appointed the first chaplains from the Sikh, Hindu, Buddhist and Muslim faiths to join the long-standing Honorary Officiating Jewish Chaplain.

But all these adjustments are subject to the over-riding imperatives of operational effectiveness and health and safety. For example, while Sikh men are normally allowed to wear turbans, some trades require specialist headgear (such as commanders' helmets in armoured fighting vehicles, combat helmets, fire-fighters' breathing apparatus with full hoods, and aircrew flying helmets), especially on operations. Turbans are incompatible with this. Male Sikh personnel can normally wear a patka under specialist headgear but even this is not possible with a flying helmet, which must be closely fitted to the contours of the head to be effective. In these circumstances, Sikh personnel may be required to have their hair cut short.

Persuading the best people to choose a career in the Armed Forces is challenging, whether men or women and whatever their ethnic and cultural background. It involves, among other things, ensuring that they feel welcome and valued. This has meant changing attitudes and behaviours, some of which were cherished as part of the traditional Service ethos. But traditions have to evolve and adapt if they are to survive. Just as wider society has come to consider that language and actions that were once commonplace are no longer acceptable, so have the Armed Forces. This is a matter of respect for others, of sensitivity, of recognising the limits on certain types of behaviour and not crossing the line. Progress comes from gaining acceptance for such changes without destroying the banter and camaraderie that fosters team spirit and underpins operational effectiveness. This is not easy and requires clear, consistent leadership from the top down. Achieving real diversity is difficult; the Armed Forces work at it continuously and direct effort and resources to promote it. And we are getting there.

The recently appointed Buddhist, Hindu, Muslim and Sikh Armed Forces Chaplains.

ESTATE

Objective: Maintain an estate of the right size and quality, managed in a sustainable manner, to achieve Defence objectives.

Public Service Agreement Target (SR2002 MoD Target 7)

Increase value for money by making improvements in the efficiency and effectiveness of the key processes for delivering military capability:

- **Identify for disposal land and buildings with a Net Book Value of over £300M (from 1 April 2002 to 31 March 2006).**

Performance Measures and Assessment

Improving the Estate – Improve Single Living Accommodation to Grade 1 standard by delivering 2,500 Grade 1 bed spaces through Project SLAM and 5,300 Grade 1 bed spaced through other projects:

- **3,570 new-build bed spaces delivered in 2005-06 through Project SLAM;**
- **3,055 new-build bed spaces delivered in 2005-06 through parallel projects.**

Improving the Estate – Improve Service Families Accommodation in the UK by upgrading 600 family houses to Standard 1 for condition:

- **1,705 Service families houses upgraded in 2005-06 of the long term stock 25,091 houses at Standard 1 for condition and 15,794 at Standard 2 for condition. Over 95% of the long term core stock now at Standard 1 or 2 for condition.**

Managing the Estate – Relocation of 3,900 posts outside of London and the South East by 2010:

- **Major Estate rationalisation programme in progress;**
- **1,229 posts so far relocated outside of London and South East.**

Managing the Estate – Achieve gross estates disposal receipts of £250M in year and identify land and buildings for disposal with cumulative value of £300M by April 2006:

- **Accrued gross disposal receipts from surplus land and property of £266M in 2005-06 (cumulative total £685M April 2003-March 2006 against cumulative target of £500M);**
- **Assets with Net Book Value of £61M transferred to Defence Estates in 2005-06 for disposal (cumulative value £456M from 1 April 2002 to 31 March 2006).**

Managing the Estate – Award Regional Prime Contracts for the Central region by September 2005 and East by October 2005:

- **Regional Prime Contract (Central) awarded 2 November 2005;**
- **Regional Prime Contract (East) awarded 16 November 2005;**
- **Housing Prime Contract for England and Wales awarded 14 November 2005;**
- **Value for Money measurement tool under development.**

Managing the Estate – Deliver the Sustainable Development strategy for the Defence Estate:

- **62% of scheduled ancient monuments in good or fair condition in 2005 (56% in 2004);**
- **79% of Sites of Special Scientific Interest assessed as in 'favourable' or 'unfavourable recovering' condition in January 2006 against target of 75%;**
- **Increased access to Defence land.**

THE DEFENCE ESTATE

299. The Ministry of Defence is one of the largest landowners in the UK with a diverse estate of some 240,000 hectares (about 1 per cent of the UK land mass) valued at some £18 billion. It comprises a built estate of around 80,000 hectares (and rights to use a further 5,400 hectares) and a rural estate of some 160,000 hectares (and rights to use about 120,000 hectares more). It includes 179 Sites of Special Scientific Interest (SSSI), around 650 listed buildings and 1,057 scheduled monuments. We spend about £1.5 billion per year on maintenance and construction, with some of these costs offset against income from tenants and other land users. Overseas there are the garrisons in Germany, Cyprus, the Falkland Islands and Gibraltar, major training facilities in Canada, Cyprus, Germany, Norway, Poland and Kenya, and other facilities in Ascension Island, Belize, Brunei, Nepal, Singapore and the United States.

IMPROVING THE ESTATE

300. The housing provided for Service personnel and their families is an important part of their overall package of terms and conditions and plays a significant role in retention and we are committed to providing high quality living conditions. The condition of living accommodation on the Defence estate is not as good as it should be. We invested some £163M during the year to take forward a range of programmes to improve both Single Living Accommodation and Service Families Accommodation, although the need to balance the resources needed against other Defence priorities has meant that we are not able make progress as fast as we would like.

Single Living Accommodation

301. Project SLAM (Single Living Accommodation Modernisation) is a Prime Contract to upgrade some 9,000 single bed spaces in the UK by 31 March 2008. It was awarded in December 2002 and construction work began in April 2003. It is providing a greatly improved living environment for single Service personnel, including mostly single rooms with en-suite facilities. Feedback has been good, and there is anecdotal evidence of single Service personnel in private lodgings requesting a return to base to take up SLAM accommodation. 3,570 bed spaces were delivered in 2005-06 against a target of 2,500, bringing the total upgraded so far to 5,582. There are also a number of other projects to modernise Single Living Accommodation in England, Scotland, Northern Ireland, Germany, Gibraltar and Cyprus aiming to upgrade about a further 21,000 single bed spaces by the end March 2008. 3,055 bed spaces were delivered in 2005-06, including over 800 in Germany, against a target of 5,300, bringing the total upgraded since 1 April 2003 to some 10,200. The shortfall against target in 2005-06 reflects delays to some projects pending decisions on the future structure and deployment of Service personnel. Schemes completed during the year included Vimy Barracks, Catterick (539); RAF Coningsby (258); RM Lympstone (412); St David's Barracks, Bicester (390); HMS Collingwood (294); Gutersloh, Germany (216); and Glencourse Barracks, Edinburgh (419).

Completed SLAM accommodation at St. David's Barracks

Service Families Accommodation

302. We currently manage some 49,000 Service Families Accommodation (SFA) properties, of which nearly 43,000 are considered to be long-term core stock. It is intended that the remainder will be handed back to Annington Homes Limited or disposed of as soon as possible. Work continued to improve the overall standard. During 2005-06 1,705 properties were upgraded to Standard 1 for Condition (costing £9.8M) against an original target of 600, bringing the total upgraded to Standard 1 since 1 April 2003 to 5,519. At April 2005, the long-term core stock was made up of 25,091 properties at Standard 1 (24,000 in April 2004), 15,794 at Standard 2 (18,000 in April 2004), 1,982 properties at Standard 3 (900 in April 2003) and 133 at Standard 4 (100 in April 2003). We plan to upgrade a minimum of 900 properties each year up to 2011.

MANAGING THE ESTATE

303. As set out in the Defence Estate Strategy *In Trust and On Trust*, a refreshed version of which was launched in March 2006, our goal is to have an estate of the right size and quality to support the delivery of Defence capability, managed and developed effectively and efficiently in line with best practice, and sensitive to social and environmental considerations. Our approach is continuing to develop to reflect Smart Acquisition principles and substantial rationalisation of Defence activities. In May 2005 the National Audit Office published its report on *Managing the Defence Estate*. This concluded that we had made considerable progress in rationalising and improving the estate, providing a more effective and more efficient estate with wider benefits for the military and for the morale of service personnel and their families, but that more was needed to strengthen the arrangements.

Rationalisation, Relocation and Disposals

304. We are taking forward an extensive programme of estate rationalisation and modernisation as part of the Department's change and efficiency goals. Projects underway include:

- the Army project to collocate the Headquarters of Land Command and the Adjutant General, probably at Andover in Hampshire;
- Project Allenby/Connaught to provide a modern working environment for the Army garrisons around Salisbury Plain;
- the creation of an integrated RAF headquarters at RAF High Wycombe in Buckinghamshire from 1 April 2006 by collocation of the headquarters of the RAF Strike and Personnel and Training Commands;
- the creation of an integrated acquisition and support orgnisation in the Bristol/Bath area, building on previous plans to collocate the headquarters of the Defence Logistics Organisation with the Defence Procurement Agency at Abbey Wood and, relocate the Defence Logistics Organisation Land and Air environment Integrated Project Teams with the Maritime environment teams;
- rationalisation of the Defence Intelligence Staff's estate;
- rationalisation of the Defence medical estate, including relocation of the Defence Medical Education and Training Agency from Aldershot to the Midlands;
- rationalisation and refurbishment of the Army training estate, including the closure during the year of the Army Technical Foundation College at Arborfield in Berkshire and absorption of its function into the Technical College at Harrogate in Yorkshire;
- rationalisation of the Defence Estate in London, including the closure and disposal of Chelsea Barracks, under a new procurement strategy, Prime Contracting Plus, that will use the value of the sites released by consolidation to fund construction and relocation costs;
- the reduction of the MoD Head Office from three buildings to two, enabling possible disposal of the Old War Office Building in Whitehall;
- follow-up to the review of Defence Airfields.

305. This programme will more than deliver on the Department's target under the Lyons Review to move at least 3,900 posts out of London and the South East by 2010. At 31 March 2006, 1,229 posts have relocated. The MoD has a strong track record of reducing or relocating out of London and the south east, having already reduced from more than 20 central London buildings to just 3 buildings in 2004. The further rationalisations outlined above and a number of smaller projects will contribute a further 3,800 to 4,100 posts over the next four years, not including any relocations resulting from implementation of the Defence Training Review. These will be offset to some degree by the creation of the new integrated Army and RAF headquarters, both of which are likely to move some posts into the South East.

306. Accrued gross Estates disposal receipts of £266M were achieved during the year against a target of £250M, bringing total receipts to £685M for the three year period up to March 2006 against the 2002 Spending Review goal of £500M. In addition, assets with a net book value of £61M were identified and transferred to Defence Estates for disposal, bringing their cumulative value from 1 April 2002 to 31 March 2006 to £456M against the 2002 Spending Review Value for Money PSA target of over £300M.

307. We have forged a good working relationship with English Partnerships fostered by the signing of a Framework Agreement in 2004 to engender collaborative working. In March 2006 Defence Estates completed the sale of the former Oakington Barracks, approximately five miles from Cambridge, to English Partnerships for £99M. The 288 hectare site will form part of the new town of Northstowe which will be developed to provide approximately 10,000 new homes.

Prime Contracting

308. Management of the majority of the Defence built estate in England and Wales is provided through a series of Regional Prime Contracts (RPCs). Some specific locations, and Service personnel accommodation management, are covered by other management arrangements. The RPC for Scotland covers built, rural and Service accommodation. We successfully completed roll-out of the five RPCs in November 2005 within a few weeks of the target date set in 2002, with the award of final contract for the Central region to Carillion Enterprise, a consortium comprising Carillion Services Ltd and Enterprise plc, and for the Eastern region to Babcock DynCorp, a consortium comprising Babcock Infrastructure Services and DynCorp International, on 2 and 16 November 2005 respectively. They became fully operational at the end of April and June 2006. A Housing Prime Contract for England and Wales to modernise service delivery for the repair and maintenance of Service Families Accommodation was awarded on 14 November 2005 to MODern Housing Solutions, a joint venture between Carillion, Enterprise and Atkins and became fully operational on 1 April 2006. The Contract covers the whole SFA estate across England and Wales, except where properties are covered by extant Private Finance Initiative (PFI) arrangements.

309. Regional Prime Contracting has a target to deliver 30% through life value for money improvements in estate management by 2013 through improved planning, supply chain management, incentivisation, continuous improvement, economies of scale and partnering. This is being measured using the Estate Performance Measurement System (EPMS) which is currently being

rolled out following the successful conclusion of pilots in early 2005, focusing initially on the areas of the estate managed under Prime Contracting. The poor availability of historical information on the estate continues to hamper assessments, and we do not expect the value for money improvements being achieved by the Scotland, South West and South East contracts to have been assessed and scored before the end of 2006. However, preliminary data from RPC Scotland, the most mature available, indicates that this level of improvement against the 2003-04 baseline may already have been achieved. This is currently being verified through a robust validation process to ensure that data standards have been applied consistently across the estate.

Housing Management

310. Around 3,000 Service Family properties are currently vacant. This is known as the housing management margin. We continue to use this, less housing earmarked for disposal in the next 12 months, as a measure of the efficiency of our housing management. However, about 6%, over 3,000 further properties, was housing held in abeyance as a result of the uncertainty arising from possible future estate rationalisation decisions and service deployments, which are at historically high level. The housing management margin increased to 13.9% from 11.2% over the year against a target of 10%.

311. The number of empty properties also reduced from 1 April 2006 as Gurkha families started taking up SFA following changes to their terms and conditions of service. A rigorous programme to identify and dispose of property for which there is no longer-term requirement continues.

312. The service to residents of Service Families Accommodation is changing significantly following the merger of the Defence Housing Executive and Defence Estates and the roll-out of the Housing Prime Contract. We are redesigning the Housing Customer Attitude Survey to be more focussed and remove factors that are outside the control of estate management, such as levels of long term detached duty and operational commitments. Work also continued to develop consistent and world-wide housing standards, charging and reporting mechanisms. While satisfaction levels are an important performance indicator we will not be able to meaningfully quantify the satisfaction levels of SFA residents until this work is completed and the new Housing Prime Contract has bedded in the delivery of services to SFA occupants. It is planned to measure the satisfaction of occupants late in 2006.

Project Aquatrine

313. Project Aquatrine is a Defence-wide 25-year PFI project to deliver water and waste water services to the Defence estate across Great Britain. It comprises three contracts covering the Midlands, Wales and the South West; Scotland; and the North, East and South-East of England. At the same time as transferring risk to the service providers it is providing increased value for money (in 2005-06 cost benefit efficiencies of over £11M were realised for the contract for the Midlands, Wales and the South West), helping to achieve our sustainability goals (a leakage reduction programme is expected to produce water savings of over 0.75M m^3 across the estate this year) and improving health and safety (new fire mains and static tanks are being installed at a number of locations).

Supplier Management

314. Defence Estates has generated a major rationalisation of its supply base, through the implementation of large-scale Prime Contract and Private Public Partnership projects. As such a significant proportion of Defence Estates business is now contracted out to a reduced number of suppliers for the medium to long term. As part of Defence Estates Supplier Management strategy we are improving the overall working relationship with suppliers and have identified a unique opportunity to work collaboratively with groups of suppliers delivering similar outputs. We have launched a collaborative supplier development programme and in November 2005 launched Supplier Associations for the Prime Contracting community and for Aquatrine. The purpose of these Associations is to create an environment to undertake business improvements, resourced by all parties, to provide tangible benefits to MoD and to industry. In the absence of a competitive atmosphere over the next few years, we are confident the Associations will greatly assist to deliver efficiencies and improve project delivery.

Sustainable Development: Stewardship, Conservation and Access

315. We work to manage the Estate in as sustainable a way as possible. Further information on this is provided in paragraphs 77-82 on sustainable development, and in the essay on Project Allenby/Connaught on page 154. Detailed reporting is set out in the *Sustainable Development Annual Report 2005.* A further strand of our sustainable development strategy is the responsible management of the diverse and nationally important archaeological and environmental assets under our control, and the provision of as much public access and recreation to Defence land as is consistent with safety and security requirements and the delivery of military capability for which that land is held. Detailed information on these is contained in the annual *Stewardship Report on the Defence Estate* and the Ministry of Defence Conservation Magazine *Sanctuary.*

An MoD biodiversity day

316. A major audit was conducted during 2005 to check the data we held on the number, status, location, ownership and management responsibility for Scheduled Ancient Monuments on the Defence estate. Over 9,000 monuments are recorded on land we own or use, of which 1,057 are scheduled. Their condition continued to improve, with 62% assessed as in good or fair condition, compared to 56% in 2004.

317. The Department has 179 Sites of Special Scientific Interest (SSSIs) covering nearly 84,000 hectares under management (more than any other landowner in the UK). We continued to make progress continues towards meeting the national target of 95% of SSSIs in 'favourable' or 'unfavourable recovering' condition by 2010, with an interim target of 75% by 1 April 2006. 79% of Defence SSSIs were assessed achieving this in January 2006.

Reflecting the quality of management, Defence Estates won a number of external awards during the year, including: the Marsh Lepidoptera Conservation Award for work on habitat management; Highly Commended at the Environment and Sustainable Technology Awards for work on integrating sustainable practices across the Estate; and two English Nature awards at Otterburn and Warcop for SSSI improvements.

318. We maintain some 1,300 kilometres of public rights of way on the Defence estate in England and Wales, and over a further 100 kilometres of other permissive routes. This last figure almost doubled with the completion of the Epynt Way in South Wales in the spring of 2006. Downloadable dossiers on selected walks complete with gradings and timings, access details, safety tips, points of interest and maps are available on the upgraded MoD Public Access website at www.access.mod.uk.

A Defence Estates official on the Epynt Way

FURTHER SOURCES OF INFORMATION

319. Additional Information on Estate is available from the following sources:

- quarterly PSA reports to HM Treasury at www.mod.uk
- UK Defence Statistics 2006 available at www.dasa.mod.uk (to be published in September 2006);
- NAO Report *Managing the Defence Estate* (HC 25 on 25 May 2005) available at www.nao.uk;
- *2005 Stewardship Report on the Defence Estate* available at www.defence-estates.mod.uk;
- *The Defence Estate Strategy 2006 – In Trust and On* Trust available at www.defence-estates.mod.uk;
- DE Corporate Plan 2006-2011 available at www.defence-estates.mod.uk;
- DE Information Booklet at www.defence-estates.mod.uk;
- MoD Public Access website at www.access.mod.uk;
- *Defence Estates Annual Report and Accounts 2005-06* at www.defence-estates.mod.uk (to be published in July 2006);
- *Defence Estates Framework Document* at www.defence-estates.mod.uk;
- *Securing the Future – UK Government sustainable development strategy*, Cm 6467 available at www.sustainable-development.gov.uk/publications/uk-strategy/uk-strategy-2005.htm;
- *Sustainable Development Annual Report 2005* available at www.mod.uk (to be published in August 2005);
- *MoD Sustainable Development Delivery Strategy for Non-Operational Energy* available at www.mod.uk;
- *MoD Sustainable Development Action Plan – February 2006* available at www.mod.uk;
- *Safety, Health and Environmental protection in the Ministry of Defence – Policy Statement by the Secretary of State for Defence* – May 2005;
- information on sustainable development at www.sustainable-development.gov.uk;
- information on Defence Estates at www.defence-estates.mod.uk;

Essay: Sustainable Production: Project Allenby/Connaught

Background

The Government's Sustainable Development strategy, Securing the Future, is applied directly to the Government Estate through the Framework for Sustainable Development on the Government Estate. Project Allenby/Connaught is a 35-year PFI project with a capital value of over £1 billion and a through-life value of around £8 billion to deliver the living and working accommodation required in Aldershot and the garrisons around Salisbury Plain (Tidworth, Bulford, Larkhill and Warminster). It will provide a modern environment with associated support services for some 18,000 personnel. It is the largest PFI project of its type in the UK. The contract was awarded to Aspire Defence Limited, (a consortium of Kellogg, Brown & Root and Carillion) on 31 March 2006.

Practical Sustainability

Sustainable development has been at the heart of Project Allenby/Connaught throughout, and the project continues to look for best practice in sustainable development for incorporation wherever possible. The steps taken from the beginning of the project and the exchange of information with other major redevelopment initiatives has ensured that it embodies a wide range of features that enhance sustainability as well as protecting the environment. Examples of these include:

- **Whole Life Costing.** These principles point towards the solutions which will be most cost-effective in the long run, rather than just providing low initial costs (for example, by replacing poorly insulated buildings that waste a lot of energy with new, well insulated buildings). Such solutions are generally more sustainable;

- **Pairing and Sharing.** Where possible facilities will be shared between occupying units, reducing both the cost and the environmental impact, for example through building designs that allow one kitchen to be shared between two messes;

- **Efficiency in Land Use.** Because the project covers a number of garrisons, it has been possible to plan land use holistically. This has enabled more units to be fitted into Tidworth Garrison, and more land to be released in Aldershot for urban development to the benefit of the wider community;

- **Archaeology, Historic Buildings and Monuments.** Military use has protected Salisbury Plain from intensive farming or urban development, so it is one of the best preserved archaeological and ecological landscapes in Europe. Detailed archive research backed up by physical investigation was undertaken with the Wiltshire County Archaeologist to identify and mitigate the impact of barracks modernisation. There are also a number of historic buildings and ancient monuments potentially affected by the project. Surveys have been commissioned to explore how these can best be incorporated into the new scheme, including where appropriate by keeping them in use, to secure their future and preserve their historic value for the community.

Assessment and Contractual Obligations

Defence policy requires environmental assessment and sustainability appraisals for all new projects. Project Allenby/Connaught implemented this principle from a very early stage. PFI bidders were required to produce their own sustainability appraisals as part of their bid submissions. They also had to produce a range of innovative sustainability proposals including combined heat and power plants, rainwater collection, solar heating, sustainable urban drainage solutions and waste disposal. Sustainability was scored specifically and was an integral part of the bid evaluation.

The contract requires Aspire Defence Limited to achieve an 'Excellent' rating for around 300 new buildings and a 'Very Good' for over 100 refurbished buildings, measured using a bespoke version of the Building Research Establishment's building design assessment method to measure the impact of buildings upon the environment. These ratings can only be achieved by incorporating measurable sustainable benefits including metering electricity, gas and water usage; using renewable energy technologies such as solar power; reducing car travel by placing living and working amenities in close proximity and linking them with cycle paths; harvesting rain water for toilet flushing; and ensuring timber used for construction is grown in managed forests. A 36-person Junior Ranks Single Living Accommodation demonstrator block was constructed at Perham Down in Hampshire before the contract was awarded. This achieved an 'Excellent' rating and specific credits under the Green Guide for EcoHomes for Carbon Dioxide emissions, reduced water consumption, and waste segregation and recycling facilities. Aspire Defence Ltd also intends to make extensive use of modular construction, which requires less energy to achieve the same quality output and reduces the construction timescale and site traffic as well as increasing flexibility.

REPUTATION

Objective: Enhance our reputation with our own people and externally.

Performance Measures and Assessment

Continuing improvement in overall ratings of our reputation of MoD and UK Armed Forces among the UK public:

- **Favourable ratings for Armed Forces of 64%, an increase from 54% in March 2005; unfavourable ratings reduced to 5% from 6% in March 2005;**
- **Favourable ratings for MoD improved to 38% from 32%; unfavourable ratings improved to 14% from 15%.**

Continuing improvement in overall scores of our reputation among Service and civilian personnel:

- **The most recent survey was conducted in Spring 2005 and showed very high levels of support for our top level objective that the MoD and Armed Forces are a force for good in the world;**
- **We plan to conduct further research later this year.**

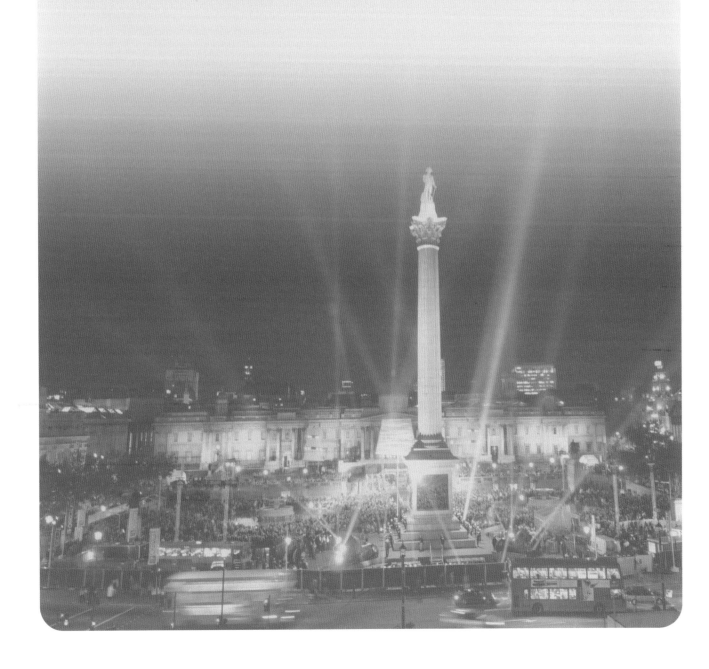

DEFENCE IN THE PUBLIC EYE

320. The work of the MoD and the Armed Forces is constantly in the public eye and we work hard to ensure that Parliament, the media and the public have an accurate perception of what we are doing and why. We have improved the MoD and single Service web-sites and our arrangements for supporting journalists on operations. The Department has responded to more requests for information under the Freedom of Information Act than any other Government department (see page 267-268). Public opinion, as reflected in the most recent survey conducted for the MoD, remains strongly favourable to the Armed Forces.

COMMUNICATING THE WORK OF THE DEPARTMENT

321. We publicise and explain the work of the Department through a number of channels. Parliament is central. The communication of Defence policy and activity in Ministerial statements, debates on Defence issues and answers to Parliamentary Questions is a key obligation of officials throughout the Department. In the first year of full operation of the Freedom of Information Act, we received 4,515 requests for information, which was significantly more than any other central Government department. Over three quarters were answered within 20 working days and it was necessary to decline only one tenth of requests made under the Act. Further information is provided in the section on Open Government at Annex F.

322. On a day-to-day basis, Defence press officers are responsible for engagement with the media and informing them of newsworthy events. Press officers also respond to questions from journalists and provide the media with the required facts. (The essay on pages 159-160 explains how). The new Defence Media Operations Centre, opened in April 2005, raised our ability to work with the media on operations: its two rapidly- deployable media teams provide early support to journalists in theatres of operation, and collect audio, film and images for supply to media organisations around the world.

323. Besides Parliament, the Press Office and the Media Operations Centre, we use a wide variety of mechanisms to get our message across. During the year, MoD exhibitions and single Service presentation teams raised public awareness of the MoD and the Armed Forces, attracting audiences in excess of 150,000 overall. The schools teams similarly helped to raise the profile of the Armed Forces and the MoD amongst young people. Increasingly, however, people learn about Defence online: the Department's and single Service web sites were well used and continue to be extensively improved; the online photographic library alone received more than 100,000,000 "hits" last year. We also continue to take our messages directly to the public, on both a day-to-day basis and through one-off events.

324. 2005 was a year of anniversaries. In July a week of events commemorated the 60th anniversary of the end of the Second World War, the finale of which took place in The Mall, where a Lancaster bomber released one million poppies in memory of those who died in the War. The commemoration of the 200th anniversary of Nelson's victory at Trafalgar unfolded in a series of events and activities culminating in a dramatic re-enactment of the battle: surveys suggest nearly half of all UK adults saw, heard or attended one or more of the events. The Services also assisted in the production of documentaries including *The Household Cavalry* and *Shipmates*, which were widely viewed and seen as informative: over half of the 16% of adults who saw the BBC documentary *Shipmates*, which went behind the scenes at Devonport Royal Naval Base, thought the programme conveyed the strong teamwork and professionalism of staff at the Base.

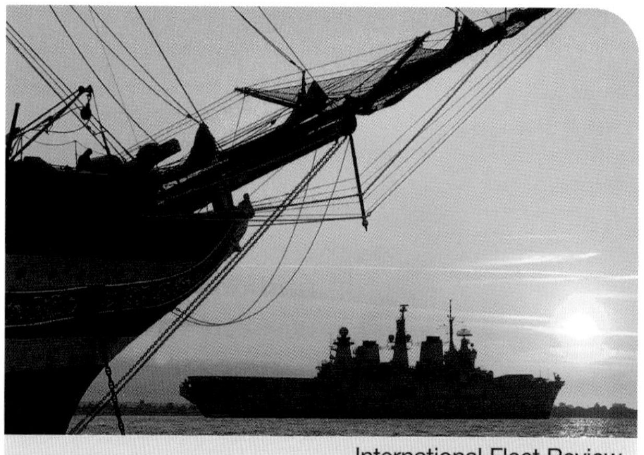

International Fleet Review

REPUTATION AMONG UK PUBLIC

325. The successful achievement of Defence objectives depends upon public support. The Department carries out regular public opinion surveys, using an independent marketing company, to test the reputation of the MoD and the Armed Forces. The most recent, carried out for the Department by Ipsos MORI in March 2006, shows a high level of public favourability towards the Armed Forces. The need for strong Armed Forces is supported by four in every five of those surveyed, and the levels of confidence in the ability of the Armed Forces to carry out their tasks and help make the world a safer place are similarly high, as Table 28 shows. On the other hand, the numbers of people who believe the Armed Forces are well equipped has returned to the levels shown by our surveys in December 2003 and there has been a reduction also in those who consider that the Armed Forces and the MoD have due regard for the environment when carrying out their activities. This was disappointing considering the Department's commitment to sustainable development (see paragraphs 77-82 and 315-318).

Table 28: External Opinion Survey results (percentage of positive replies)		March 2006	March 2005	Change
Favourability of overall impression of UK Armed Forces and MoD				
Favourable	Armed Forces	64	54	+ 10
	MoD	38	32	+ 6
Unfavourable	Armed Forces	5	6	- 1
	MoD	14	15	- 1
Neither	Armed Forces	31	39	- 8
	MoD	49	53	- 4
The requirement for Defence and Defence tasks				
UK needs strong Armed Forces		80	81	- 1
Confidence in the ability of UK Armed Forces to defend UK		85	82	+ 3
UK Armed Forces help make the world a safer place		73	71	+ 2
Confidence in the ability of UK Armed Forces to defend overseas territories		81	74	+ 7
Confidence in the ability of UK Armed Forces to protect UK Overseas economic interests		70	61	+ 9
Characteristics of the Armed Forces and Ministry of Defence				
UK Armed Forces have the highest professional standards		69	70	- 1
UK Armed Forces are well equipped		37	53	- 16
UK Armed Forces look after their people		61	63	- 2
UK Armed Forces recruit, train and promote their best people regardless of race, gender, religion or sexual orientation		50	56	- 6
UK Armed Forces make a positive contribution to local communities		44	47	- 3
MoD and UK Armed Forces carry out their activities with due regard for the environment		26	36	- 10
MoD is as open as it can be about its activities		31	37	- 6
MoD gives taxpayer value for money (previously "spends taxpayers' money wisely")		34	26	+ 8

INTERNAL COMMUNICATION

326. Good internal communication is vital. It is inseparable from our determination to remain a top class employer who values its people. We are committed to keeping all of our staff, military and civilian, in touch with the latest developments in Defence and the Forces, providing our people with information which is honest, straightforward and timely. Our internal research confirms that the best way to disseminate important information is through the chain of command (or line-management), by the routine cascade from managers to their staff. We support commanders and line managers in briefing their people through a range of corporate publications that complement our official guidance, notices, instructions and briefings:

- The three Armed Services have their own websites, intranets and official publications (RN Broadsheet and Navy News, SOLDIER, RAF News), along with separate channels for internal briefing;
- The MoD maintains a corporate in-house news and information service which provides electronic briefing notes, updates to our public website and intranet and which produces Focus, our monthly Defence newspaper;
- Other constituent parts of the Department, from the largest agencies to smallest branches and units, have their own internal channels for disseminating messages;
- Our major internal change programmes have their own bespoke communication plans, making use of the above channels to get their messages across, along with posters, road shows and other media.

327. We believe our in-house corporate publications to be among the best in their class. For 2005, both halves of the MoD's corporate news service – paper and electronic – picked up separate Communicators In Business "Awards of Excellence" in their respective classes. SOLDIER gained four similar awards, including awards for best news photograph and for best feature, whilst Navy News was runner-up in the best feature category, and RAF News was recognised in the best externally-available newspaper category. In March 2006, the Royal Navy's IC DVD 'Two-Six' picked up Gold and Silver awards at the International Visual Communications Association ceremony, benchmarked against the industry's finest.

REPUTATION AMONG SERVICE AND CIVILIAN PERSONNEL

328. We periodically monitor how our own people feel about Defence and the Armed Forces. The most recent information we have (from Spring 2005) showed very high levels of support among Service personnel and MoD civil servants for our top level objective that the MoD and Armed Forces are a force for good in the world. Detailed results are available from the MoD website. We aim to conduct further research later this year.

FURTHER SOURCES OF INFORMATION

329. Additional Information on Reputation is available from the following sources:
- detailed Opinion Surveys published on www.mod.uk;
- Defence image database at www.defenceimagedatabase.mod.uk;
- *Navy News* at www.navynews.co.uk;
- *Soldier Magazine* at www.soldiermagazine.co.uk;
- *RAF News* at www.rafnews.co.uk.

Essay: Press Reporting of Operations

The world has witnessed highly significant changes to the size and nature of the media in recent years. Competing national and global news organisations have grown rapidly in number. Digital technology means ever faster transmission of reports, images and film, to satisfy a sharp increase in public appetite for 24-hour news. The mobile telephone can capture footage that in minutes becomes the focus of breaking news, and in turn can broadcast that news back to its owner. We are responding to these changes, as we must. The Armed Forces are a continual source of media interest, generating coverage which in turn influences their public reputation, locally, nationally and throughout the world. Media reports can impact on the security of personnel deployed in theatre, and the environment in which they do their business.

Military operations present difficult and often dangerous work for journalists. The MoD has raised its efforts to understand their requirements, and to provide better support to them in their coverage. Although journalists usually work to an editorial agenda, experience has shown that where we provide them with adequate support in theatre, their reports reflect a better understanding of the reality of operations. A major development has been the establishment of the Defence Media Operations Centre at RAF Uxbridge in Middlesex. Comprising largely military personnel, its main task is to have two 10-strong Joint Media Operations Teams (JMOT) ready to move at 48 hours' notice to support reporters and film crews as they arrive in theatre.

In October 2005, in the wake of the devastating earthquakes in Pakistan-controlled Kashmir, a JMOT deployed with UK Forces, to support the large numbers of media arriving in the region. Liaising with the UK and Pakistani authorities, the team arranged to airlift reporters and film crews into some of the worst affected – and otherwise inaccessible – areas. This led to vivid reporting on the humanitarian crisis, reaching the homes of potential aid donors throughout the world. The arrival of the England cricket team in Pakistan further illustrated the ability of media operations teams on the ground to harness creative opportunities. Michael Vaughan and Marcus Trescothick agreed to help distribute aid to the stricken villages of Bagh and Rawalakot in an RAF Chinook, extending the media coverage into a number of specialist sport news channels.

The media operations teams are equipped with state-of-the-art technology, including handheld cameras, Steady Cam, and the Avid Pro editing suite, to capture audio, film and stills of the British Forces in theatre. This enables us to supply news organisations throughout the world with accurate, high-quality material that would otherwise be difficult to obtain. In eight months from April 2005, more than 1,500 MoD film clips reached around 30 countries, including footage of the Royal Navy rescue of a Russian submarine off the Kamchatka Peninsula.

More robust media operations arrangements in-theatre have been backed up with improvements in Head Office in Whitehall. The press office 'operations team' has been strengthened, press officers are encouraged to gain experience of working in-theatre, and an enhanced planning team produces media plans for forthcoming events, increasingly in close liaison with other Whitehall departments.

The Iraqi parliamentary elections in December 2005, for instance, posed opportunities but also difficulties and danger for Western journalists. The Department for International Development, the Foreign Office, MoD and Iraqi officials together developed a handling plan for getting reporters and film crews to locations around the country. A media operations team deployed to Baghdad where, working with military authorities, and liaising with the US State Department to ensure consistency, they were able to ensure comprehensive coverage.

Early contact with journalists to explain fully the background to an operation and its practical challenges usually reaps benefits. Advance planning for the making of Jane Corbin's 19 March Panorama report on Iraq allowed us to arrange an interview with the Defence Secretary, background briefings from government officials and an escorted 10-day programme of interviews and visits. It resulted in a report which, while critical of Iraq's infrastructure and security situation, was fair and balanced.

A media crew and JMOT minders take cover during a mortar attack in Iraq

Media imperatives remain balanced between information, newsworthiness and entertainment. There is a continual challenge for MoD to keep up with the pace of reporting, which is accelerating as the number of competing media organisations grows. Lack of support and information can have an adverse effect on news coverage, as illustrated by the rapidly unfolding events in Basra on 19 September 2005, during negotiations to release two members of the British Forces from Jameat police station. Lack of clarity over what had happened, combined with dramatic footage of the petrol-bombing of British armoured vehicles outside the station that were broadcast globally within minutes of the incident, and rumours of insurgents working within the Iraqi security forces, led to conflicting reports and adverse speculation over the future of the British Forces in Basra. This proved particularly challenging for the press office in Whitehall in their handling of journalists' enquiries. But it also showed how such challenges can be overcome where an effort is made to help the media. Soon after the incident, interviews were arranged with the two soldiers filmed escaping from their blazing vehicle. These generated favourable human interest stories detailing the soldiers' courageous handling of the situation.

The media continue to present new challenges and new opportunities. The growth of broadband internet, in particular, offers the potential for more sophisticated provision of electronic news. Work to create more dynamic working relations with the UK regional media continues. And in Iraq and Afghanistan, the post-conflict growth of radio, television and print periodicals is providing greater scope to communicate with local populations in the areas where we operate. We will continue to develop our practices to make best use of this fast-changing environment.

Departmental Resource Accounts

2005-06

SECTION 2:

Notes to the Accounts

THE ANNUAL REPORT

History and Background

The present Ministry of Defence (MoD), the Department, was formed by the amalgamation in 1964 of the Ministry of Defence, the Admiralty, the War Office and the Air Ministry, and the inclusion in 1971 of the Ministry of Aviation Supply. In 1973, the operations of the Atomic Weapons Establishment were transferred from the UK Atomic Energy Authority to the MoD.

Principal Activity

The principal activity of the Department is to deliver security for the people of the United Kingdom and the Overseas Territories by defending them, including against terrorism, and act as a force for good by strengthening international peace and stability. This is achieved by working together to produce battle-winning people and equipment that are:

- fit for the challenge of today,
- ready for the tasks of tomorrow, and
- capable of building for the future.

Further definition of the Departmental Objectives in terms of outputs is given in the Statement of Operating Costs by Departmental Aim and Objectives and in its supporting Note to the Accounts – Note 24.

Departmental Boundary[1]

At 31 March 2006, the Department consisted of 13 (2004-05:12) Top Level Budget (TLB) Holders (detailed in Note 2 to the accounts – The Analysis of Net Resource Outturn) responsible for providing forces and support services required for a modern defence force. Within these TLBs, there were 55 (2004-05: 69) reporting entities known as management groupings; the reduction is a result of the ongoing process of reform of the finance function: the 'Simplify and Improve' initiative.

There are 20 on-vote Defence Agencies (listed in Note 36), a reduction of 6 from 2004-05 following the removal of agency status on 1 April 2005 from: the Warship Support Agency, the Medical Supplies Agency, the Defence Dental Agency, Queen Victoria School, the Defence Geographic and Imagery Intelligence Agency and the Defence Intelligence and Security Centre. Defence Agencies publish their own accounts. All on-vote agencies are also management groupings, except for the Defence Procurement Agency and Defence Estates which are TLBs, and the Disposal Services Agency and Naval Recruiting and Training Agency, which form part of larger management groupings. Further information relating to the Defence Agencies can be found at Annex E.

Also included within the Departmental Boundary are Advisory Non-Departmental Public Bodies (NDPBs) sponsored by the Department; these are listed at Note 36.

There are 5 (2004-05: 5) Executive Defence Agencies established as Trading Funds, and owned by the Secretary of State for Defence, at 31 March 2006. These Trading Funds produce their own accounts and fall outside the Departmental Boundary. Further details are at Note 15 – Investments and Note 32 – Related Party Transactions.

The Department also sponsors 6 Executive Non Departmental Public Bodies (NDPBs), which are self accounting and produce their own accounts. They receive Grants-in-Aid from the MoD and fall outside the Departmental Boundary. Further details are at Note 32 – Related Party Transactions.

The Oil and Pipelines Agency is a Public Corporation sponsored by the Department, which falls outside the Departmental Boundary

On 10 February 2006, QinetiQ Group plc was successfully floated on the London Stock Exchange, via an Initial Public Offering (IPO). The IPO completed the process of transforming the MoD in-house research and development organisation into an international defence technology and security company. QinetiQ Group plc is outside the Departmental Boundary; details of the MoD's remaining shareholding in the company are set out at Note 15 – Investments and Note 32 – Related Party Transactions.

With effect from 1 April 2005, the provisions for civil nuclear liabilities were transferred to the Nuclear Decommissioning Authority; sponsored by the Department of Trade and Industry. The effect of this 'Machinery of Government Change' has been reflected by re-stating the relevant opening balances and prior year operating cost statement. Further details are at Note 33 – Restatement of Balance Sheet and Operating Cost Statement at 31 March 2005.

[1]The Departmental Boundary in this context relates to the boundary of the Departmental Resource Accounts.

Pension Liabilities

The transactions and balances of the Armed Forces Pension Scheme (AFPS) (including the Non-Regular Permanent Staff Pension Scheme, the Army Careers Officers Pension Scheme and the new Reserve Forces Pension Scheme) and the Armed Forces Compensation Scheme are not consolidated in these financial statements. The report and accounts of the AFPS are prepared separately; further information is available on the Website: *www.official-documents.co.uk/document/hc0506/hc02/0286/0286.asp.*

The Department's share of the transactions and balances of other pension schemes to which employees belong (e.g. under Civil Service Pension (CSP) arrangements, the Department of Health, Social Services and Public Safety Superannuation Scheme and the Teachers' Superannuation Scheme) is also not consolidated in these accounts; separate accounts are prepared for the schemes and details can be found on the following websites:
www.civilservice-pensions.gov.uk/scheme_information/facts_and_figures/index.asp
www.dfes.gov.uk/aboutus/reports/
www.official-documents.co.uk/document/hc0506/hc04/0492/0492.asp

Further information on the various pension schemes can be found in the Remuneration Report and at Note 9 – Staff Numbers and Costs.

Future Developments

The Department has comprehensive efficiency and change programmes that extend right across the Department and affect every employee. The details of many of these programmmes are set out in the section on Efficiency and Change in the Annual Performance Report, which forms the first part of the MoD Annual Report and Accounts.

Progress on the collocation of the operational Command headquarters and the personnel & training headquarters of the three Services has continued. The Fleet and 2nd Sea Lord organisations merged on 1 April 2006 and collocated in a unified Headquarters in Portsmouth, creating a single Naval Top Level Budget. The first stage of the collocation of the headquarters of Strike Command and RAF Personnel and Training Command at High Wycombe will be complete by October 2006. Project Hyperion is taking forward the re-organisation of the Army's Land and Adjutant General Commands with progressive collocation to a new Land Forces Headquarters planned to be completed by March 2009.

The process of organisation review continues to identify opportunities to reduce the number of on vote Agencies. With effect from 1 April 2006, agency status was removed from: the Naval Recruiting and Training Agency, the Army Training and Recruiting Agency and the RAF Training Group Defence Agency as these training organisations became an integral part of their respective Services' Top Level Budgets. The MoD currently has in hand a major programme of efficiency and business change including extensive organisational restructuring and rationalisation. As a result of this and other factors, the number of agencies is likely to continue to reduce in the future.

The Joint Personnel Administration (JPA) will modernise the personnel management and administration of the Armed Forces by harmonising and simplifying a range of personnel policies and processes and by introducing new information systems. JPA began its roll-out, to the RAF, in April 2006.

The Defence Resource Management Programme aims to simplify and improve current financial processes, structures and systems to reduce costs and improve decision-making. As part of the Programme, a Shared Service Centre for accounts receivable was established in December 2005 and extended to cover fixed asset processing in April 2006.

From April 2006, all intangible and tangible fixed assets and related provisions and reserves will be transferred to Single Balance Sheet Owners based on the category of asset managed:

- Land and Buildings – Defence Estates
- Single Use Military Equipment – Defence Logistics Organisation
- Plant & Machinery – Defence Logistics Organisation
- Transport – Defence Logistics Organisation
- IT & Communications – Defence Communication Services Agency
- Assets Under Construction (excluding Land & Buildings) – Defence Procurement Agency

Management

The Ministers who had responsibility for the Department during the year and the composition of the Defence Management Board (DMB) during the year ended 31 March 2006 are shown on pages 171 to 172 in the Remuneration Report.

Fixed Assets

Changes in fixed asset values during the year are summarised in Notes 13, 14 and 15 (Intangible Assets, Tangible Fixed Assets and Investments) to the accounts. Note 1 – Statement of Accounting Policies provides details of the accounting policies relating to fixed assets.

Research and Development

Research and development expenditure is incurred mainly for the future benefit of the Department. Such expenditure is primarily incurred on the development of new fighting equipment and on the improvement of the effectiveness and capability of existing fighting equipment.

In accordance with SSAP13, "Accounting for Research and Development" (as adapted for the public sector by HM Treasury's Financial Reporting Manual (FReM), paragraphs 5.3.6 to 5.3.8), amounts spent on research are not capitalised, and certain development expenditure is expensed. The amounts are included at Note 10 – Other Operating Costs.

Capitalised development expenditure is included in Intangible Assets, where appropriate, and shown in Note 13.

Net Expenditure

The Operating Cost Statement shows net expenditure of £34,393,535,000 which has been charged to the General Fund. Cash voted by Parliament and drawn down for the provision of Defence Capability (RfR 1), Conflict Prevention (RfR 2) and War Pensions Benefits (RfR 3) amounting to £31,262,178,000 has been credited to the General Fund (Note 21).

Dividends

Details of any dividends and loan interest received on investments can be found at Notes 11, 12 and 15 (Income, Net Interest Payable and Investments) to the accounts.

Payments to Suppliers

The Department's bills, with the exception of some payments to suppliers by units locally, are paid through the Defence Bills Agency (DBA). In 2005-06, the DBA met its target by paying 99.99% of all correctly submitted bills within eleven calendar days, ensuring that the Department is in compliance with its statutory obligation under the Late Payment of Commercial Debts (Interest) Act 1998. Commercial debt interest paid during the year amounted to £14,708.89 and included interest paid by units locally of £48 (2004-05: £63).

Departmental Reporting Cycle

The MoD's main Departmental Report presented to Parliament each year comprises the Ministry of Defence Annual Performance Report (which forms the first section of the Annual Report and Accounts and sets out the MoD's performance, against the objectives stated in the Statement of Operating Costs by Departmental Aim and Objectives, over the year and developments since the year end, where appropriate) and The Government's Expenditure Plans: Ministry of Defence, which sets out planned expenditure over the following year. The MoD's financial performance is also reported to Parliament in the explanatory memorandum to the Main Estimates, and in the Public Expenditure Outturn White Paper. Performance against Public Service Agreement and Efficiency targets is reported to Parliament during the year in the Autumn Performance Report and The Government's Expenditure Plans: Ministry of Defence.

Post Balance Sheet Events

A Ministerial announcement on 10 May 2006, set out the outcome of the work on the composition and location of the post-normalisation garrison in Northern Ireland. This included the associated timelines for further base closures and announced the start of consultation with the trades unions on the future requirement for civilian staff for a peacetime garrison.

On 3 July 2006, the Secretary of State announced publication of the MoD's "Enabling Acquisition Change" report. This included a recommendation that the Defence Procurement Agency and the Defence Logistics Organisation should be merged to create a new organisation whose core function is delivery of equipment and support operations to the Front Line. It is the intention that the majority of the recommendations in the report will be implemented by April 2007, although the bedding in of the new intergrated procurement and support organisation will not be complete until April 2008.

Financial Instruments

The Department does not trade or enter into any speculative transactions in foreign currencies. Forward contract commitments entered into to cover future expenditure in foreign currencies are stated in Note 28 – Financial Instruments.

Provision of Information and Consultation with Employees

The MoD has a strong Whitley committee structure through which employees' representatives, in the form of recognised industrial and non industrial trades unions (TUs), are consulted on and informed of all matters likely to affect our civilian personnel. This structure is supported by formal policy and procedures for consulting and informing TUs. We also advocate the development of informal relationships with the TUs to discuss ideas together. Our policy makes clear that consulting the TUs is not a substitute for dealing with personnel direct, and vice versa. Managers and project leaders, for example, are encouraged to use all media available, including cascade briefings, newsletters and intranet websites/email. In respect of Service personnel, the process operates through the chain of command, with no formal representation through the TUs. Additional information on communication, internal and external, is provided in the Reputation section of the Annual Performance Report which forms the first part of this Annual Report and Accounts.

MANAGEMENT COMMENTARY

Performance

The Annual Performance Report forms the first part of the MoD Annual Report and Accounts and provides the detailed information set out, as best practice, in the Accounting Standards Board's (ASB's) Reporting Statement: Operating and Financial Review.

The Performance Report uses the Defence Balanced Scorecard structure to:

- describe Defence strategies, objectives and activities, and how they are managed and delivered in the legislative, regulatory and external environments in which we operate;
- provide a forward looking view of performance and development for the reporting year, with sections on Current and Future Operations as well as Future Capabilities;
- set out information on the availability and use of resources, covering: finance, manpower and estate as well as aspects such as reputation and the Wider Markets Initiative.

The Annual Performance Report also describes some of the risks and uncertainties which might affect performance.

The Statement on Internal Control describes the Department's risk and control framework and its relationship to the Performance Management System. The Departmental approach to Performance Management is detailed in Annex D.

Environmental, Social, Community, Employee and Other Matters

The preface to the Annual Report and Accounts summarises senior managers' views of how the document sets out the Department's work to realise the Defence Vision, highlighting all relevant matters. Some specific aspects mentioned in the ASB's Reporting Statement that are covered by the Performance Report are:

- **Social and Community Issues** – included in the sections on: Current Operations e.g. Crisis Response Operations and Military Aid to the Civil Authorities; Wider Government e.g. Defence in the Wider Community and Young People: Building Skills and Raising Expectations; and the essay on Defence Youth Policy.
- **Environmental** – aspects are included in the Sustainable Development sections under Estate and Wider Government. Defence Estates also produce an annual publication about conservation of the natural and historic environment on the Defence Estate. The publication, Sanctuary, illustrates how the MoD is undertaking its responsibility for stewardship of the estate in the UK and overseas through its policies and their subsequent implementation; the latest publication is available on the website: *www.defence-estates.mod.uk/publications/sanctuary/sanctuary2005.pdf.*
- **Employees** – information is provided in the sections on: Manpower, Personnel Management, Health and Safety and Future Personnel Plans and the essays on Diversity and the Care of Injured Personnel. Information on policy and numbers of disabled staff can be found in the Manpower section and at Annex F – Government Standards.
- **Performance Indicators** – these are included at the start of each section of the Performance Report where the Objective, Public Service Targets, Performance Measures and the Assessment against the measures are set out. Additional information can be found in the MoD Departmental Plan 2005-2009 available on the Website: *www.mod.uk/DefenceInternet/AboutDefence/CorporatePublications/BusinessPlans* and in the Summary of performance against SR2004 Public Service Agreement Objectives and Targets at the beginning of the Performance Report.
- **Contractual Arrangements** – some of the Department's major contractual commitments are detailed in Note 27 to the accounts – Private Finance Initiative (PFI) Commitments. The Defence Science and Technology Laboratory, the UK Hydrographic Office, the Met Office, the Defence Aviation Repair Agency and ABRO are Executive Defence Agencies financed by Trading Fund; they provide essential services to the Department. Further information on Trading Funds is at Annex E to the Annual Report and Accounts. Details of significant contracts relating to the management of the Defence Estate are included in the Estate section of the Performance Report.

- **Spending Review** – the financing implications of significant changes following the Department's Spending Review are set out in The Government's Expenditure Plans 2005-06 to 2007-08: Ministry of Defence which, with the MoD Annual Report and Accounts, comprise the MoD's Departmental Report. The Government's Expenditure Plans 2005-06 to 2007-08: Ministry of Defence and the MoD Investment Strategy are available on the websites: *http://www.mod.uk/DefenceInternet/AboutDefence/CorporatePublications/BusinessPlans/GovernmentExpenditurePlans* and *http://www.mod.uk/DefenceInternet/AboutDefence/CorporatePublications/PolicyStrategy/DefenceDepartmentalInvestmentStrategy.htm*

- **Contingent Liabilities** Details of Contingent Liabilities disclosed under Financial Reporting Standard (FRS) 12 and additional liabilities included for Parliamentary Reporting and Accountability are at Notes 29 and 30 to these accounts.

Financial Position

The Statement of Parliamentary Supply – Summary of Resource Outturn on Page 187 compares Estimate and Outturn (net total resources). A detailed explanation of the variances against the Departmental Expenditure Limit is shown in paragraphs 263-264 within Resources in the Performance Report.

Request for Resources (RfR) 1, Provision of Defence Capability, provides for expenditure primarily to meet the Ministry of Defence's operational support and logistics services costs and the costs of providing the equipment capability required by defence policy. Within RfR1, the Estimate and Outturn for Operating Appropriations in Aid are shown as equal amounts. Any Appropriations in Aid in excess of the estimate are shown at Note 6, and these will be surrendered to the Consolidated Fund. This RfR is made up from three different controls:

- Resource DEL, which consists of items such as pay, equipment support costs, fuel and administrative expenses, as well as non cash items such as depreciation, cost of capital and movements in the level of provisions;

- Annually Managed Expenditure, which covers programmes that are demand-led, or exceptionally volatile in a way that could not be controlled by the Department, and where the programmes are so large that the Department could not be expected to absorb the effects of volatility in its programme, such as movements in nuclear provisions; and

- Non Budget costs, items of expenditure which are subject to Parliamentary but not Treasury control, and therefore outside DEL and AME. The majority of the costs relate to changes in the discount rates for pensions and other long term liabilities.

The net outturn is £32,737,691,000 against an Estimate of £34,664,525,000, a variance of £1,926,834,000 underspent. The variations were underspends of £374,656,000 against Resource DEL, £263,013,000 in AME, and £1,289,165,000 in Non Budget. The principal explanations for the underspend were reviews of fixed assets, capital spares and stock, resulting in lower depreciation and other impairment charges. The underspend in AME was due principally to the transfer of civil nuclear liabilities to the newly formed Nuclear Decommissioning Authority, and that in Non Budget to the lower than expected charges when the discount rate was changed, and again the transfer of nuclear liabilities to the Nuclear Decommissioning Authority.

RfR2, Conflict Prevention, shows net outturn of £1,055,848,000 against an Estimate of £1,101,276,000, a variance of £45,428,000. A contingency of £69,000,000 was included in the Spring Supplementary Estimate for reasons of prudence as the often rapidly changing operational situation means that costs are difficult to forecast. In the event, only a proportion of this contingency was needed.

RfR3, War Pensions Benefits shows net outturn of £1,068,595,000 against an Estimate of £1,072,972,000, an underspend of £4,377,000. This RfR provides for the payment of war disablement and war widows' pensions in accordance with relevant legislation, and this is all Annually Managed Expenditure. The costs of administering war pensions are borne by RfR1.

The non-operating Appropriations in Aid show a net outturn of £374,320,000 against an overly ambitious Estimate of £607,041,000.

The Net Cash Requirement shows a net outturn of £30,603,297,000 against an Estimate of £31,501,992,000, an underspend of £898,695,000. This is because the creditors at the end of the year were higher than had been forecast at the time the Spring Supplementary Estimate was submitted, and there was £146,000,000 of contingency in RfR2, for resource costs and urgent operational requirements, that in the event was not required.

Other Areas

The Department's Accounts include a note (Note 31) on Losses and Special Payments. The nature of the losses and special payments, as defined in Government Accounting, varies from year to year depending on the circumstances arising and decisions made by the Department during the year. Cases brought forward from last year are shown separately in order properly to identify the cases arising during the year. Further details on this Statement are included in the Resources Section of the Annual Performance Report.

The Department is required to have a professional revaluation of its tangible fixed assets every five years, and manages this process through a rolling programme. The current revaluation programme is due to complete in 2007-08 and is currently under review to ensure that it is being carried out effectively and at minimum cost.

Details of directorships and other significant interests held by Ministers are set out in The Register of Lords' Interests and The Register of Members' Interests which are available on the UK Parliament website:
http://www.parliament.uk/about_commons/register_of_members__interests.cfm

Details of directorships and other significant interests held by Defence Management Board members are included at Note 32 – Related Party Transactions.

Auditor

The financial statements for the Department are audited by the Comptroller and Auditor General under the Government Resources and Accounts Act 2000. The Certificate and Report of the Comptroller and Auditor General on the financial statements are set out on pages 185 to 186. The audit fee is disclosed in Note 10 – Other Operating Costs.

Statement as to Disclosure of Information to Auditors

So far as I, the Accounting Officer, am aware, there is no relevant audit information of which the Department's auditors are unaware, and I have taken all the steps that I ought to have taken to make myself aware of any relevant audit information and to establish that the Department's auditors are aware of that information.

Bill Jeffrey
Accounting Officer **11 July 2006**

REMUNERATION REPORT

Remuneration Policy

The Review Body on Senior Salaries provides independent advice to the Prime Minister and the Secretary of State for Defence on the remuneration of senior civil servants and senior officers of the Armed Forces.

The Review Body also advises the Prime Minister from time to time on the pay, pensions and allowances of Members of Parliament; on Peers' allowances; and on the pay, pensions and allowances of Ministers and others whose pay is determined by the Ministerial and Other Salaries Act 1975.

In reaching its recommendations, the Review Body has regard to the following considerations:

- the need to recruit, retain and motivate suitably able and qualified people to exercise their different responsibilities;
- regional/local variations in labour markets and their effects on the recruitment and retention of staff;
- Government policies for improving the public services including the requirement on departments to meet the output targets for the delivery of departmental services;
- the funds available to departments as set out in the Government's departmental expenditure limits; and
- the Government's inflation target.

The Review Body takes account of the evidence it receives about wider economic considerations and the affordability of its recommendations.

Further information about the work of the Review Body can be found at *www.ome.uk.com.*

There is an established departmental procedure for the appointment of all Non-Executive Directors. This requires a visibly fair and open recruitment and selection process with appointment on merit, thus mirroring the Civil Service Commissioners' Recruitment Code for permanent employees to the Civil Service.

For the Non-Executive Directors appointed to the Defence Management Board, the Department has employed recruitment consultants to search for suitable candidates based upon a specification drawn up by senior officials. Short listed candidates are then interviewed by a selection panel (Permanent Under Secretary and Chief of the Defence Staff) with the successful candidate chosen on merit and appointed to the Board for a period of three years.

Performance and Reward

The basic salary and annual increases of the civilian members of the Defence Management Board (DMB), which could include a bonus payment, are performance related and are set by the Permanent Secretaries Remuneration Committee and the MoD's Main Pay Committee.

Pay and management arrangements for members of the Senior Civil Service (SCS) reward individuals for delivery and personal achievement. These arrangements include an objective-setting regime complementary to the Department's performance management system and a performance-related incremental pay system.

Up to two thirds of the SCS population will receive a bonus with the highest level of award limited to the top ten percent assessed as making the greatest contribution; the ceiling for the bonus payments is five percent of the SCS paybill.

All senior military officers (except for Legal Branch 2-star officers, medical and dental officers and those in the Chaplaincy branches) are paid under the Performance Management and Pay System. Depending on their performance, individuals can be awarded a double increment, a single increment or no increment and progress accordingly up the incremental pay range for their rank. The award of increments is recommended by the Senior Officers' Remuneration Committee, chaired by the Department's Permanent Under Secretary.

Whilst Non-Executive remuneration is not directly linked to performance, in part to avoid any suggestion that an employee/employer relationship exists, Non-Executive Directors' (NED) performance should nevertheless be reviewed annually. The aim of any review is to consider the impact of the NED on the performance of the board, recognise the contribution of the NED and identify ways this could be improved, and provide feedback.

Senior Managers' Contracts

Civil Service appointments are made in accordance with the Civil Service Commissioners' Recruitment Code, which requires appointments to be on merit on the basis of fair and open competition but also includes the circumstances when appointments may otherwise be made. Further information about the work of the Civil Service Commissioners can be found at *www.civilservicecommissioners.gov.uk.*

Unless otherwise stated below, the officials covered by this report hold appointments which are open-ended until they reach the normal retiring age of 60. Early termination, other than for misconduct, would result in the individual receiving compensation as set out in the Civil Service Compensation Scheme.

The Chief of Defence Procurement (CDP) and the Chief Scientific Adviser (CSA) are recruited on three year fixed term appointments. The conditions covering the termination of their employment are set out in their contract documents. The contract for CDP has been renewed for a further two years and now ends in 2008.

Non-Executive Directors are not employees and, therefore, do not have a contractual relationship with the Department but rather are appointees who receive a Letter of Appointment setting out amongst others: their role, period of appointment, standards and any remuneration.

The Chief of the Defence Staff, Vice Chief of the Defence Staff, Single-Service Chiefs of Staff and Chief of Defence Logistics are appointed on the recommendation of the Secretary of State for Defence to the Prime Minister. The final approval of the appointee lies with Her Majesty The Queen.

Senior Military members of the Management Board hold appointments which are competed for by the 3 Services. Once selected for the appointment, they will usually hold the post for between 3 and 4 years.

Management

Ministers who had responsibility for the Department during the year were:

Secretary of State for Defence

The Right Honourable Dr John Reid MP was appointed as Secretary of State for Defence on 6 May 2005; prior to this, the Secretary of State for Defence was The Right Honourable Geoffrey Hoon MP.

Minister of State for the Armed Forces

The Right Honourable Adam Ingram MP.

Parliamentary Under Secretary of State for Defence and Minister for Defence Procurement

Lord Drayson was appointed as Parliamentary Under Secretary of State for Defence and Minister for Defence Procurement on 10 May 2005, replacing The Lord Bach of Lutterworth.

Parliamentary Under Secretary of State for Defence and Minister for Veterans

Don Touhig MP was appointed as Parliamentary Under Secretary of State for Defence and Minister for Veterans on 10 May 2005, replacing Ivor Caplin MP.

Recent Ministerial Changes

On 6 May 2006, The Right Honourable Des Browne MP was appointed as Secretary of State for Defence, replacing The Right Honourable Dr John Reid MP, and Tom Watson MP was appointed Parliamentary Under Secretary of State for Defence and Minister for Veterans, replacing Don Touhig MP.

The composition of the Defence Management Board (DMB), as at 31 March 2006 was:

Permanent Under Secretary of State
Bill Jeffrey CB
(appointed 21 November 2005, following the retirement of Sir Kevin Tebbit KCB CMG).

Chief of the Defence Staff
General Sir Michael Walker GCB CMG CBE ADC Gen
(appointed 2 May 2003).

First Sea Lord and Chief of the Naval Staff
Admiral Sir Jonathon Band KCB ADC
(appointed 7 February 2006, replacing Admiral Sir Alan West GCB DSC ADC).

Chief of the General Staff
General Sir Mike Jackson GCB CBE DSO ADC Gen
(appointed 1 February 2003).

Chief of the Air Staff
Air Chief Marshal Sir Jock Stirrup GCB AFC ADC DSc FRAeS FCMI RAF
(appointed 1 August 2003).

Vice Chief of the Defence Staff
General Sir Timothy Granville-Chapman KCB CBE ADC Gen
(appointed 22 July 2005, replacing Air Chief Marshal Sir Anthony Bagnall KCB OBE FRAeS RAF).

Second Permanent Under Secretary of State
Ian Andrews CBE TD
(appointed 4 March 2002).

Chief of Defence Procurement
Sir Peter Spencer KCB
(appointed 1 May 2003 and re-appointed, for a 2 year period, on 1 May 2006).

Chief of Defence Logistics
General Sir Kevin O'Donoghue KCB CBE
(appointed 1 January 2005).

Chief Scientific Adviser
Professor Sir Roy Anderson FRS
(appointed 1 October 2004).

Finance Director
Trevor Woolley
(appointed to the Defence Management Board 24 June 2004).

Non-Executive Directors
Charles Miller Smith, Chairman of Scottish Power.
*Philippa Foster Back OBE, Director of the Institute of Business Ethics.

*Chairman of the Defence Audit Committee.

Recent Changes to the Defence Management Board
Air Chief Marshal Sir Jock Stirrup GCB AFC ADC DSc FRAeS FCMI RAF was appointed Chief of the Defence Staff on 28 April 2006.
Air Chief Marshal Sir Glenn Torpy KCB CBE DSO ADC BSc(Eng) FRAeS RAF was appointed Chief of the Air Staff on 13 April 2006.

Paul Skinner, Chairman of Rio Tinto plc and Rio Tinto Ltd was appointed Non Executive Director on 1 June 2006.

Ministerial Salaries, Allowances and Taxable Benefits

(This section has been subject to audit)

	2005-06 Salary* £	2005-06 Benefits-in-kind (to nearest £100)	2004-05 Salary £	2004-05 Benefits-in-kind (to nearest £100)
Secretary of State for Defence: The Rt Hon Dr John Reid MP (from 6 May 05)	67,653	Nil		
Full year equivalent salary	*74,902*			
The Rt Hon Geoffrey Hoon MP (to 6 May 05)	7,450	700	72,862	7,300
Full year equivalent salary	*74,902*			
Minister of State for the Armed Forces: The Rt Hon Adam Ingram MP	38,854	Nil	37,796	Nil
Parliamentary Under Secretary of State and Minister for Defence Procurement: Lord Drayson (from 10 May 05) †	Nil	Nil		
The Lord Bach of Lutterworth (to 9 May 05) ††	10,983	Nil	97,608	Nil
Full year equivalent salary	*102,138*			
Parliamentary Under Secretary of State for Defence and Minister for Veterans: Don Touhig MP (from 10 May 05)	26,320	Nil		
Full year equivalent salary	*29,491*			
Ivor Caplin MP (to 9 May 05)	3,171	Nil	28,688	Nil
Full year equivalent salary	*29,491*			

*Ministers who moved to different Departments were paid by MoD up to the end of the month in which they left; their new Department commenced paying them thereafter. Salary disclosures only cover the period during which individuals served as Ministers within the MoD.

† Lord Drayson does not receive the ministerial salary of £69,138 to which he is entitled.

†† Lords Ministers' Night Subsistence paid to The Lord Bach of Lutterworth was £3,548 in 2005-06 (2004-05: £30,353) and is included in the salary figures disclosed.

Ministers who, on leaving office, have not attained the age of 65 and are not appointed to a relevant Ministerial or other paid office within three weeks, are eligible for a severance payment. One payment was made in 2005-06 (2004-05 – Nil).

Ministers' Salary

'Salary' includes: gross salary; performance pay or bonuses; overtime; reserved rights to London weighting or London allowances; recruitment and retention allowances; private office allowances and any other allowance to the extent that it is subject to UK taxation.

The figures above are based on payments made by the Department and thus recorded in these accounts. In respect of Ministers in the House of Commons, the Department bears only the cost of the additional Ministerial remuneration; the salary for their services as an MP – £59,095 pa with effect from 1 April 2005 (£57,485 pa with effect from 1 April 2004) and various allowances to which they are entitled are borne centrally. The arrangements for Ministers in the House of Lords are different in that they do not receive a salary but rather an additional remuneration, which cannot be quantified separately from their Ministerial salaries. This total remuneration, as well as the allowances to which they are entitled, is normally paid by the Department and is therefore shown in full above.

Benefits-in-kind for Ministers

Ministers' private use of official cars is exempt under the rules governing the definition of taxable benefits-in-kind. Mr Hoon was provided with living accommodation and the value of the benefit is calculated in accordance with HM Revenue & Customs regulations. The value of the accommodation is exempt from tax but a taxable benefit is calculated in respect of the ancillary services (e.g. maintenance and utilities) provided; the value of the benefit is limited to 10% of Ministerial salary.

Ministerial Pensions

(This section has been subject to audit)

Figures for **2005-06 in bold**. The real increase in the value of the accrued pension compared to the 2004-05 value, is shown in italics (in bands of £2,500).

	Total Accrued Pension at Retirement as at 31 Mar 06 £000	CETV* at 31 Mar 05 or Date of Appointment if Later £000	CETV at 31 Mar 06 or on Cessation of Appointment if Earlier £000	Real Increase in CETV £000
Secretary of State for Defence:				
The Rt Hon Dr John Reid MP (from 6 May 05)	**10-15**	**141**	**181**	**28**
The Rt Hon Geoffrey Hoon, MP (to 6 May 05)	**10-15** *0-2.5*	**101****	**102**	**1**
Minister of State for the Armed Forces:				
The Rt Hon Adam Ingram MP	**5-10** *0-2.5*	**95****	**119**	**17**
Parliamentary Under Secretary of State and Minister for Defence Procurement:				
Lord Drayson (from 10 May 05)†	**Nil**	**Nil**	**Nil**	**Nil**
The Lord Bach of Lutterworth (to 9 May 05)	**5-10** *0-2.5*	**101**	**103**	**1**
Parliamentary Under Secretary of State for Defence and Minister for Veterans:				
Don Touhig MP (from 10 May 05)	**0-5**	**41**	**50**	**5**
Ivor Caplin MP (to 9 May 05)	**0-5** *0-2.5*	**21**	**22**	**0**

† Lord Drayson is not a member of the Parliamentary Contributory Pension Fund.
* CETV – Cash Equivalent Transfer Value.
** The factors used to calculate the CETV were revised on 1 April 2005 on the advice of the scheme's actuary. The CETV figures for 31 March 2005 have been recalculated using the new factors and in two cases this has led to changes to the figures published last year.

Pension benefits for Ministers are provided by the Parliamentary Contributory Pension Fund (PCPF). The scheme is statutory based (made under Statutory Instrument SI 1993 No 3253, as amended).

Those Ministers who are Members of Parliament are also entitled to an MP's pension under the PCPF. The arrangements for Ministers provide benefits on an 'average salary' basis with either a 1/50th or 1/40th accrual rate, taking account of all service as a Minister. The accrual rate has been 1/40th since 15 July 2002 but Ministers, in common with all other members of the PCPF, can opt to increase their accrual rate from 5 July 2001, or retain the 1/50th accrual rate and the lower rate of employee contribution.

Benefits for Ministers are payable at the same time as MPs' benefits become payable under the PCPF or, for those who are not MPs, on retirement from Ministerial office on or after age 65. Pensions are increased annually in line with changes in the Retail Prices Index. Members pay contributions of 6% of their Ministerial salary if they have opted for the 1/50th accrual rate, and 9% if they have opted for the 1/40th accrual rate. There is also an employer contribution paid by the Exchequer representing the balance of cost. This is currently 24% of the Ministerial salary.

The Cash Equivalent Transfer Value (CETV)

This is the actuarially assessed capitalised value of the pension scheme benefits accrued by a member at a particular point in time. The benefits valued are the member's accrued benefits and any contingent spouse's pension payable from the scheme. It is a payment made by a pension scheme or arrangement to secure pension benefits in another pension scheme when the member leaves a scheme and chooses to transfer the pension benefits they have accrued in their former scheme. The pension figures shown relate to the benefits that the individual has accrued as a consequence of their total Ministerial service, not just their current appointment as a Minister. CETVs are calculated within the guidelines and framework prescribed by the Institute and Faculty of Actuaries.

The Real Increase in the Value of the CETV

This reflects the increase in CETV effectively funded by the employer. It takes account of the increase in accrued pension due to inflation, contributions paid by the Minister (including the value of any benefits transferred from another pension scheme or arrangement) and uses common market valuation factors for the start and end of the period.

Defence Management Board – Salaries, Allowances and Taxable Benefits in Kind

(This section has been subject to audit)

	2005-06 Salary* £000	2005-06 Benefits-in-kind (to nearest £100)	2004-05 Salary £000	2004-05 Benefits-in-kind (to nearest £100)
Permanent Under Secretary of State Bill Jeffrey CB (from 21 Nov 05) *Full year equivalent salary*	55-60 *155-160*	10,800		
Permanent Under Secretary of State Sir Kevin Tebbit KCB CMG (to 11 Nov 05)** *Full year equivalent salary*	115-120 *180-185*	25,500	170-175	32,600
Chief of the Defence Staff General Sir Michael Walker GCB CMG CBE ADC Gen	200-205	38,000	185-190	33,400
First Sea Lord and Chief of the Naval Staff Admiral Sir Jonathon Band KCB ADC (from 7 Feb 06) *Full year equivalent salary*	20-25 *140-145*	3,900		
First Sea Lord and Chief of the Naval Staff Admiral Sir Alan West GCB DSC ADC (to 6 Feb 06) *Full year equivalent salary*	120-125 *145-150*	23,400	135-140	22,100
Chief of the General Staff General Sir Mike Jackson GCB CBE DSO ADC Gen	170-175	28,100	160-165***	22,500
Chief of the Air Staff Air Chief Marshal Sir Jock Stirrup GCB AFC ADC DSc FRAeS FCMI RAF	145-150	27,600	135-140	22,300
Vice Chief of the Defence Staff General Sir Timothy Granville-Chapman KCB CBE ADC Gen (from 22 Jul 05) *Full year equivalent salary*	95-100 *140-145*	18,400		

	2005-06 Salary* £000	2005-06 Benefits-in-kind (to nearest £100)	2004-05 Salary £000	2004-05 Benefits-in-kind (to nearest £100)
Vice Chief of the Defence Staff Air Chief Marshal Sir Anthony Bagnall KCB OBE FRAeS RAF (to 21 July 05) *Full year equivalent salary*	45-50 *145-150*	8,500	140-145	24,800
Second Permanent Under Secretary of State Ian Andrews CBE TD	135-140	25,700	130-135	29,000
Chief of Defence Procurement Sir Peter Spencer KCB	135-140	29,400	125-130	31,100
Chief of Defence Logistics General Sir Kevin O'Donoghue KCB CBE *Full year equivalent salary*	135-140	Nil	30-35 *110-115*	Nil
Chief Scientific Adviser Professor Sir Roy Anderson FRS *Full year equivalent salary*	135-140	18,900	60-65 *125-130*	10,900
Finance Director Trevor Woolley *Full year equivalent salary*	125-130	Nil	80-85 *105-110*	Nil
Non-Executive Directors	**Fees**		**Fees**	
Charles Miller Smith	25-30	Nil	25-30	Nil
Philippa Foster Back OBE	25-30	Nil	25-30	Nil

* Salary includes gross salary, performance pay and allowances paid.
** Sir Kevin Tebbit received a payment from the Civil Service Compensation Scheme.
*** The prior year salary figure has been restated.

Benefit in kind figures for civilian members of the DMB represent the value obtained from the private use of official cars. For Service members of the DMB, the benefit in kind represents the value obtained from the use of Official Service Residences. The Department has an arrangement with the HM Revenue and Customs where MoD pays the tax liability that would ordinarily be paid by the individual on the benefit in kind. The tax liability consists of income tax and, where applicable, employees' National Insurance Contributions. This tax liability is included in the figures disclosed to arrive at the full value of the benefit to the individual.

Defence Management Board – Pension Benefits

(This section has been subject to audit)

2005-06 figures are in bold. The real increase in the pension, from 2004-05, and where applicable the real increase in the lump sum payment, are shown in italics.

	Total Accrued Pension at Retirement as at 31 Mar 06 £000	CETV at 31 Mar 05 or Date of Appointment if Later* £000	CETV at 31 Mar 06 or on Cessation of Appointment if Earlier £000	Real Increase or (Decrease) in CETV £000
Permanent Under Secretary of State Bill Jeffrey CB (from 21 Nov 05)	Pension **65-70** *2.5-5* Lump Sum **195-200** *7.5-10*	**1,125**	**1,212**	**69**
Permanent Under Secretary of State Sir Kevin Tebbit KCB CMG (to 11 Nov 05)	Pension **75-80** *0-2.5* Lump Sum **225-230** *5-7.5*	**1,317**	**1,388**	**41**
Chief of the Defence Staff General Sir Michael Walker GCB CMG CBE ADC Gen	Pension **100-105** *2.5-5* Lump Sum **300-305** *5-10*	**1,533**	**1,604**	**52**
First Sea Lord and Chief of the Naval Staff Admiral Sir Jonathon Band KCB ADC (from 7 Feb 06)	Pension **70-75** Lump Sum **215-220**	**1,418**	**1,434**	**10**
First Sea Lord and Chief of the Naval Staff Admiral Sir Alan West GCB DSC ADC (to 6 Feb 06)	Pension **70-75** *2.5-5* Lump Sum **215-220** *10-12.5*	**1,331**	**1,405**	**69**
Chief of the General Staff General Sir Mike Jackson GCB CBE DSO ADC Gen	Pension **70-75** *0-2.5* Lump Sum **220-225** *5-7.5*	**1,134**	**1,161**	**30**
Chief of the Air Staff Air Chief Marshal Sir Jock Stirrup GCB AFC ADC DSc FRAeS FCMI RAF	Pension **70-75** *2.5-5* Lump Sum **215-220** *10-12.5*	**1,382**	**1,462**	**68**

	Total Accrued Pension at Retirement as at 31 Mar 06 £000	CETV at 31 Mar 05 or Date of Appointment if Later* £000	CETV at 31 Mar 06 or on Cessation of Appointment if Earlier £000	Real Increase or (Decrease) in CETV £000
Vice Chief of the Defence Staff General Sir Timothy Granville-Chapman KCB CBE ADC Gen (from 22 Jul 05)	Pension **70-75** Lump Sum **210-215**	**1,241**	**1,184**	**45**
Vice Chief of the Defence Staff Air Chief Marshal Sir Anthony Bagnall KCB OBE FRAeS RAF (to 21 Jul 05)	Pension **70-75** *0-2.5* Lump Sum **215-220** *0-2.5*	**1,188**	**1,182**	**(7)**
Second Permanent Under Secretary of State Ian Andrews CBE TD	Pension **50-55** *2.5-5* Lump Sum **125-130** *5-7.5*	**686**	**789**	**73**
Chief of Defence Procurement Sir Peter Spencer KCB	Pension **5-10** *0-2.5* Lump Sum **N/A**	**47**	**75**	**33**
Chief of Defence Logistics General Sir Kevin O'Donoghue KCB CBE**	Pension **65-70** *10-12.5* Lump Sum **205-210** *30-32.5*	**1,104**	**1,298**	**190**
Chief Scientific Adviser Professor Sir Roy Anderson FRS	Pension **0-5** *0-2.5* Lump Sum **N/A**	**12**	**39**	**32**
Finance Director Trevor Woolley	Pension **40-45** *0-2.5* Lump Sum **130-135** *5-7.5*	**581**	**641**	**31**
Non-Executive Directors Charles Miller Smith Philippa Foster Back OBE	 N/A N/A	 N/A N/A	 N/A N/A	 N/A N/A

* The CETV as at 31 Mar 05 for members of the Principal Civil Service Pension Scheme has been recalculated on the advice of the Scheme Actuary.
** The prior year calculation of pension was incorrect. The comparison above reflects the increase in pension and lump sum in relation to the correctly calculated 2004-05 figures.

Principal Civil Service Pension Scheme (PCSPS)

Pension benefits are provided through the Civil Service pension arrangements. From 1 October 2002, civil servants may be in one of three statutory based 'final salary' defined benefit schemes (classic, premium, and classic plus). The schemes are unfunded with the cost of benefits met by monies voted by Parliament each year. Pensions payable under classic, premium, and classic plus are increased annually in line with changes in the Retail Prices Index. New entrants after 1 October 2002 may choose between membership of premium or joining a good quality 'money purchase' stakeholder arrangement with a significant employer contribution (partnership pension account).

Employee contributions are set at the rate of 1.5% of pensionable earnings for classic and 3.5% for premium and classic plus. Benefits in classic accrue at the rate of 1/80th of pensionable salary for each year of service. In addition, a lump sum equivalent to three years' pension is payable on retirement. For premium, benefits accrue at the rate of 1/60th of final pensionable earnings for each year of service. Unlike classic, there is no automatic lump sum although members may give up (commute) some of their pension to provide a lump sum. Classic plus is essentially a variation of premium, but with benefits in respect of service before 1 October 2002 calculated broadly in the same way as in classic.

The partnership pension account is a stakeholder pension arrangement. The employer makes a basic contribution of between 3% and 12.5% (depending on the age of the member) into a stakeholder pension product chosen by the employee from a selection of approved products. The employee does not have to contribute but, where they do make contributions, the employer will match these up to a limit of 3% of pensionable salary (in addition to the employer's basic contribution). Employers also contribute a further 0.8% of pensionable salary to cover the cost of centrally-provided risk benefit cover (death in service and ill health retirement).

Further details about the Civil Service pension arrangements can be found at the website *www.civilservice-pensions.gov.uk.*

Armed Forces Pension Scheme (AFPS)

From 6 April 2005, a new Armed Forces Pension Scheme (known as AFPS 05) was introduced for all new members of the Armed Forces; those in service before this date have been given the opportunity to transfer, from AFPS-75, to the new scheme. Both schemes are defined benefit, salary-related, contracted out, occupational pension schemes. The AFPS is non-contributory for members; the costs of benefits accruing for each year of service are met by the employer at an 'all ranks' rate approximately equivalent to 31% of total pay. Members are entitled to a taxable pension for life and a tax-free pension lump sum if they leave the Armed Forces at or beyond either the Early Departure Point or the Immediate Pension Point. If a scheme member leaves before these points, they will be entitled to a preserved pension and related lump sum.

Further details about Armed Forces Pensions can be found at the website *www.mod.uk/DefenceInternet/AboutDefence/Issues/Pensions/*

Cash Equivalent Transfer Value

A Cash Equivalent Transfer Value (CETV) is the actuarially assessed capitalised value of the pension scheme benefits accrued by a member at a particular point in time. The benefits valued are the member's accrued benefits and any contingent spouse's pension payable from the scheme. A CETV is a payment made by a pension scheme or arrangement to secure pension benefits in another pension scheme or arrangement when the member leaves a scheme and chooses to transfer the benefits accrued in their former scheme. The pension figures shown relate to the benefits that the individual has accrued as a consequence of their total membership of the pension scheme, not just their service in a senior capacity to which disclosure applies. The pension details include the value of any pension benefit in another scheme or arrangement which the individual has transferred to the AFPS or Civil Service pension arrangements and for which a transfer payment commensurate with the additional pension liabilities being assumed has been received. They also include any additional pension benefit accrued to the member as a result of their purchasing additional years of pension service in the scheme at their own cost.

CETVs are calculated within the guidelines and framework prescribed by the Institute and Faculty of Actuaries. The factors used to calculate the CETV for members of the PCSPS were revised on 1 April 2005 on the advice of the Scheme Actuary. The CETV figures for 31 March 2005 have been recalculated using the new factors (in some cases this has led to changes to the figures published last year) and restated on the same basis as the CETV figures for 31 March 2006.

Real Increase in CETV

This reflects the increase in CETV effectively funded by the employer. It takes account of the increase in accrued pension due to inflation, contributions paid by the employee (including the value of any benefits transferred from another pension scheme or arrangement) and uses common market valuation factors for the start and end of the period.

Bill Jeffrey
Accounting Officer **11 July 2006**

STATEMENT OF ACCOUNTING OFFICER'S RESPONSIBILITIES

Under the Government Resources and Accounts Act 2000, HM Treasury has directed the Ministry of Defence to prepare for each financial year resource accounts detailing the resources acquired, held or disposed of during the year and the use of resources by the Department during the year.

The accounts are prepared on an accruals basis and must give a true and fair view of the state of affairs of the Department and of its net resource outturn, resources applied to objectives, recognised gains and losses, and cash flows for the financial year.

In preparing the accounts, the Accounting Officer is required to comply with the requirements of the *Government Financial Reporting Manual* and in particular to:

- observe the Accounts Direction issued by HM Treasury, including the relevant accounting and disclosure requirements, and apply suitable accounting policies on a consistent basis;

- make judgements and estimates on a reasonable basis;

- state whether applicable accounting standards, as set out in the *Government Financial Reporting Manual,* have been followed, and disclose and explain any material departures in the accounts;

  and

- prepare the accounts on a going-concern basis.

HM Treasury has appointed the Permanent Head of Department as Accounting Officer of the Department. The responsibilities of an Accounting Officer, including responsibility for the propriety and regularity of the public finances for which the Accounting Officer is answerable, for keeping proper records and for safeguarding the Department's assets, are set out in the Accounting Officers' Memorandum issued by HM Treasury and published in *Government Accounting.*

STATEMENT ON INTERNAL CONTROL

1. Scope of responsibility

As Accounting Officer, I have responsibility for maintaining a sound system of internal control that supports the achievement of Departmental policies, aims and objectives, set by the Department's Ministers, whilst safeguarding the public funds and Departmental assets for which I am personally responsible, in accordance with the responsibilities assigned to me in Government Accounting.

During the Financial Year 2005/06, the Department's outputs were delivered through 13 Top Level Budget areas, each managed by a military or civilian Top Level Budget (TLB) Holder, together with 5 Trading Fund Agencies. The Department also has 6 executive Non-Departmental Public Bodies (NDPB) and 1 Public Corporation with delegated responsibilities. Included within the TLBs are 20 on-vote Defence Agencies whose Chief Executives are responsible for producing annual accounts which are laid before Parliament but which also form part of the Departmental Resource Accounts. TLB Holders operate within a framework of responsibilities delegated by me. To assist me in assessing the adequacy of control arrangements across the Department, TLB Holders submit to me an annual statement of Assurance, endorsed by their Audit Committee and Management Board, also covering the Agencies for which they are responsible[2]. Both the Veterans' Agency (VA) and Armed Forces Pensions Administration Agency (AFPAA) are administered within the Central TLB. The VA manages the War Pensions and Benefit Programme (WPB), and AFPAA the Armed Forces Pensions and Compensation scheme (AFPS/AFCS). The Agencies' Chief Executives are directly accountable for the delivery of these services. The 5 MoD Trading Funds (the Defence Aviation Repair Agency, ABRO, the Defence Science and Technology Laboratory (Dstl), the UK Hydrographic Office, and the Met Office) fall outside the Departmental Accounting Boundary and their Chief Executives are Accounting Officers in their own right. They therefore publish their own SICs together with their Annual Accounts. Given their close integration into the Department's business, and their extensive use of Departmental personnel and assets, their Chief Executives also provide to me the SIC prepared for their annual Accounts. Although sponsored by the Department, the 6 NDPBs and Public Corporation also fall outside the Departmental Boundary and their accounts are also published separately. The NDPBs operate within a financial memorandum agreed between their respective Boards of Trustees and the Department. The Public Corporation (Oil and Pipelines Agency) has a Board of Directors on which the Department is represented.

Ministers are involved in the delivery of outputs, including the management of risks to delivery, through the Defence Council which is chaired by the Secretary of State for Defence and includes all the senior executive members of the Defence Management Board (DMB). Ministers also chair a variety of internal Boards which review the performance of the Trading Funds, the primary on-vote Agencies, including the Defence Procurement Agency (DPA) and Defence Estates (DE) which are also TLBs, and other elements of MoD business such as change, Acquisition and Environment and Safety. In particular, all 5 Trading Funds report to Advisory Boards chaired by MoD Ministers. Ministers are consulted on all key decisions affecting Defence, including major investment decisions and on operational matters. The Chief of Defence Staff is the Government's and the Secretary of State's principal advisor on military operations and is responsible for the maintenance of military operational capability and for the preparation and conduct of military operations, including managing the risks to successful outcomes. The Chiefs of Staff Committee is chaired by the Chief of Defence Staff and is the main forum in which the collective military advice of the Chiefs is obtained on operational issues. The individual Service Chiefs also advise the Chief of Defence Staff, the Secretary of State and, when required, the Prime Minister on the operational employment of their Service.

2. The purpose of the system of internal control

The system of internal control is designed to manage risk to a reasonable level rather than to eliminate all risk of failure to achieve policies, aims and objectives; it can therefore provide only reasonable and not absolute assurance of effectiveness. The system of internal control is based on an ongoing process designed to identify and prioritise the risks to the achievement of Departmental policies, aims and objectives, to evaluate the likelihood of those risks being realised and the impact should they be realised, and to manage them efficiently, effectively and economically. The system of internal control has been in place in the Department for the year ended 31 March 2006 and up to the date of approval of the annual report and accounts, and accords with Treasury guidance.

[2] For the Defence Procurement Agency and Defence Estates, which are both agencies and Top Level Budgets, this is discharged by submission of the Statement on Internal Control prepared for their own annual Accounts.

3. Capacity to handle risk

Active management of risk is fundamental to the effective achievement of Defence objectives, and is central to the way business is conducted within the Department. It informs operational decision making, contingency planning, investment decisions and the financial planning process. Risk forms an integral element of the DMB's performance reviews. Guidance on the Department's approach to risk is detailed in a Joint Service Publication[3], which is periodically reviewed and updated. This sets out the Department's corporate governance and risk management policy statement and strategy to be cascaded down through TLB Holders, and provides extensive guidance to staff on definitions, criteria and methods available for risk assessment and management. It is made available to all personnel in either hard copy or via the Department's intranet. Individual training, at both awareness and practitioner level, is available to all staff via the Department's in-house training provider.

4. The risk and control framework

The Department's Performance Management System provides the strategic framework for the consideration of risks within the Defence Balanced Scorecard and lower level scorecards, offering a starting point for the identification, evaluation, control and reporting of risk against a balanced assessment of Departmental objectives. Key Departmental objectives, performance indicators and targets are defined annually by the DMB and cascaded to TLB Holders through Service Delivery Agreements. Performance is monitored and discussed quarterly at DMB and lower level management board meetings, including explicit consideration of key risks. The Department's risk appetite is determined through the advice on operations given to Ministers, through decisions taken as part of the Department's bi-annual planning round including assessing any gaps against Planning Assumptions, and demonstrated through the limits and controls placed on individual investment projects as part of the Department's Investment Approval process and the total number of projects.

5. Review of effectiveness

As Accounting Officer, I have responsibility for reviewing the effectiveness of the system of internal control. My review of the effectiveness of the system of internal control is informed by the work of the internal auditors and the executive managers within the Department who have responsibility for the development and maintenance of the internal control framework, and comments made by the external auditors in their management letter and other reports. I have been advised on the implications of the result of my review of the effectiveness of the system of internal control by the DMB and the Defence Audit Committee (DAC) and a plan to address weaknesses and ensure continuous improvement of the system is in place.

The following processes are in operation in order to maintain and review the effectiveness of the system of internal control:

- A Defence Management Board, which meets approximately monthly to manage the plans, performance and strategic direction of the Department, comprising the senior members of the Department and two external independent members.

- A Defence Audit Committee, chaired by an external independent member of the DMB, which has adopted a risk-based approach to internal control and is placed at the heart of the assurance process, co-ordinating the activities of internal audit, and drawing on reports from pan-Departmental process owners and specialist assurance sources, including:

  - 2nd Permanent Under Secretary, as the Chair of the Defence Environment and Safety Board
  - the Chief of Defence Logistics
  - the Finance Director
  - the Deputy Chief of the Defence Staff (Personnel)
  - the Civilian Personnel Director
  - the Science and Technology Director
  - the Director General Media and Communication

[3]Joint Service Publication 525.

- the Director General Security and Safety as the Departmental Security Officer
- the Director of Defence Acquisition
- the Director of Operational Capability
- Defence Internal Audit, including the Defence Fraud Analysis Unit
- the National Audit Office

- A Departmental risk register, supported by operational-level risk registers, which complements the Defence Balanced Scorecard. Departmental risks are routinely reviewed by the DMB in the context of its regular reviews of Departmental programmes.

- Through TLB Holders, a cascaded system for ensuring compliance with legal and statutory regulations. Each TLB holder is supported by an Audit Committee, including and, in all bar one case[4], chaired by non-executive directors and at which representatives from the internal and external auditors are present. Like the DAC these committees focus their activities to provide advice on wider-business risk and assurance processes.

- A new Business Management System, with responsibility for the effective and efficient operation of the key pan-Departmental processes, such as Planning and Human Resources (military and civilian), including the identification of risks within these processes and the maintenance of effective controls to manage them, assigned to functional heads or process owners. Process Owners are responsible directly to the DMB.

- Through TLB Holders, a cascaded system for ensuring that business continuity plans are in place, and that these plans are tested on a regular basis.

- An annual risk-based programme of internal audit provided by Defence Internal Audit (DIA), who are the primary source of independent assurance, which is complemented by the activity of the Directorate of Operational Capability (DOC), which provides independent operational audit and assurance to the Secretary of State and the Chief of Defence Staff. On the basis of the audit work conducted during the year, DIA offered Substantial Assurance that the systems of internal control, risk management and governance reviewed are operating effectively across the Department.

- The Department's external audit function is provided by the Comptroller and Auditor General, supported by staff from the National Audit Office (NAO). The Accounting Officer and NAO staff see all DAC papers and attend its meetings, and there was no relevant audit information that the NAO were not already aware. Additionally the Accounting Officer held periodic private discussions with Internal Audit, and the NAO see all relevant Top Level Budget (TLB) papers and attend TLB Audit Committee meetings.

- Annual Reports providing measurable performance indicators and more subjective assessments on the Health of Financial Systems from all TLB Holders and key functional specialists. Improvements have continued to be made to our financial control during the year. The Department has delivered its outputs within the resources voted by Parliament despite the additional workload generated by Operations. The Department remained within the Treasury's Total Departmental Expenditure Limit but, owing to an accounting adjustment that arose from review after the year end, the specific Departmental Capital Expenditure Limit was exceeded.

- Centres of Excellence in key areas – including Change, Equipment and Estates, integrating Office of Government Commerce (OGC) processes, tools and structures into existing Departmental management and control processes – to ensure that high-risk mission-critical projects and programmes carried out by the Department do not suffer from any of the common causes of failure identified by the OGC and the National Audit Office.

- A dedicated team to co-ordinate, and appropriate mechanisms to strengthen, the management of scientific risks, particularly to Service personnel health, and in health, safety and environmental matters.

- An effective governance structure and performance management system that addresses the risks arising from the introduction of the general right of access to information from January 2005 under the Freedom of Information Act.

Bill Jeffrey
Accounting Officer

11 July 2006

[4]The General Officer Commanding Northern Ireland (GOCNI)'s Audit Committee is chaired by the TLB Civil Secretary, but contains two Non-Executive Directors with direct access to the Management Board and TLB Holder.

THE CERTIFICATE OF THE COMPTROLLER AND AUDITOR GENERAL TO THE HOUSE OF COMMONS

I certify that I have audited the financial statements of the Ministry of Defence for the year ended 31 March 2006 under the Government Resources and Accounts Act 2000. These comprise the Statement of Parliamentary Supply, the Operating Cost Statement and Statement of Recognised Gains and Losses, the Balance Sheet, the Cashflow Statement and the Statement of Operating Costs by Departmental Aim and Objectives and the related notes. These financial statements have been prepared under the accounting policies set out within them.

Respective responsibilities of the Accounting Officer and auditor

The Accounting Officer is responsible for preparing the Annual Report and the financial statements in accordance with the Government Resources and Accounts Act 2000 and HM Treasury directions made thereunder and for ensuring the regularity of financial transactions. These responsibilities are set out in the Statement of Accounting Officer's Responsibilities.

My responsibility is to audit the financial statements in accordance with relevant legal and regulatory requirements, and with International Standards on Auditing (UK and Ireland).

I report to you my opinion as to whether the financial statements give a true and fair view and whether the financial statements and the part of the Remuneration Report to be audited have been properly prepared in accordance with HM Treasury directions issued under the Government Resources and Accounts Act 2000. I also report whether in all material respects the expenditure and income have been applied to the purposes intended by Parliament and the financial transactions conform to the authorities which govern them. I also report to you if, in my opinion, the Annual Report is not consistent with the financial statements, if the Department has not kept proper accounting records, if I have not received all the information and explanations I require for my audit, or if information specified by HM Treasury regarding remuneration and other transactions is not disclosed.

I review whether the statement on pages 182 to 184 reflects the Department's compliance with HM Treasury's guidance on the Statement on Internal Control, and I report if it does not. I am not required to consider whether the Accounting Officer's statements on internal control cover all risks and controls, or to form an opinion on the effectiveness of the Department's corporate governance procedures or its risk and control procedures.

I read the other information contained in the Annual Report and consider whether it is consistent with the audited financial statements. I consider the implications for my report if I become aware of any apparent misstatements or material inconsistencies with the financial statements. My responsibilities do not extend to any other information.

Basis of audit opinion

I conducted my audit in accordance with International Standards on Auditing (UK and Ireland) issued by the Auditing Practices Board. My audit includes examination, on a test basis, of evidence relevant to the amounts, disclosures and regularity of financial transactions included in the financial statements and the part of the Remuneration Report to be audited. It also includes an assessment of the significant estimates and judgments made by the Accounting Officer in the preparation of the financial statements, and of whether the accounting policies are most appropriate to the Department's circumstances, consistently applied and adequately disclosed.

I planned and performed my audit so as to obtain all the information and explanations which I considered necessary in order to provide me with sufficient evidence to give reasonable assurance that the financial statements and the part of the Remuneration Report to be audited are free from material misstatement, whether caused by fraud or error and that in all material respects the expenditure and income have been applied to the purposes intended by Parliament and the financial transactions conform to the authorities which govern them. In forming my opinion I also evaluated the overall adequacy of the presentation of information in the financial statements and the part of the Remuneration Report to be audited.

Opinions

In my opinion:

- the financial statements give a true and fair view, in accordance with the Government Resources and Accounts Act 2000 and directions made thereunder by HM Treasury, of the state of the Department's affairs as at 31 March 2006 and the net cash requirement, net resource outturn, resources applied to objectives, recognised gains and losses and cashflows for the year then ended;
- the financial statements and the part of the Remuneration Report to be audited have been properly prepared in accordance with HM Treasury directions issued under the Government Resources and Accounts Act 2000; and
- in all material respects the expenditure and income have been applied to the purposes intended by Parliament and the financial transactions conform to the authorities which govern them.

I have no observations to make on these financial statements.

John Bourn
Comptroller and Auditor General **12 July 2006**

National Audit Office
157-197 Buckingham Palace Road
Victoria
London SW1W 9SP

STATEMENT OF PARLIAMENTARY SUPPLY

Summary of Resource Outturn 2005-06

		Estimate			Outturn			2005-06 Net Total Outturn compared to Estimate Savings/ (Excess)	2004-05 Outturn Restated
Request for Resources	Note	Gross Expenditure £000	A-in-A * £000	Net Total £000	Gross Expenditure £000	A-in-A * £000	Net Total £000	£000	£000
1	2	36,011,095	1,346,570	34,664,525	34,084,261	1,346,570	32,737,691	1,926,834	30,514,128
2	2	1,101,276	–	1,101,276	1,055,848	–	1,055,848	45,428	938,181
3	2	1,072,972	–	1,072,972	1,068,595	–	1,068,595	4,377	1,109,521
Total resources	3	38,185,343	1,346,570	36,838,773	36,208,704	1,346,570	34,862,134	1,976,639	32,561,830
Non operating cost A-in-A				607,041			374,320	232,721	287,435

* Appropriation-in-Aid (A-in-A)

The prior year costs have been restated to reflect the transfer of responsibility for certain nuclear decommissioning from the MoD to the Nuclear Decommissioning Authority. Movements are detailed at Note 33.

Net Cash Requirement 2005-06

	Note	Estimate £000	Outturn £000	2005-06 Net Total Outturn compared to Estimate Savings/(Excess) £000	2004-05 Outturn £000
Net Cash Requirement	4	31,501,992	30,603,297	898,695	29,624,275

Summary of Income Payable to the Consolidated Fund

(In addition to appropriations in aid, the following income relates to the Department and is payable to the Consolidated Fund (cash receipts being shown in italics)).

	Note	Forecast 2005-06 Income £000	Forecast 2005-06 Receipts £000	Outturn 2005-06 Income £000	Outturn 2005-06 Receipts £000
Total	5	–	–	468,599	*470,388*

The notes on pages 193 to 245 form part of these accounts

Further analysis of the variances between Estimate and Outturn is at Note 2 and a summary of the overall financial position, including an explanation of the main variances identified above, is provided both in the Management Commentary and the following paragraphs. A detailed explanation of the Department's financial performance in relation to HM Treasury's Departmental Expenditure Limits is included within Resources in the Performance Report.

RfR 1, Provision of Defence Capability, provides for expenditure primarily to meet the Ministry of Defence's operational support and logistics services costs and the costs of providing the equipment capability required by Defence policy. Within RfR1, the Estimate and Outturn for Operating Appropriations in Aid are shown as equal amounts. Any Appropriations in Aid in excess of the Estimate are shown at Note 6, and these will be surrendered to the Consolidated Fund.

The net outturn is £32,737,691,000 against an Estimate of £34,664,525,000, a variance of £1,926,834,000 underspent. Principal explanations for the underspend were reviews of fixed assets, capital spares and stock resulting in lower depreciation and other impairment charges. The underspend in nuclear provisions was due principally to the transfer of nuclear liabilities to the newly formed Nuclear Decommissioning Authority, and a lower than expected charge for the unwinding of the discount on provisions, following the discount rate change from 3.5% to 2.2%.

RfR2, Conflict Prevention, shows net outturn of £1,055,848,000 against an Estimate of £1,101,276,000, a variance of £45,428,000. A contingency of £69,000,000 was included in the Spring Supplementary Estimate for reasons of prudence as the often rapidly changing operational situation means that costs are difficult to forecast. In the event, only a proportion of this contingency was needed.

RfR3, War Pensions Benefits shows net outturn of £1,068,595,000 against an Estimate of £1,072,972,000 an underspend of £4,377,000. This RfR provides for the payment of war disablement and war widows' pensions in accordance with relevant legislation. The costs of administering war pensions are borne by RfR1.

The non-operating Appropriations in Aid show a net outturn of £374,320,000 against an overly ambitious Estimate of £607,041,000.

The Net Cash Requirement shows net outturn of £30,603,297,000 against an Estimate of £31,501,992,000, an underspend of £898,695,000. This is because the creditors at the end of the year were higher than had been forecast at the time the Spring Supplementary Estimate was submitted, and there was £146,000,000 of contingency in RfR2, for resource costs and urgent operational requirements, that in the event was not required.

OPERATING COST STATEMENT

for the year ended 31 March 2006

	Note	2005-06 £000	2004-05 Restated £000
Staff costs	9	11,254,851	10,995,642
Other operating costs	10	20,171,162	19,595,404
Gross operating costs		**31,426,013**	**30,591,046**
Operating income	11	(1,390,997)	(1,416,807)
Net operating cost before interest		**30,035,016**	**29,174,239**
Net interest payable	12	1,252,150	131,294
Cost of capital charge	21	3,106,369	3,025,892
Net operating cost		**34,393,535**	**32,331,425**
Net resource Outturn	3	**34,862,134**	**32,561,830**

The prior year costs have been restated to reflect the transfer of responsibility for certain nuclear decommissioning from the MoD to the Nuclear Decommissioning Authority. Movements are detailed at Note 33.

Statement of Recognised Gains and Losses

for the year ended 31 March 2006

	Note	2005-06 £000	2004-05 £000
Net gain on revaluation of fixed assets and stocks	22	(2,425,832)	(4,521,891)
Net gain on revaluation of investments	22	(242,590)	–
Receipts of donated assets and (gain)/loss on revaluation	22	(111,753)	(440,664)
Recognised gains for the financial year		**(2,780,175)**	**(4,962,555)**
Prior year adjustment	33	(4,348,036)	
Recognised gains since the last Annual Accounts		**(7,128,211)**	

The notes on pages 193 to 245 form part of these accounts.

BALANCE SHEET

as at 31 March 2006

		31 March 2006		31 March 2005 Restated	
	Note	£000	£000	£000	£000
Fixed Assets					
Intangible assets	13	22,982,695		22,647,823	
Tangible fixed assets	14	71,774,958		69,608,889	
Investments	15	514,132		347,108	
			95,271,785		**92,603,820**
Current Assets					
Stocks and work-in-progress	16	6,052,227		6,095,363	
Debtors	17	2,921,155		2,849,378	
Cash at bank and in hand	18	1,018,245		438,411	
		9,991,627		**9,383,152**	
Creditors: amounts falling due within one year	19	6,449,389		6,000,880	
Net current assets			**3,542,238**		**3,382,272**
Total assets less current liabilities			**98,814,023**		**95,986,092**
Creditors: amounts falling due after more than one year	19	1,057,601		809,895	
Provisions for liabilities and charges	20	6,274,944		5,182,680	
			7,332,545		5,992,575
Net assets			**91,481,478**		**89,993,517**
Taxpayers' equity					
General fund	21		72,490,177		69,254,944
Revaluation reserve	22		16,635,683		18,719,510
Donated assets reserve	22		2,113,028		2,019,063
Investment reserve	22		242,590		–
			91,481,478		**89,993,517**

The balances at 31 March 2005 have been restated to reflect the transfer of responsibility for certain nuclear decommissioning from the MoD to the Nuclear Decommissioning Authority. Movements are detailed at Note 33.

Bill Jeffrey
Accounting Officer

11 July 2006

The notes on pages 193 to 245 form part of these accounts.

CASH FLOW STATEMENT

for the year ended 31 March 2006

	Note	2005-06 £000	2004-05 Restated £000
Net cash outflow from operating activities	23.1	(23,865,060)	(22,966,281)
Capital expenditure and financial investment	23.2	(6,222,278)	(6,246,193)
Payments of amounts due to the Consolidated Fund		(736,501)	(237,175)
Financing	23.4	31,403,673	29,575,496
Increase in cash at bank and in hand	23.5	579,834	125,847

The notes on pages 193 to 245 form part of these accounts.

STATEMENT OF OPERATING COSTS BY DEPARTMENTAL AIM AND OBJECTIVES

for the year ended 31 March 2006

Aim

The principal activity of the Department is to deliver security for the people of the United Kingdom and the Overseas Territories by defending them, including against terrorism; and to act as a force for good by strengthening international peace and stability.

In pursuance of this aim, the Department has the following objectives:

	2005-06			2004-05		
	Gross £000	Income £000	Net £000	Gross Restated £000	Income £000	Net Restated £000
Objective 1: Achieving success in the tasks we undertake	3,984,890	(420,801)	3,564,089	3,725,324	(335,767)	3,389,557
Objective 2: Being ready to respond to the tasks that might arise	27,526,586	(925,270)	26,601,316	25,950,299	(1,016,681)	24,933,618
Objective 3: Building for the future	3,204,461	(44,926)	3,159,535	2,963,087	(64,359)	2,898,728
	34,715,937	(1,390,997)	33,324,940	32,638,710	(1,416,807)	31,221,903
Paying war pensions and allowances	1,068,595	–	1,068,595	1,109,522	–	1,109,522
Total	35,784,532	(1,390,997)	34,393,535	33,748,232	(1,416,807)	32,331,425

See additional details in Note 24.

The prior year costs have been restated to reflect the transfer of responsibility for certain nuclear decommissioning from the MoD to the Nuclear Decommissioning Authority. Movements are detailed at Note 33.

The notes on pages 193 to 245 form part of these accounts.

NOTES TO THE ACCOUNTS

1 Statement of Accounting Policies

Introduction

1.1 These financial statements have been prepared in accordance with the generic Accounts Direction issued by HM Treasury under reference DAO(GEN)01/06 on 16 January 2006 and comply with the requirements of HM Treasury's Financial Reporting Manual (FReM). In order to reflect the particular circumstances of the Department, the following exceptions to the FReM have been made:

The Operating Cost Statement is not segmented into programme and non-programme expenditure, with the agreement of HM Treasury.

The FReM's requirement for Departments to prepare accounts that present the transactions and flows for the financial year and the balances at the year end between "core" department and the consolidated group in respect of the Operating Cost Statement (and supporting notes) and Balance Sheet (and supporting notes) has not been applied. With the agreement of HM Treasury, the agencies falling within the Departmental Boundary are on-vote and embedded within the Departmental chain of command; they are, therefore, treated as an integral part of the "core" Department. So, throughout these accounts, the consolidated figures for the Ministry of Defence (including its on-vote agencies) are deemed to be those for the "core" Department.

Accounting Convention

1.2 These financial statements are prepared on an accruals basis under the historical cost convention, modified to include the revaluation of certain fixed assets and stocks.

Basis of Preparation of Departmental Resource Accounts

1.3 These financial statements comprise the consolidation of the Department, its Defence Supply Financed Agencies and those Advisory NDPBs sponsored by the Department which are not self-accounting. The Defence Agencies and the Advisory NDPBs sponsored by the Department are listed in Note 36.

1.4 Five of the Department's agencies are established as Trading Funds. They, therefore, fall outside Voted Supply and are subject to a different control framework. Consequently, the Department's interests in the Trading Funds are included in the financial statements as fixed asset investments. Executive NDPBs operate on a self-accounting basis and are not included in the consolidated accounts. They receive grant-in-aid funding from the Department which is treated as an expense in the Operating Cost Statement.

1.5 The Department's interest in QinetiQ, formerly a Self-Financing Public Corporation, is included in the financial statements as a fixed asset investment.

1.6 The Armed Forces Pension Scheme (AFPS) is not consolidated within these financial statements. Separate accounts are prepared by the AFPS.

1.7 Machinery of Government changes which involve the merger of two or more Departments into one new Department, or the transfer of functions or responsibility of one part of the public service sector to another, are accounted for using merger accounting in accordance with Financial Reporting Standard (FRS) 6.

Net Operating Costs

1.8 Costs are charged to the Operating Cost Statement in the period in which they are incurred and matched to any related income. Costs of Contracted-Out Services are included net of related VAT. Other costs are VAT inclusive, although a proportion of this VAT is recovered via a formula agreed with HM Revenue and Customs. Surpluses and deficits on disposal of fixed assets and stock are included within Note 10 – Other Operating Costs.

1.9 Income from services provided to third parties is included in operating income, net of related VAT.

Fixed Assets

1.10 Through the application of the Modified Historical Cost Accounting Convention (MHCA), the Department's fixed assets are expressed at their current value to the Department. The Department achieves this through the application of prospective indices which are produced by the Defence Analytical Services Agency. These indices are applied to the fixed assets, falling within the categories listed below, at the start of each financial year and look ahead to the subsequent balance sheet date. With the exception of Land and Buildings, the indices are also adjusted to reflect the actual change in prices in the prior year as compared to the earlier prediction.

- Land (by region and type);
- Buildings – Dwellings (UK and specific overseas indices);
- Buildings – Non Dwellings (UK and specific overseas indices);
- Single Use Military Equipment – Sea Systems;
- Single Use Military Equipment – Air Systems;
- Single Use Military Equipment – Land Systems;
- Plant and Machinery;
- Transport – Fighting Equipment;
- Transport – Other;
- IT and Communications Equipment – Office Machinery and Computers; and
- IT and Communications Equipment – Communications Equipment.

1.11 Additionally, all fixed assets are subject to a quinquennial revaluation by external professional valuers in accordance with FRS15.

1.12 Assets under construction are valued at cost and are subject to indexation. On completion, they are released from the project account into the appropriate asset category.

1.13 The Department's policy on the capitalisation of subsequent expenditure under FRS15 is to account separately for material major refits and overhauls when their value is consumed by the Department over a different period to the life of the corresponding core asset and where this is deemed to have a material effect on the carrying values of a fixed asset and the depreciation charge. Subsequent expenditure is also capitalised where it is deemed to enhance significantly the operational capability of the equipment, including extension of life, and when it is incurred to replace or restore a component of an asset that has been treated separately for depreciation purposes.

Intangible Assets

1.14 Pure and applied research costs are charged to the Operating Cost Statement in the period in which they are incurred.

1.15 Development costs are capitalised where they contribute towards defining the specification of an asset that will enter production. Development costs not capitalised are charged to Other Operating Costs. The development costs are amortised over the planned operational life of that asset type, e.g. class of ship or aircraft, on a straight-line basis. Amortisation commences when the asset type first enters operational service within the Department. If it is decided to withdraw the whole or a significant part of an asset type early, then a corresponding proportion of any remaining unamortised development costs is written off to the Operating Cost Statement along with the underlying tangible fixed assets. For the purposes of development costs, a significant withdrawal of assets is deemed to be 20% or greater of the net book value of the underlying asset class.

1.16 On the grounds of materiality, the Department has not fully complied with the FReM emissions cap and trade scheme accounting requirements. Instead of registering an asset and liability in respect of its holding of allowances and obligation to deliver allowances, the Department has simply reflected purchases and sales of allowances as an expense and income respectively in the Operating Cost Statement. All other costs associated with the scheme, such as compliance checking, are also charged to the Operating Cost Statement.

Tangible Fixed Assets

1.17 The useful economic lives of tangible fixed assets are reviewed annually and adjusted where necessary. The capitalisation threshold is normally £10,000. The £10,000 threshold is applied when deciding whether to register an asset on the Fixed Asset Register (FAR). The decision to record an asset on a FAR normally takes place at the point when the asset is initially acquired.

1.18 In these financial statements, guided weapons, missiles and bombs (GWMB) and capital spares are categorised as fixed assets and subject to depreciation. The depreciation charge in the Operating Cost Statement also includes the cost of GWMB fired to destruction. The principal asset categories and their useful economic lives, depreciated on a straight line basis, are:

	Category	Years
Land and Buildings	Land Buildings, permanent Buildings, temporary Leasehold	Indefinite, not depreciated Useful economic life 5 – 20 Shorter of expected life and lease period
Single Use Military Equipment (including GWMB)		Operational life (on a pooled basis for GWMB)
Plant, Machinery and Transport	Plant and Machinery Specialised Vehicles (includes non-fighting vessels and aircraft) Other standard vehicles	5 – 15 Operational life 3 – 5
IT and Communications Equipment	Computers Satellites Communications Equipment	3 – 7 Operational life Operational life
Operational Heritage Assets *		As other tangible fixed assets
Capital Spares	Items of repairable material retained for the purpose of replacing parts of an asset undergoing repair, refurbishment, maintenance, servicing, modification, enhancement or conversion.	Operational life (on a pooled basis, consistent within the life of the prime equipment supported)

*Operational Heritage Assets are included within the principal asset category to which they relate.

Donated Assets

1.19 Donated assets (i.e. those assets that have been donated to the Department or assets for which the Department has continuing and exclusive use but does not own legal title and for which it has not given consideration in return) are capitalised at their current valuation on receipt and are revalued/depreciated on the same basis as purchased assets.

1.20 A donated assets reserve represents the value of the original donation, additions, any subsequent professional revaluation and indexation (MHCA) or a professional valuation. Amounts equal to the donated asset depreciation charge, impairment costs and deficit/surplus on disposal arising during the year, are released from this reserve to the Operating Cost Statement.

Impairment

1.21 The charge to the Operating Cost Statement in respect of impairment arises on the decision to sell a fixed asset and take it out of service; on transfer of a fixed asset into stock; on reduction in service potential and where the application of MHCA indices causes a downward revaluation below the depreciated historical cost and which is deemed to be permanent in nature. Impairment also includes the cost of capital spares that are embodied into a fixed asset, as part of a major refit and overhaul, but which cannot be capitalised in accordance with FRS 15. Any reversal of an impairment cost is recognised in the operating cost statement to the extent that the original charge, adjusted for subsequent depreciation, was recognised in the Operating Cost Statement. The remaining amount is recognised in the revaluation reserve.

Disposal of Tangible Fixed Assets

1.22 Disposal of assets is principally handled by two specialist agencies: Defence Estates for property assets and the Disposal Services Agency for non-property assets.

1.23 Property assets identified for disposal are included at the open market value with any resulting changes in the net book value charged to the Operating Cost Statement under Impairment or credited to the revaluation reserve as appropriate. On subsequent sale, the surplus or deficit is included in the Operating Cost Statement under surplus/deficit on disposal of fixed assets.

1.24 Non-property assets are subject to regular impairment reviews. An impairment review is also carried out when a decision is made to dispose of an asset and take it out of service. Any write down in value to the net recoverable amount (NRA) is charged to the Operating Cost Statement under Impairment or credited to the revaluation reserve as appropriate. The surplus or deficit at the point of disposal is included in the Operating Cost Statement under surplus/deficit on disposal of fixed assets. Non-property assets, where the receipts on sale are anticipated not to be separately identifiable, are transferred to stock at their NRA and shown under assets declared for disposal. Any write down on transfer is included in the Operating Cost Statement under Impairment.

1.25 Disposals exclude fixed assets written off and written on. These items are included within Other Movements in Notes 13 and 14 (Intangible and Tangible Fixed Assets).

Leased Assets

1.26 Assets held under finance leases are capitalised as tangible fixed assets and depreciated over the shorter of the lease term or their estimated useful economic lives. Rentals paid are apportioned between reductions in the capital obligations included in creditors, and finance charges charged to the Operating Cost Statement. Expenditure under operating leases is charged to the Operating Cost Statement in the period in which it is incurred. In circumstances where the Department is the lessor of a finance lease, amounts due under a finance lease are treated as amounts receivable and reported in Debtors.

Private Finance Initiative (PFI) Transactions

1.27 Where the substance of the transaction is that the risks and rewards of ownership remain with the Department, the assets and liabilities are reported on the Department's Balance Sheet. Unitary charges in respect of on-balance sheet PFI deals are apportioned between reduction in the capital obligation and charges to the Operating Cost Statement for service performance and finance cost. Where the risks and rewards are transferred to the private sector, the transaction is accounted for in the Operating Cost Statement through service charges in accordance with FRS 5 and Treasury Guidance.

1.28 Where assets are transferred to the Private Sector Provider, and the consideration received by the Department is in the form of reduced unitary payments, the sales value is accounted for as a prepayment. This prepayment is then reduced (charged to the Operating Cost Statement) over the course of the contract as the benefits of the prepaid element are utilised.

Investments

1.29 Investments represent holdings that the Department intends to retain for the foreseeable future. Fixed asset investments are stated at market value where available; otherwise they are stated at cost. In the case of Trading Funds and other public bodies/corporations not consolidated into the Department's resource accounts, the value of loans, public dividend capital and other interests held by the Department are recorded at historic cost. In February 2006, QinetiQ Group plc became a listed company. The MoD's investment in QinetiQ Group plc is now recorded at market value. Details on the QinetiQ Group plc investment are given in Note 15. Investments may either be equity investments, held in the name of the Secretary of State for Defence, or medium or long-term loans made with the intention of providing working capital or commercial support.

1.30 Joint Ventures would be accounted for using the Gross Equity method of accounting. Under this method, the Department's share of the aggregate gross assets and liabilities underlying the net equity investments would be shown on the face of the Balance Sheet. The Operating Cost Statement would include the Department's share of the investee's turnover. The Department currently has no Joint Ventures.

Stocks and Work-in-Progress

1.31 Stock is valued at current replacement cost, or historic cost if not materially different. Provision is made to reduce cost to net realisable value (NRV) where there is no expectation of consumption or sale in the ordinary course of the business. Stock provision is released to the operating costs on consumption, disposal and write-off.

1.32 Internal Work-in-Progress represents ongoing work on the manufacture, modification, enhancement or conversion of stock items. This is valued on the same basis as stocks. External Work-in-Progress represents ongoing work on production or repair contracts for external customers. This is valued at the lower of current replacement cost and NRV.

1.33 Assets declared for disposal include stock held for disposal and those non-property fixed assets identified for disposal where receipts are not anticipated to be separately identifiable.

1.34 Stocks written-off, included within other operating costs, represents the book value of stock which has been scrapped, destroyed or lost during the year, and adjustments to agree the book values with the figures shown on the supply systems.

Provisions for Liabilities and Charges

1.35 Provisions for liabilities and charges have been established under the criteria of FRS 12 and are based on realistic and prudent estimates of the expenditure required to settle future legal or constructive obligations that exist at the Balance Sheet date.

1.36 Provisions are charged to the Operating Cost Statement unless they have been capitalised as part of the cost of the underlying facility where the expenditure provides access to current and future economic benefits. In such cases, the capitalised provision will be depreciated as a charge to the Operating Cost Statement over the remaining estimated useful economic life of the underlying asset. All long-term provisions are discounted to current prices using the rate advised by HM Treasury. The rate for financial year 2005-06 is 2.2% (3.5% for 2004-05). The discount is unwound over the remaining life of the provision and shown as an interest charge in the Operating Cost Statement.

Reserves

1.37 The Revaluation Reserve reflects the unrealised element of the cumulative balance of revaluation and indexation adjustments on fixed assets and stocks (excluding donated assets and those financed by Government grants). The Donated Asset Reserve reflects the net book value of assets that have been donated to the Department.

1.38 The General Fund represents the balance of the taxpayers' equity.

1.39 The Investment Reserve represents the value of the Departmental investment in QinetiQ Group plc on flotation, and the subsequent movement in market valuation as at 31 March 2006.

Pensions

1.40 Present and past employees are mainly covered by the Civil Service pension arrangements for civilian personnel and the AFPS for Service personnel. There are separate scheme statements for the AFPS and Civil Service pensions as a whole.

1.41 Both the AFPS and the main Civil Service pension schemes are unfunded defined benefit pension schemes, although the Department accounts for the schemes in its accounts as if they were defined contribution schemes in accordance with the HM Treasury FReM. The employer's charge is met by payment of a superannuation contribution adjusted for past experience (SCAPE), formerly known as an accruing superannuation liability charge (ASLC), which is calculated based on current pay of serving personnel. The SCAPE represents an estimate of the cost of providing future superannuation protection for all personnel currently in pensionable employment. In addition, civilian personnel contribute 1.5% of salary to fund a widow/widower's pension if they are members of Classic and 3.5% if they are members of Premium. The Department's Balance Sheet will only include a creditor in respect of pensions to the extent that the contributions paid to the pension funds in the year fall short of the SCAPE and widow/widower's pension charges due. Money purchase pensions delivered through employer-sponsored stakeholder pensions have been available as an alternative to all new Civil Service entrants since October 2002.

1.42 The pension schemes undergo a reassessment of the SCAPE contribution rates by the Government Actuary at three-yearly intervals. Provisions are made for costs of early retirement programmes and redundancies up to the normal retirement age and are charged to the Operating Cost Statement.

1.43 The Department operates a number of small pension schemes for civilians engaged at overseas locations. Since 1 April 2003, they have been accounted for in accordance with FRS 17 – *Retirement Benefits.*

1.44 The disclosures required under FRS 17 are included in the Remuneration Report.

Early Departure Costs

1.45 The Department provides in full for the cost of meeting pensions up to normal retirement age in respect of military and civilian personnel early retirement programmes and redundancies announced in the current and previous years. Pensions payable after normal retirement age are met by the Armed Forces Pension Scheme for military personnel and the Civil Service pension arrangements for civilian personnel.

Cost of Capital Charge

1.46 A charge, reflecting the cost of capital utilised by the Department, is included in the Operating Cost Statement and credited to the General Fund. The charge is calculated using the HM Treasury standard rate for financial year 2005-06 of 3.5% (2004-05: 3.5%) in real terms on all assets less liabilities except for:

- Donated assets and cash balances with the Office of HM Paymaster General (OPG), where the charge is nil.
- Liabilities for the amounts to be surrendered to the Consolidated Fund and for amounts due from the Consolidated Fund, where the charge is nil.
- Assets financed by grants, where the charge is nil.
- Additions to heritage collections where the existing collection has not been capitalised, where the charge is nil.

1.47 The cost of capital charge on the fixed asset investments in the Trading Funds and in the Self Financing Public Corporation is calculated at a specific rate applicable to those entities, and is based on their underlying net assets.

Foreign Exchange

1.48 Transactions that are denominated in a foreign currency are translated into Sterling using the General Accounting Rate ruling at the date of each transaction. US$ and Euros are purchased forward from the Bank of England. Monetary assets and liabilities are translated at the spot rate applicable at the Balance Sheet date and the exchange differences are reported in the Operating Cost Statement.

1.49 Overseas non-monetary assets and liabilities are subject to annual revaluation and are translated at the spot rate applicable at the Balance Sheet date and the exchange differences are taken to the revaluation reserve for owned assets, or the donated asset reserve for donated assets.

2. Analysis of Net Resource Outturn

Request for Resources 1: Provision of Defence Capability	Other Current Expenditure	Grants	Operating Appropriation -in-Aid	Total Net Resource Outturn	Total Net Resource Estimate	Total Net Outturn Compared With Estimate	Total Net Resource Outturn Restated
	2005-06						2004-05
	£000	£000	£000	£000	£000	£000	£000
TLB HOLDER							
Commander-in-Chief Fleet	3,610,461	–	(16,826)	**3,593,635**	3,601,440	7,805	3,571,021
General Officer Commanding (Northern Ireland)	580,639	–	(1,131)	**579,508**	587,276	7,768	626,427
Commander-in-Chief Land Command	5,829,642	130	(196,210)	**5,633,562**	5,548,474	(85,088)	5,340,560
Commanding-in-Chief RAF Strike Command	4,071,158	–	(27,662)	**4,043,496**	4,044,594	1,098	3,502,913
Chief of Joint Operations	605,655	–	(27,226)	**578,429**	536,080	(42,349)	499,452
Chief of Defence Logistics	8,044,821	772	(305,560)	**7,740,033**	8,224,444	484,411	7,412,637
2nd Sea Lord/Commander-in-Chief Naval Home Command	814,472	3,223	(39,960)	**777,735**	747,520	(30,215)	762,524
Adjutant General's Command	1,971,534	15,662	(38,572)	**1,948,624**	1,942,270	(6,354)	1,788,072
Air Officer Commanding-in-Chief Personnel & Training Command	1,058,556	7,235	(158,662)	**907,129**	862,304	(44,825)	1,127,137
Central	2,625,112	158,814	(295,053)	**2,488,873**	2,681,190	192,317	2,405,077
Defence Estates *	1,298,979	–	(233,000)	**1,065,979**	1,147,560	81,581	746,444
Defence Procurement Agency **	2,885,790	–	(6,707)	**2,879,083**	4,238,067	1,358,984	1,995,350
SIT (Science, Innovation, Technology)	497,948	3,658	(1)	**501,605**	503,306	1,701	506,109
Total (RFR 1)	**33,894,767**	**189,494**	**(1,346,570)**	**32,737,691**	34,664,525	1,926,834	30,283,723
Excess Operating Appropriations in Aid ***							215,889
Items treated as CFERs to be allocated ***							14,516
Total (RFR 1)	**33,894,767**	**189,494**	**(1,346,570)**	32,737,691	**34,664,525**	**1,926,834**	30,514,128

* Defence Estates is a new TLB created from a Management Group within Central TLB
** Defence Procurement Agency prior year figure restated to reflect the transfer to the Nuclear Decommissioning Authority
*** For 2005-06 these items are reported within the appropriate TLB Total Net Resources

Request for Resources 2: Conflict Prevention	Other Current Expenditure	Grants	Operating Appropriation -in-Aid	Total Net Resource Outturn	Total Net Resource Estimate	Total Net Outturn Compared With Estimate	Total Net Resource Outturn Restated
	2005-06						2004-05
	£000	£000	£000	£000	£000	£000	£000
Programme Expenditure: Sub-Saharan Africa*	36,419	–	–	**36,419**	30,520	(5,899)	–
Programme Expenditure: Rest of the World*	73,552	–	–	**73,552**	82,220	8,668	133,176
Peace Keeping: Rest of the World	945,877	–	–	**945,877**	988,536	42,659	805,005
Total (RFR 2)	**1,055,848**	**–**	**–**	**1,055,848**	1,101,276	45,428	938,181

* 2004-05 Programme Expenditure was not disclosed by geographic area within the Estimates or Outturn.

Request for Resources 3: War Pensions Benefits	Other Current Expenditure	Grants	Operating Appropriation -in-Aid	2005-06 Total Net Resource Outturn	Total Net Resource Estimate	Total Net Outturn Compared With Estimate	2004-05 Total Net Resource Outturn Restated
	£000	£000	£000	£000	£000	£000	£000
War Pensions Benefits Programme costs	–	1,064,862	–	**1,064,862**	1,068,466	3,604	1,101,504
War Pensions Benefits Programme costs – Far Eastern Prisioners of War	–	3,730	–	**3,730**	4,500	770	8,010
War Pensions Benefits Programme costs – British Limbless ex-Servicemen's Association	–	3	–	**3**	6	3	7
Total (RFR 3)	**–**	**1,068,595**	**–**	**1,068,595**	1,072,972	4,377	1,109,521

	Other Current Expenditure	Grants	Operating Appropriation -in-Aid	2005-06 Total Net Resource Outturn	Total Net Resource Estimate	Total Net Outturn Compared With Estimate	2004-05 Total Net Resource Outturn Restated
	£000	£000	£000	£000	£000	£000	£000
Total Net Resource Outturn	**34,950,615**	**1,258,089**	**(1,346,570)**	**34,862,134**	36,838,773	1,976,639	32,561,830

Provision of Defence Capability (RfR1)

2.1 Principal explanations for the underspend on RfR1 were reviews of fixed assets, captial spares and stock resulting in lower depreciation and other impairment charges. The underspend in AME was due principally to the transfer of nuclear liabilities to the newly formed Nuclear Decommissioning Authority, and that in Non Budget to the lower than expected charges when the discount rate was changed, and again the transfer of nuclear liabilities to the Nuclear Decommissioning Authority. A detailed explanation of the variances against the Departmental Expenditure Limit is shown in paragraphs 263-264 within Resources, in the Performance Report.

Conflict Prevention (RfR2)

2.2 The following table shows the conflict prevention costs summarised by each of the Operations, and compared against the Estimate (voted funding) for the year.

Operation	Resource Costs	Capital Costs	2005-06 Total	2004-05 Outturn
	£000	£000	£000	£000
Peace Keeping Expenditure				
Afghanistan	148,117	51,231	199,348	67,034
Iraq	797,760	159,838	957,598	909,930
Programme Expenditure				
Balkans	62,679	174	62,853	86,560
Global pool *	10,873	–	10,873	
African pool *	36,419	–	36,419	48,499
Total RfR2	**1,055,848**	**211,243**	**1,267,091**	**1,112,023**
Total Estimate	1,101,276	329,997	1,431,273	1,173,035
Difference – savings/(excess)	45,428	118,754	164,182	61,012

*2004-05 African and Global Pool Expenditure was not disclosed by geographic area within the Estimates or Outturn

A breakdown of cost for the three main Operations is shown in the following table, alongside the Departmental Allocation for the year and the Outturn for 2004-05.

	Total Outturn 2005-06								
	Iraq			Afghanistan			Balkans		
	Total Outturn £000	Total Departmental Allocation 2005-06 £000	Outturn 2004-05 £000	Total Outturn £000	Total Departmental Allocation 2005-06 £000	Outturn 2004-05 £000	Total Outturn £000	Total Departmental Allocation 2005-06 £000	Outturn 2004-05 £000
Resource Cost (by area)									
Direct costs									
Service manpower	80,237	80,278	115,590	7,575	7,172	14,898	11,509	11,640	15,960
Civilian manpower	14,213	11,688	13,889	1,627	1,116	996	4,949	7,336	7,614
Infrastructure costs	81,407	84,082	87,550	10,522	25,663	7,197	12,633	13,954	15,912
Equipment support	220,232	243,097	198,273	24,399	14,832	6,488	7,840	7,339	4,399
Other costs and services	111,186	103,984	110,169	37,595	46,070	19,863	11,824	16,935	32,480
Income	10,054	3,812	2,110	7,792	5,917	(2,054)	2,369	(9,209)	(8,681)
Stock consumption	218,920	202,936	156,280	57,171	33,918	10,178	9,332	8,566	7,642
Contingency	–	55,000	–	–	14,000	–	–	–	–
Indirect costs									
Stock write-off	51	44	1,559	(2)	(2)	9	–	–	–
Provisions	1,560	3,000	6,192	–	–	–	(437)	87	299
Depreciation and amortisation (inc Urgent Operational Requirements – UORs)	33,611	15,577	41,270	1,255	1,596	177	2,376	6,944	8,608
Fixed asset write-off	21,848	30,000	8,000	–	–	–	–	–	–
Cost of capital	4,441	4,594	6,186	183	162	185	284	408	444
Total	**797,760**	**838,092**	**747,068**	**148,117**	**150,444**	**57,937**	**62,679**	**64,000**	**84,677**
Capital Cost (by area)									
Capital addition including UORs and Recuperation)	159,838	199,944	162,862	51,231	53,053	9,097	174	–	2,430
Net Book Value of fixed asset disposals	–	–	–	–	–	–	–	–	(547)
Contingency	–	60,000	–	–	17,000	–	–	–	–
Total	**159,838**	**259,944**	**162,862**	**51,231**	**70,053**	**9,097**	**174**	**-**	**1,883**
Total by Operation	**957,598**	**1,098,036**	**909,930**	**199,348**	**220,497**	**67,034**	**62,853**	**64,000**	**86,560**

2.3 In accordance with the accounting principles agreed with HM Treasury, the Department has identified the costs of operations on the basis of net additional costs. Expenditure such as wages and salaries for permanently employed personnel are not included as these costs would have been incurred in the normal course of business. Costs of activities such as training and exercises which would have been incurred, but which have been cancelled due to operational commitments, have been deducted.

Negative numbers are shown in brackets. However, when comparing outturn against Estimate, excesses are shown in brackets.

The "positive income" figures in the operational costs represent income foregone (loss of receipts) as a result of those operations. The major loss of receipt falls into two areas: those from the Sultan of Brunei in respect of withdrawal of the services of the Gurkha Regiment whilst it was deployed in Afghanistan and the loss of anticipated messing charges for those military personnel based in the UK and Germany that were deployed to Iraq.

2.4 Comments on Major Changes in Cost

Between 2004-05 and 2005-06:

a. The reduction in service manpower costs in 2005-06, in both Iraq and Afghanistan, is the result of managing existing resources to reduce the requirement for Territorial Army support.

b. The increase in equipment support and stock consumption costs in 2005-06 in Afghanistan is the result of the planned expansion of operations into Helmand province.

c. The increase in stock consumption costs in 2005-06 in Iraq is the result of increased use of armament stores and fuel.

Between 2005-06 Outturn and Estimate:

d. The increase in depreciation and amortisation costs in Iraq between the sum allocated and final Outturn is the result of depreciation of Urgent Operational Requirements (UORs) which are purchased for specific operational purpose and often have short life spans.

e. The Request for Resources is based upon forecast costs two third of the way through the financial year. Due to the often rapidly changing operational situation it is prudent to include a contingency figure within the request; this is based on prior year's outturn and UOR costs which give an indication of potential short notice operational equipment requirements.

f. When the capital Estimate was prepared, it was based on UORs that had been financially approved. Not all UORs were subsequently delivered prior to the end of the financial year, resulting in an underspend against capital costs.

War Pensions Benefits – Programme Costs (RfR3)

2.5 The Chief Executive of the Veterans Agency is not a Top Level Budget Holder, but exercises all the responsibilities for the programme costs. There was an underspend of £4,377,000 against this RfR.

3. Reconciliation of Net Resource Outturn to Net Operating cost

			2005-06	2004-05
	Outturn	Supply Estimate	Outturn Compared with Estimate	Outturn Restated
	£000	£000	£000	£000
Net Resource Outturn (Statement of Parliamentary Supply)	34,862,134	36,838,773	1,976,639	32,561,830
– Less income scored as Consolidated Fund Extra Receipts and included in operating income and interest (inc. excess operating Appropriation-in-Aid) (Note 5)	(468,599)		468,599	(230,405)
Net Operating Cost	**34,393,535**	36,838,773	2,445,238	32,331,425

Net Resource Outturn is the total of those elements of expenditure and income that are subject to Parliamentary approval and included in the Department's Supply Estimate. Net operating cost is the total of expenditure and income appearing in the Operating Cost Statement. The Outturn against the Estimate is shown in the Statement of Parliamentary Supply.

4. Reconciliation of Resources to Cash Requirement

	Note	Estimate £000	Outturn £000	Savings/ (Excess) £000
Resource Outturn	2	36,838,773	34,862,134	1,976,639
Capital:				
*Purchase of fixed assets:				
– RfR 1	13/14	7,058,578	6,906,906	151,672
– RfR 2	13/14	329,997	211,243	118,754
– RfR 1 Capitalised provisions	13/14	–	43,178	(43,178)
– Investments	15	–	6,000	(6,000)
Non operating cost A-in-A:				
Proceeds on sale of fixed assets	10/13/14	(510,000)	(299,317)	(210,683)
Proceeds on redemption of shares	23.2	(27,857)	(21,766)	(6,091)
Repayment of loans made to the Trading Funds and QinetiQ	15	(69,184)	(53,237)	(15,947)
Accruals adjustments:				
Non-cash transactions-				
Included in operating costs	23.1	(8,725,882)	(7,276,465)	(1,449,417)
Included in net interest payable	12	(2,318,484)	(1,211,110)	(1,107,374)
Capitalised provisions shown above			(43,178)	43,178
		(11,044,366)	(8,530,753)	(2,513,613)
Cost of capital charge	23.1	(2,284,067)	(3,106,369)	822,302
*Changes in working capital other than cash, excluding movements on creditors falling due after one year		414,788	399,153	15,635
* Increase in creditors falling due after one year			(247,705)	247,705
*Use of provisions for liabilities and charges	20	795,330	374,039	421,291
Adjustment for movements on cash balances in respect of collaborative projects	23.5		59,791	(59,791)
Net cash requirement	23.5	**31,501,992**	**30,603,297**	**898,695**

* Stated to include accruals within the movements in the year

5. Analysis of income payable to the Consolidated Fund

In addition to Appropriations-in-Aid, the following income relates to the Department and is payable to the Consolidated Fund (cash receipts being shown in italics).

	2005-06 Forecast		2005-06 Outturn	
	Income £000	Receipts £000	Income £000	Receipts £000
Operating income and receipts – excess A-in-A Request for Resources 1	–	–	76,272	*76,272*
Operating income and receipts – excess A-in-A Request for Resources 2	–	–	16,062	*16,062*
Other operating income and receipts not classified as A-in-A	–	–	20,283	*20,283*
Subtotal operating income and receipts payable to the Consolidated Fund	–	–	112,617	*112,617*
Other amounts collectable on behalf of the Consolidated Fund (QinetiQ sale CFER)	–	–	355,982	*357,771*
Total income payable to the Consolidated Fund	–	–	468,599	*470,388*

6. Reconciliation of income recorded within the Operating Cost Statement to operating income payable to the Consolidated Fund

	Note	2005-06 £000	2004-05 £000
Operating Income		1,390,997	1,416,807
Income included within other operating costs			
– Refunds of formula based VAT recovery		31,669	71,603
– Foreign exchange gains		9,711	–
– Other		(11)	–
Interest Receivable		26,821	304
Gross Income		**1,459,187**	**1,488,714**
Income authorised to be appropriated in aid		(1,346,570)	(1,258,309)
Operating Income payable to the Consolidated Fund	5	**112,617**	**230,405**

7. Non-Operating income – Excess A in A

	2005-06 £000	2004-05 £000
Principal repayments of voted loans	53,237	25,187
Proceeds on disposal of fixed assets	321,083	415,455
Non-operating income – excess A-in-A	–	153,207

8. Non-Operating income not classified as A in A

	Income £000	Receipts £000
The Department has no non-operating income not classified as A-in-A	–	–

9. Staff Numbers and Costs

9.1 The average number of full-time equivalent persons employed during the year was: Service 203,290 (2004-05: 210,180) and Civilian 95,750 (2004-05: 96,780[5]). Source: Defence Analytical Services Agency.

	Permanent Staff	Temporary Staff	Armed Forces	Ministers	2005-06 Total	2004-05 Total
Analysis of Staff Numbers	94,626	1,120	203,290	4	**299,040**	306,960

In order to align with the total pay costs incurred during the year, shown below, the calculation of the average number of staff uses monthly statistics to identify an average employed for the year. The staff numbers quoted reflect the numbers of personnel employed in organisations within the Departmental Boundary for the Annual Accounts (see page 163) and therefore exclude those within the Trading Funds. The numbers reported within the Performance Report include employees in the MoD Trading Funds. More information on the Department's staff numbers, and the statistical calculations used, is available on the website: *http://www.dasa.mod.uk.*

9.2 The aggregate staff costs, including grants and allowances paid, were as follows:

	2005-06 £000	2004-05 £000
Salaries and Wages	8,603,882	8,470,881
Social Security costs	644,726	619,673
Pension costs	1,751,740	1,486,848
Redundancy and severance payments	254,503	418,240
	11,254,851	**10,995,642**
Made up of:		
Service	8,262,776	8,047,195
Civilian	2,992,075	2,948,447
	11,254,851	**10,995,642**

Principal Civil Service Pension Scheme

9.3 The Principal Civil Service Pension Scheme (PCSPS) is an unfunded multi-employer defined benefit scheme. The Ministry of Defence is unable to identify its share of the underlying assets and liabilities. The Scheme Actuary (Hewitt Bacon Woodrow) valued the scheme as at 31 March 2003. Details can be found in the resource accounts of the Cabinet Office: Civil Superannuation *(www.civilservice-pensions.gov.uk).*

9.4 For 2005-06, total pension contributions of £345,182,000 were payable in respect of the various schemes in which MoD civilian staff were members. Contributions to the PCSPS in the year were £309,639,000 (2004-05: £240,854,000) at rates in the range of 16.2 to 25.6 percent of pensionable pay, based on salary bands (the rates in 2004-05 were between 12% and 18.5%); the scheme actuary reviews employer contributions every four years. From 2006-07, the salary bands will be revised and the rates will be in a range between 17.1% and 26.5%. The contribution rates are set to meet the cost of the benefits accruing, to be paid when the member retires, not the benefits paid during the period to existing pensioners.

9.5 Employees can opt to open a partnership pension account, a stakeholder pension with an employer contribution. Employer contributions are age-related and range from 3% to 12.5% of pensionable pay. Employers also match employee contributions up to 3% of pensionable pay. In addition, employer contributions of 0.8% of pensionable pay were payable to the PCSPS to cover the cost of the future provision of lump sum benefits on death in service and ill health retirement of these employees.

[5] The 2004-05 average full-time equivalent civilian staff number has been restated following the identification of an error in the classification of personnel employed within one of the MoD Trading Funds. The consequence is a reduction in the average number of civilian personnel for 2004-05 from 97,540 shown in the 2004-05 Annual Report and Accounts to 96,780.

Armed Forces Pension Scheme

9.6 From 6 April 2005, the new Armed Forces Pension Scheme (known as AFPS 05) was introduced for all new members of the Armed Forces; those in service before this date have been given the opportunity to transfer to the new Scheme. The AFPS is an unfunded, non-contributory, defined benefit, salary-related, contracted out, occupational pension scheme. A formal valuation of the AFPS was carried out as at 31 March 2005 by the scheme's actuary, the Government Actuary's Department. Scheme members are entitled to a taxable pension for life and a tax-free pension lump sum if they leave the Regular Armed Forces at or beyond normal retirement age; those who have at least two years service who leave before age 55 will have their pensions preserved until age 65. Pensions may be payable to the spouse, civil partner, partner or to eligible children. Death-in-service lump sums are payable subject to nomination. There are no attributable ill-health benefits under the AFPS 05; these will be considered under the War Pensions Scheme (WPS) or the new Armed Forces Compensation Scheme (AFCS).

9.7 AFPS 05 includes an Early Departure Payment for those who leave before age 55 providing they have at least 18 years service and are at least 40 years of age. The Early Departure Payment Scheme pays a tax-free lump sum and income of between 50% and 75% of preserved pension between the date of the individual's departure from the Armed Forces and age 55. The income rises to 75% of preserved pension at age 55 and is index linked. At age 65, the Early Departure payments stop and the preserved pension and preserved pension lump sum are paid.

9.8 For 2005-06 total employers' pension contributions payable were £1,406,558,000. This figure includes £1,404,451,000 payable to the AFPS, (2004-05 £1,245,994,000) based on rates determined by the Government Actuary. For 2005-06, the rates were 34.3% of total pay (33.8% for 2004/05) for officers and 21.3% (18.2% for 2004/05) for other ranks. The contribution rates reflect benefits as they are accrued, not costs actually incurred in the period, and reflect past experience of the scheme. Further information on the Armed Forces Pension Scheme and the Armed Forces Compensation Scheme can be found at the website: *www.mod.uk/DefenceInternet/AboutDefence/Issues/Pensions/.*

Other Pension Schemes

9.9 The Armed Forces Pension Scheme incorporates three smaller pension schemes: the Non-Regular Permanent Staff Pension Scheme (NRPSPS), the Army Careers Officers Pension Scheme (ACOPS) and the new Reserve Forces Pension Scheme (RFPS). The membership of these schemes is 0.48% of the AFPS total membership and the employers' contributions are included in the AFPS figure at note 9.8.

9.10 Certain other employees are covered by schemes such as the Department of Health, Social Services and Public Safety Superannuation Scheme and the Teachers' Superannuation Scheme. The figure for total employers' pension contributions at note 9.4 includes contributions in respect of these schemes.

10. Other Operating Costs

	2005-06 £000	2004-05 Restated £000
Operating expenditure:		
– Fuel*	369,463	238,579
– Stock consumption	1,038,865	1,079,123
– Surplus arising on disposal of stock (net)	(16,372)	(25,214)
– Provisions to reduce stocks to net realisable value	(165,851)	227,498
– Stocks written off (net)	758,698	703,558
– Movements: includes personnel travelling, subsistence/relocation costs and movement of stores and equipment**	820,690	710,644
– Utilities	291,347	241,111
– Property management	1,747,294	1,509,085
– Hospitality and entertainment	5,364	6,450
– Accommodation charges	307,138	340,113
– Equipment support costs	3,614,442	3,623,327
– Increase/(Decrease) in nuclear and other decommissioning provisions (Note 20)***	(94,964)	(316,024)
- IT and telecommunications	755,249	678,250
– Professional fees	552,917	565,138
– Other expenditure	1,736,028	1,861,022
– Research expenditure and expensed development expenditure	994,480	996,421
Depreciation and amortisation:		
– Intangible assets (Note 13)	1,314,570	1,023,665
– Tangible owned fixed assets (Note 14)	5,236,589	5,128,204
- Donated assets depreciation – release of reserve	(57,991)	(49,473)
- Tangible fixed assets held under finance leases (Note 14)	4,685	3,660
Impairment on fixed assets (Notes 13 & 14):		
– Arising on Quinquennial valuation	254,156	110,000
– Arising on Other items	182,344	(335,339)
Impairment – release of reserve	(23,696)	(12,835)
(Surplus) arising on disposal of tangible and intangible fixed assets		
– Tangible and Intangible fixed assets	(458,384)	(52,079)
– Donated assets – release of reserve	(20,975)	(1,541)
Fixed assets (written on) – net	(301,805)	(85,648)
Investment writedown on share conversion	4,774	–
Capital project expenditure write off/(write on)	(22,145)	25,851
Bad debts written off	8,398	(5,411)
Increase in bad debts provision	1,439	920
Rentals paid under operating leases	192,488	228,515
Auditors' remuneration – audit work only ****	3,500	3,300
Grants-in-Aid	61,087	63,079
Exchange differences on foreign currencies: net deficit/(surplus)	8,207	14,728
War Pensions Benefits	1,069,133	1,096,727
Total Other Operating Costs	**20,171,162**	**19,595,404**

* The prior year figure for Fuel has increased by £57,205,547 to reflect a more accurate disclosure of all expenditure on fuel (excluding utilities). A corresponding reduction is shown in Stock Consumption.
** The prior year figure for Movements has increased by £287,874,734 to reflect a more accurate disclosure of all personnel movements. A corresponding reduction is shown in Other Expenditure.
*** The prior year figure for the movement in nuclear decommissioning provision has increased by £104,768,000 following the transfer to the Nuclear Decommisioning Authority.
**** Auditors' remuneration: No charge is made for non-audit work carried out by the auditors.

11. Income

	RfR 1	RfR2	2005-06 £000 Total	2004-05 £000 Total
Income Souce				
External Customers				
Rental income – property	49,444		49,444	54,618
Receipts – personnel	55,171		55,171	52,798
Receipts – sale of fuel	56,559		56,559	57,406
Receipts – supplies and services	176,466		176,466	174,177
Receipts – personnel related	175,369		175,369	168,626
Receipts – provision of families accommodation	180,779		180,779	178,319
Receipts – NATO/UN/US Forces/Foreign Governments	300,341	16,062	316,403	347,745
Other	193,634		193,634	180,328
Other Government Departments, Trading Funds and QinetiQ				
Rental income – property	440		440	2,680
Receipts – personnel related	3,281		3,281	17,662
Reverse tasking	26,384		26,384	28,473
Dividends from Investments (Note 15.4)	39,387		39,387	28,387
Income from provison of goods and services	113,218		113,218	122,773
Other	4,462		4,462	2,815
	1,374,935	**16,062**	**1,390,997**	**1,416,807**

12. Net Interest Payable

	2005-06 £000	2004-05 Restated £000
Interest receivable:*		
– Bank interest	(21,553)	(18,529)
– Loans to Trading Funds	(4,664)	(5,523)
– Loan to a Self Financing Public Corporation – QinetiQ**	(603)	(1,109)
– Other interest receivable	(1)	(2)
	(26,821)	(25,163)
Interest payable:		
– Bank interest	18	25
– Loan interest	3,348	3,417
– Unwinding of discount on provision for liabilities and charges (Note 20)***	1,211,110	147,851
– Finance leases and PFI contracts	64,480	5,164
– Late payment of Commercial debts	15	–
	1,278,971	156,457
Net interest payable	**1,252,150**	131,294

* Interest receivable of which £765,000 is payable to Consolidated Fund (£304,000 in 2004-05).

** for the period to Feb 06 prior to flotation.

*** The increase in the unwinding of the discount is as a result of the change in discount rate from 3.5% to 2.2% with effect from 1 Apr 05

The prior year figure for unwinding of discount on provisions for liabilities and charges has decreased by £142,106,000 following the transfer to the Nuclear Decommissioning Authority.

13. Intangible Assets

	Single use Military Equipment £000	Others £000	Total £000
Cost or Valuation			
At 1 April 2005	27,992,914	448,966	28,441,880
Additions	1,350,720	199,248	1,549,968
Impairment	(7,201)	(23,313)	(30,514)
Revaluations	366,104	13,838	379,942
Other movements	(1,295,504)	371,802	(923,702)
At 31 March 2006	28,407,033	1,010,541	**29,417,574**
Amortisation			
At 1 April 2005	(5,713,858)	(80,199)	(5,794,057)
Charged in Year	(1,270,657)	(43,913)	(1,314,570)
Impairment	(5,549)	8,201	2,652
Revaluations	(64,536)	(3,256)	(67,792)
Other movements	677,057	61,831	738,888
At 31 March 2006	(6,377, 543)	(57,336)	**(6,434,879)**
Net Book Value:			
At 31 March 2006	**22,029,490**	**953,205**	**22,982,695**
At 1 April 2005	22,279,056	368,767	22,647,823

Note:
i) Intangible asset valuations are based on the actual costs incurred over time where available, or derived by applying a ratio to the tangible fixed asset valuations based on the historical relationship between development and production costs. The intangible asset valuations were indexed using the appropriate Gross Domestic Product (GDP) deflator to determine the opening balance sheet valuation;
ii) Intangible assets include development expenditure in respect of fixed assets in use and assets under construction where the first delivery into operational use of the asset type has taken place;
iii) Additions on intangible and tangible fixed assets (Note 14) include accruals amounting in total to £2,514,869,000 (2004-05: £2,246,205,000); and
iv) Other movements comprise reclassifications to tangible fixed assets and transfers to operating costs.

14. Tangible Fixed Assets

	Dwellings £000	Other Land and Buildings	Single Use Military Equipment (SUME)	Plant and Machinery	Transport	IT and Comms Equipment	Assets under Construction (SUME)	Assets under Construction (Others)	Total
	£000	£000	£000	£000	£000	£000	£000	£000	£000
Cost or Valuation									
At 1 April 2005 Restated	2,838,959	17,607,893	58,143,194	6,443,132	8,551,289	1,467,527	11,715,475	741,716	107,509,185
Additions	611	30,194	401,991	63,878	12,580	180,401	4,253,950	624,576	5,568,181
Capitalised provisions	–	25,370	17,808	–	–	–	–	–	43,178
Donations	12,331	37,887	–	5,188	–	–	–	–	55,406
Impairment	(9,716)	(154,946)	68,954	(28,026)	(293,063)	(207,807)	(3,692)	(1,193)	(629,489)
Disposals	(1,619)	(198,477)	(1,067,310)	(26,694)	(8,385)	(65)	–	–	(1,302,550)
Revaluations	160,068	1,021,504	1,929,311	85,843	(187,937)	(38,354)	152,589	12,771	3,135,795
Other movements	389,104	(861,726)	1,073,283	(664,226)	136,560	65,986	(3,523,988)	(314,738)	(3,699,745)
At 31 March 2006	3,389,738	17,507,699	60,567,231	5,879,095	8,211,044	1,467,688	12,594,344	1,063,132	110,679,961
Depreciation									
At 1 April 2005	(348,421)	(2,001,726)	(27,578,261)	(2,968,608)	(4,568,829)	(434,451)	–	–	(37,900,296)
Charged in year	(86,044)	(609,794)	(3,446,561)	(391,890)	(471,923)	(235,062)	–	–	(5,241,274)
Impairment	4,636	23,014	119,082	17,863	7,328	48,925	–	–	220,848
Disposals	251	4,874	1,066,598	26,652	7,196	65	–	–	1,105,636
Revaluations	(38,954)	(237,772)	(1,198,983)	(35,943)	295,761	25,050	–	–	(1,190,841)
Other movements	(8,510)	857,172	1,960,312	746,954	431,325	113,671	–	–	4,100,924
At 31 March 2006	(477,042)	(1,964,232)	(29,077,813)	(2,604,972)	(4,299,142)	(481,802)	–	–	(38,905,003)
Net Book Value:									
At 31 March 2006	**2,912,696**	**15,543,467**	**31,489,418**	**3,274,123**	**3,911,902**	**985,886**	**12,594,344**	**1,063,132**	**71,774,958**
At 1 April 2005	2,490,538	15,606,167	30,564,933	3,474,524	3,982,460	1,033,076	11,715,475	741,716	69,608,889

Note:

i) Additions on intangible assets (Note 13) and tangible fixed assets include accruals amounting in total to £2,514,869,000 (2004-05: £2,246,205,000).

ii) Other movements comprise reclassifications between tangible fixed asset categories, intangible assets, assets under construction, stock and transfers to operating costs.

iii) The prior year cost for other Land and Buildings has been reduced by £25,705,000 to reflect the transfer of a capitalised provision to the Nuclear Decommissioning Authority.

iv) Fixed Assets as at 31 March 2006 include capitalised provisions at cost of £195,698,000 (Restated 2004-2005: £219,677,000).

14.1 The net book value of tangible fixed assets by each major class of asset includes an amount of £522,190,000 (2004-05 £660,448,000) in respect of assets held under finance leases and PFI contracts. Detail by asset category is as follows:

	Dwellings	Other Land and Buildings	Plant and Machinery	Fighting Equipment Transport	Other Transport	IT and Comms Equipment	Total
	£000	£000	£000	£000	£000	£000	£000
Gross Cost:							
At 31 March 2006	**31,479**	**341,841**	**102,534**	**84,993**	**8,077**	**54,913**	**623,837**
At 1 April 2005	28,204	450,358	95,915	51,814	47,907	62,792	736,990
Accumulated Depreciation:							
At 31 March 2006	**8,438**	**15,480**	**9,014**	**57,250**	**2,395**	**9,070**	**101,647**
At 1 April 2005	4,382	11,324	4,388	44,716	3,867	7,865	76,542

14.2 Analysis of Land and Buildings

	Freehold	Long lease	Short lease	Beneficial Use*	Total
	£000	£000	£000	£000	£000
Net Book Value:					
At 31 March 2006	**17,072,700**	**267,245**	**63,041**	**2,090,735**	**19,493,722**
Restated At 1 April 2005	16,639,415	248,469	50,232	2,001,336	18,939,452

*Relates to properties that are being used by the Department where no legal title is held. Such properties have been valued on the same basis as all other properties used by the Department.

The net book values at 31 March 2006 and 1 April 2005 include assets under construction of £1,037,559,000 and £842,748,000 respectively.

The balance as at 1 April 05 for Freehold has been reduced by £25,705,000 following the transfer of a capitalised provision to the Nuclear Decommissioning Authority.

14.3 2005 – 06 Quinquennial Revaluation

a. All categories of fixed assets, except Intangibles, Assets under Construction and Capital Spares, are subject to a quinquennial revaluation, which is being conducted on a rolling programme. During 2005-06, 22% of Land and Buildings were re-valued by two external organisations: the Valuation Office Agency, who dealt with the UK estate, and GVA Grimley, who were responsible for the overseas estate. These valuations were undertaken in accordance with the Royal Institute of Chartered Surveyors Appraisal and Valuation Manual and were on the basis of the existing use value to the Department. Due to the specialised nature of the Departmental estate, the majority of assets were valued using the Depreciated Replacement Cost method.

b. As a result of the valuations undertaken in 2005-06, the net increase to Land and Buildings was £269,423,000. Impairments charged to the Operating Cost Statement were £87,882,000. Impairments incurred as a result of the 2002-03 quinquennial review have been reversed through the Operating Cost Statement in 2005-06 to the sum of £10,008,000.

c. 70% of Plant and Machinery, IT and Transport was professionally re-valued on a Depreciated Replacement Cost basis in 2005-06 by the Valuation Office Agency valuers: the net decrease in net book value from these valuations (£56,188,000) is reflected in these accounts. Impairments of £162,232,000 have been charged to the Operating Cost Statement.

d. Much of the overseas Plant and Machinery, IT & Communications Equipment and Transport were valued by GVA Grimley during 2005-06. The movement in the net book value of assets valued was a decrease of £10,908,000. Impairments charged to the Operating Cost Statement are £5,656,000. Impairments that originated in the 2002-03 quinquennial review have been reversed through the Operating Cost Statement in 2005-06 to the sum of £5,610,000.

15. Investments

	Trading Funds		Other Investments	QinetiQ	Total
	Public Dividend Capital	Loans			
	£000	£000	£000	£000	£000
Balance at 1 April 2005	184,254	87,390	1	75,463	347,108
Additions					
Met Office		6,000			6,000
Disposals (share conversions and shares sold in the Initial Public Offering (IPO))				(28,329)	(28,329)
Loan Repayments					
QinetiQ				(45,886)	(45,886)
Defence Aviation Repair Agency (DARA)		(4,840)			(4,840)
UK Hydrographic Office (UKHO)		(357)			(357)
ABRO		(2,154)			(2,154)
Revaluations				242,590	242,590
Balance at 31 March 2006	**184,254**	**86,039**	**1**	**243,838**	**514,132**
Balance at 1 April 2005	184,254	87,390	1	75,463	347,108

Public Dividend Capital and Loans at 31 March 2006 were held in the following Trading Funds:

	Public Dividend Capital	Loans	Interest Rates
	£000	£000	% p.a.
Defence Science Technology Laboratory (Dstl)	50,412	–	
Met Office	58,867	6,000	4.45
UK Hydrographic Office	13,267	10,993	8.375
Defence Aviation Repair Agency	42,303	45,350	4.20 – 5.00
ABRO	19,405	23,696	5.625
Balance at 31 March 2006	**184,254**	**86,039**	

Analysis of loans repayable by instalments:

	Due within one year	Due after one year	Total
	£000	£000	£000
Met Office	1,100	4,900	6,000
UK Hydrographic Office	387	10,606	10,993
Defence Aviation Repair Agency	4,840	40,510	45,350
ABRO	2,154	21,542	23,696
Balance at 31 March 2006	**8,481**	**77,558**	**86,039**

15.1 Investment in QinetiQ Group plc.

	£000	Total £000
Balance at 1 April 2005		75,463
Repayment of Long Term Loan		(45,886)
Balance After repayment of Long Term Loan		29,577
Disposals		
Redemption of Preferences Shares	(21,766)	
Write-down on share conversions	(4,774)	(26,540)
Balance after share redemption and conversions		3,037
Book Value of the shares sold in the IPO		(1,789)
Value of the remaining shareholding before revaluations		1,248
Revaluations		
Revaluation of the remaining shares to the IPO market price of 200p per share		248,522
Balance of investment at the IPO market price		249,770
Write-down in the value of the shares to a market price of 195.25p as at 31 March 06		(5,932)
Balance at 31 March 2006		**243,838**

As part of the process of preparing for the Initial Public Offering (IPO) in QinetiQ Group plc, and in accordance with the company's Articles of Association, the outstanding loan with MoD (£45,886,023) was repaid. This reduced MoD's investment from £75,463,551 (at 1 April 2005) to an investment valued at £29,577,528 and consisting of various types of shares.

This investment was further reduced on the redemption, by MoD, of its Redeemable Cumulative Preference Shares for £21,765,524 leaving an investment that consisted of a mixture of Ordinary and Convertible Shares (with a book value of £7,812,004). The Company then undertook a series of share redemptions, conversions and bonus issues, in accordance with the Articles of Association, which resulted in MoD holding 303,770,800 of the new class of Ordinary Shares with a nominal value of £3,037,708. The book value of MoD's investment was written-down to this amount prior to the IPO.

On 10 February 2006, MoD sold 178,885,355 of its shares, for 200p per share, as part of the IPO. The book value of the shares sold was £1,788,853.55. The balance of the shareholding (124,885,445 shares) had a book value of £1,248,854.45 (£3,037,708.00 – £1,788,853.55). This remaining shareholding was revalued, at 200p per share (a total valuation of £249,770,890 as at 10 February 2006, an increase in the book value of the investment of £248,522,035.55).

Fees associated with the sale of shares (e.g. stamp duty and commission paid) were £10,617,824.75 and are included as Professional Fees under Other Operating Costs. (Further details of Other Operating costs can be found at Note 10 to the accounts).

The total raised from the IPO was £357,770,710 (178,885,355 shares sold at 200p per share). This amount has been treated as a Consolidated Fund Extra Receipt which was payable, in full, to HM Treasury.

On 31 March 2006, the 124,885,445 shares held were valued at 195.25p per share: a reduction in the total value of the investment, compared to the 200p per share value on flotation, of £5,932,058.64. The Department's remaining shareholding in QinetiQ Group plc is 124,885,445 (19.3%) Ordinary Shares (nominal value 1p each) which, at 31 March 06, were valued at a market price of 195.25p per share; a total market value of £243,838,831.36. Holders of Ordinary Shares in QinetiQ Group plc are entitled to receive notice of, attend, speak and vote at general and extraordinary meetings of the company and have one vote for every share owned.

The Department also holds one Special Share in QinetiQ Group plc, and one Special Share in each of two of its subsidiary companies, QinetiQ Holdings Limited and QinetiQ Limited. The Special Shares can only be held by the Crown and give the Government the right to: implement and operate the Compliance System, prohibit or restrict QinetiQ from undertaking activities which may lead to an unmanageable conflict of interest that would be damaging to the defence or security interests of the United Kingdom, and to veto any transaction which may lead to unacceptable ownership of the company. The Special Shareholder must receive notice of, and may attend and speak at, general and extraordinary meetings. The Special Shares carry no voting rights, except to enforce certain aspects of the compliance regime. The shareholder has no right to share in the capital or profits of the company other than – in the event of liquidation – to be repaid the capital paid up in respect of the shares before other shareholders receive any payment.

15.2 Other investments.

Investments, including Special Shares, were held in the following at 31 March 2006:

	7.5% Non-cumulative Irredeemable Preference Shares at £1 each
Chamber of Shipping Limited	688 Shares
British Shipping Federation Limited	55,040 Shares

	Preferential Special Shares at £1 each
Devonport Royal Dockyard Limited	1 Share
Rosyth Royal Dockyard Limited	1 Share
AWE plc	1 Share
AWE Pension Trustees Limited	1 Share
QinetiQ Group plc	1 Share
QinetiQ Holdings Limited	1 Share
QinetiQ Limited	1 Share
BAE Systems Marine (Holdings) Limited	1 Share

	Non Preferential Shares of £1 each
International Military Services Limited	19,999,999 Shares

The Department has a 100% interest in the non-preferential shares of International Military Services Limited, a company registered in England. International Military Services Limited ceased trading on 31 July 1991. Following settlement of outstanding contracts, the company will be liquidated. The Department has written down the value of the investment to nil.

The 7.5% Non-cumulative Irredeemable Preference Shares in Chamber of Shipping Limited and British Shipping Federation Limited are valued at 1p each reflecting the value at which shares would be recovered by the two companies should membership by the Department be ceded, as laid down in the Articles of Association of the respective companies.

Special Shares confer on the Secretary of State for Defence special rights regarding ownership, influence and control, including voting rights in certain circumstances, under the individual Articles of Association of the relevant companies in which the shares are held. Further detailed information can be obtained from the companies' individual annual reports and accounts, which can be obtained from:

Company	Registration number
Devonport Royal Dockyard Limited, Devonport Royal Dockyard, Devonport, Plymouth PL1 4SG	02077752
Rosyth Royal Dockyard Limited, c/o Babcock BES, Rosyth Business Park, Rosyth, Dunfermine, Fife KY11 2YD	SC101959
AWE plc, AWE Aldermaston, Reading, Berkshire RG7 4PR	02763902
AWE Pension Trustees Limited, AWE Aldermaston, Reading, Berkshire RG7 4PR	02784144
QinetiQ Group plc, 85 Buckingham Gate, London SW1E 6PD	04586941
QinetiQ Holdings Limited, 85 Buckingham Gate, London SW1E 6PD	04154556
QinetiQ Limited, 85 Buckingham Gate, London SW1E 6PD	3796233
BAE Systems Marine (Holdings) Limited, Warwick House, PO Box 87, Farnborough Aerospace Centre, Farnborough, Hants GU14 6YU	01957765

15.3 Net Assets of Trading Funds

The reported net assets, after deducting loans due to MoD, of the investments held in Trading Funds at 31 March 2006 and 31 March 2005 were:

	31 March 2006 £000	31 March 2005 £000
UK Hydrographic Office	49,207	43,150
Met Office	188,293	175,753
Defence Aviation Repair Agency	82,904	76,877
Defence Science and Technology Laboratory	218,000	198,900
ABRO	47,598	53,496
Total	**586,002**	**548,176**

15.4 Dividends from Investments

The following dividends, shown as income in Note 11, were received in the accounting periods ended 31 March 2005 and 31 March 2006:

	31 March 2006 £000	31 March 2005 £000
QinetiQ	6,091	5,759
UK Hydrographic Office	6,296	19,628
Met Office	Nil	Nil
Defence Aviation Repair Agency	12,000	Nil
Defence Science and Technology Laboratory	3,000	3,000
ABRO	12,000	Nil
Total	**39,387**	**28,387**

16. Stocks and Work in Progress

	31 March 2006 £000	31 March 2005 £000
Work in progress	34,244	28,861
Raw materials and consumables	6,015,687	6,064,180
Assets declared for disposal	2,296	2,322
	6,052,227	**6,095,363**

17. Debtors

17.1 Analysis by type

	31 March 2006 £000	31 March 2005 Restated £000
Amounts falling due within one year		
Trade debtors	177,539	211,854
Deposits and advances	54,355	53,186
Value Added Tax	320,544	277,354
Other debtors	275,363	187,263
Staff loans and advances	41,921	33,085
Prepayments and accrued income	506,324	636,303
Current part of PFI prepayment	156,716	193,229
	1,532,762	**1,592,274**
Amounts falling due after one year		
Trade debtors	28,000	49,693
Deposits and advances	26	–
Other debtors	2,431	97,250
Prepayments and accrued income	1,357,936	1,110,161
Total Debtors	**1,388,393**	**1,257,104**

Note:
i) Other debtors include loans for house purchase and other loans made to staff amounting to £92,291,269 (2004-05: £85,299,668). The number of staff with house purchase loans was 11,712 (2004-05:12,558).
ii) Prepayments falling due after one year include an amount of £391,000,000 in respect of an adjudication decision where an appeal is pending: the amount represents an amount paid into an Escrow Account in the financial year 2002-03 and interest earned on it since that date.
iii) The prior year balance for prepayments and accrued income falling due within one year has been reduced by £21,521,000 following the transfer to the Nuclear Decommissioning Authority.

17.2 Intra-Government Balances

	Amounts falling due within one year £000		Amounts falling due after more than one year £000	
	2005-06	2004-05	2005-06	2004-05
Balances with other central government bodies	366,301	337,142	30,143	60,514
Balances with local authorities	1,433	2,375	–	–
Balances with NHS Trusts	12,864	10,136	–	–
Balances with public corporations and trading funds	7,576	38,637	–	301
Subtotal: intra-government balances	388,174	388,290	30,143	60,815
Balances with bodies external to government	1,144,588	1,203,984	1,358,250	1,196,289
Total debtors at 31 March	**1,532,762**	**1,592,274**	**1,388,393**	**1,257,104**

The 2004-05 "Amounts falling due within one year" balance with other central government bodies has been restated to include the VAT debtor.

18. Cash at Bank and in Hand

	2005-06 £000	2004-05 £000
Balance at 1 April	438,411	312,564
Net Cash Inflow/(Outflow):		
Received from Consolidated Fund	31,262,178	29,497,000
Utilised	(30,682,344)	(29,371,153)
Increase during year	579,834	125,847
Balance at 31 March	**1,018,245**	**438,411**
The following balances at 31 March were held at:		
Office of HM Paymaster General	684,585	277,775
Commercial Banks and Cash in Hand	333,660	160,636
Balance at 31 March	**1,018,245**	**438,411**

Note:
The cash at bank balance includes £256,381,000 (2004-05: £196,590,000) of sums advanced by foreign governments to the Department on various collaborative projects where the United Kingdom is the host nation. Advances made by foreign governments for the procurement of defence equipment on their behalf are also included in this amount. The corresponding liability for these advances is shown under creditors due within one year.

19. Creditors

19.1 Analysis by type

	31 March 2006	31 March 2005 Restated
	£000	£000
Amounts falling due within one year		
VAT	36,320	(13)
Other taxation and social security	240,255	215,375
Trade creditors	546,569	709,356
Other creditors (Note ii)	351,519	344,645
Payments received on account	25,920	22,115
Accruals and deferred income	4,465,599	4,444,563
Current part of finance leases	4,378	4,914
Current part of imputed finance lease element of on-balance sheet PFI contracts	15,168	16,409
Current part of NLF loans (Note i)	1,797	1,695
Amounts issued from the Consolidated Fund for supply but not spent at year end (Note iii)	658,881	(127,275)
Consolidated Fund extra receipts due to be paid to the Consolidated Fund – Received	102,983	369,096
	6,449,389	**6,000,880**
Amounts falling due after more than one year		
Other creditors	101,618	37,441
Accruals	176,686	558
Finance leases	2,639	10,507
Imputed finance lease element of on-balance sheet PFI contracts	642,523	651,757
NLF loans (Note i)	48,335	50,132
Loans – other	85,800	59,500
	1,057,601	**809,895**

The prior year balances for trade creditors and accruals and deferred income, have been reduced by £2,238,000 and £72,495,000 respectively, following the transfer to the Nuclear Decommissioning Authority.

Note:
i) Loans are from the National Loans Fund in respect of the Armed Forces Housing Loans. These are fully repayable between years 2012 and 2028, with the last instalment due on 20 February 2028. Interest on the loans is payable at rates ranging from 4.25% to 7% per annum.
ii) Included in other creditors are amounts advanced by foreign governments to the Department in respect of various collaborative projects where the United Kingdom is the host nation and for the procurement of defence equipment on their behalf of £256,381,000 (2004-05 – £196,590,000).
iii) The amount comprises amounts drawn down from the Consolidated Fund of £31,262,178,000 less Net Cash Requirement (Statement of Parliamentary Supply) of £30,603,297,000

19.2 Intra-Government Balances

	Amounts falling due within one year £000		Amounts falling due after more than one year £000	
	2005-06	2004-05	2005-06	2004-05
Balances with other central government bodies	806,936	257,762	134,135	50,132
Balances with local authorities	781	1,216	–	–
Balances with NHS Trusts	2,938	14,485	–	–
Balances with public corporations and trading funds	66,884	287,243	3,874	–
Subtotal: intra-government balances	877,539	560,706	138,009	50,132
Balances with bodies external to government	5,571,850	5,440,174	919,592	759,763
Total creditors at 31 March	**6,449,389**	**6,000,880**	**1,057,601**	**809,895**

The 2004-05 balances with other central Government bodies has been restated to include creditors with the Considated Fund and the National Loans Fund.

20. Provisions for Liabilities and Charges

	Nuclear Decom-missioning	Other Decom-missioning And Restoration Costs £000	Early Retirement Commit-ments £000	Other £000	Total £000
At 1 April 2005 (Restated)	3,290,637	110,883	467,622	1,313,538	5,182,680
Increase in Provision	112,306	32,016	172,185	293,767	610,274
Unwinding of discounting	1,114,871	4,002	26,329	65,908	1,211,110
Amounts released	(205,821)	(17,755)	(40,530)	(132,604)	(396,710)
Reclassifications	–	(2,699)	–	1,150	(1,549)
Amounts capitalised	43,178	–	–	–	43,178
Utilised in year	(55,683)	(8,876)	(99,095)	(210,385)	(374,039)
At 31 March 2006	**4,299,488**	**117,571**	**526,511**	**1,331,374**	**6,274,944**

The balance as at 1 April 2005 for nuclear decommissioning has been reduced by £4,320,528,000 following the transfer to the Nuclear Decommissioning Authority.

Analysis of amount charged/(credited) to Operating Cost Statement

	2005-06 £000	2004-05 Restated £000
Charged/(credited) to:		
Property management	10,334	6,066
Staff costs	274,509	407,621
Nuclear and Other Decommissioning provisions	(95,111)	(316,024)
War Pensions Benefits	2,200	(10,355)
Other costs	21,632	131,141
Net interest (receivable)/payable	1,211,110	147,850
	1,424,674	**366,299**
Made up of:		
Increase	610,274	809,522
Release	(396,710)	(591,073)
	213,564	218,449
Unwinding of discount *	1,211,110	147,850
Net increase in provisions	**1,424,674**	**366,299**

* The 2005-06 charge for the unwinding of discount is higher due to the change in discount factor from 3.5% to 2.2% in this year.

The prior year costs for nuclear and other decommissioning provisions has increased by £104,786,000 and costs for net interest payable have decreased by £142,106,000 following the transfer to the Nuclear Decommissioning Authority.

Nuclear Decommissioning

20.1 Nuclear decommissioning provisions relate principally to the cost of facility decommissioning and the treatment and storage of nuclear waste arising from operations at MoD sites, operations of Royal Navy submarines and for the Departmental share of planning and constructing a national repository for the eventual disposal of that waste.

On 1 April 2005, the Nuclear Decommissioning Authority (NDA), a newly formed organisation sponsored by the Department of Trade and Industry, took over the responsibility for decommissioning and clear-up of civil nuclear sites. As a result, the MoD liabilities at 1 April 2005 relating to civil nuclear sites and the associated value of provisions and funding for decommissioning costs were transferred to the NDA. The liabilities for the decommissioning of other MoD sites and for the disposal of submarine waste have been retained by MoD. The MoD retains responsibility for the Atomic Weapons Establishment (AWE).

The liabilities include the costs associated with decommissioning and care and maintenance of redundant facilities (the conditioning, retrieval and storage of contaminated materials), research and development and the procurement of capital facilities to handle the various waste streams.

Calculation of the provision to cover the liabilities is based on schedules of information received by the MoD from major decommissioning contractors. These schedules are based on technical assessments of the processes and methods likely to be used in the future to carry out the work. Estimates are based on the latest technical knowledge and commercial information available, taking into account current legislation, regulations and Government policy. The amount and timing of each obligation are therefore sensitive to these factors. These sensitivities and their likely effect on the calculation and amount of the liabilities are reviewed on an annual basis.

The latest estimate of the undiscounted cost of dealing with the MoD's nuclear liabilities is £9,753,827,000 (Restated 2004-2005: £9,127,164,000).

The estimate of £4,299,488,000 at 31 March 2006 represents £9,863,904,000 discounted at 2.2% to the balance sheet date and expressed in 2005-06 money values.

The estimated timescale over which the costs will need to be incurred is as follows:

	31 March 2006 £000
Up to 3 years	311,855
From 4 – 10 years	864,766
Beyond 10 years	3,122,867
Total	**4,299,488**

Provisions have been made to cover the costs associated with the research, development and construction of the NIREX Deep Waste Repository (DWR). The provisions have been based on advice provided by NIREX.

However, the policy for the disposal of intermediate and high level waste has yet to be clarified following the previous Government's rejection, in May 1997, of planning consent for the proposed Deep Waste Repository. Pending the current Government's consideration of a House of Lords Sub Committee report on the means of disposing of radioactive waste, the UK holders of such waste are working on the assumption that a repository will not be available earlier than 2040. This will necessitate the continued provision of interim storage.

During 2005-06, a formal review has been undertaken of the AWE nuclear provision incorporating an assessment of the risks and assumptions which underpin the provision calculations and the level of contingency within it. Progress made since 2000 against the original plans was also examined. The outcome of this review was the decision to retain the provision at the current level until the next quinquennial review due in 2007.

Other Decommissioning and Restoration

20.2 Other decommissioning and restoration provisions relate primarily to contaminated sites where the Department has a constructive or a legal obligation to restore the sites for normal use and for the decommissioning of certain fighting equipment and GWMB. During 2005-06, a provision of £20,111,000 was created for environmental liabilities at the former Defence Evaluation and Reseach Agency (DERA) test ranges, currently operated by QinetiQ Group plc.

Early Retirement Pensions

20.3 Where the Department implements an early departure scheme, provision is made for future liability payable to civilian early retirees. During 2005-06, provisions were created for the early departure of civilian employees in Northern Ireland (£42,975,000) as a result of "normalisation", within the DLO (£80,682,000), and within the Central TLB (£10,222,000) to extend the Departmental scheme announced in 2004-05.

Other

20.4 Other provisions include costs arising from the disposal of fixed assets; redundancy and relocation costs associated with reorganisation and restructuring and amounts payable under guarantees, litigation and contractual arrangements. Provisions created during 2005-06 include £153,044,000 arising from Army restructuring of the Home Service officers and soldiers of the Royal Irish Regiment following Northern Ireland normalisation, an increase of £66,756,000 for legal claims, and £13,560,000 for ABRO restructuring. The pension provision for locally employed personnel overseas has been increased by £46,290,000 on advice from the Government Actuary's Department. Existing provisions include those concerning an adjudication decision where an appeal is pending (£368,000,000).

21. General Fund

	2005-06 £000	2004-05 Restated £000
Balance at 1 April	69,254,944	68,129,653
Net Parliamentary Funding – Drawn Down	31,262,178	29,497,000
Year end adjustment – Supply Creditor/(Debtor) – current year	(658,881)	127,275
Net Transfer from Operating Activities		
– Net Operating Costs	(34,393,535)	(32,331,425)
– CFERs paid and repayable to Consolidated Fund	(470,388)	(383,612)
Non-cash charges:		
– Cost of Capital (OCS)	3,106,369	3,025,892
– Auditors' Remuneration (Note 10)	3,500	3,300
Transfer from Revaluation Reserve (Note 22)	4,450,319	1,094,062
Transfer from Donated Asset Reserve (Note 22)	(64,329)	92,799
Balance at 31 March	**72,490,177**	**69,254,944**

The prior year net operating costs transferred from operating activity have decreased by £78,714,000 following the transfer to the Nuclear Decommissioning Authority. The balance as at 1 April 2004 is also restated from £64,028,508,000 as a result of the transfer.

22. Reserves

	Revaluation Reserve £000	Donated Asset Reserve £000	Investment Reserve £000
At 1 April 2005	18,719,510	2,019,063	–
Arising on revaluation during the year (net)	2,425,832	56,346	–
Arising on revaluation on flotation of QinetiQ	–	–	248,522
Arising on valuation of year end market values	–	–	(5,932)
Additions during the year	–	55,407	–
Transfers and reclassifications	(59,340)	20,545	–
Transferred (to) / from Operating Cost Statement	–	(102,662)	–
Transferred (to) / from General Fund	(4,450,319)	64,329	–
At 31 March 2006	**16,635,683**	**2,113,028**	**242,590**

22.1 Following the Quinquennial Review of asset valuations during 2002, the MoD rebased the land and building assets with new gross costs and lives, within TLB asset registers. This resulted in a loss of direct linkage between individual assets and the revaluation reserve held on the Fixed Asset Registers (FARs). Off-line records continued to be maintained by TLBs.

22.2 The MoD estate was subject to a subsequent full professional revaluation review during 2004-05, and a further 22% review during 2005-06. The resultant movements in valuations were significantly reduced from those experienced in 2002. It is considered that future movements in the valuation of the estate will remain fairly constant and that the requirement for significant impairment reversals will not arise.

22.3 In preparation for the transfer of assets to Single Balance Sheet Owners from 1 April 2006 and the centralised processing of assets within the Shared Service Centre, and in light of the difficulties experienced in trying to maintain the off-line records, the unsupported revaluation reserve within the general ledger has been written-off to the general fund. The net transfer to the general fund is £2,898,000,000.

23. Notes to the Cash Flow Statement

23.1 Reconciliation of operating cost to operating cash flows

	Note	2005-06 £000	2004-05 Restated £000
Net operating cost	OCS	34,393,535	32,331,425
Non-cash transactions:			
– Depreciation and amortisation charges	10	(6,497,853)	(6,106,056)
– Impairment in value of fixed assets	10	(412,804)	238,174
– Provisions to reduce value of stock to its net realisable value	10	165,851	(227,498)
– Stocks written off – net	10	(758,698)	(703,558)
– Auditors' remuneration	10	(3,500)	(3,300)
– Surplus/(deficit) arising on disposal of tangible fixed assets	10	123,377	53,620
– Surplus/(deficit) arising on disposal of investments (QinetiQ)	10	355,982	–
– Fixed Assets written on – net	10	301,805	85,648
– Capital project expenditure written on/(off)	10	22,145	(25,851)
– Amounts written off investments	10	(4,774)	–
– Movement in provisions for liabilities and charges (excluding capitalised provisions)	20	(212,014)	(218,797)
– Unwinding of discount on provisions for liabilities and charges	20	(1,211,110)	(147,850)
– Cost of capital	21	(3,106,369)	(3,025,892)
		(11,237,962)	(10,081,360)
Increase/(decrease) in stocks/WIP		255,844	288,489
Increase/(decrease) in debtors		71,777	95,478
Less movements in debtors relating to items not passing through the OCS		–	–
(Increase)/decrease in creditors		(696,215)	(696,529)
Less movements in creditors relating to items not passing through the OCS		600,926	636,629
Use of provisions		477,154	392,149
Net cash outflow from operating activities		**23,865,060**	**22,966,281**

The prior year figure for the movement in provisions for liabilities and charges has decreased by £104,786,000 following the transfer to the Nuclear Decomissioning Authority.

23.2 Analysis of capital expenditure and financial investment

	Note	2005-06 £000	2004-05 Restated £000
Intangible fixed asset additions	13	1,549,968	1,579,884
Tangible fixed asset additions	14	5,568,181	5,489,495
Less movement on fixed asset accruals & creditors		(169,781)	(482,544)
Proceeds on disposal of tangible fixed assets		(299,316)	(266,912)
Proceeds of redemption of Redeemable Preference Shares in QinetiQ		(21,766)	(48,543)
Proceeds of Shares in QinetiQ		(357,771)	–
Loans made to Trading Funds	15	6,000	–
Repayment of loans made to the Trading Funds and QinetiQ	15	(53,237)	(25,187)
Net cash outflow from investing activities		**6,222,278**	**6,246,193**

23.3 Analysis of capital expenditure and financial investment by Request for Resources

	Capital expenditure £000	Loans etc £000	A in A £000	Net Total £000
Request for Resources 1	6,737,125	(47,237)	(321,082)	6,368,806
Request for Resources 2	211,243	–	–	211,243
Request for Resources 3	–	–	–	–
Paid to the Consolidated Fund Extra Receipts (QinetiQ flotation)	–	–	(357,771)	(357,771)
Net movements in debtors/creditors	169,781	–	–	169,781
Total 2005-06	**7,118,149**	**(47,237)**	**(678,853)**	**6,392,059**
Total 2004-05	7,092,316	(25,187)	(415,455)	6,651,674

23.4 Analysis of financing

	Note	2005-06 £000	2004-05 Restated £000
From the Consolidated Fund (Supply) – current year	21	31,262,178	29,497,000
From the Consolidated Fund (Supply) – prior year	21	127,275	80,095
Advances from the Contingencies Fund		1,839,814	–
Repayments to the Contingencies Fund		(1,839,814)	–
Repayment of loans from the National Loans Fund		(1,695)	(1,599)
Capital elements of payments in respect of finance leases and on-balance sheet PFI contracts		(10,385)	–
Loans – Other		26,300	–
Net financing		**31,403,673**	29,575,496

23.5 Reconciliation of Net Cash Requirement to increase in cash

	Note	2005-06 £000	2004-05 Restated £000
Net cash requirement		(30,603,297)	(29,624,275)
From the Consolidated Fund (Supply) – current year	23.4	31,262,178	29,497,000
From the Consolidated Fund Supply – prior year	23.4	127,275	80,095
Amounts due to the Consolidated Fund received and not paid	19	102,983	369,096
Amounts due to the Consolidated Fund received in the prior year and paid over		(369,096)	(222,659)
Movement on Collaborative balances		59,791	26,590
Increase in cash		**579,834**	125,847

24. Notes to the Statement of Operating Costs by Departmental Aim and Objectives

The net costs of the Departmental Objectives are determined as follows:

Objective 1: Achieving success in the tasks we undertake

This objective comprises the following:

	2005-06			2004-05		
	Gross £000	Income £000	Net £000	Gross £000	Income £000	Net £000
Operations	**1,055,848**	**(16,062)**	**1,039,786**	938,449	(268)	938,181
Other military tasks	**1,751,704**	**(53,287)**	**1,698,417**	1,849,803	(86,019)	1,763,784
Contributing to the community	**566,648**	**(72,362)**	**494,286**	457,294	(62,328)	394,966
Helping to build a safer world	**610,690**	**(279,090)**	**331,600**	479,778	(187,152)	292,626
Total	**3,984,890**	**(420,801)**	**3,564,089**	3,725,324	(335,767)	3,389,557

Costs are identified as follows:

- **Operations** comprises the additional costs incurred deploying the Armed Forces in military operations, e.g. in Iraq and Afghanistan, over and above the costs of maintaining the units involved at their normal states of readiness;
- **Other military tasks** include ongoing military commitments, e.g. to security in Northern Ireland and Overseas Commands, and the costs of identifying and countering the threat of terrorist attack on the UK mainland, and of maintaining the integrity of UK waters and airspace;
- **Contributing to the community** includes ongoing support activities, e.g. search and rescue, administration of cadet forces. In addition, it includes the costs of assistance to other Government Departments and agencies, e.g. in counter drugs operations;
- **Helping to build a safer world** includes the costs of Defence diplomacy undertaken to build confidence and security with our allies. It also includes the Department's support of wider British interests.

Objective 2: Being ready to respond to the tasks that might arise

The costs of delivering the military capability to meet this objective are analysed among force elements of the front line commands, including joint force units where these have been established, and a small number of centrally managed military support activities.

In addition to the direct operating costs of the front line units, they include the attributed costs of logistical and personnel support, identified by reference to the output costs of supplier Management Groupings.

In common with all objectives, these also contain a share of the costs of advising Ministers and accountability to Parliament, and apportioned overheads for head office functions and centrally provided services. The total comprises the full costs, including support services, of force elements grouped under the following headings:

	2005-06 Gross £000	2005-06 Income £000	2005-06 Net £000	2004-05 Gross £000	2004-05 Income £000	2004-05 Net £000
Royal Navy						
Aircraft carriers	363,720	(9,392)	354,328	362,268	(15,507)	346,761
Frigates and Destroyers	1,385,909	(30,940)	1,354,969	1,614,503	(66,014)	1,548,489
Smaller warships	424,510	(11,840)	412,670	509,040	(22,819)	486,221
Amphibious ships	296,158	(5,935)	290,223	348,724	(8,594)	340,130
Strategic sealift	43,742	(2,675)	41,067	40,097	(1,929)	38,168
Fleet support ships	347,915	(3,473)	344,442	413,254	(5,150)	408,104
Survey and other vessels	74,755	(2,389)	72,366	106,285	(3,797)	102,488
Naval aircraft	1,170,120	(31,482)	1,138,638	1,224,695	(31,763)	1,192,932
Submarines	3,441,777	(48,510)	3,393,267	2,351,571	(45,064)	2,306,507
Royal Marines	550,066	(10,153)	539,913	552,325	(12,555)	539,770
	8,098,672	(156,789)	7,941,883	7,522,762	(213,192)	7,309,570
Army						
Field units	8,696,394	(204,079)	8,492,315	7,683,884	(166,992)	7,516,892
Other units	2,204,945	(218,263)	1,986,682	1,927,205	(191,669)	1,735,536
	10,901,339	(422,342)	10,478,997	9,611,089	(358,661)	9,252,428
Royal Air Force						
Strike/attack and offensive support aircraft	1,832,257	(54,774)	1,777,483	2,424,992	(76,478)	2,348,514
Defensive and surveillance aircraft	2,409,986	(61,914)	2,348,072	2,303,701	(75,409)	2,228,292
Reconnaissance and maritime patrol aircraft	620,778	(15,043)	605,735	512,340	(23,002)	489,338
Tankers, transport and communications aircraft	1,304,193	(56,750)	1,247,443	1,064,852	(36,427)	1,028,425
Future capability	20,370	(372)	19,998	14,908	(314)	14,594
Other aircraft and RAF units	886,603	(36,854)	849,749	764,418	(48,798)	715,620
	7,074,187	(225,707)	6,848,480	7,085,211	(260,428)	6,824,783
Centre Grouping						
Joint and multinational operations	495,378	(21,187)	474,191	544,794	(21,333)	523,461
Centrally managed military support	491,589	(92,020)	399,569	437,110	(148,012)	289,098
Maintenance of war reserve stocks	465,421	(7,225)	458,196	749,333	(15,055)	734,278
	1,452,388	(120,432)	1,331,956	1,731,237	(184,400)	1,546,837
Total Objective 2	27,526,586	(925,270)	26,601,316	25,950,299	(1,016,681)	24,933,618

Most groupings are self explanatory. The following, however, should be noted:

- **Smaller warships** includes mine hunting and offshore patrol vessels;
- **Amphibious ships** includes assault ships providing platforms for landing craft and helicopters, and Royal Fleet Auxiliary landing support ships;
- **Strategic sealift** is the Roll-On Roll-Off ferry facility supporting the Joint Rapid Reaction Force;
- **Fleet support ships** includes Royal Fleet Auxiliary ships providing tanker and replenishment support to warships;
- **Survey and other vessels** includes ocean and coastal survey and ice patrol ships;
- **Naval aircraft** include Sea King, Lynx and Merlin helicopters deployed in anti-submarine, airborne early warning, Royal Marine support, and reconnaissance and attack roles;
- **Submarines** includes the operating costs of submarines, nuclear weapons systems and logistical support of nuclear propulsion, including nuclear decommissioning; (The costs of submarines reported in 2005-06 include the increased cost incurred following the change in the discount rate, from 3.5% to 2.2%, applied to the Department's provisions for nuclear decommissioning).

- **Army – Field units** includes 1 (UK) Armoured Division, 3 (UK) Division, Joint Helicopter Command and Theatre troops;

- **Army – Other units** includes Regional Divisions and Land support and training;

- **Strike/attack and offensive support aircraft** includes Tornado GR1/GR1A/GR1B/GR4/GR4A, Joint Force Harrier and Jaguar aircraft deployed in strike/attack and offensive support roles;

- **Defensive and surveillance aircraft** includes Typhoon, Tornado F3 and Sentry AEW1 aircraft deployed in UK air defence, and NATO and UN peacekeeping commitments;

- **Reconnaissance and maritime patrol aircraft** includes Canberra and Nimrod R1 aircraft deployed on reconnaissance, and Nimrod MR2 aircraft on maritime patrol. (Tornado GR1A/4A included in *strike/attack and offensive support aircraft* also undertake reconnaissance roles);

- **Tankers, transport and communications aircraft** includes C-17, Hercules, Tristar and VC10 aircraft providing air transport and air to air refuelling, and smaller transport aircraft (BAe 125/146 and Squirrel helicopters) used in a rapid communications role;

- **Future capability** includes the development and use of geographic information.

- **Other aircraft and RAF units** includes ground forces (e.g. the RAF Regiment) and miscellaneous aircraft not included elsewhere;

- **Joint and multinational operations** includes Chief of Joint Operations HQ and the costs less receipts of UK participation in NATO;

- **Centrally managed military support** includes intelligence operational support and Special Forces; and

- **Maintenance of war reserve stocks** includes the holding costs and charges of munitions and other stocks, above the levels required for planned consumption.

Objective 3: Building for the future

This objective comprises the following elements:

	2005-06			2004-05		
	Gross £000	Income £000	Net £000	Gross Restated £000	Income £000	Net Restated £000
Research	**1,041,105**	**(159)**	**1,040,946**	996,421	(318)	996,103
Equipment programme	**2,163,356**	**(44,767)**	**2,118,589**	1,966,666	(64,041)	1,902,625
Total	**3,204,461**	**(44,926)**	**3,159,535**	2,963,087	(64,359)	2,898,728

The prior year gross cost for the equipment programme has been reduced by £78,714,000 following the transfer to the Nuclear Decommissioning Authority.

- **Research** comprises the costs, including capital charges, of the Science, Innovation, Technology TLB, and research expenditure incurred by other TLBs; and

- **Equipment Programme** refers to the administration and programme costs, primarily of the Defence Procurement Agency, associated with specifying requirements for and procurement of fighting equipment and other assets. The values of fixed asset additions are shown in Notes 13 and 14.

Attribution to Objectives

Gross expenditure of £27,929,750,000 (78.1%) (2004-05 – 72.8%) and Operating Income of £883,844,000 (63.5%) (2004-05 – 55.8%) were allocated to tasks, force elements or activities directly supporting the Objectives. The rest was apportioned in one of two ways:

i. by means of cost attributions to "customer" Management Groupings, using local output costing systems to identify the full local costs of services provided. Cost attributions from suppliers are analysed onward to final outputs on advice from the recipients. If specific advice is not given, attributed costs are assumed to follow the same pattern as locally incurred expenditure:

ii. as an element of central overhead, shared among objectives in proportion to all other attributions. The force elements etc. described above receive a share of the expenditure and income components of these overheads, on the basis of their net costs. The central overheads comprised:

	2005-06			2004-05		
	Gross £000	Income £000	Net £000	Gross £000	Income £000	Net £000
Support for Ministers and Parliament	**19,155**	**(87)**	**19,068**	15,830	(43)	15,787
Departmental corporate services	**825,530**	**(280,807)**	**544,723**	1,686,358	(263,904)	1,422,454
Strategic management	**303,154**	**(7,208)**	**295,946**	353,073	(2,214)	350,859

- **Support for Ministers and Parliament** includes provision of advice to Ministers and the costs, wherever incurred in the Department, of dealing with Parliamentary business;
- **Departmental corporate services** comprises internal support functions, e.g. payment of bills, payroll administration, housing and medical care for service personnel, and costs of Departmental restructuring; and
- **Strategic management** comprises Departmental Head Office policy-making functions in strategic, personnel, scientific and medical matters.

The reduction in costs for Departmental Corporate Services in 2005-06 is due in part to the income on disposal from the flotation of QinetiQ (£355,982,000), the inclusion of the corporate civilian redundancy provision (£187,000,000) and the RAF Personnel and Training Command provision for military redundancy and restructuring (£148,000,000) in 2004-05 and the realignment of housing costs to all TLBs.

Capital employed

The deployment of the Department's capital in support of its objectives does not follow the pattern of operating costs. Net assets totalling £72,541,390,000 (79.3%) support the military capability required to meet Objective 2. The remainder comprises assets wholly attributable to tasks within Objective 1 (£3,709,146,000 – 4.0%), and intangible assets, fighting equipment and other assets under construction, and assets related to equipment procurement within Objective 3 (£15,246,655,000 – 16.7%), and payment of War Pensions Benefits (-£15,711,000).

25. Capital Commitments

Capital commitments, for which no provision has been made in these financial statements, were as follows:

	31 March 2006 £000	31 March 2005 £000
Contracted but not provided for	**18,906,646**	20,446,744

26. Financial Commitments

Commitments under operating leases:

	Land and Buildings		Other	
	31 March 2006	31 March 2005 Restated	31 March 2006	31 March 2005
	£000	£000	£000	£000
The Department was committed to making the following payments during the next year in respect of operating leases expiring:				
Within one year	11,458	5,118	9,860	16,137
Between two and five years	14,811	10,382	167,785	145,328
After five years	155,575	148,623	755,075	642,446
	181,844	**164,123**	**932,720**	**803,911**

The prior year figures have been restated due to an omission in the 2004-05 Note in respect of operating leases in Germany.

The prior year "Other – after five years" figure has been restated to include the Strategic Sealift project.

Obligations under finance leases:

	2005-06	2004-05
	£000	£000
Rentals due within 1 year	4,378	4,914
Rentals due after 1 year but within 5 years	2,639	8,019
Rentals due thereafter	–	2,488
	7,017	**15,421**

The movement between 2004-05 obligations and the 2005-06 obligations is as a result of the reclassification of a finance lease to an operating lease.

27. Private Finance Initiative (PFI) Commitments

27.1 The payments made during the year in respect of on and off Balance Sheet PFI transactions were £869,512,000 (2004-05: £728,465,000).

27.2 The service payments which the Department is committed to make during the year 2006-07 are analysed below by time-bands specifying the period in which the individual commitment expires:

	31 March 2006 £000	31 March 2005 £000
In the 2nd to 5th years	81,912	186,883
In the 6th to 10th years	236,188	117,687
In the 11th to 15th years	213,235	132,590
In the 16th to 20th years	54,519	54,447
In the 21st to 25th years	240,046	190,569
In the 26th to 30th years	11,600	86,967
In the 31st to 35th years	120,350	28,339

27.3 The following information is provided for those schemes assessed as off Balance Sheet:

Project Description	Capital Value* £000	Contract Start**/ End Dates	
Training, Administration and Financial Management Information System (TAFMIS): Provision of training administration and financial management information systems to the Army Training and Recruiting Agency (ATRA)	41,000	Aug 1996	Nov 2009
Hazardous Stores Information System (HSIS): Provision of an information management service for hazardous stores safety datasheets with 2,000 users	1,000	Oct 1997	Oct 2007
Defence Fixed Telecommunications System (DFTS): Integration of 50 fixed telecommunications networks used by the Armed Forces and MoD, including the delivery of voice, data, LAN interconnect and other WAN services	70,000	Jul 1997	Jul 2012
Electronic Messaging Service: Interoperability of messaging services for the Army	33,000	Apr 1997	Apr 2007
Medium Support Helicopter Aircrew Training Facility (MSHATF): Provision of 6 flight simulator training facilities, covering three different types of helicopter, at RAF Benson	114,000	Oct 1997	Oct 2037
Hawk Synthetic Training Facility: Provision of replacement simulator training facilities at RAF Valley	19,000	Dec 1997	Dec 2015
Joint Services Command and Staff College (JSCSC): Design and delivery of a new tri-Service Command and Staff Training College infrastructure and supporting services, including single residential accommodation and married quarters. (Of the total amount, £64 million relates to on-balance sheet)	92,800	Jun 1998	Aug 2028
Attack Helicopter Training Service: Provision of full mission simulator, 3 field deployable simulators, ground crew, maintenance and armament training	165,000	Jul 1998	Sep 2027
Family Quarters Yeovilton: Provision of married quarters accommodation for 88 Service families at RNAS Yeovilton	8,200	Jul 1998	Jul 2028
RAF Lyneham Sewage Treatment: Refurbishment of existing sewage treatment facilities, serving a population of 7,000, to meet regulatory standards at RAF Lyneham	3,800	Aug 1998	Aug 2023
Tidworth Water and Sewerage: Pathfinder project providing water, sewerage and surface water drainage, serving a population of 12,000 military and dependants at Tidworth.	5,000	Feb 1998	Aug 2018
RAF Mail: Provision of informal messaging services for the RAF	12,000	Nov 1998	Nov 2008

Project Description	Capital Value* £000	Contract Start**/	End Dates
Fire Fighting Training Units: Provision of fire fighting training for the Naval Recruiting and Training Agency (NRTA)	22,500	Apr 1999	Jan 2021
Light Aircraft Flying Training: Provision of flying training and support services for Air Experience Flying (AEF) and University Air Squadron (UAS) Flying Training	20,000	Apr 1999	Mar 2009
Tornado GR4 Synthetic Training Service: Provision of aircraft training service at RAF Marham and RAF Lossiemouth	61,700	Jun 1999	Jun 2031
Army Foundation College: Provision of teaching and training facilities for the further vocational education and military training of high-quality school leavers	73,400	Feb 2000	Dec 2029
RAF Cosford/RAF Shawbury Family Quarters: Provision of married quarters accommodation for 145 Service families at RAF Cosford and RAF Shawbury	15,100	Mar 1999	Jun 2025
Central Scotland Family Quarters: Provision of married quarters accommodation for 164 Service Families in Central Scotland	24,700	Aug 1999	Jan 2021
Tri-Service Material Handling Equipment: Provision of Tri-Service materials handling capability	35,000	Jun 2000	Jun 2010
Commercial Satellite Communication Service (INMARSAT): Provision of world-wide commercial satellite communication system for Royal Navy Ships.	2,600	Mar 2001	Mar 2008
E3D Sentry Aircrew Training Service: E3D Sentry simulators instructors and maintainers at RAF Waddington	6,900	Jul 2000	Dec 2030
Lynx MK 7 and 9 Aircrew Training Service: Provision for simulator training facility for Lynx MK 7 and 9 helicopter aircrew	15,400	Jul 2000	Jul 2025
Tri-Service White Fleet: Provision, management and maintenance of support vehicles in the UK	40,000	Jan 2001	Jan 2011
Family quarters at Wattisham: Provision of married quarters accommodation for 250 service families	34,200	May 2001	Mar 2028
Family quarters at Bristol / Bath / Portsmouth: Provision for married quarters accommodation for 317 service families	78,000	Nov 2001	Sep 2028
Defence Housing Executive Information Systems (DOMIS): Provision for a management information system for the Defence Housing Executive	11,600	Oct 2001	Sep 2010
Marine Support to Range and Aircrew Training: Provision of management, manning, operation and maintenance of Air Support Craft and Range Safety Craft	11,800	Dec 2001	Dec 2012
Astute Class Training: Provision of a training environment for crewmen and maintainers to support Astute Class submarines for 30 years	79,600	Sep 2001	Jan 2037
Strategic Sealift (RoRo): Provision of strategic sealift services based on six RoRo ferries in support of Joint Rapid Reaction Force (JRRF) deployments	175,000	Jun 2002	Dec 2024
Material Handling Equipment: Provision of tri-service material handling equipment for Army, Navy and RAF storage depots	9,000	Aug 2002	Jul 2010
Aquatrine Project A: Provision of water and waste water services	154,000	Apr 2003	Nov 2028
Aquatrine Project B: Provision of water and waste water services	86,400	Sep 2004	Mar 2030
Aquatrine Project C; Provision of water and waste water services	363,600	Oct 2004	Mar 2030
Hayes Records and Storage: Pan-Government Records Management and Archive Services	11,100	Sep 2003	Sep 2028
Defence Sixth Form College: Development of a sixth form college to help meet the future recruitment requirements in the Armed Forces and MoD Civil Service	20,000	Jun 2003	Aug 2033
Colchester Garrison: Redevelopment, rebuilding and refurbishment to provide accommodation and associated services (messing, education, storage, workshops)	539,000	Feb 2004	Feb 2039
Skynet 5: Range of satellite services, including management of existing Skynet 4 satellites	1,360,930	Oct 2003	Feb 2020
C Vehicles: Provision of Earthmoving and Specialist plant, Engineer Construction Plant and Material Handling Equipment and support services	114,436	Jun 2005	Jun 2021
Portsmouth 2 Housing: Provision of 148 Family Quarters in Portsmouth	27,092	Oct 2005	Oct 2030

* The capital value is based on private sector partners' capital investment, where known, or otherwise the capital value of the public sector comparator.

** The date when the contracts were signed.

27.4 The following PFI projects are treated as on balance sheet. The service payment commitments for the year 2005-06 are included in the table shown at 27.2.

Project Description	Contract end date	Contract end date
Defence Helicopter Flying School: Provision of helicopter flying training services	Apr 1997	Mar 2012
RAF Lossiemouth Family Quarters: Redevelopment and reprovision of 279 family quarters	Jun 1998	Aug 2020
Joint Services Command and Staff College: Command and Staff College for military and civilian personnel	Jun 1998	Aug 2028
RAF Fylingdales: Provision of guaranteed power supply	Dec 1998	Dec 2023
Main Building Refurbishment: Redevelopment and management services for MoD Main Building	May 2000	May 2030
Naval Communications: Submarine fleet communications service	Jun 2000	Dec 2030
Defence Electronic Commerce Service: Strategic partnership to deliver e-business environment to share information between MoD and trading partners	Jul 2000	Jul 2010
Defence Animal Centre: Redevelopment of new office and residential accommodation, animal husbandry and training support	Aug 2000	Nov 2026
Heavy Equipment Transporters: Provision of vehicles to replace existing fleet and meet future requirements	Dec 2001	Jul 2024
Field Electrical Power Supplies: Provision of generator sets to support operational electrical requirements in the field	Jul 2002	Jun 2022
Devonport Armada Single Living Accommodation: Provision of Support Services and Fleet Accommodation Centre services at Devonport Naval Base	Jul 2004	Mar 2029
Project Allenby/Connaught: Rebuild, refurbishment, management and operation of facilities for service accommodation at Aldershot, Tidworth, Bulford, Warminster, Larkhill and Perham Down	Mar 2006	Mar 2041

* * The dates when the contracts were signed.

No specific contingent liabilities have been identified in respect of the PFI contracts listed above.

28. Financial Instruments

FRS 13, Derivatives and Other Financial Instruments, requires disclosure of the role which financial instruments have had during the period in creating or changing the risks an entity faces in undertaking its activities. Because of the largely non-trading nature of its activities and the way in which government Departments are financed, the Department is not exposed to the degree of financial risk faced by business entities. Moreover, financial instruments play a much more limited role in creating or changing risk than would be typical of the listed companies to which FRS 13 mainly applies. Financial assets and liabilities are generated by day-to-day operational activities and are not held to change the risks facing the Department in undertaking its activities.

Liquidity risk

The Department's revenue and capital resource requirements are voted annually by Parliament and are, therefore, not exposed to significant liquidity risks.

Interest rate risk

A significant proportion of the Department's financial assets and liabilities carry nil or fixed rates of interest. The exposure to interest risk is, therefore, not significant.

Foreign currency risk

The Department enters into forward purchase contracts annually with the Bank of England to cover the majority of its foreign exchange requirements for the following year. The details of the outstanding foreign currency contracts are as follows:

	Foreign currency	Weighted average exchange rate	31 March 2006 Sterling	31 March 2005 Sterling
	US$/Euro 000	(=£1)	£000	£000
			2006/2007 delivery	2005/2006 delivery
US Dollar	1,986,000	1.8426	1,077,839	892,182
Euro	1,524,000	1.3931	1,093,972	962,769
			2007/2008 delivery	2006/2007 delivery
US Dollar	1,813,000	1.7552	1,032,949	836,864
Euro	1,541,000	1.4197	1,085,456	990,699
Total			4,290,216	3,682,514

The 31 March 2006 mid-market closing rates for US Dollar and Euro were £/$ 1.7346 and £/Euro 1.433 respectively.

Fair values

Financial assets
The Department's financial assets include investments in, and loans made to, MoD agencies funded through a Trading Fund and QinetiQ. The net assets of these bodies (excluding MoD loans) and the interest rates applicable to these loans are shown in Note 15. Other financial assets' fair values approximate to their book values.

Financial liabilities
The Department's liabilities include loans from the National Loans Fund, obligations under finance leases and PFI contracts and a loan from the Atomic Weapons Establishment amounting in total to £800,640,000 (2004-05: £794,914,000). The fair values of these liabilities will be different from their book values but since these represent only 4.8% of the gross liabilities and provisions, the impact on the Department's net assets will not be material. The fair values of provisions for liabilities and charges are not materially different to their book values, which are stated after discounting at the Treasury rate of 2.2%. Other liabilities' fair values approximate to their book values.

29. Contingent Liabilities and Contingent Assets Disclosed under FRS 12

29.1 Contingent Liabilities

Contingent liabilities estimated at some £1,575,055,000 (2004-05: £1,607,000,000) have been identified. This comprises site restoration liabilities of some £400,000,000 (2004-05: £400,000,000) relating to the British Army Training Units in Canada and indemnities, that are quantifiable, of £979,500,000 (2004-05:£1,036,000,000) granted to contractors and suppliers.

The Department holds a number of sites where it may be necessary to carry out remediation work in respect of contamination. It is not cost effective or practicable to identify all levels of contamination at individual sites nor to assess the likely cost of any remediation work necessary. As any liability cannot, therefore, be quantified it is not appropriate to include a provision in accordance with FRS 12.

The Department has identified a contingent liability for compensation payments arising from the underpayment of pensions under the Armed Forces Pension Scheme. The scope and scale of the underpayments are currently being assessed as part of a programme of work called Project Collins. The payment of compensation has not yet been agreed and the amounts involved (if any) will be dependent on a number of factors to be considered as part of the project. Until this work is completed, any potential liability cannot be quantified; so, a provision in accordance with FRS12 is not appropriate.

29.2 Contingent Assets

A US salvage company, Odyssey Marine Exploration, has found what is believed to be the wreck of HMS Sussex, which sank in the Western Mediterranean in 1694 carrying gold and silver coins estimated to be valued at the time at £1 million. If confirmed as HMS Sussex, the wreck and its contents are legally the property of Her Majesty's Government.

A licensing agreement was signed on 27 September 2002 between the Disposal Services Agency of the Ministry of Defence, on behalf of Her Majesty's Government, and Odyssey for further archaeological exploration of the wreck of HMS Sussex and recovery of artefacts et cetera. Under the agreement, the net proceeds of the sale of coins and other marketable artefacts will be shared between the two parties. Insufficient certainty exists at present as to the presence or value of any potential recovery of artefacts to quantify the contingent asset.

30. Contingent Liabilities not required to be disclosed under FRS 12 but included for Parliamentary Reporting and Accountability

30.1 Quantifiable (Unrestricted)

The MoD has entered into the following quantifiable contingent liabilities by offering guarantees, indemnities or by giving letters of comfort. None of these is a contingent liability within the meaning of FRS12 since the likelihood of a transfer of economic benefit in settlement is too remote.

	1 April 2005 £000	Increase in year £000	Liabilities crystallised in year £000	Obligation expired in year £000	31 March 2006 £000	Amount reported to Parliament by Departmental minute £000
UNRESTRICTED						
Indemnities						
Residual liability for the remediation of unidentified contamination in parts of the former Rosyth Naval Base which has been sold to Rosyth 2000 plc.	Up to 1,000				1,000	1,000
Termination liabilities arising out of MoD's association with the Research Council under the Joint Grants Scheme.	10,035 (Note i)			(10,035)	–	10,035
Liabilities arising from insurance risk of exhibits on loan to the Army, Navy and RAF Museums.	2,125	601 (Note ii)			2,726	2,726

Explanation of movement

Note:

i. The liability at 1 April 2005 has been restated to reflect a downward review of the obligation in 2004-05 by £7,585,000.

ii. Increase in the number of exhibits and indemnities issued through the Department for Culture, Media and Sport scheme.

Reconciliation between disclosed amount and amount reported to Parliament

The MoD conducts a review of its outstanding liabilities annually to ensure that all its liabilities have been properly recorded under the requirements of Resource Accounting and Government Accounting. Until 2003-04, unclassified liabilities which were reportable to Parliament under Government Accounting were published in the annual Supplementary Statement to the Consolidated Fund and National Loans Fund accounts. The Finance Act 2003 repealed the requirement for this publication. Restricted liabilities continue to be reported annually to Parliament.

30.2 Quantifiable (Restricted)

Details on restricted indemnities are not given because they are sensitive due to commercial confidentiality and/or national security.

30.3 Unquantifiable

The MoD has entered into the following unquantifiable contingent liabilities by offering guarantees, indemnities or by giving letters of comfort. None of these is a contingent liability within the meaning of FRS12 since the likelihood of a transfer of economic benefit in settlement is too remote.

Unrestricted Indemnities

- Indemnity given in relation to the disposal of Gruinard Island in the event of claims arising from the outbreak of specific strains of anthrax on the Island.
- Indemnity to Devonport Royal Dockyards Ltd (DRDL) in respect of nuclear risks under the Nuclear Installations Act 1965.
- Indemnity to the Babcock Group in respect of nuclear risks under the Nuclear Installations Act 1965.
- Indemnities to DRDL and the Babcock Group in respect of non-nuclear risks resulting from claims for damage to property or death and personal injury to a third party.

Restricted Indemnities

- Details on restricted liabilities are not given because they are sensitive due to commercial confidentiality and national security.

These liabilities are unquantifiable due to the nature of the liability and the uncertainties surrounding them.

31. Losses and Special Payments

CLOSED CASES: these comprise losses and special payments which have been formally signed off to date subsequent to a satisfactory completion of all the case work relating to the loss or special payment. Closed cases, therefore, include some cases which in the previous year were shown under Advance Notifications.	Arising in 2005-06 £000	Reported in 2004-05 as Advanced Notifications £000
Total (excluding gifts, special payments and War Pensions Benefits) under £250,000 each: 13,739 cases	14,602	
Total (excluding gifts, special payments and War Pensions Benefits) over £250,000 each: 13 cases (detailed below)	30,527	262,851
Bookkeeping losses and adjustments		
Clearance of obsolete balances for old, completed projects. Amounts written off. (DPA)	16,551	
Claims waived or abandoned		
Following an annual review of the Service Level Agreement, a claim for Service Level Failure Charges against EDS has been waived. Originally £660k, the sum has been reduced following finalisation of payment terms. (Central)		548
Stores and other losses		
An issue of 2 Power Units was made to 62 Stores Squadron in support of Operation TELIC. The unit subsequently raised a Discrepancy Report as a result of nil receipt. An in depth investigation has been able to track the issue into Theatre but the unit had subsequently returned to peacetime location. The stores have not been accounted for in Theatre and, therefore, formal write-off action is required with a conclusion that the stores have been lost in Theatre or used by other units but not accounted for. (DLO)	747	
HMS Penzance. Loss of Minesweeping and Dan laying stores whilst undertaking an exercise. The vehicle was lost owing to a lack of battery power which prevented the drag rope being released and the Emergency Release procedure being effective. During the run, the battery drain was excessive and unusually fast, given the demands placed on the vehicle. Full "on receipt" checks had been completed on 16 Mar 05. The vehicle operators took the correct actions when trying to surface the vehicle. (FLEET)	394	
Loss of TALON Satellite Communication equipment deployed to Operation TELIC. Remedial measures were taken and, since the incident, internal procedures for the issue and receipt of equipment have been reviewed. (LAND)	332	
Tornado engine spares destroyed by fire, caused by a short circuit in cabling in module repair bay at RAF Marham. Provision of an automatic fire detection system has been approved and should be installed during financial year 2006-07. (STC)		352
Fruitless Payments		
In the wake of Hurricane Katrina, which made landfall on the US Gulf coast states of Louisiana, Mississippi and Alabama on the 29th August 2005, the UK responded to an urgent US request on the 4th September 2005 to send 500,000 Operational Ration Packs (ORPs) to aid the relief effort. 475,185 ORPs were airlifted by the Defence Logistics Organisation to the US authorities at Little Rock Airbase between the 5th and 7th September 2005. The decision to gift the ORPs was made by the then PUS, a decision endorsed by the Treasury, and a departmental minute to that effect was laid before Parliament. The Treasury, however, directed that only the ORPs could be gifted and the transportation costs of £1,981,975 would have to be written off. Staff from the Department are in discussions with the Cabinet Office about putting in place a process that seeks to ensure that MoD would not be left to pick up the costs if a similar event occurs in the future. (DLO)	1,982	
Constructive Losses		
The Tornado F3 Mid-Life Fatigue Programme (MLFP) was designed to modify those parts of the aircraft structure that, on predicted usage, would reach a fatigue life limit prior to the fleet planned Out of Service Date (OSD). A study carried out concluded that those parts of the aircraft originally identified no longer had an impact on the aircraft's ability to reach OSD and so, to prevent further nugatory expenditure, the decision was taken in December 2003 to terminate the Tornado F3 MLFP. Negotiations were conducted with the prime contractor EADS to agree the level of consequential costs associated with the termination of the contract. Financial provision for the termination costs was made in the 2003-04 accounts and, following a contract amendment in February 2005, final payment of £10.521M was made in March 2005. (DLO)	10,521	
This constructive loss arose from the UK Government decision not to proceed into production for the medium range anti-tank guided weapons system (MR TRIGAT). There is also a loss (on which negotiations are continuing) in connection with the long range (LR TRIGAT) project (see Advance Notifications). (DPA)		105,343
Loss due to a new building at AWE that was not fit for purpose and cannot be utilised in any other capacity (total loss £148M):		
1) A loss of £83m has been incurred in respect of plant and equipment within the building. (DPA)		82,983
2) A loss of £65m has been incurred following the impairment of the building. (DPA)		64,672
A Post Project Evaluation was conducted during 2004-05 and a Learning from Experience day was held to ensure that lessons have been learnt and procedures have been changed in order to try to prevent any similar reoccurrence.		
A delay in the production of helicopter training course material resulted in courses not being run leading to a write-off of £8M. Lessons learnt include improvements to the design and acceptance processes for training material to avoid such delays in the future. (DPA)		8,369

CLOSED CASES (contined)	Arising in 2005-06 £000	Reported in 2004-05 as Advanced Notifications £000
The relocation of HMS OSPREY to RNAS Yeovilton involved the construction of a new office block for 847 Squadron. The roof of the building, which was completed in 1999, obscured the view of the end of the runway from the Aircraft Control Tower, causing a potential flight safety hazard. Re-design and construction of a new roof was required to address this. (FLEET)		584
Gifts		
Total under £250,000 each: 18 cases	265	
Total over £250,000 each: 5 cases (detailed below)	44,591	
Infrastructure and Police vehicles to the Government of Iraq. Details of the transfer were notified to the House of Commons in a Departmental Minute dated 9th January 2006. (CJO)	19,600	
Infrastructure, Vehicles and Communications equipment to the Government of Iraq. Details of the transfer were notified to the House of Commons in a Departmental Minute dated 12th October 2005. (CJO)	15,500	
MoD Pattern Room to the Royal Armouries Leeds. Details of the transfer were notified to the House of Commons in a Departmental Minute dated 14th June 2001. The effective date of transfer was September 2005. (DPA)	6,000	
Operational Ration Packs to the Government of the USA in aid of Hurricane Katrina. Details of the transfer were notified to the House of Commons retrospectively in a Departmental Minute dated 6th February 2006. The costs of transportation were written off as a fruitless payment. (DLO)	3,115	
Non-Lethal Equipment, EOD to the Government of Nepal. Details of the transfer were notified to the House of Commons in a Departmental Minute dated 13th July 2005. (Central)	376	
International Courtesy Rules		
Supplies and services provided on a reciprocal basis to Commonwealth and Foreign Navy vessels during visits to British Ports at Clyde, Portsmouth, Devonport and Gibraltar (Central)	1,723	
Transfer of properties below market value		
In December 2004, the MoD gained Parliamentary approval to gift some surplus land in Aldershot to the English Churches Housing Group to provide short-term accommodation units for Service leavers considered at risk of social exclusion immediately after discharge. The value of the land is £350k and the gifting took place during the year. (This was notified in FY 04/05 and reported as a gift in the annual accounts). (DE)	350	
Special Payments		
Total under £250,000 each: 606 cases (of which 2 cases were due to maladministration).	498	
Total over £250,000 each: 3 cases (detailed below)	575	85,076
During 2004-05, the Contractor refurbishing the Officer's Mess at RAF Valley entered a claim for prolongation and disruption of work after payment penalties for over-running the completion date were applied. The likely compensation was estimated at £445k and a provision was made in the accounts in March 2005. The eventual compensation was agreed at £575k and this amount was paid in full to the contractor during 2005-06. (PTC)	575	
HM Treasury agreed an ex-gratia payment of up to £84,500,000 to Swan Hunter subject to completion of certain contractual conditions relating to the construction of two Landing Ship Dock (Auxiliary). Total paid to 31 Mar 06 was £84.5m. The MoD originally placed a contract for four LSD(A). There is a possible claim for £63.8M for delay and dislocation costs relating to the other two ships (see Advance Notifications). (DPA)		84,500
This loss relates to a settlement payment made to a service provider as a result of a termination of contract due to technical reasons relating to Defence Information Infrastructure requirements. (DLO)		576

CLOSED CASES (contined)	Arising in 2005-06 £000	Reported in 2004-05 as Advanced Notifications £000
War Pensions Benefits (WPB):		
Claims Abandoned-WPB		
Irrecoverable overpayments of war pensions relating to 2,785 cases amounting to £506,421 (2004-05: 2,147 cases amounting to £836,000) were written off. These represent overpayments of pensions which occur due to a number of reasons outside of the Agency's control; this represented 0.05% of the total war pension payments budget of £1.07Bn. All overpayments are recorded as amounts outstanding and action is taken to recover these amounts. In the 2005-06 financial year, over £1.6M of overpayments were recovered. However, where the overpayment was found to be irrecoverable, the decision was taken to waive the amount owed.	506	
Special Payments-WPB		
Total number of payments made during the year were 943 (2004-05: 1,626) and amounted to £5,815,084 (2004-05: £12,120,619). These payments were for War Disability Pensions, and were made under the authority of Treasury dispensing instruments but outside the scope of the Service Pension order. These relate to the following payments:		
(a) Far Eastern Prisoners of War Ex-gratia payments		
In the 2000 pre-budget speech, the Chancellor of the Exchequer announced that ex-gratia awards of £10,000 would be paid to surviving members of British groups held prisoner by the Japanese during the Second World War or their surviving spouses.		
Although the large majority of cases have been paid in previous financial years, 63 claims were processed and paid in the 2005-06 financial year. The total payment amounted to £630,000.	630	
Following a Judicial Review announced in November 2003, the scheme was expanded to allow payments to qualifying Gurkhas in Nepal. In the 2005-06 financial year, 90 successful claims were processed totalling £900,000. A further £2.2 million was charged to the Operating Cost Statement by way of provision to reflect the likely payments in the 2006-07 financial year.	3,100	
(b) Empire Air Training Scheme Pensions		
These Payments relate to members of the Royal Australian Air Force who were trained under the Empire Air Training Scheme and were subsequently selected for service in the RAF. The British Government agreed in June 1942 that it would contribute towards pensions in respect of disablement or death due to the service with the RAF.		
In 2005-06 the total number of cases were 335 (2004-05: 380 cases) and the cost amounted to £1,466,066 (2004-05: £1,625,924).	1,466	
(c) Noise Induced Sensorineural Hearing Loss		
In 2005-06, 219 cases (2004-05: 246 cases) were paid under the Dispensing Instruments and the total amount payable was £523,676 (2004-05: £558,470). The figure was arrived at through a scan of the War Pensions Computer System (WPCS).	524	
(d) Crown Agents Supplementation payments		
Crown Agents Financial Services make payments to ex-members of the colonial forces who are resident in the UK and who have been awarded a disablement pension by the colonial government. The payment is a supplementation amount that increases the disablement pension to the rate equivalent to a UK war pension.		
The Veterans Agency re-imburses Crown Agents Financial Services for these payments. In 2005-06, the total number of cases was 16 (2004-05: 19 cases) and the amount payable was £95,340 (2004-05: £126,224).	95	

ADVANCE NOTIFICATIONS: these comprise losses and special payments, which arose during 2005-06 and prior years, but where the cases have not yet been formally signed off to date. A formal sign off cannot take place until all the work necessary to establish the validity of the loss or special payment, and the exact amount thereof, has been satisfactorily concluded. The amounts shown below are, therefore, only the best estimates, and are reflected in these accounts where appropriate. It is likely that, in many instances, the final value of these losses and special payments will differ from the estimates below when they are reported as closed in future years. Should the final value be less than £250,000, they will not be separately identified.	Arising in 2005-06 £000	Reported and arising in prior years £000
Notified in prior years		
This constructive loss arose from the UK Government decision not to proceed into production for the long range anti-tank guided weapons system (LR TRIGAT). (DPA)		205,000
The value of 8 Chinook Mk3 helicopters has been written down by £205m under prudent accounting practices while the MoD establishes a way forward for the programme. The write down has arisen because, although the terms of the contract had been met, the helicopters do not currently meet the operational requirement and could not acquire Military Aircraft Release. (DPA)		205,000
Slippage in the construction programme for two Landing Ship Dock (Auxiliary) caused delay in supplying design information and equipment to a contractor. This resulted in a claim on the MoD relating to the associated delay and dislocation costs. (DPA)		63,800
The extended range ordnance modular charge system (ERO/MCS) was cancelled due to technical difficulties with the MCS that could not be resolved. This produced an estimated constructive loss. In 2003-04 the loss was estimated at £34.5m. (DPA)		32,798
Uncleared balances in respect of Income Tax and National Insurance balances to be written off in the books of the Armed Forces Personnel Administration Agency (AFPAA). (Central)		1,479
A food component was withdrawn from Operational Ration Packs (ORP) following discovery in tests that deterioration of the product's packaging could over time compromise the safety of the contents. The Contractor accepted liability in principle for this defect and agreed to supply a replacement product utilising an alternative packaging arrangement, at no cost to MoD, subject to being able to develop a replacement product that could be warranted fully fit for purpose. This development work is continuing and, if successful, will substantially mitigate the overall loss to the Department brought about by a combination of loss of use of the original product and the cost of its removal/destruction. (DLO)		1,400
Metropole Building re-wire project. Bad Debt provision for legal dispute between MoD and former contractor which remains unresolved. Case is currently with the Treasury Solicitor and negotiations are ongoing. (Central)		500
A constructive loss arose in respect of the Voice Monitoring and Analysis Facility (VMAF) due to several factors including a limited capability and a change in policy placing the onus on contractors to provide their own capability testing. Changes in procurement policy will ensure that losses of a similar nature do not occur again. (DLO)		434

ADVANCE NOTIFICATIONS (continued)	Arising in 2005-06 £000	Reported and arising in prior years £000
Notified during the year		
Bookeeping Losses and Adjustments		
A detailed reconciliation of the Fixed Asset Register with the General Ledger for the Central Top Level Budget is underway, and this advance notification represents the maximum value of the bookkeeping adjustment that may have to be made. This unreconcilied balance has arisen over a period of several years. The issue will be fully resolved during 2006-07, as part of the transfer of assets and balances to the Single Balance Sheet Owners. (Central)	9,367	
In preparation for the implementation of the Order to Cash system a reconcilliation was undertaken of debtor balances. This highlighted a number of problems where prepaid amounts were duplicated against income and debtor balances and balances could not be reconciled. The duplications have now been reconciled to the current Defence Bills Debtor balance, and the adjustment should be written off as a book-keeping loss. Work is on-going to try to reconcile other balances – however, there may be a need to write off the final unreconciled amounts. The figure quoted is the best estimate of the amount that may be written off. (Central)	6,175	
Claims waived or abandoned		
A potential claim against a contractor on the ASTOR programme has been abandoned resulting in a loss, but other benefits have been secured in compensation. (DPA)	28,000	
A commercial compensation package agreed as a result of slippage to the delivery dates by the contractor and the unavailability of components for the COBRA programme has resulted in a potential write-off. (DPA)	548	
Service Level Failure Charges against EDS waived. Final amount is expected to be agreed by September 2006. (AFPAA). (Central)	1,022	
Stores and other losses		
Item of aircraft spares transferred from the Westlands Managed store in RNAS Culdrose to HMS WESTMINSTER conducting RP1 in Rosyth Naval Base. There is a clear audit trail confirming receipt by Ship's staff in Rosyth. However, on running a weekly Issue Transaction Summary (ITS) (Stores equivalent of a bank statement listing all issues to a unit from external sources), the item had not been brought to Ship's charge and cannot be located. (FLEET)	630	
Constructive losses		
A potential loss arose as the result of the UK Government decision to reduce the number of Nimrod MRA4 procured from 18 to 12. (DPA)	32,600	
Cancellation of the Alternative Launcher Drive System (ALDS) programme has resulted in a potential write-off. (DPA)	4,000	
A constructive loss arose as a result of a settlement between the Agency and a manufacturer for the provision of Manportable Remote Control Vehicles (MRCVs). (DPA)	1,117	
An agreement was breached with a Contractor that required contracts for nuclear cores to be placed within a certain timeframe rendering MoD liable to pay default costs. (DPA)	562	
Special Payments		
A contractor is claiming extra costs resulting from the late delivery of unusable Global Positioning System chips in respect of the Storm Shadow missile programme, purchased via Foreign Military Sales. However, the MoD is attempting to re-claim from the supplier of the Government Furnished Equipment via the US courts. A related write off of £1.8M for Variation of Price (VoP) was recorded in the 2004-05 accounts. (DPA)	4,000	
There is a possible extra contractual payment of £3.8m resulting from the late supply of Government Furnished Equipment to the TITAN & TROJAN project. (DPA)	3,800	
There is a possible ex-gratia payment in settlement of the Armoured Vehicle Training Service PFI procurement strategy. (DPA)	2,900	
Following the closure of the last RAF base in Germany (RAF Brüggen), it was decided that the UK would withdraw from the Central European Pipeline System. This resulted in payments of £2.069M during FY 2005-06, to ensure that the UK has no further involvement or liability in respect of the Central European Pipeline System. (DLO)	2,069	

32. Related Party Transactions

32.1 The Defence Science and Technology Laboratory, the UK Hydrographic Office, the Met Office, the Defence Aviation Repair Agency and ABRO operate as Executive Defence Agencies financed by Trading Fund.

The Initial Public Offering for QinetiQ Group plc completed the transformation of the MoD's in-house research and development organisation into an international defence technology and security company. MoD retains a 19.3% shareholding in the company and also holds a Special Share; further details can be found at Note 15 – Investments, to these accounts. The MoD also appoints a Non-Executive Director to QinetiQ's Board; the appointment is currently held by Mr Colin Balmer. (Until 18 Jan 06, the appointment was held by Mr Trevor Woolley – MoD's Finance Director).

The Navy Army Air Force Institutes (NAAFI) and the Oil and Pipelines Agency are Public Corporations.

The Trading Funds, QinetiQ, the Oil and Pipelines Agency and NAAFI are regarded as related parties outside the Departmental Boundary with which the Department has had material transactions. All transactions are carried out on terms which are contracted on an arms length basis, and are subject to internal and external audit.

Oil and Pipelines Agency (Public Corporation)
Agency Fees: £1,747,000 (2004-2005: £1,625,000)
VAT recovery £305,725 (2004-2005: £284,375).
Director Defence Fuels Group is a member of the Board of Directors.

32.2 The following are Executive NDPBs of the MoD. They are designated NDPBs under the National Heritage Act 1983 and produce their own annual accounts, in accordance with the Charities (Accounts and Reports) Regulations 1995, on an accruals basis, and are regarded as related parties. During the year, each Executive NDPB had a material transaction with the Department, as listed below:

Fleet Air Arm Museum
Grant-in-Aid: £579,036 (2004-2005: £564,448)

Assistant Chief of Staff Aviation, CinCFleet, Whale Island; Assistant Director Joint Manoeuvre, MoD, London; Director Logistics (Rotary Wing) RNAS Yeovilton; Commanding Officer RNAS Culdrose and Commanding Officer RNAS Yeovilton are members of the Board of Trustees.

National Army Museum
Grant-in-Aid: £4,871,546 (2004-2005: £5,151,170)
The Department is not represented on the Board.

Royal Air Force Museum
Grant-in-Aid: £7,104,192 (2004-2005: £7,026,895)
The Department is not represented on the Board.

Royal Marines Museum
Grant-in-Aid: £783,252 (2004-2005: £704,839)
Director Royal Marines and Regimental Sergeant Major, Royal Marines Corps are members of the Board of Trustees.

Royal Naval Museum
Grant-in-Aid: £1,025,044 (2004-2005: £1,143,901)
Naval Base Commander Portsmouth and Chief of Staff (Warfare) CinCFleet were members of the Board of Trustees during the financial year.

Royal Navy Submarine Museum
Grant-in-Aid: £548,317 (2004-2005: £649,314)
Rear Admiral Submarines is a member of the Board of Trustees.

Other

32.3 Mr Ian Andrews, Second Permanent Under Secretary of State, is a trustee of the Imperial War Museum. Mr Charles Miller Smith, a Non-Executive Director on the Defence Management Board, is also the Chairman of Scottish Power. The Imperial War Museum and Scottish Power are therefore regarded as related parties of the Ministry of Defence and transactions between the organisations during the year were:

			£000
Imperial War Museum	Various transactions-Payments		48
	Various transactions-Receipts		12
Scottish Power	Various transactions-Payments		1,825

During the year various works of art and other items were transferred to and from the Imperial War Museum. No value was attributed to these items.

The Department also pays a number of grants to other bodies outside the Departmental Boundary. These include Grants-in-Aid to the Royal Hospital Chelsea, Skill Force and the Commonwealth War Graves Commission.

In addition, the MoD has had a number of transactions with other government departments and central government bodies. Most of the transactions have been with: the Foreign & Commonwealth Office, the Cabinet Office, HM Revenue & Customs, the Department for International Development, the Home Office, the Treasury Solicitor, the Office of Communications, the National School of Government and the Department for Work and Pensions.

Joint Ventures

32.4 Within the Departmental accounting boundary, see page 163 for further information, the Department does not have any Joint Ventures. Some of the Trading Funds have set up Joint Ventures and the Department is involved in collaborative projects with various foreign countries for the development and production of fighting equipment.

33. Restatement of Balance Sheet and Operating Cost Statement at 31 March 2005

The transfer of responsibility for the decommissioning costs for civil nuclear sites, from the MoD to the Nuclear Decommisioning Authority (NDA), is a Machinery of Government change. In accordance with the HM Treasury's Financial Reporting Manual, the transfer is accounted for under merger accounting rules, requiring the restatement of the opening Balance Sheet and prior year's Operating Cost Statement, Cash Flow Statement, Statement of Operating Costs by Departmental Aim and Objectives and associated Notes to the Accounts.

Balance Sheet	Published Balance at 31 March 2005 £000	Transfer to the NDA £000	Restated Balance at 31 March 2005 £000
Fixed Assets			
Intangible Assets	22,647,823	–	22,647,823
Tangible Fixed Assets – capitalised provision	69,634,594	(25,705)	69,608,889
Investments	347,108	–	347,108
Current Assets			
Stocks and work-in-progress	6,095,363	–	6,095,363
Debtors – prepayment	2,870,899	(21,521)	2,849,378
Cash at bank and in hand	438,411	–	438,411
Creditors: amounts falling due within one year	6,075,613	(74,733)	6,000,880
Creditors: amounts falling due after more than one year	809,896	–	809,896
Provisions for liabilities and charges	9,503,208	(4,320,528)	5,182,680
Net assets	85,645,481	4,348,036	89,993,517
Taxpayers' equity			
General fund	64,906,908	4,348,036	69,254,944
Revaluation reserve	18,719,510	–	18,719,510
Donated assets reserve	2,019,063	–	2,019,063
	85,645,481	4,348,036	89,993,517

Operating Cost Statement	Published 2004-05 £000	Movements arising from the transfer to NDA £000	Restated 2004-05 £000
Staff costs	10,995,642	–	10,995,642
Other operating costs	19,700,190	(104,786)	19,595,404
Gross operating costs	30,695,832	(104,786)	30,591,046
Operating income	(1,416,807)	–	(1,416,807)
Net operating cost before interest	29,279,025	(104,786)	29,174,239
Net interest payable	273,399	(142,106)	131,294
Cost of capital charge	2,857,714	168,178	3,025,892
Net operating cost	32,410,138	(78,714)	32,331,425

34. Post Balance Sheet Events

Subsequent to the year end, a Ministerial announcement on 10 May 2006 set out the outcome of the work on the composition and location of the post-normalisation garrison in Northern Ireland, associated time-lines for further base closures, and announced the start of consultation with the trade unions on the future requirement for civilian support staff for the peacetime garrison.

On 3 July 2006, the Secretary of State announced publication of the MoD's "Enabling Acquisition Change" report. This included a recommendation that the Defence Procurement Agency and the Defence Logistics Organisation should be merged to create a new organisation whose core function is delivery of equipment and support operations to the Front Line. It is the intention that the majority of the recommendations in the report will be implemented by April 2007, although the bedding in of the new integrated procurement and support organisation will not be complete until April 2008.

35. Non-Operational Heritage Assets

35.1 The Department owns a range of non-operational heritage assets from historically significant defence equipment, through archive information, to museum and art collections. In accordance with HM Treasury's Financial Reporting Manual (FReM), non-operational heritage assets are valued except where the cost of the valuation outweighs the benefits that the knowledge of the valuation would deliver or where it is not possible to establish a sufficiently reliable valuation.

On the above basis, no non-operational heritage assets, except land, were valued at the year-end.

35.2 The scope and diversity of the holdings of non-operational heritage assets which are not valued are illustrated by the examples detailed in the table below:

Item	Location	Description
HMS Victory	Portsmouth	HMS Victory is the world's oldest commissioned warship and is most famous for her role as Lord Nelson's Flagship at the Battle of Trafalgar. HMS Victory is open to the public, details are available at: http://www.hms-victory.com
Army Historic Aircraft Flight	Middle Wallop	Formed in 1977, the flight consists of seven aircraft and makes public appearances between May and September. Further information can be found at: http://www.deltaweb.co.uk/haf/index.htm
Battle of Britain Memorial Flight	RAF Coningsby	The Memorial Flight operates 11 mainly World War II aircraft that appear at several hundred public events each year and can also be viewed at their hangar at RAF Coningsby. Further information is available at: http://www.deltaweb.co.uk/bbmf/history.html
Enigma Machine	RAF Cosford	Cryptographic equipment captured during WW2 and used by Bletchley Park to assist in the breaking of German signal traffic.
MoD Art Collection	Various locations	The MoD Art Collection comprises approximately 800 works of fine art and 250 antiques such as clocks and furniture. Many other miscellaneous items, such as photographs and manuscripts are contained in the archive. At the core of the collection are works commissioned by (and bequeathed to) the Admiralty during the 19th century, and those given to the Admiralty and to the War Office by the War Artists Commission at the end of the Second World War. Items from the MoD art collections are displayed in conference rooms and senior officers' accommodation throughout the Defence estate. The most important items are on permanent public display in the National Maritime Museum and on temporary loan to many other public museums and galleries.
Records and artworks	London, Taunton	The Admiralty and Institute of Naval Medicine Libraries and the Air Historical Branch (London) comprise text and records of historical and research items. Although not open to the public, access is available on application.
Artefacts, records and artworks	Various locations	Over one hundred Regimental and Corps Museums and collections exist across the country. Ownership of the buildings and contents of the museums varies between the MoD, local authorities and regimental associations. The museums, which are open to the public, trace the history of the regiments and comprise displays of uniforms, weapons, medals and records. Further information is available at: http://www.army.mod.uk/museums/index.htm

36. Entities within the Departmental Boundary

The entities within the boundary during 2005-06 were as follows:

Executive Agencies

Armed Forces Personnel Administration Agency
Army Training and Recruiting Agency
British Forces Post Office
Defence Analytical Services Agency
Defence Bills Agency
Defence Communication Services Agency
Defence Estates
Defence Medical Education Training Agency
Defence Procurement Agency
Defence Storage and Distribution Agency
Defence Transport and Movements Agency
Defence Vetting Agency
Disposal Services Agency
Duke of York's Royal Military School
Ministry of Defence Police and Guarding Agency
Naval Recruiting and Training Agency
Pay and Personnel Agency
RAF Training Group Defence Agency
Service Children's Education
Veterans Agency

Advisory Non-Departmental Public Bodies

Advisory Committee on Conscientious Objectors
Advisory Group on Medical Countermeasures
Animal Welfare Advisory Committee
Armed Forces Pay Review Body
Central Advisory Committee on War Pensions
Dartmoor Steering Group
Defence Nuclear Safety Committee
Defence Scientific Advisory Council
National Employer Advisory Board
Nuclear Research Advisory Council
Review Board for Government Contracts
War Pensions Committees

Independent Monitoring Board – Independent Board of Visitors for Military Corrective Training Centre

Other Entities

The Reserve Forces and Cadet Associations (formerly TAVRA)

37. Votes A Statement – Statement of Approved Maximum Armed Forces Numbers

37.1 Votes A provide the formal mechanism by which Parliament sets limits for and monitors the maximum numbers of personnel retained for service in the Armed Forces. They are presented to the House shortly before the start of each financial year (late February), and form part of the Parliamentary Supply process.

37.2 Votes A numbers represent uppermost limits for Service manpower; they neither predict actual strengths nor act as a control over numbers in the Services. The Vote includes a contingency margin to cover unforeseen circumstances. Manpower levels are monitored routinely, and if it is anticipated that the numbers could be breached, then a Supplementary Estimate may be required to increase the limit. There was no requirement to raise a Supplementary estimate in 2005-06.

37.3 The tables included below compare, for each service, the numbers voted by the House of Commons with the maximum numbers maintained and the date at which this peak occurred.

37.4 Maximum numbers of personnel to be maintained for Service with the Armed Forces:

	Numbers voted by the House of Commons	Maximum numbers maintained	Peak Dates
Officers, Men & Women for NAVAL SERVICE	44,180	39,943	1 Apr 2005
Officers, Men & Women for ARMY SERVICE	128,945	116,812	1 Apr 2005
Officers, Men & Women for AIR FORCE SERVICE	56,140	51,992	1 Apr 2005

37.5 Maximum numbers of personnel to be maintained for service with the Reserve Forces:

	Numbers voted by the House of Commons	Maximum numbers maintained	Peak Dates
Reserve Naval and Marine Forces	17,200	14,712	1 Apr 2005
Reserve Land Forces	84,000	70,650	1 Nov 2005
Reserve Air Forces	23,050	14,164	1 Apr 2005

37.6 Maximum numbers of personnel to be maintained for service as special members with the Reserve Forces:

	Numbers voted by the House of Commons	Maximum numbers maintained	Peak Dates
Special Members of the Reserve Naval Forces	300	182	1 Jan 2006
Special Members of the Reserve Land Forces	6,000	112	1 Oct 2005
Special Members of the Reserve Air Forces	550	88	1 Nov 2005

Annexes

Annex A

ACCOUNTABILITY TO PARLIAMENT

Ministers have accounted to Parliament during 2005-06 on all aspects of the Department's business. 3,883 Parliamentary Questions were tabled. Defence Ministers participated in six debates on Defence issues in the House of Commons and six in the House of Lords, responded to 18 Adjournment Debates and two urgent questions in the House of Commons, and made 11 oral statements to the House of Commons and six to the House of Lords. They also made 136 written statements to the House of Commons and the House of Lords. Details are published in Hansard, and a full list of Defence debates and oral and written statements is available on www.mod.uk.

EVIDENCE TO HOUSE OF COMMONS DEFENCE COMMITTEE

Since 1 April 2005 the Ministry of Defence has given evidence to the House of Commons Defence Committee on a number of occasions covering a wide range of issues and the Government has responded to a number of the Committee's reports. All Committee publications, including published evidence given to the Committee, are available at www.parliament.uk/parliamentary_committees/defence_committee.cfm

SESSION 2005-06

House of Commons Defence Committee Reports (Government Responses are listed in brackets after the report they relate to)

First Report HC 747 (HC 1021)	***Armed Forces Bill***	*published 8 December 2005*
Second Report HC 554 (HC 926)	***Future Carrier and Joint Combat Aircraft Programmes***	*published 21 December 2005*
Oral evidence Tuesday 1 November 2005 HC556-I	***Introductory evidence sessions with the Secretary of State for Defence***	*published 17 January 2006*
Third Report HC 557 (HC 1000)	***Delivering Front Line Capability to the RAF***	*published 18 January 2006*
Fourth Report HC 980 (HC1136)	***Costs of peace – keeping in Iraq and Afghanistan: Spring Supplementary Estimates 2005-06***	*published 16 March 2006*
Fifth Report HC558	***The UK Deployment to Afghanistan***	*published 6 April 2006*
Sixth Report HC822 (HC1293)	***Ministry of Defence Annual Report and Accounts 2004-05***	*published 20 April 2006*
Seventh Report HC824	***The Defence Industrial Strategy***	*published 10 May 2006*

The Defence Committee also undertook a number of visits to military establishments both in the UK and overseas as part of its inquiries, as shown in the table below.

Table 29: Defence Committee visits to military establishments		
Date of Visit	**Establishment**	**Related Inquiry**
16 Nov 05	RAF Marham	Delivering Front Line Capability to the RAF
21 Nov 05	DARA St Athan	Delivering Front Line Capability to the RAF
23-24 Nov 05	UK Support Command (Germany)	The UK deployment to Afghanistan/ Familiarisation visit
8 Dec 05	PJHQ Northwood	Familiarisation visit
26 Jan 06	Defence Procurement Agency	Familiarisation visit
9 Feb 06	Fleet Command HQ	Familiarisation visit
27 Feb 06	Land Command HQ	Familiarisation visit
9 Mar 06	Strike Command HQ	Familiarisation visit
22-23 March 06	Bishopspark School, Paderborn and King's Secondary School, Gutersloh, Germany	Educating Service Children

EVIDENCE TO SELECT COMMITTEES OF THE HOUSE OF COMMONS AND HOUSE OF LORDS

Since 1 April 2005 the Ministry of Defence has also given written and oral evidence on various issues to a number of Select Committees of the House of Commons and House of Lords, as shown below.

SESSION 2005-06

Reports (Government Responses are listed in brackets after the report)

HoC Constitutional Affairs Committee
HC 731 ***The Office of the Judge Advocate General*** *published 12 December 2005*

Health Committee
HC 485 vols i-iii ***Smoking in Public Places*** *published 19 December 2005*

Public Administration Committee
HC 735 ***A Debt of Honour*** *published 18 January 2006*

Lords EU Committee
HL 125 ***Current Developments in European Defence Policy*** *published 3 March 2006*

Joint Committee on Human Rights
HL 133/HC954 ***Implementation of the Strasbourg Judgements:*** *published 8 March 2006*

EVIDENCE TO PUBLIC ACCOUNTS COMMITTEE AND REPORTS

We have also given evidence to the Public Accounts Committee, as shown in the tables below.

SESSION 2004-05

Reports (Government Responses are listed in brackets after the report)

Eighth Report HC 386 (Cm 6577)	***Ministry of Defence: Battlefield Helicopters***
Twenty-Sixth Report HC 70 (Cm 6668)	***Ministry of Defence: The Rapid Procurement of Capability to Support Operations***

SESSION 2005-06

Reports (Government Responses are listed in brackets after the report)

Third Report HC 410 (Cm 6712)	***Ministry of Defence: Major Projects Report 2004***
Twenty-Sixth Report HC 667 (Cm 6775)	***Ministry of Defence: Assessing and Reporting Military Readiness Report***

MoD Evidence

Major Projects Report 2005

HC 889-i	Oral Evidence given by Mr Bill Jeffrey CB, Permanent Under Secretary of State, Sir Peter Spencer KCB, Chief of Defence Procurement and Lieutenant General Sir Robert Fulton KBE, Deputy Chief of Defence Staff Equipment Capability, Ministry of Defence.

Progress in Combat Identification

HC 70-i	Evidence given by Mr Bill Jeffrey CB, Permanent Under Secretary of State and Air Vice Marshal Stephen Dalton CB, Capability Manager (Information Superiority) and Senior Responsible Owner for Combat Identification, Ministry of Defence.

Annex B

ORGANISATION AND MANAGEMENT OF DEFENCE

Secretary of State and Ministers

1. The Secretary of State for Defence is responsible for the formulation and conduct of Defence policy. He is supported by a Minister of State for the Armed Forces, and two Parliamentary Under-Secretaries of State.

Strategic Control

2. Beneath Ministers lies the top management of the MoD, comprising eleven senior officials and Service officers. The Secretary of State has two principal advisers: the Permanent Under Secretary of State (PUS), and the Chief of the Defence Staff (CDS). They share responsibility for much of the Department's business, reflecting the input that both military and civilian personnel make to political, financial, administrative and operational matters. The PUS has primary responsibility for policy, finance and administration in the Department. He is the MoD's Principal Accounting Officer and is personally accountable to Parliament for the expenditure of all public money voted for Defence purposes. CDS is the professional head of the Armed Forces and the principal military adviser to the Secretary of State and the Government. PUS and CDS each have a deputy; the Second Permanent Under Secretary of State (2nd PUS), and the Vice Chief of the Defence Staff (VCDS). They jointly head the Central Staff or Head Office.

3. Defence is managed through a system of high level boards and committees that provide corporate leadership, with strategic control and direction flowing from the Defence Council, the Defence Management Board (DMB) and the Chiefs of Staff Committee. This ensures that the Department operates as one entity.

The Defence Council

4. The Defence Council is the senior Departmental committee. It is chaired by the Secretary of State, and comprises the other Ministers, the PUS and CDS, and other senior Service officers and officials. It provides the formal legal basis for the conduct of Defence through powers vested in it by statute and Letters Patent.

The Service Boards

5. Administration of the single Services and their personnel is delegated to the Service Boards (the Admiralty, Army and Air Force Boards) from the Defence Council. The Service Boards are chaired by Ministers and monitor Service performance as well as exercising quasi-judicial functions, such as discipline and redress of grievance.

The Defence Management Board

6. The DMB is the highest, non-ministerial committee in the MoD. Chaired by PUS, it is essentially the main corporate board of the MoD, providing senior level leadership and strategic management of Defence. Its role is support the PUS as Accounting Officer to deliver the Defence aim set out in the Public Service Agreement; it also owns the Defence Vision. The Board is made up of the non-Ministerial members of the Defence Council, the Department's Finance Director and two external, independent members. The DMB is responsible for:

- **The role of Defence** – providing strategic direction, vision and values;
- **Objectives and targets** – establishing the key priorities and Defence capabilities necessary to deliver the MoD's Departmental objectives;
- **Resource allocation and strategic balance of investment** – to match Defence priorities and objectives; and
- **Performance management** – managing and driving corporate performance.

The Chiefs of Staff Committee

7. The Chiefs of Staff Committee is chaired by CDS and is the main forum in which the collective military advice of the Chiefs is obtained on operational issues, and through which CDS discharges his responsibility for the preparation and conduct of military operations.

Service Executive Committees

8. Service Executive Committees (SECs) assist their Service Chiefs in their roles as members of the DMB and in their operational and management advisory roles within the Department. The Committees bring together, under their respective single Service Chief of Staff, the operational and personnel commanders for each service, and are responsible for translating Defence-wide objectives into priorities and targets for each Service. The Committees are:

- The Navy Board;
- The Executive Committee of the Army Board; and
- The Air Force Board Standing Committee.

Figure 9: Top level committee structure

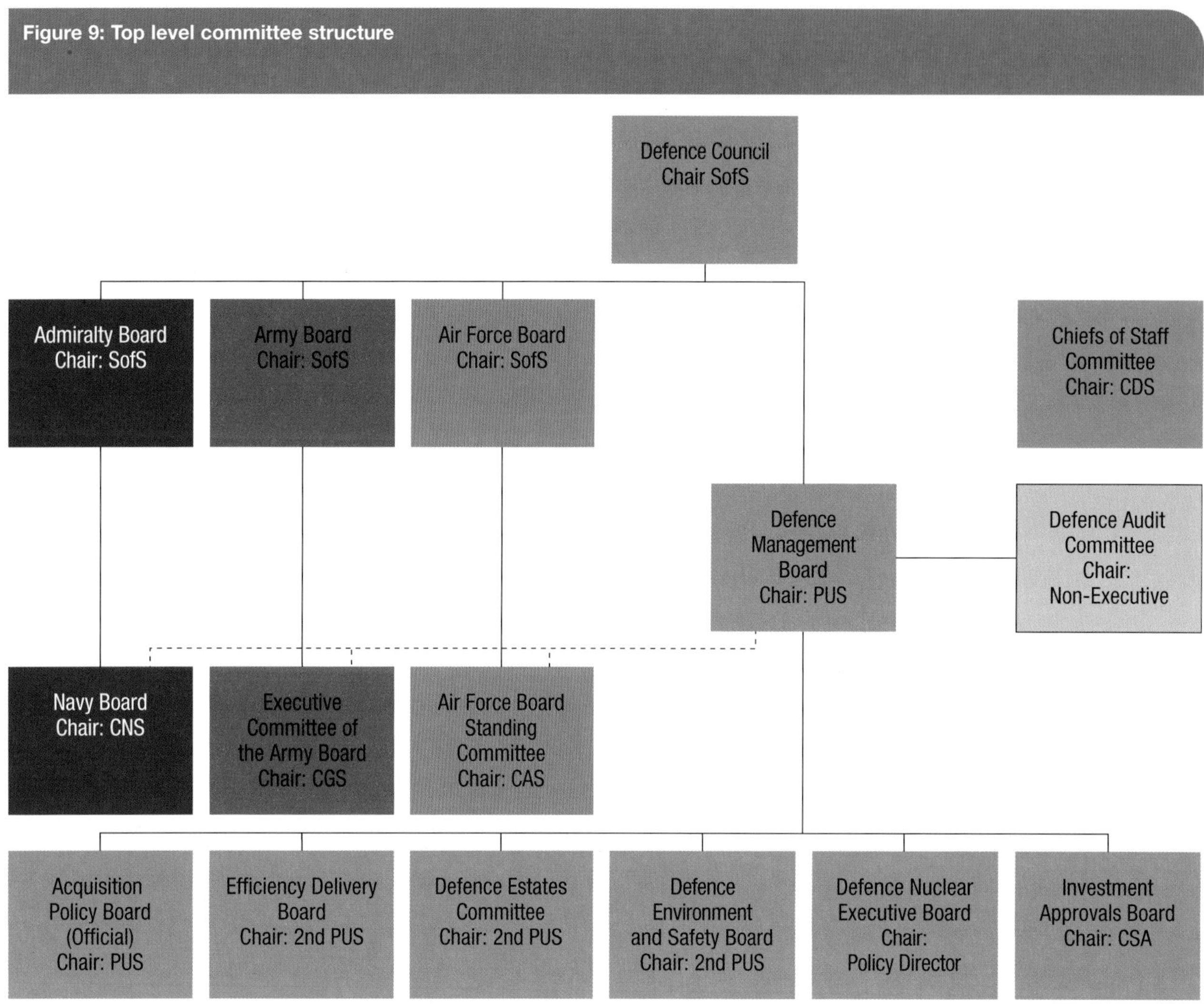

The Head Office

9. The Head Office is responsible for leading the Defence contribution to the development of the Government's foreign and security policy and wider HMG objectives, and for translating those objectives into Departmental policy and the Defence capability needed to deliver it. The Head Office has four main roles:

- Advising Government on Defence
- Making Policy and Setting Departmental Strategy
- Planning and Resource Allocation
- Management of Defence

10. There are a number of departmental high level processes which define standards and requirements for key activities (such as personnel and financial management) which take place across the various business units, to ensure that they operate consistently and effectively across Defence. These enabling processes do not deliver specific outputs, but condition how that delivery is carried out. The Business Management System was introduced in April 2005 to enable better management of a range of these. In the first instance it identified six enabling pan-Departmental processes, for logistics; civilian workforce; Service personnel; communications; financial management; and commodity procurement. A further three Head Office enabling functions were also defined, for planning and resourcing, the strategic context, and the peace-conflict cycle. A senior Process Owner was appointed for each process, accountable to the Defence Management Board for ensuring that their process is efficient and effective, coherent with other processes and functions, and is implemented consistently across all Top Level Budget organisations. This brought greater clarity, coherence and accountability to the way the Department is managed by defining the interconnection between these processes, the roles and responsibilities of the senior military and civilian process owners responsible for them, and their relationship with Top Level Budget Holders and Senior Responsible Owners responsible for specific outputs.

[1] This has now been reduced to 12 TLBs with the merger of the Commander in Chief Fleet and the Chief of Naval Personnel to form the Fleet Joint TLB on 1 April 2006.

Top Level Budgets and Agencies

11. Most Defence activity takes place outside the Head Office and is managed through thirteen[1] Top Level Budget (TLB) holders, (shown in figure 10) and five Trading funds not included in the TLB structure. PUS grants each TLB holder extensive delegated powers over personnel, infrastructure and budget. The Army and Air Force have separate TLBs for their Operational and Personnel commands. The Navy merged their two TLBs on 1 April 2006 to form a single Fleet TLB.

12. The other TLBs are Defence rather than single Service organisations:

- Chief of Joint Operations, who is responsible for the planning and execution of joint (tri-Service) operations, and for the management of Permanent Joint Operating Bases in Cyprus, Gibraltar, the Falkland Islands and Diego Garcia;
- The Defence Procurement Agency, which procures equipment for all three Services;
- The Defence Logistics Organisation, the sole authority for providing logistics support to the Armed Forces;
- The Central TLB, including the Head Office and providing corporate services to other TLBs;
- The Science, Innovation and Technology TLB, headed by the Chief Scientific Adviser, who is responsible for delivering expert advice and developing scientific and technological solutions to satisfy MoD's needs and problems; and,
- Defence Estates, which delivers estate maintenance, works and services, and manages service housing.

13. Each TLB holder has a 'contract' with MoD Head Office, known as a Service Delivery Agreement, which specifies the outputs required of that TLB, the resources they are given to deliver these outputs, and the authority delegated to TLB holders by the PUS. Within the TLB structure are a range of agencies, spanning the bulk of Defence support activity, including logistics, training and corporate services such as bill paying and policing (see Annex E). The Secretary of State owns and is ultimately accountable for the performance of Defence agencies and Trading Funds.

Figure 10: Top Level Budget structure of the Ministry of Defence

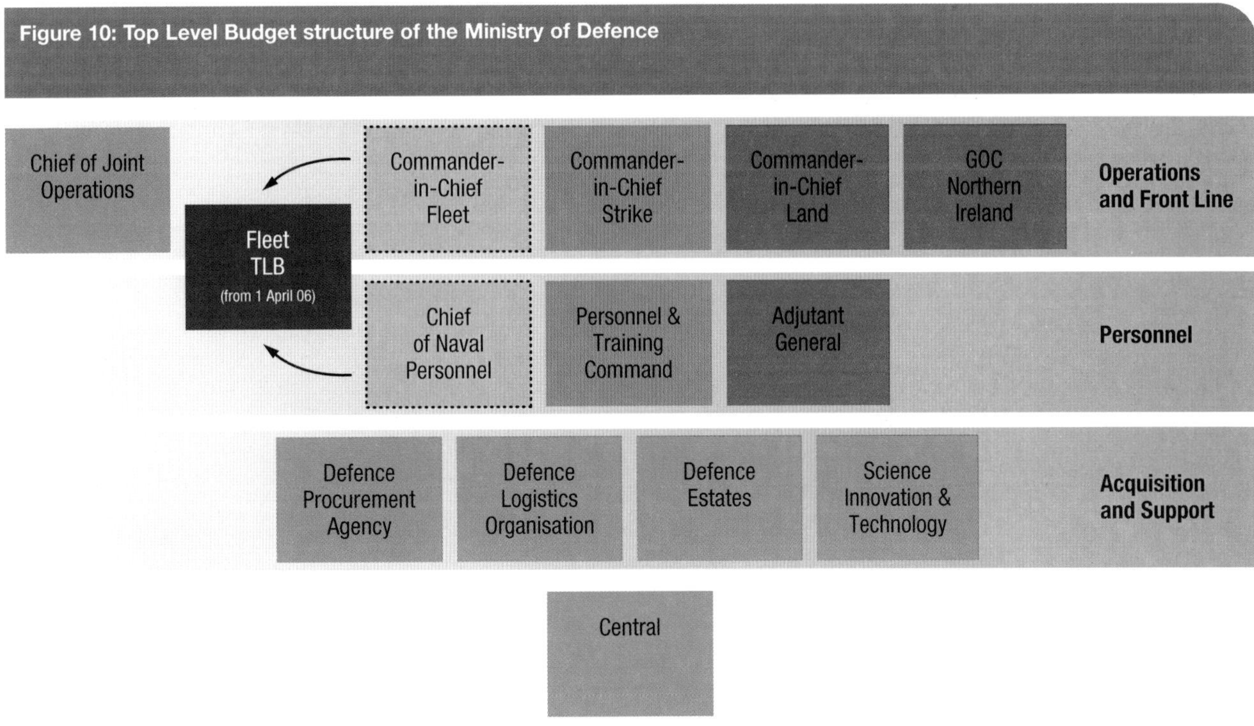

Annex C

PSA TARGET 2: DETAILED ASSESSMENT AGAINST PERFORMANCE INDICATORS

A. Afghanistan: On Course

By end 2007-08: Accountable and democratic structures for Afghanistan's governing institutions and armed forces, representing Afghanistan's ethnic diversity, and operating with respect for human rights.

- During 2005-06 parliamentary and provincial elections were held and the National Assembly was inaugurated. There was an acceleration in Security Sector Reform notably in disarmament, demobilisation and reintegration. The UN played a leading role. The UK contributed funding, expertise and military resources including some $20m since 2002 for disarmament, demobilisation and reintegration;

- The planning for the deployment to Helmand reflects multi-disciplinary civil-military approach. The UK focus has been on the importance of accelerating security sector reform, to ensure long-term capacity building of Afghan institutions as the international community's exit strategy, in G8 fora and through EU/Afghanistan Joint Declaration. This focus further emphasised in Afghanistan Compact, the framework document for the international community's engagement over next 5 years;

- The UK announced on 26 January 06 the deployment of an additional 3,300 troops to Southern Afghanistan, as part of the expansion of the NATO-led International Security Assistance Force (ISAF). The UK has agreed to lead a Provincial Reconstruction Team in Helmand Province, which will be supported by a UK Taskforce. This, in addition to the 1,000 strong deployment of the Headquarters Group of the Allied Rapid Reaction Corps, which is due to lead the ISAF from May 2006 for nine months, will increase the total UK commitment to Afghanistan from around 1,000 in January 06 to a peak of 5,700 in mid 2006, and reducing, as the initial deployment of engineers withdraws, to below 4,700 by the Autumn.

B. Balkans: On Course

By end 2007-08: Western Balkan states at peace within and between themselves and continuing on the path to closer integration with the EU and NATO.

- The UK continues to provide considerable military, political and financial support, both multilaterally (through EU and NATO) and bilaterally, to help support the process of integration, particularly focussing on Kosovo's final status process. Since 1 April 2005 an average of some 1,050 UK regular service personnel have been deployed in Bosnia and Kosovo;

- Bosnia-Herzegovina (BiH) and Serbia-Montenegro opened EU Stabilisation and Association Agreements. Former Yugoslav Republic of Macedonia awarded EU candidate status. Progress towards Partnership for Peace and NATO membership is less apparent, mostly due to states not having achieved outstanding conditions e.g. full International Criminal Tribunal for Yugoslavia co-operation.

- UK was instrumental in securing BiH police reform. Several Departments and law enforcement agencies continue to tackle organised crime in the Balkans.

- The MoD, in collaboration with volunteers from the UK Fire service, led a Global Conflict Prevention Pool funded project to establish an amalgamated fire and emergency response service for the ethnically divided communities of East and West Mostar in BiH. Through retraining demobilised soldiers from the Bosnian Armed Forces, the new Brigade not only provided a much needed enhanced service to the community but, also engaged representatives of all ethnicities in the city, going some way to help the process of post-conflict reconciliation and reconstruction in Mostar.

C. Democratic Republic of Congo (DRC): On Course

By end 2007-08: Reduced cross border interference in Eastern DRC, a stable government in Kinshasa overseeing accountable security services and a reduction in militia operating outside such democratic government control. (This target will focus on DRC but will necessarily take account of wider Great Lakes conflict dynamics).

- The DRC Transitional Government has until June 2006 to successfully organise free and fair elections, merge various armed forces into a national army, and demobilise those wanting to return to civil life. Elections are on track, but army integration is moving at a slower pace.

- The UK is one of several key actors in Security Sector Reform in DRC. The UK has offered DRC Government $5million to support newly integrated brigades, once they have implemented EUSEC's recommendations to speed up disarmament, integration and to improve the transparency of paying its soldiers.

- The UK continues to support MONUC's (UN mission in DRC) robust approach to protecting civilians and tackling armed groups in the DRC, particularly in the volatile East and Northeast.

D. Iraq: On Course

By end 2007-08: A stable, united and law abiding state, within its present borders, co-operating with the international community, no longer posing a threat to its neighbours or to international security, abiding by all its international obligations and providing effective, representative and inclusive government all its people.

- Despite serious security challenges, political progress has been made in 2005-06. With support from the UK, the constitution drafting process was completed, and successful elections were held in December 2005 for a new permanent Iraqi Government. The International Mission for Iraqi Elections found that the election had generally met international standards.

- Progress has also been achieved in the reconstruction and conflict resolution effort. With international partners, the UK continues to focus on Security Sector Reform and capacity building, including training and mentoring the Iraqi Police, Army, Navy, and Border Enforcement and increasingly Iraqis are taking the lead; supporting the Iraqi PM's office and Cabinet and Committee system; and providing grants to grass-roots Iraqi civil society.

- Significant risks remain, notably from the continuing insurgency, sectarianism, and in the economy. Following the elections a Government of National Unity has now been formed, which should be better able to tackle the key security and economic challenges facing Iraq.

- Since 1 April 2005 an average of some 8,000 service personnel have been deployed in Iraq to assist the Iraqi Government in providing security and building the capability and capacity of the Iraqi Security Forces so that they may take responsibility for their own security.

E. Middle East Peace Process: Slippage

By end 2007-8: Maximising the opportunity of Israeli withdrawal from Gaza and parts of the West Bank, significant progress towards a negotiated settlement resulting in the emergence of an independent, democratic, and viable Palestinian state with a reformed security sector, living side by side in peace and security with Israel.

- The UK continued to work closely with the Quartet to encourage a return to the Roadmap, following the successful Israeli disengagement from Gaza in the summer.

- The UK also worked closely with the US and international partners on Palestinian security sector reform, but such work was suspended following Hamas' surprise victory in the January elections. International donors have reviewed their support to the new Government against its commitment to the principles of non-violence, recognition of Israel, and acceptance of previous agreements and obligations, including the Roadmap. Work with Israeli NGOs was stepped up during the year, helping raise awareness of key MEPP issues.

- The MoD has provided a Military Liaison Officer who was working closely with the Palestinian National Security Forces, to support their short-term capacity and work towards longer-term reform, through training, advice and provision of equipment. Whilst the Hamas elections take place, he has assisted the US Security Co-ordinator General Dayton's office to act as Military Planner.

F. Nepal: Slippage

By end 2007-08: A stable Nepal with a durable ceasefire in place with the Maoists, democratic institutions restored with respect for human rights and significant progress towards a constitutional settlement.

- UK objectives were thrown off course by the King's surprise takeover of power in February 2005, despite pre-emptive warnings by the international community. Efforts to persuade the King to reverse this step have failed. The UK and international partners have helped to persuade Maoists to extend 3-month autumn unilateral ceasefire. The King declined to respond or accept the Maoist/party agreement. The ceasefire expired in January 2006 and the violence resumed.

- The UK led high level EU Troika registered united EU message of support for multi-party democracy. The Government supported UN's human rights monitoring operation, which appears to have contributed to improvements in human rights, including a reduced number of illegal detentions, although abuse remains at a high level.

- HMG gifted bomb disposal kit was used to diffuse hundreds of Maoist improvised explosive devices, which could have killed and injured many people.

G. Nigeria: On Course

By end 2007-08: Local and central government effectively managing and resolving conflict and a reduction in the number of people affected by conflict.

- There has been significant communal fighting between Muslim and Christian ethnic groups in Plateau and Kano states since the late nineties, with communal fighting of a lesser magnitude in the Niger Delta Region. Both situations have seen a worrying upsurge in early 2006.

- The UK has supported co-ordination between government and civil society and funds ongoing work on inter-faith peacebuilding. The Government is currently scoping the possibility of UK support to conflict prevention in the Niger Delta region.

H. Sierra Leone: On Course

By end 2007-08: Ongoing stable and democratic government overseeing accountable security services and a reduction in regional militia.

- Due to past and ongoing involvement, the UK continues to play an unusually influential role.

- The UK continued to support the enhancement of the capacities, skills and resources of the Sierra Leone Armed Forces, Police and state security structures, such as the Office of National Security. Crucial given the draw down of UNAMSIL at the end of the 2005. Future advice and training now falls to International Military Advisory and Training Team (including some 90 UK Service personnel) and DFID (for the police). Over £18m of Africa Conflict Prevention Pool programme budget was channelled into Sierra Leone in FY2005-06.

I. Sudan: Slippage

By end 2007-08: A fully implemented comprehensive peace agreement between the Government of Sudan and the SPLM, progress towards a stable and democratic government, a reduction in militia operating outside democratic control, and a reduction in the number of deaths through violent conflict.

- Prospects for peace in Sudan remain fragile given ongoing crisis in Darfur, instability in East and enormous challenge of implementing North-South peace agreement.

- The UK has provided technical assistance to Sudanese parties on DDR planning in North/South peace process, leading donor discussions on support for military security transition through a multilateral International Military Advisory Team.

- The UK gave financial support to, and maintained an observer presence at Abuja Peace Talks. In January 2006 Foreign Secretary addressed parties, delivering a tough message about lack of progress, helping to inject new energy into talks.

- In FY2005-06, HMG provided almost £30m support for African Union Mission in Sudan funding the purchase of vehicles, rapid deployment kits and covered costs of airlifting Nigerian battalions into Darfur through NATO.

J. UN Peacekeeping: On Course

By end 2007-08: All potential UN peacekeeping missions should follow the principles of integrated and comprehensive planning set out in the Brahimi Report of 2000, incorporating these from the onset of the planning process and carrying them forward into mission deployment with appropriate training of personnel and systematic processes for learning lessons and applying best practice.

- All new mandates take account of the multi-dimensional nature of UN missions based on Brahimi principles. The UK worked towards adopting UNSCR 1649, which called for an integrated strategy for the disarmament, resettlement and repatriation of foreign combatants incorporating military, political, social and justice-related aspects.

- The UK engagement played an important part in the decision to establish UN Peacebuilding Commission (PBC); and has hosted a conference to examine how PBC will fulfil its mandate, attended by UN experts, World Bank, academics and senior officials from member states.

- The Government supported the 5th Civilian/Military Peacekeeping Training Exercise (Mapex) to develop capacity, and enhance understanding of complex Peace Support Operations through study of operational planning, co-ordination and conduct.

K. UN Peacekeeping: Ahead

By end 2007- 08: A 5% increase in the number of states contributing effective peacekeepers to regional and international Peace Support Operations (PSOs) under a UN mandate, with adjustment where necessary for changes in the demand for peacekeepers.

- 108 countries are contributing 69,800 peacekeepers to UN missions: a 12.5% increase in the number of countries involved and a 31% increase in the number of peacekeepers. G8 countries are on track to achieve Sea Island target of training 75,000 peacekeepers (mainly in Africa) by 2010.

- The UK continues to provide training to build PSO capacity. For example, the British Embassy Hanoi led a seminar to support Vietnam's preparedness to contribute to PSOs, following on from their recent agreement in principle to do so. Vietnam will soon decide about when and where to participate in UN PSO activity.

L. African Peacekeeping: On Course

By end 2007-08: Increased capacity in the African Union (AU) and sub-regional security organisations to manage peacekeeping missions.

- The UK support instrumental in developing of African Union's (AU) Peace and Security Architecture. HMG played a key role in co-ordinating donor resources and technical inputs on the African Standby Force (ASF) agenda.

- Regionally HMG's technical and financial support focused on Economic Community Of West African States, Eastern Africa Standby Brigade (EASBRIG) and, where possible, Southern African Development Community.

- The UK funded a military consultant to advise the AU when drafting the roadmap for the ASF. UK has supported the workshop process taking forward several key aspects of the ASF's development, acting as lead partner and delivering technical advice and funding for the EASBRIG-led ASF Logistics workshop, and also providing UK military personnel in an advisory role to most of the other workshop streams.

Annex D

PERFORMANCE MANAGEMENT

1. Since 2000, the strategic management of the MoD has been underpinned and facilitated by the Defence Balanced Scorecard. At the highest conceptual level, the Defence Balanced Scorecard is a framework that helps the DMB to translate strategy into operational objectives that drive both behaviour and performance. For Defence, this strategy is articulated in the Departmental Plan, which sets out the department's top level strategic objectives, including our Public Service Agreement (PSA) targets. The Defence Balanced Scorecard tells the DMB how well Defence is doing in terms of the objectives that underpin the Plan. Ultimately, this assessment tells the DMB whether Defence is 'succeeding' and gives them with an insight into the department's ability to achieve the Defence Vision.

2. The first Balanced Scorecards were devised, principally by Robert Kaplan and David Norton, for private sector – financially driven – organisations. As a public sector organisation, with outputs not expressed in financial terms, we have adapted their model to better reflect the nature of Defence. Accordingly, the Defence Balanced Scorecard has the four perspectives that summarise the breadth of Defence activity and cover the whole of the MoD's principal areas of business; Purpose, Resources, Enabling Processes and Future Capabilities. This generic structure is shown in Figure 11.

Figure 11: Top level 2005 Balanced Scorecard

Are we fit for today's challenges and ready for tomorrow's tasks?

Are we making the best use of our resources?

RESOURCES

Defending the United Kingdom and its interests: acting as a force for good in the world

Are we a high performing organisation?

ENABLING PROCESSES

Are we building for the future?

FUTURE CAPABILITIES

3. There are a number of strategic objectives in each perspective – and 17 in total. Performance against each of the objectives is assessed on a quarterly basis. Against each objective, targets setting out required levels of performance are agreed with those in the Department who are responsible for achieving the objectives – for delivery. Detailed performance indicators and metrics are also agreed. The performance indicators we use are a mixture of lag indicators (which inform the Board about actual achievements) and lead indicators (which are used to encourage different behaviours). Assessments may be quantitative or qualitative, and will either be provided by objective sources or subjected to lower level scrutiny and audit – by Front Line Commands or the Resources and Plans Directorates, for example. Agreeing the objectives, targets, performance indicators and metrics is an annual exercise, conducted prior to the publication of the Departmental Plan.

4. The DMB receives a detailed performance report four times a year. For each objective in the Departmental Plan, the report will include an assessment of actual performance from the previous and current quarter, and a forecast of performance at the end of the next three to four financial years. Analysis of the issues highlighted by the performance assessments is included in the report, together with an assessment of the key risks that could jeopardise the achievement of objectives. The strategic risk information represented is a result of gathering the most significant risks from the TLBs and Process Owners into a consolidated Departmental Risk Register. This register associates individual risks with particular objectives from the Departmental Plan. The overall 'weight' of risk against each of these objectives is then assessed and presented graphically to the DMB. The information, and assessments, that the DMB receive are used to inform board discussion and decision – they may, for example, support decisions to adjust strategic direction and priorities, or the reallocation of resources. And as the Department's performance against PSA targets is assessed in the Defence Balanced Scorecard, the assessments are also used to inform reports to Parliament, No 10, HM Treasury and the Cabinet Office.

5. Our approach, and the data systems underpinning it, have been subject to thorough review over the last four years, first in 2002 by the Department's internal auditors and then in 2003-04 by the NAO, who conducted an external review of our reporting arrangements for the 2002 Spending review PSA targets. More specifically:

- our Conflict Prevention assessments (PSA Target 2) draw on a wide range of international statistics and reporting. In October 2005 the NAO published a report on Joint Targets, including the Joint Target for Conflict Prevention shared by the MoD, FCO and DFID;
- during 2004-05 the NAO conducted a further review specifically into our arrangements for assessing and reporting military readiness (PSA Target 3). Their report, published in June 2005, concluded that we had a good, and continuously improving, system for reporting readiness levels which compares well with that of other countries, such as the United States and Australia, and has been proven over time. They also noted that recent operations have largely validated the accuracy of the readiness reporting system. We have since made a number of further improvements recommended by the NAO in the way we report readiness. In January 2006, the Public Accounts Committee published their own, follow-on, report into our readiness reporting systems and found that we have a sophisticated system for defining, measuring, and reporting the readiness of the Armed Forces.
- the personnel statistics used to measure performance against out manning balance targets (PSA Target 5) are produced quarterly by the Defence Analytical Services Agency to the standard required for National Statistics;
- the NAO audit every year the reported performance against the PSA procurement targets. In addition, the NAO's annual Major Projects Report sets out forecast performance, costs and timings for the MoD's 20 largest equipment programmes (PSA Target 6). The most recent report, MPR 2005, published in November 2005, shows forecast cost savings of £699 million for the MoD's top 20 major equipment programmes; and
- the financial data underpinning assessment of our value for money (SR2002 PSA Target 7) and efficiency (SR2004 Efficiency Target) targets ultimately derive from the Departmental Resource Accounts, on which the NAO has now given an unqualified opinion for three years. Within that, Defence Internal Audit validate our logistics efficiency data every year, and their reports are visible to the NAO.

We are currently awaiting the outcome of the NAO's audit of the data systems that underpin our reporting against the 2004 Spending Review PSA targets.

6. Our approach to strategic management and performance reporting continues to attract interest from wider audiences, including other Government departments, local authorities and other nations' Ministries or Departments of Defence. In addition, we are regularly invited to address, and take part in, international strategic and performance management symposia. This interaction is important to us because it gives us the chance to share ideas and pick up examples of other good practice. In this way we can continue to improve the strategic management of the Department.

Annex E

DEFENCE AGENCY PERFORMANCE

Table 30: Defence Agency Performance

Name	Overall Performance Number and % of targets achieved. 05/06	04/05	03/04	Year on Year Performance – number and % of targets met which were directly comparable with the previous year. 05/06	04/05	Relative performance against comparable targets in 04/05 (better/same/worse)
Armed Forces Personnel Administration Agency	9/10 90%	8/8[2] 100%	9/9 100%	7/8 88%	8/8 100%	3/4/1
Army Training and Recruiting Agency[1]	1/4 25%	1/4[2] 25%	4/5 80%	1/4 25%	1/4 25%	1/1/2
British Forces Post Office	6/6 100%	6/7[2] 86%	n/a	5/5 100%	5/5 100%	1/2/2
Defence Analytical Services Agency	8/10 80%	8/8[2] 100%	7/8 88%	4/5 80%	5/5 100%	2/1/2
Defence Bills Agency	6/6 100%	6/6 100%	6/6 100%	6/6 100%	6/6 100%	4/0/2
Defence Communication Services Agency	5/5 100%	6/7 86%	6/7 86%	4/4 100%	4/4 100%	1/0/3
Defence Estates	15/22 68%	10/15 67%	10/11 91%	4/6 67%	4/6 67%	3/0/3
Defence Medical Education and Training Agency	3/6 50%	5/7 71%	7/7 100%	3/5 60%	4/5 80%	1/2/2
Defence Procurement Agency	7/7 100%	7/8[2] 88%	2/5 40%	7/7 100%	7/7 100%	4/0/3
Defence Storage and Distribution Agency	6/6 100%	6/6 100%	2/6 33%	6/6 100%	6/6 100%	4/1/1
Defence Transports and Movements Agency	5/6 83%	5/6 83%	3/3 100%	5/6 83%	5/6 83%	2/3/1
Defence Vetting Agency	11/16 69%	6/12 50%	8/17 47%	9/13 69%	8/13 62%	9/2/2
Disposal Services Agency	5/6 83%	5/6[2] 83%	4/4 100%	2/2 100%	2/2 100%	2/0/0
Duke of York's Royal Military School	4/6 67%	5/8 63%	6/8 75%	2/4 50%	3/4 75%	2/0/2
MoD Police and Guarding Agency	3/8 38%	4/9[2] 44%	2/8 25%	0/4 0%	1/4 25%	1/1/2
Naval Recruiting and Training Agency[1]	5/7 71%	5/8 63%	4/7 57%	5/7 71%	4/7 57%	2/1/4
Pay and Personnel Agency	8/8 100%	9/9[2] 100%	5/6 83%	3/3 100%	3/3 100%	1/0/2
Service Children's Education	27/34 79	18/34[2] 53%	5/16 31%	25/32 78%	17/32 53%	18/7/7
RAF Training Group Defence Agency[1]	6/8 75%	3/7[2] 43%	5/7 71%	5/7 71%	3/7 43%	4/2/1
Veterans Agency	7/7 100%	7/7 100%	5/6 83%	6/6 100%	6/6 100%	3/3/0

Notes:

[1] Agency status was removed on 1 April 2006

[2] Where there are multiple elements to a Key Target, these have been counted separately. The number of key targets for these agencies for 2004/05 has been revised to ensure consistency.

Organisational Changes

From 1 April 2006 the Pay and Personnel Agency became part of the new People, Pay and Pensions Agency and Agency status was removed from the three Service Training Agencies (the Army Training and Recruiting Agency, the Naval Recruiting and Training Agency and the RAF Training Group Defence Agency).

Armed Forces Personnel Administration Agency

The year saw an exceptionally intense level of activity throughout the Agency which has culminated in the implementations of both Joint Personnel Administration (JPA) across the RAF and the new Compensation and Pension System (CAPS) in the weeks immediately preceding the end of the year. At the heart of both systems are AFPAA-developed technical solutions which, although based on standard commercial packages, have still required substantial configuration in order to support the new, harmonised personnel processes for the Armed Forces. In order to be able to utilise these technical solutions to best effect, AFPAA itself has had to undergo a fundamental transformation which will only complete when JPA is implemented across the Army in March 2007. The transformation programme has included a fundamental review of end-to-end processes, changes to the organisational structure and improvements to the working environment. A training programme was developed and delivered to all AFPAA staff which promoted the values and behaviours required to underpin the future success of the Agency in delivering a wide range of customer services to the highest possible standard. The agency narrowly missed one key target, relating to error rates on pay, as a consequence of single incident affecting about 7,500 individuals.

Army Training and Recruiting Agency

This was the last year of operation for ATRA prior to loss of Agency status as part of the changes proposed under the merger of the LAND and AG top level budget areas.

During the period of this report ATRA performed well against its key targets but the reduced recruiting levels of the two previous years influenced the inflow to the Field Army. The recruiting environment continued to be challenging, particularly for the Infantry and Royal Artillery, and as a consequence the agency missed three of its key targets, one narrowly. However Officer Regular Commissions Board passes are above target levels and soldier enlistments have improved and continue to show encouraging signs as a direct result of advertising. The publication of the Blake Report has provided further focus to ATRA's work already in hand to reduce risk in training, instigated as a result of Director Operational Capability, House of Commons Defence Committee and Adult Learning Inspectorate reports. ATRA's focus has continued to be to improve the number and quality of soldiers completing Phase 2 training.

British Forces Post Office

The efficient distribution of personal mail to Defence personnel deployed on operations has been the main effort of all staff employed at the BFPO's central sorting office in North West London. Demanding performance targets have been met against a backdrop of continued operational intensity and significant demands for efficiencies in all areas. The single most strategically important development during the year was the formal announcement of the 'preferred bidder' to construct the new facility for all of BFPO's London based activities at RAF Northolt. The relocation of BFPO from its home of over 40 years has been anticipated for a number of years as part of the necessary redevelopment of the MoD estate in London. This announcement enabled the detailed planning to commence in earnest for the relocation, which is expected to be achieved during the summer of 2007.

Defence Analytical Services Agency

DASA was charged with having more impact on policy and decision making within the MoD and for the first time this year this was explicitly reflected in its targets – interpreted as the delivery of new products and services, and the engagement of new Departmental customers. The Agency's performance in these respects has been very positive with a significant amount of new work being identified. Some common themes in this new work has enabled DASA to better focus efforts to have more impact on policy and decision making in MoD in the future – this is reflected in DASA's Corporate Plan for 2006-07, specifically in the development of its Information Strategy. DASA missed two of its Key Targets one as a result of an error in a statistical press release relating to one of its major outputs where no tolerance is allowed. However, overall performance was excellent, most targets being exceeded, including customer satisfaction at 96%.

Defence Bills Agency

The Defence Bills Agency met or exceeded all its key targets. This was the fourth consecutive year that the Agency maintained this level of performance, but this year's was particularly notable because of the additional pressures and challenges it faced with the introduction of the new Order to Cash process which went live in December 2005. New debt procedures introduced in late 2004 allowed the Agency to surpass the Key Debt Target by some 8%, bringing debt figures to historically low levels. During the year the Agency also dealt with an 8% increase in the number of bills received and retained accreditation to Charter Mark and the new Investors In People Standard.

Defence Communication Services Agency

From April 2005, Key Target 1 (Service Assurance) is an aggregated index for service delivery against a revised Product Portfolio that takes into account both the quantity and quality of services delivered. An enhanced Agency performance measurement process was successfully embedded with approximately 800 metrics as opposed to the 250 reported against in previous years. These adjustments underpin the increasing utility and flexibility of Customer Supplier Agreements and support the increasingly mature position of these agreements as the foundation upon which customer/supplier relationships across Defence are based. Before 2005-06 the rationale underpinning Key Target 5 (Project delivery) was measurement of a steadily decreasing percentage of new projects that would exceed their time, cost and performance targets – the target incorporated a decreasing profile in recognition of Agency project management expertise improving over time. This Key Target has now been refocused to measure the percentage of new projects that are successfully delivered to time, cost and performance targets.

Defence Estates

Details relating to Defence Estates can be found on pages 149 to 153.

Defence Medical Education and Training Agency

DMETA continued fully to meet the Commanders in Chief requirements for Secondary Care Personnel for operations and exercises. In addition there has been a significant improvement in Key Target 2 (to ensure that DMETA staff achieve their annual mandatory military training) compared with 2004-05 as a result of local initiatives at MoD Health Units to identify opportunities for training and to ensure that staff can be made available. The Agency narrowly missed three of its key targets on: annual mandatory individual military training for DMETA staff (whilst at the same time showing a significant improvement in performance against the previous year); initial training that meets the requirements, professional standards and timescales defined by the single Services; and customer confidence. The latter is measured against the baseline established last year. For this first year it has only been possible to measure performance over a 9-month period in order to be able to report performance at the end of the year. In future years a full 12 months data will be available on which to calculate confidence ratings.

Defence Procurement Agency

Details relating to the Defence Procurement Agency can be found on Pages 77 to 80.

Defence Storage and Distribution Agency

DSDA continued to deliver successfully against its Key Performance Targets through 2005-06. It maintained the very high customer service levels in its explosive business area and significantly exceeded the performance recorded for the previous period in its non-explosive business area. In this latter area, demand for DSDA Services has been in excess of that forecast by Customers in terms of issues and receipt activity, up by 4.75% (£107k) and 7.25% (£34k) respectively. As the increase in output activity was met from within budget limits performance figures are in excess of 100%. During the year, the DSDA "Do Different Option" was the successful bid in the Future Defence Supply Chain initiative (FDSCi). The Agency has started the process of delivery against some very tough targets and has agreed the incorporation of its '7 day delivery' aspirations into the FDSCi Performance Indicators, with the target of achieving its aim by October 2007.

Defence Transport and Movements Agency

This was an extremely busy year for the Agency with the need to deliver strategic transport and movements in support of operations never more important. The tempo of operational activity was high throughout the period and remained significantly above the routine of steady state. To achieve this, the Agency ensured that the operational output of DTMA was not obscured by other non-operational, but nevertheless vital Agency requirements; the operational output continues to underpin all that the Agency does. However, the business needs of the Agency were not ignored demonstrated by the positive feedback that DTMA has received through Customer Surveys and the successful achievement of five of the key targets. The agency missed one key target relating to reducing the average unit cost of output.

Defence Vetting Agency

The arrival of a new Chief Executive in September 2005 enabled the Agency to complete a fundamental review of its vision and business strategy. At the centre of this strategy is the creation of a single vetting process and a new supporting management structure which will enable the DVA to be recognised as the lead authority on vetting process and risk based assessment across Government. The single vetting process will also ensure improved value for money and enable the agency to meet its vision of a shared service provider for national security vetting. Business development will be critical to the delivery of the DVA vision. Greater efficiency and effectiveness will be achieved through closer relationships with customers, competitors, and suppliers. The Agency also began implementation of the work which will enable it to be formally accredited as a Charter Mark organisation. The Agency missed five of its key targets/sub-targets relating to completion time for clearances, despite a reduction in the average completion times.

Disposal Services Agency

Prior to 1 April 2005, the DSA was part of the Defence Exports Services Organisation (DESO). Its main customer was the Defence Logistics Organisation (DLO), with the relationship articulated primarily through the DLO's Head of Specialisation (Disposal & Sales). On 1 April 2005 the Head of Specialisation (Disposal & Sales) amalgamated with the DSA, and the ownership of the merged Agency moved from DESO to the DLO. During its first year, despite changes in structure and a new Chief Executive, the new DSA has met or exceeded four of its five Key Targets. The remaining Target, to meet the standards of Internal Business Agreements, was only just missed.

The Duke of York's Royal Military School

The Duke of York's Royal Military School has academic and financial targets. The academic targets now match the cohorts and are benchmarked against national data. The financial targets ensure financial efficiency and mirror the expectation of wider community involvement. Key achievements over the year included improved academic achievement at GCSE and A Level, maintenance of financial efficiency and increased community involvement. The school missed two key targets relating to GCSE average points score and average cost per pupil.

Ministry of Defence Police and Guarding Agency

The Agency set a series of challenging and demanding Key Targets for 2005-06 based on its defined outputs within its business plan and to support the delivery of long term Critical Success Factors. The Agency has taken on a target for International Policing, agreed with the Foreign and Commonwealth Office, which was met. However the agency missed five of its key targets, relating to crime solving rate, customer tasking, efficiency and recruitment (2 key targets). Of these, the agency just failed to meet its target for recruiting female staff despite a substantial improvement on the previous year's performance.

Naval Recruiting and Training Agency

This was the last year of operation for NRTA prior to loss of Agency status as part of a wider reorganisation of the Royal Navy's Top Level Budget structure. The change of status facilitates this reorganisation but also provides the opportunity to create in due course a single Naval Training Command responsible for the delivery of all training activity, including those too closely entwined with front-line operations to be included within an Agency. The year was moderately successful in terms of key targets, with five out of seven achieved this year. It missed its targets for outputs from initial training and Royal Naval Reserve trained strength. The Royal Marine recruiting target, missed by a margin in 2004-05, was changed for 2005-06 to a more realistic but still challenging figure, and was achieved. The eighth 2004-05 target, comparing the cost of the HQ overhead with the 2003-04 baseline figure, could not sensibly be assessed this year owing to the scale of change ahead of the wider TLB reorganisation.

Pay and Personnel Agency

This was the last year of the Pay and Personnel Agency. In April 2006 the agency became part of the new People, Pay and Pensions Agency (PPPA). All the 2005-06 Key Targets were achieved during a time of considerable change and preparations leading to the launch and Initial Operating Capability for the new agency. Overall this was a good year with challenging targets in terms of ensuring current operations such as pay, pensions and expenses payments continued to be delivered and Key Targets for timeliness and accuracy, responsiveness and for unit costs were achieved. In addition improvements were made to the hardware platforms on which the systems depend and a new automated call distribution system for the People Service Centre was introduced. These measures helped to improve the reliability of these systems both for our own staff and for customers.

Service Children's Education

The key aim of Service Children's Education is to provide a quality educational service, from Foundation Stage to Sixth Form, to the children of Service personnel accompanying their parents on postings overseas. To that end the Key Targets focus heavily on comparisons between the Agency's academic performance in relation to developments and achievements within mainstream schooling in the United Kingdom. The Agency continued to make significant progress in this core area of business with improvements across all Key Stages. Of the current 12 sub-targets relating to Standard Assessment at Key Stages 1-3, SCE met or exceeded the National average in 9. When compared with Local Education Authorities in the UK, SCE are within the top 15 (of 150) at Key Stages 1 and 3 and within the top 40 at Key Stage 2. The results of "higher achievers" again see SCE at or above the National average in 10 of the 12 sub-targets with GCSE results within the upper UK quartile and "A"-Level results (from an extremely small cohort) only 1% below the UK figure.

RAF Training Group Defence Agency

This was the last year of operation for TGDA prior to loss of Agency status as part of the collocation and rationalisation of the Royal Air Force's Headquarters. The agency's plan for 2005-06 focussed on delivering both standing and in-year priorities. The agency met all of its key targets within set tolerances with the exception of reducing the cost of training by improving first-time pass rates; and Initial Flying Training. Although the Initial Flying Training target was marginally outside the set tolerance, this will have no lasting operational effect and the shortfall will be recouped where essential this year. The main effort for 2005-06 for the core HQ was the restructuring of the Group and the preparation for transfer to High Wycombe as part of the Co-located Headquarters. This remained largely on track, although a number of areas of risk remain.

Veterans Agency

The Agency achieved all its key targets in 2005-06. Key achievements included reducing the average clearance time for claims to war pension by a further 8.8% to 52 working days and for claims from war widows by a further 4.6% to 21 working days; and the successful introduction of the new Armed Forces Compensation Scheme in April 2005, with a 100% claims accuracy rate achieved. The Agency received its second CIPFA/Price Waterhouse Coopers Public Accountability Award in June 2005.

MOD BUSINESS OWNERSHIP

The following sections give a performance overview of each of the MoD Trading Funds; ABRO, Defence Aviation Repair Agency (DARA), Defence Science and Technology Laboratory (DSTL), Met Office and the United Kingdom Hydrographic Office (UKHO). In addition to these businesses, the MoD also retains a 19.3% shareholding of QinetiQ following its privatisation this year; further detail can be found at paragraphs 272-273 within the main body of the report.

Trading Funds

Table 31: Defence Trading Fund Performance

Name	Overall Performance Number and % of targets achieved.			Year on Year Performance – number and % of targets met which were directly comparable with the I previous year.		Relative performance against comparable targets in 04/05 (better/same/worse)
	05/06	04/05	03/04	05/06	04/05	
ABRO	4/5 80%	3/5 60%	5/5 100%	3/4 75%	3/4 75%	2/1/1
Defence Aviation Repair Agency (DARA)	3/4 75%	5/5 100%	4/4 100%	1/2 50%	0/0 0%	0/1/1
Defence Science and Technology Laboratory (DSTL)	7/10 70%	7/7 100%	7/7 100%	3/5 60%	5/5 100%	2/1/2
Met Office	5/5 100%	3/6[1] 50%	6/7 86%	1/1 100%	1/1 100%	0/0/1
UK Hydrographic Office (UKHO)[2]	3/6[3] 50%	4/6 67%	5/7 71%	2/4 50%	3/4 75%	3/0/1

Notes:
[1] Previously reported as 4/7 because 2 sub-elements had been counted independently.
[2] Previous years adjusted as sub-elements are no longer counted independently
[3] The three remaining targets were partially achieved

ABRO

ABRO (formally known as the Army Base Repair Organisation) is the Defence engineering business that provides repair, re-manufacture and engineering of land based equipment in support of UK Armed Forces. In addition, subject to delivering against its obligations to the broader MoD customer, ABRO is required to grow the long-term value of the business using its core skills and surplus capacity to diversify into other Defence and civil markets.

2005-06 has been a challenging year for ABRO: it has had to react to changes in the Defence industry driven by the modernisation of logistics support to the front line. As a result, in July 2005, the first phase of a rationalisation programme was announced reducing ABRO's workforce by up to 294 to reflect a downturn in its workload. Plans for the second phase of rationalisation programme were announced in November 2005. They involved up to 1226 redundancies across all of ABRO's sites together with the closure of its Donnington armoured vehicle and engine facilities, focussing in-depth maintenance and repair of the armoured vehicle fleet at ABRO Bovington site (Dorset). Also proposed was the closure and reprovision in new facilities of ABRO's large one-stop shops at Warminster (Wiltshire) and Colchester (Essex) and an extension of in-barracks working which enables engineering support services to be delivered closer to the customer. In addition, there would be a significant rationalisation of the Head Office in Andover. However, in March 2006, following a reassessment of the likely threat on deployed operations, it was decided that the depth-repair programme for the FV430 fleet should be extended, resulting in extra work for ABRO's armoured vehicle repair centre at Bovington. As a consequence, repair work on Warrior and Combat Vehicle Reconnaissance (Tracked) will remain at ABRO's current Donnington facility for the medium term. ABRO confirmed in March 2006 that the rationalisation of its one-stop shops at Warminster and Colchester would proceed as planned with up to 339 redundancies.

Against the background of uncertainty created by rationalisation programme, ABRO performed well. It exceeded its revenue target of £128M (2004/05: £150M) and successfully delivered the first phase of the rationalisation programme. This, coupled with a more sustained flow of work from the DLO, saw an improvement in net profit from -£5.3M to £4.47M and, Return on Capital Employed from -5.3% to 4.0%. However, performance in 2004/5 was adversely affected by the need to establish £10M in obsolete stock provisions as a result of weak material control and consequent escalation in stock holdings.

Going forward, the key challenges for ABRO will be to develop and implement successfully the remainder of its rationalisation programme, play a positive role in the MoD/BAE Partnering Agreement and other wider changes to the armoured vehicle market place, and use its core Defence and civilian markets.

Defence Aviation Repair Agency

The Defence Aviation Repair Agency (DARA) provides deep level maintenance, repair and overhaul (MRO) services for military aircraft, systems and components. As a Trading Fund, it also has freedom to compete for other commercial work. MoD work accounts for the vast majority of DARA's revenue, either directly with the MoD or as a sub-contractor to Defence Original Equipment Manufacturers. A key objective of DARA is to provide a responsive, flexible and highly competitive service to the UK Armed Forces. The future direction of DARA was the issue dominating the reporting period. The culmination of which produced a number of preferred options, which the Minister for the Armed Forces announced to Parliament on 8 November 2005, which was later ratified on 2 February 2006. In summary the decision was to:

- Close DARA's fast jet business at St Athan by April 2007
- Close DARA's engines business at Fleetlands by April 2007
- Prepare for the possible sale of DARA's VC10, Rotary and Components businesses at St Athan, Fleetlands and Almondbank
- Retain in MoD ownership DARA's electronics business at Sealand

The cumulative effect on manpower levels means that a further 725 jobs will be lost across DARA, with up to 50 from reductions to DARA's corporate headcount. Despite this, DARA has continued to meet and at times, exceed MoD customer requirements achieving 3 out of its 4 Key performance targets.

The year has seen DARA's Rotary business transform its operations and embrace 'lean' principles within a 'pulse line' environment. The results have been impressive. The first helicopter platform to enter the pulse line during April 2005 was the Lynx. The Chinook and Sea King platforms followed and with invaluable support from stakeholders and experts in developing 'lean' principles and 'pulse line' activities, DARA is achieving and delivering outputs that would have been unimaginable 18 months ago.

The business, under UK accounting rules, is required to recognise any costs arising from the impending closure of the Fast Jet and Engines businesses, which adversely affected the operating profit and DARA has, for the first time, posted an operating loss of £3.3m in its accounts. Return on Capital Employed (ROCE) performance subsequently fell from 6.7% in 2004-05 to -2.43% in 2005-06.

Work is underway to test market interest in DARA's Rotary, Components and VC10 Tanker businesses. No decision has been taken to sell these businesses and any interest will be measured against criteria to test whether sale might deliver improved effectiveness, value for money for Defence and a better long-term future for employees.

Defence Science and Technology Laboratory

Defence Science and Technology Laboratory's (DSTL) core role is to provide independent and objective, high quality scientific, analytical, technological and engineering advice and services to the MoD and UK Armed Forces. It carries out only work which must be done in Government. Its mission is to create the winning edge for UK Forces and Government through the best use of science and technology, by delivering timely advice and solutions to the government's most important Defence and national security related problems in the most efficient and effective manner.

Although turnover remained static during 2005/06 at £353million, net profit for the DSTL (excluding Ploughshare) rose from £20.2M in 2004/05 to £21.8M in 2005/06. The ROCE fell rom 9.4% for 2004/05 to 8.8%. Manpower charge rates continued to be held below the target for the fifth consecutive year indicating a reduction in real terms of the cost to customers. DSTL's wholly owned technology management company, Ploughshare Innovations Ltd, successfully completed its first full year of operations.

Looking to the future, DSTL is undertaking a major change programme to create an integrated laboratory for the future known as "i-lab". This links a number of strategic improvement programmes. It is progressing well, with the most significant issue over the next three years being to rationalise the DSTL estate to three core sites in order to (a): reduce fragmentation of DSTL's science and technology capability base to maximise synergy and coherence of delivery to customers; (b) sustain DSTL's long-term future by minimising overheads and reducing unnecessary duplication in laboratories, facilities and support functions; and (c) rationalise the sourcing of facilities management services to one contract. Successful delivery of i-lab will be a key objective for the new Chief Executive, who will be appointed in the course of 2006-07.

Met Office

The Met Office provides the official national meteorological service for the UK, and is a world-leading provider of climate-prediction, environmental and weather-related services in the UK and around the world. In July 2005 the Met Office published a five year Corporate Plan which set out the intention to develop an even stronger role for the Met Office within government, to provide a more cost-effective public meteorolgical service, and to achieve significant commercial growth.

During 2005-06, the Met Office published its first ever winter forecast based on a statistical method analysis of sea temperature patterns in the North Atlantic. A successful media campaign ensured 71% public awareness of the winter forecast among the general public. The final figures for the full winter period revealed that mean temperatures were the lowest since 1996-07 for England and Wales and that all regions of the country had a drier than average winter, in line with the forecast made.

Turnover in 2005-06 was £170.4m (2004-05: £165.6m). The profit for the financial year fell from £12.3m in 2004-05 to £9.5m, largely due to an exceptional profit of £4.0m in 2004-05 arising on the disposal of freehold sites in Bracknell and in part because of a requirement to write-off a past investment in *weatherXchange,* a failed Joint Venture Company which went into administration in October 2005. Although ROCE fell from 7.6% in 2004/05 to 5.3%, it remained above the 3.5% target.

The key challenge for the Met Office going forward is the full delivery of its Corporate Plan. During 2006-07 it will seek to develop stronger, output-based relationships with all its government customers, and begin to implement a major new commercial strategy. In the course of 2006-07, it is expected to appoint both a new Chairman and Chief Executive to the Met Office.

UK Hydrographic Office

The UK Hydrographic Office (UKHO) exists to help preserve the safety of life at sea. The hydrographic information it provides is crucial to support operations by the Royal Navy around the world. The UKHO also plays a central role in discharging the UK's treaty obligations to provide hydrographic services for waters of UK national responsibility, as required under international convention. In addition, it is a highly profitable commercial business.

Once again, the UKHO had a very successful year's trading and has continued to provide exceptional service to the Defence Customer. Net profit (£9.3M 2004/5 to £9.9M 2005/6) and ROCE (16.2% 2004/5 to 17.2% 2005/6) rose on the back of the growth of commercial sales – both paper and digital. The UKHO has developed and agreed a new, more market-orientated strategy. This has resulted in a number of changes, including the reorganisation of the UKHO to create new, market-facing divisions.

During 2005-06, Admiralty Holdings Limited, acquired SevenCs, a German company which produces key software for the display of electronic navigational charts on board ship. Working with SevenCs will enable the UKHO to better meet the needs of the mariner. In addition UKHO has secured a record number of reciprocal agreements with Hydrographic Offices around the world for the wider use of their data.

The challenge for the future for UKHO is to develop a commercial approach which will position it well in the digital market. Delivering this will be the top priority for the new Chief Executive, who takes up appointment in July 2006, following the retirement of Dr Wyn Williams – who has led the UKHO through five years of sustained growth.

FURTHER INFORMATION

Further details on Trading Funds can be found in individual Trading Fund annual reports and accounts at:
- ABRO – *http://www.abrodev.co.uk/*
- DARA – http://www.daranet.co.uk/
- DSTL – *http://www.dstl.gov.uk/*
- Met Office – *http://www.met-office.gov.uk/*
- UKHO – *http://www.ukho.gov.uk*

Annex F

GOVERNMENT STANDARDS

Fraud

The previously enhanced Departmental emphasis on the deterrence and detection of fraud, theft and irregularity was further reinforced during the year. The Defence Fraud Analysis Unit (DFAU) undertook a pan-MoD programme of 153 presentations to an aggregate audience of 7,900 staff. This helped to sustain a high level of internal disclosure which contributed significantly to the record total of 382 recorded cases with an estimated value of £1.65M compared to £5.01M in the previous year. The most significant increase was attributed to cases of suspected exploitation of assets including abuse of electronic working practices and internet access. In order to improve the reporting and investigative process, action was put in hand to create a central Departmental reporting cell managed by Defence Police Authorities and the DFAU. When fully operational, this will provide a 'one stop shop' for the reporting of all suspicions and rapid allocation of cases to the appropriate investigative authority. Concomitant with this, the Departmental policy of zero tolerance regarding fraud, theft and irregularity received fresh endorsement by PUS and CDS. This will be promulgated to all TLB holders, Command/Civil Secretaries and Agency Chief Executives.

Bill Payment

The table below shows the targets and performance achieved in settling bills relating to Defence.

Table 32: Bill Paying Performance — Proportion of Bills Settled within Thirty Calendar Days

	2005-06		2004-05	
	Target	Achieved	Target	Achieved
Defence Bills Agency	99.9% (within 11 days)	99.99% 5,621,028 invoices representing £20.18Bn	9.98% (within 11 days)	99.98%
ABRO	100%	96% 70,959 invoices representing £74.2M	100%	96.00%
Defence Aviation Repair Agency	100%	96.38% 14,922 invoices representing £165.4M	100%	95.41%
Defence Science and Technology Laboratory	98.00%	98.4% 36,742 invoices representing £238.5M	98.00%	98.30%
Met Office	99.00%	99.48% 12,689 invoices representing £57.909M	99.00%	98.73%
UK Hydrographic Office	100%	98.8% 12,998 invoices representing £48.64M	100%	98.70%

[1]DBA's target is to pay 99.98% of correctly presented bills within 11 calendar days of receipt as part of the Department's 30 day payment target.

Open Government

In the first year of full operation of the Freedom of Information (FOI) Act, MoD received significantly more requests for information than any other central government department. This inevitably presented some challenges, but the preparatory programme of work to raise awareness and establish effective operating procedures helped to ensure that staff were ready to cope with the demand. Requests were logged and managed using the Access to Information Toolkit, which has now rolled out to some 1,000 users. While there is room for improvement, the analysis of performance shows that in 2005 over three-quarters of requests were answered within 20 working days (see Note 1 to Table 33) and that it was necessary to refuse information in reply to only 16% of requests. The key statistics in Table 33 are drawn from a comprehensive summary published by the Department for Constitutional Affairs (www.foi.gov.uk/reference/StatisticsAndReports.htm), which allows MoD's performance to be compared in detail with that of other government departments. To provide an immediate comparison, the final column of Table 33 provides the average statistics in relation to timeliness and openness for all Departments of State.

Table 33: Requests for information under the Freedom of Information Act in 2005 Category	MoD Performance	Average for Government Departments
Number of requests received	4,604	
Of these –		
% of requests answered within 20 working days	77% (1)	70%
% of requests answered 'in time' (2)	83%	81%
% of requests that were late	17%	19%
Total 'resolvable requests' (3)	4,094	
Of these –		
% of resolvable requests where information was granted in full	71%	60%
% of resolvable requests where information was withheld in full	16%	21%

Notes:

(1) The 2004-05 report (paragraph 169) said that in the first 3 months of 2005, 81% of requests had been answered within 20 working days. The correct statistic for the period is 71%; the figure of 81% relates to requests answered 'in time' (see Note (2))

(2) 'In time' means that the timescale for response has been extended under the terms of s.10 of the FOI Act

(3) 'Resolvable requests' are all those where it was possible to provide a substantive response. They exclude requests which are lapsed or 'on-hold', where the information was not held, and where it was necessary to provide advice and assistance since in each of these cases it would not have been possible to resolve the request in the form it was asked.

Comparative data will be available in the Department for Constitutional Affairs report for the first quarter of 2006, but Table 34 provides a summary of MoD performance in this period.

Table 34: Requests for information under the Freedom of Information Act from January to March 2006

Category	
Number of requests received	905
Of these –	
% of requests answered within 20 working days	77%
% of requests answered 'in time' (1)	81%
% of requests that were late	18%
Total 'resolvable requests' (2)	803
Of these –	
% of resolvable requests where information was granted in full	69%
% of resolvable requests where information was withheld in full	11%

Notes
(1) 'In time' means that the timescale for response has been extended under the terms of s.10 of the FOI Act
(2) 'Resolvable requests' are all those where it was possible to provide a substantive response. They exclude requests which are lapsed or 'on-hold', where the information was not held, and where it was necessary to provide advice and assistance since in each of these cases it would not have been possible to resolve the request in the form it was asked.

In the final months of 2004 and during 2005, about 1,200 staff attended a 2-day FOI course developed specifically for MoD. Reflecting the growing FOI knowledge and experience within business areas, this basic training has now been reshaped into a one day course. In addition, targeted events continue to be arranged to address specific training requirements. This included seminars held in London and Bristol in December 2005 to raise awareness of the responsibilities of senior managers. Work to develop MoD's Publication Scheme also continued. A number of new Classes of Information have been added and the Publication Scheme was re-launched in January 2006 on MoD's new-look FOI website.

Further progress has been made in re-establishing access to the information contained in records affected by asbestos contamination in the basement of the Old War Office Building. In early 2005, a pilot project was carried out during which various working practices were tested as a prelude to the initiation of a full scale project. The full project to scan the affected files commenced in December 2005. Following successful scanning, the original files will be destroyed in accordance with health and safety regulations. It is anticipated that the scanning project will last about eighteen months from commencement of the contract. During the project, there will be the opportunity to access data required for business purposes when necessary, including outstanding FoI requests.

The routine review and transfer of records to The National Archives (TNA) has continued. In addition, MoD has continued to support TNA in dealing with FOI requests for files that are held by TNA but not available to the public. During 2005, a programme of re-review released more than 4,600 such files to general access.

Ministerial Correspondence

Table 35 shows Departmental and agency performance in replying to correspondence from Members of Parliament, Members of Devolved Legislatures, Members of the European Parliament and Peers during 2005-06.

Table 35: Ministry of Defence Ministers and Agency Chief Executives' Performance in Replying to Ministerial Correspondence	Target set for despatch (working days)	Number of letters received for answer	Percentage of replies within target
Ministry of Defence (excluding Defence Agencies)	15	5,583	80
Defence Agencies			
ABRO	15	1	100
Armed Forces Personnel Administration Agency	15	201	99
Army Training and Recruiting Agency	15	–	–
British Forces Post Office	15	–	–
Defence Analytical Services Agency	15	–	–
Defence Aviation Repair Agency	15	–	–
Defence Bills Agency	10	–	–
Defence Communication Services Agency	15	–	–
Defence Dental Services	15	–	–
Defence Estates	15	2	100
Defence Medical Education and Training Agency	15	–	–
Defence Procurement Agency	15	–	–
Defence Science and Technology Laboratory	15	–	–
Defence Storage and Distribution Agency	15	2	100
Defence Transport and Movements Agency	15	–	–
Defence Vetting Agency	7	4	100
Disposal Services Agency	15	1	0
Duke of York's Royal Military School	15	–	–
Ministry of Defence Police	15	–	–
Naval Recruiting and Training Agency	15	–	–
Pay and Personnel Agency	10	2	100
RAF Training Group Defence Agency	15	–	–
Service Children's Education	15	–	–
The Met Office	15	6	100
UK Hydrographic Office	15	–	–
Veterans Agency	15	199	98

Sponsorship

Table 36 satisfies the Cabinet Office requirement to publish details of individual commercial sponsorship deals that are valued in excess of £5,000, VAT exclusive, and where they supplement Government funding of any Departmental core business.

Table 36: Sponsorship between 1 Apr 2005 and 31 March 2006

Activity	TLB	Individual Sponsors	Company Contribution £ VAT EX
Royal Naval Presentation Team	Fleet	Jaguar	25,532
Yeovilton Runway		Team South West Racing	50,000
RNAS Culdrose Air Days		Lockheed Martin	19,500
Yeovilton Air Day		Rolls Royce	12,500
		Westlands Helicopters	18,200
		Aerosystems	5,700
Trafalgar 200	2SL	Lockheed Martin	114,500
		BP Shipping Ltd	100,000
		Augusta Westland	213,500
		BAE Systems	300,000
		EDS	250,000
		History Channel	25,000
		Kellogg, Brown & Root	100,000
		Lloyds Register	10,000
		London Development Agency	100,000
		NAAFI	11,500
		P&O Nedlloyd	50,000
		P&O	100,000
		Rolls Royce Marine	350,000
		Serco Denham	39,500
		Thales	258,500
		The Drapers Company	5,000
		Vosper Thorneycroft	100,000
		Vosper Thorneycroft Education & Skills	15,000
Army School of Physical Training	AG	Technogym	10,000
Blue Eagles		Breitling UK	21,500
		Special Event Services	30,000
		GM UK (SAAB)	15,000
		EDS	25,000
White Helmets		Paradigm Services	6,000
		LF Harris International	10,000
		Willow Financial Consultants	5,000
Royal Regiment of Wales Regimental Promotion	Land	Brains Brewery	15,000
Exercise Cambrian Patrol		Red Bull	14,000
The Rheindahlen & Elmpt Bulletin		Mitsubishi Motors Bruggen	16,121
Exercise Rhino Caterer 04		ESS Support Services Worldwide	10,000
Exercise Spartan Hike		NAAFI	5,000
RAF Aerobatic Display Team	PTC	BAE Systems	25,690
		Breitling	12,265
		Total/Fina/Elf	5,315
		BP Air	18,000
RAF Hercules Display Team	STC	Land Rover UK	11,328
RAF Typhoon Display Team		BAE Systems	5,178
Demonstration And Shake-down Operation programme	DLO	Babcock Naval Services	7,500
		Industrial Marine Engineering Services Ltd	5,000
		Mass Consultants Ltd	5,000
WWII 60th Anniversary Commemorations	Centre	Newsdesk Publications	20,000
		Cobra Beer	15,000
DESO Symposium		Barclays Capital	13,500
		Newsdesk	40,000
TOTAL			**2,640,329**

Advertising

Royal Navy Advertising and Public Relations expenditure for 2005-06 was £9.7M, including some £0.4M spent in relation to Trafalgar 200. The Army Recruiting Group marketing and advertising spend in 2005-06, for both the Regular and Territorial Army, was £38.4M (£33.5M in 2004-05[1]). This encompasses television and press advertising, the production of DVDs, leaflets, pamphlets and brochures as well as overarching production and design costs. The total RAF marketing spend for 2005-06 was £7.6M, including £2.0M spent on advertising. Marketing and advertising undertaken included a national TV campaign supported by radio, press and online advertising, response handling, youth sports sponsorships, exhibitions and events, educational programmes, recruiting publications and films, the RAF Careers website, customer relationship marketing, promotional items and marketing research.

Better Regulation

There is currently one piece of MoD sponsored legislation being considered by Parliament: The Armed Forces Bill (see page 90). In addition, the Armed Forces Bill (Parliamentary Approval for Participation in Armed Conflict) and Pardon for Soldiers of the Great War Bill, which are neither supported by the Department nor supported by the Government, are also being considered by Parliament. The Department held 13 public consultations in the past year; 12 of these were performed by Defence Estates, and the other by the Met Office. A Regulatory Impact Assessment regarding Surface Warship Support was performed, and is published on www.mod.uk.

Civilian Recruitment

The MoD has a legal obligation to the Civil Service Commissioners to publish summary information about our recruitment processes and the use of permitted exceptions to the principles of fair and open competition and selection on merit. The information published in the Table 37 also helps meet these requirements. The Department's recruitment figures for 2005-06 are at paragraph 296 of this report and include figures for permanent and temporary (casual) recruitment. The following information on the use of permitted exceptions has been collated separately and does not include figures for temporary (casual) recruitment. Table 37 contains information about the MoD's recruitment in the last 12 months; it includes details of the number of individuals who were appointed, their background and their appointment circumstances. The MoD is required to recruit under various Government initiatives such as New Deal. This scheme was introduced to give long term unemployed people the opportunity to be able to apply for a job without the minimum qualifications. New Deal campaigns are run for New Deal candidates only. The MoD also operates a Guaranteed Interview Scheme for disabled people: applicants with a disability who apply for a vacancy in the Department have the opportunity to declare their disability on their application form, providing they meet the minimum entry requirements, they are able to claim a Guaranteed Interview. All permanent recruitment campaigns are subject to fair and open competition; exceptions to this are short term casual staff who will not be eligible to apply for a permanent post or be established in their temporary role. Exceptions also apply to individuals with specialist knowledge of PPP/PFI, which the Department needs.

[1] Due to an error, the Army's 2004-05 advertising spend mistakenly quoted the whole of Headquarters Recruiting Group's budget. The figure for 2004-05 should have read £33.452M.

Table 37: Civilian Recruitment[1]

	2005-06		2004-05		2003-04	
	Non-Industrial	Industrial	Non-Industrial	Industrial	Non-Industrial	Industrial
Appointments of less than 12 months in respect of those posts specified in Annex A of the CSCRC.	**0**	**0**	0	0	0	0
Extensions up to a maximum of 24 months, of appointments originally made for a period of less than 12 months (with reasons). [2]	**28**	**2**	28	3	21	1
Recurrent short term appointments.	**2**	**27**	31	60	21	40
Short term appointments where highly specialised skills are required. [3]	**10**	**0**	16	0	4	0
Appointments under Government programmes to assist the long term unemployed. [4]	**0**	**0**	1	0	5	0
Secondments. [5]	**6**	**0**	4	0	20	1
Extensions to secondments (with reasons). [6]	**3**	**0**	4	0	1	0
Re-appointments of former civil servants.	**35**	**4**	95	28	110	11
Transfers of staff with their work (not under Transfer of Undertakings Protection of Employment).	**2**	**3**	20	1	28	3
Transfers of staff from other public services without work (excluding public bodies staffed exclusively by civil servants). [7]	**2**	**0**	78	0	95	0
Appointments of surplus acceptable candidates to shortage posts.	**3**	**0**	3	0	7	0
Appointments of disabled candidates under modified selection arrangements.	**3**	**1**	11	2	9	1
Supported employment appointments.	**0**	**0**	3	0	0	3
Number of exceptions reserved for the Commissioners' use.	**0**	**0**	0	1	0	0
Any appointments exceptionally approved by the Commissioners under the Orders in Council, outside the terms of the Code.	**0**	**0**	0	0	0	0

Notes:

[1] Figures for all years exclude Locally Employed Civilians and Royal Fleet Auxiliary. Figures for 2004/05 do not include ABRO. The exception categories reflect the information required to be published in the revised Civil Service Commissioners' Recruitment Code. Historical data is provided where possible.

[2] The majority of these extensions were to meet short-term requirements to whilst permanent replacements were sought. Fair and open competition has been used wherever possible.

[3] This shows the number of staff recruited where the requirement was short term and required specialist skills and where holding an open competition would not have identified any further candidates.

[4] An exception approved by the Commissioners following the launch of the Governments Welfare to Work – New Deal Programme. Figures exclude those New Deal candidates recruited through normal open and fair competition.

[5] Excludes other Government departments, but includes for example, local authorities, hospitals, etc.

[6] Extension due to a requirement to utilise one individual's knowledge of PPP/PFI.

[7] Figures for 2003/04 include 82 MDP Police officers transferred from Home Office Police Forces. Figures for 2004/05 include 74 Police Officers transferred from Home Office Police Forces.

ANNEX G

DEFENCE EQUIPMENT PROGRAMME AND COLLABORATIVE PROCUREMENT

Major Projects are defined as the twenty largest equipment projects that have passed their main investment decision point (Main Gate) and the ten largest equipment projects that have passed their initial investment decision (Initial Gate), by value of forecast spend remaining. The list of Major Projects was set at 1 April 2005, and the list below includes information for the end of the financial year, 31 March 2006. The following tables show key performance information of Major Projects that have passed Main Gate approval, broken down by capability area. The precise definition of In Service Date (ISD) varies with different equipment although, in general terms, it can be taken to refer to the date on which the equipment is expected to be available and supportable in service in sufficient quantity to provide a useable operational capability. The dates quoted for ships and submarines are based on the acceptance date from the contractor of the First of Class, not the date by which the equipment (or specified number of pieces of equipment) will contribute to the operational capability of the Royal Navy.

Battlespace Manoeuvre

The Battlespace Manoeuvre area incorporates capabilities designed to provide direct battlefield engagement, theatre airspace, tactical mobility, expeditionary logistics support, nuclear, biological and chemical defence, battlefield engineering, special projects and combat service support. While most of the equipment will be utilised by the Army, it also covers significant capabilities used by other services and joint organisations, for example the RAF's Typhoon and assets that will belong to the Joint Helicopter Command.

Table 38: Capability Manager Battlespace Manoeuvre Equipment Programme

Post Main Gate Projects

Equipment	Description	Current Forecast Cost (£millions)	Current Forecast ISD	Quantity Required Current
Ground Manoeuvre				
C Vehicle PFI	Commercial provision of 'C' Class vehicles	702	2006	n/a
Panther Command and Liaison Vehicle	Protected tactical mobile command vehicle	201	2007	401
Terrier	Armoured earthmoving vehicle	296	2008	65
Trojan and Titan	Armoured engineering vehicles	336	2006	66
Light Forces Anti-Tank Guided Weapon System	Anti-armour firepower system	305	2005	378
Next Generation Light Anti-armour Weapon	Short range anti-armour weapon	314	2007	14,002
Expeditionary Logistics & Support				
A400M	Heavy transport aircraft	2,616	2011	25
Support Vehicle (Cargo and Recovery)	Cargo and recovery vehicles and trailers	1,338	2008	4851 Cargo 288 Recovery 69 Trailers
Theatre Airspace				
Beyond Visual Range Air-to-Air Missile (BVRAAM)	Air-to-Air missile	1,204	2013	Note 1
Typhoon	Fighter Aircraft	Note 2	2003	232

Notes:
(1) Weapon numbers are classified
(2) Current forecast cost for Typhoon is classified due to commercial sensitivities

Precision Attack

The Precision Attack area covers the above-water and underwater battlespaces, and deep target attack. It contains programmes ranging from Paveway IV (a precision guided bomb) to nuclear submarines and artillery systems, for delivery to all three services. The table below does not reflect major equipment programmes where orders have not yet been placed, such as the future aircraft carriers.

Table 39: Capability Manager Battlespace Manoeuvre Equipment Programme

Post Main Gate Projects

Equipment	Description	Current Forecast Cost (£millions)	Current Forecast ISD	Quantity Required Current
Above-Water Effect				
Type 45 Destroyer	Anti-air warfare destroyer	5,997	2009	6
Under-Water Effect				
Astute Class Submarine	Attack submarine	3,652	2009	3
Nimrod Maritime and Reconnaissance Attack Mk4	Reconnaissance and attack patrol aircraft	3,516	2010	12
Sting Ray	Life extension and capability enhancement	592	2006	Note 1
Deep Target Attack				
Brimstone	Advanced Air-Launched Anti-Armour Weapon	911	2005	Note 1
Guided Missile-Launch Rocket System (GMLRS)	Rocket weapon system	263	2007	4080
Joint Combat Aircraft (JCA)	Attack aircraft	1,913	Note 2	Note 2
Precision Guided Bomb (PGB)	Air-launched munition	341	2007	2303

Notes:

(1) Weapon numbers are classified

(2) Joint Combat Aircraft Main Gate Business Case was tailored for development only to match the US procurement cycle. Approval for ISD and quantities required approval will be sought as part of Main Gate Production Business Case in 2006.

Information Superiority

This capability area covers intelligence, surveillance, target acquisition and reconnaissance, and command, control and information infrastructure. Most projects are inherently tri-service in nature.

Table 40: Capability Manager Information Superiority Equipment Programme

Post Main Gate Projects

Equipment	Description	Current Forecast Cost (£millions)	Current Forecast ISD	Quantity Required Current
Command, Control and Information Infrastructure				
Bowman	Tactical voice and data communications	2,014	2004	43,000 radios
Common Battlefield Application Toolset, Infrastructure andarmoured Platform Battlefield Information System Application	Bowman related hardware and software systems	339	2005	Not applicable

COLLABORATIVE PROCUREMENT

A list of collaborative programmes is published on the MoD website. We made progress on a number of collaborative procurement issues.

European Defence

We supported the work of the **European Defence Agency** across a range of projects and initiatives on the Agency's armaments and industry/market workstrands. We played a pivotal role in EU Defence Ministers' agreement in November 2005 to the introduction of the Code of Conduct on Defence Procurement, designed to increase the transparency of European defence equipment acquisition. In December 2005 the **European Commission** issued a communication on the findings from its Green Paper on Defence Procurement. Its proposals for an Interpretive Communication and a Defence Directive were scrutinised by Defence and other Government Departments' officials. We agreed that the Government would work with the Commission while ensuring that UK interests are protected. These initiatives were scrutinised by the House of Lords European Scrutiny Committee.

OCCAR (Organisation Conjoint de Coopération en matiers d'Armement)

We continue to play a strong role in ensuring that OCCAR meets its corporate and programme targets in managing collaborative equipment programmes. We placed particular emphasis on the effectiveness and application of financial management and risk management processes and practices. On OCCAR managed programmes, the first engine tests were successfully run on the A400M programme; further deliveries of the COBRA (Counter-Battery Radar) system were made to the British Army; and two firings were successfully undertaken on the Principal Anti-air Missile System programme.

Letter of Intent (LoI) Framework Agreement

As part of the six nation LoI focus on recognising European industry's efforts to restructure, we worked closely with partners to remove barriers to industrial and equipment co-operation. Achievements included agreement on guidelines on levy waivers between LoI nations, and a declaration facilitating the transit of military goods from one LoI nation to another through the territory of a third. We continued to pursue assimilation of appropriate LoI outputs into the European Defence Agency.

United States of America

Through a number of fora, including the **Bilateral Defence Acquisition Committee**, we worked closely with the US Departments of Defense and State to press for the improved information and technology exchange essential on a number of programmes. Minister (DP) emphasised to the Senate Armed Services Committee in March 2006 the importance of sharing information and technology, particularly for UK operational sovereignty for the Joint Strike Fighter.

Collaborative Equipment Programmes

We continued to make progress across the wide range of collaborative equipment programmes. In particular, while we have not entered into a full collaborative programme with France to align our requirements for future aircraft carriers, we have agreed to share our current design as a potential basis for France's future carrier. France will make payments in respect of UK's investment in the project to date and share the further costs during 2006. Opportunities for shared procurements will also be explored. A Memorandum of Understanding between the two countries was signed in March 2006, and a number of French Government, navy and industry members are now located in Bristol with the UK's Aircraft Carrier Alliance.

Annex H

NON DEPARTMENTAL PUBLIC BODIES

The Department sponsors six executive and twelve advisory Non-Departmental Public Bodies (NDPBs), a Public Corporation and an Independent Monitoring Board. Discussion is ongoing regarding the classification of a couple of other bodies with links to the department. A brief description of the Executive NDPBs is set out below. Details of their funding from the Defence Budget and total gross expenditure can be found at Note 32 to the Departmental Resource Accounts on page 241. More detailed information on these and the other bodies sponsored by the department can be found at the MoD website at www.mod.uk.

Executive NDPBs

The Department's Executive NDPBs are all museums with charitable status, which retain close links with the Armed Forces. The Financial Memorandum setting out the arrangement between the Department and these bodies on the conditions governing payment and expenditure of the Grants in Aid made by the MoD is in the process of being revised. In addition, following a review of the Executive NDPBs by the MoD's internal audit team, it is intended to draw up a Memorandum of Understanding clarifying the relationship between the department, the sponsor braches and the museums; and reflecting their independent status under charity law.

All the museums contributed to the successful World War Two 60th Anniversary celebrations in St James's Park in July, which attracted over 85,000 visitors. In addition:

- The Fleet Air Arm Museum continued to develop its relationship with the Defence and aerospace industries and the educational community, to encourage young people to consider careers either in engineering and/or the services. The finals of "Flying Start Challenge" were held at the museum for the third year running, and there was a major presence in the "Imagineering" marquee at the Royal Bath and West Show. The 1944 Chance Vought Corsair was returned to display after three years detailed forensic investigation and restoration, gaining international recognition for the archaeological attention to detail;

- The Royal Naval Museum attracted 264,000 visitors in 2005, a 17% increase on 2004, plus a further 10,00 visitors during the International Festival of the Sea. A three year online project was launched to give access to 15,000 items from the museum's collections;

- The Royal Navy Submarine Museum opened a new exhibit area;

- For the fifth year running, the Royal Marines Museum was awarded Quality Assured Visitor Attraction Status by Visit Britain. A special exhibition linked to Trafalgar 200 helped attract more visitors to the main site, and a new outstation at the RM Commando Training Centre in Devon raised total visitor numbers;

- The National Army Museum made a number of changes to improve access to its collections in line with government policy, including further measures for compliance with the Disability Discrimination Act. Examples include completion of a "kidszone" gallery providing educational opportunities for the younger audience and installation of a new state of the art lighting system. In association with the Discovery Channel a new exhibition on battlefield archaeology was opened displaying items recovered from First World War;

- The RAF Museum completed a new Air Cadets exhibition at Hendon. A major expansion of the Cosford site is currently underway with the construction of a new Cold War Exhibition. The museum launched a Modern Apprenticeship Scheme for historic aircraft maintenance at Cosford, including training provided by the Defence College of Aeronautical Engineering.

Annual Public Appointment Plan

The Committee on Standards in Public Life recommended in its Tenth Report that departments produce annual plans setting out policy and practice relating to public appointments. The MoD's Annual Public Appointment Plan includes diversity figures and targets that previously included in the now discontinued Cabinet Office publication *Delivering Diversity in Public Appointments*.

Policy

The MoD is committed to following the Code of Practice of the Commissioner for Public Appointments. All MoD Non-Departmental Public Bodies, Public Corporationand Independent Monitoring Board are encouraged to follow the Code of Practice whether or not an appointment is Ministerial and therefore formally within the remit. In practice the majority of MoD public appointments are Ministerial. The Department is fully committed to improving diversity throughout its workforce and this is reflected in our approach to filling public appointments. Paragraphs 283-284 and 294-295 set out the initiatives and actions we have taken to improve diversity. MoD public appointments are made entirely on merit. Remuneration is based on the sum needed to attract suitably qualified candidates and to reflect the time commitment and regularity of work involved in the position.

Report on Achievement of Objectives

The diversity targets for public appointments to MoD Non-Departmental Public Bodies, Public Corporation and Independent Monitoring Board to achieve during the period of this Annual Report and the actual figures achieved by our public appointees to Non-Departmental Public Bodies are shown in Table 41 below. We are currently considering whether to move to a unified recruitment centre serving the whole Department. This could benefit our public appointments by widening the field of potential candidates, and particularly by identifying the best ways to communicate with minority groups. We are also participating in a mentoring programme focused on the Hindu, Muslim and Sikh communities being run by the Department for Work and Pensions.

Within the overriding principle of selection based on merit, we aim to raise the representation of women, people from ethnic minority groups and disabled people within our public appointments to MoD NDPBs, Public Corporation and Independent Monitoring Board in line with the Government's long-term objectives of equal representation of men and women, pro-rata representation of people from ethnic minority groups and the increased participation of disabled people. We also promote the benefits of diversity within their membership. Our public appointment diversity targets for the next three years are shown below.

Table 41: Diversity targets for public appointments to MoD Non-Departmental Public Bodies, Public Corporation and Independent Monitoring Board

		2005-06	2007	2008	2009
Women	Target	30%	32%	35%	35%
	Achieved	18%			
Ethnic minorities	Target	3.5%	3.5%	4%	4.5%
	Achieved	0.5%			
Disabled people	Target	15%	5.5%	5.5%	6%
	Achieved	5.2%			

The future targets for both women and ethnic minorities are related to the overall Departmental Diversity Targets set out in Table 26 on page 145. The future targets for disabled people in our public appointments have been reduced to a more realistic figure than the 15% for the period of this Annual Report, since on the anticipated future recruitment and reappointment figures of just under 16% of the total number of appointees per year; the target of 15% is unrealistic and unachievable.

GLOSSARY

1SL/CNS: First Sea Lord and Chief of the Naval Staff. Professional head of the Navy. Member of the Defence Management Board, the Admiralty Board and the Chiefs of Staff Committee and Chair of the Navy Board. Currently held by an officer of the rank of Admiral.

2nd PUS: 2nd Permanent Under Secretary. The Deputy to the Permanent Under Secretary. Member of the Defence Council and Defence Management Board, the Admiralty, Army and Air Force Boards and their executive committees, the Acquisition Policy Board, the Investment Approvals Board, the Defence Audit Committee, official chair of the Defence Environment and Safety Board, and joint head, with the Vice Chief of the Defence Staff, of the Central Top Level Budget organisation.

2SL/CNH: Second Sea Lord and Commander-in-Chief Naval Home Command.
The Royal Navy's Principal Personnel Officer, of the rank of Vice Admiral, and a member of the Admiralty and Navy Boards. Also known as the Chief of Naval Personnel. He has responsibility for maintaining operational capability by providing correctly trained manpower through recruitment into the Royal Navy and Royal Marines and individual training. He is also Commander in Chief Naval Home Command responsible for all non DLO Naval real estate.

ABRO. A Trading Fund Agency of the MoD formally known as Army Base Repair Organisation. ABRO provides engineering support (including complex repair and servicing, re-manufacture and assembly) and fleet management services to the MoD, the defence industry and other commercial businesses for land based equipment ranging from radios to main battle tanks.

ACPP: Africa Conflict Prevention Pool. The arrangements jointly run by the MoD, FCO and DfID to deliver the Government's conflict prevention objectives in Africa. The ACPP has an annual budget of £60M.

Activity levels. The proportion of regular military personnel deployed on operations and other military tasks.

Admiralty Board. The Admiralty Board is chaired by the Secretary of State for Defence and delegated by the Defence Council to administer the activities and personnel of the Royal Navy.

AFB: Air Force Board. The Air Force Board is chaired by the Secretary of State for Defence and delegated by the Defence Council to administer the activities and personnel of the Royal Air Force.

AFBSC: Air Force Board Standing Committee. The AFBSC conducts the day-to-day business of managing the Royal Air Force on behalf of the Air Force Board. It brings together, under the Chief of the Air Staff (CAS), the RAF operational and personnel commanders, and supports the CAS in his executive role, his management and operational advisory roles, and as the professional head of the RAF.

AFCS: Armed Forces Compensation Scheme. A scheme, introduced from 6 April 2005, for members and ex-members of the Regular Armed Forces (including Gurkhas) and Reserve Forces, to pay compensation for injuries, illnesses or deaths which are caused by service on or after 6 April 2005. In the event of a Service person's death caused by service, benefits are payable to eligible dependants.

AFPS: Armed Forces Pension Scheme. The non-contributory defined benefits pension scheme covering all members of the Armed Forces.

AG: Adjutant General.
a) The Army's Principal Personnel Officer, of the rank of Lieutenant General, and a member of the Army Board and the Executive Committee of the Army Board. He has responsibility for providing trained army officers and other ranks through recruitment into the Army and individual training. He also provides education services to children of all members of the Services on long-term foreign postings.

b) The Top Level Budget (TLB) organisation managed by the Adjutant General.

ALI: Adult Learning Inspectorate. The ALI is a statutory non-departmental public body that inspects and reports on the quality of education and training for adults and young people funded by public money.

AME: Annually Managed Expenditure. Spending included in Total Managed Expenditure that does not fall within Departmental Expenditure Limits (DELs), such as nuclear provisions and War Pension Benefits. Expenditure in AME is generally less predictable and/or controllable than expenditure within DELs.

AMP: Air Member for Personnel. The RAF's principal personnel officer, of the rank of Air Marshal, a member of the Air Force Board and Air Force Board Standing Committee, and head of the RAF Personnel and Training Command. He is responsible for providing trained RAF officers and other ranks through recruitment into the RAF and individual training.

Anti-surface weapons. Weapons designed to attack targets on the surface of the land or sea.

APB: Acquisition Policy Board. The MoD's top level board, chaired by the Minister for Defence Procurement or, in his absence, the PUS. It oversees the development of defence acquisition policy and processes and defence industrial policy, and reviewing and monitoring the coherence of acquisition performance targets.

Apprentices. New entrants to the Armed Forces undertaking training in particular skilled trades.

Appropriations-in-aid. Receipts used to offset expenditure. They generally arise from the provision of repayment services, the sale of surplus goods or of equipment purchased on behalf of the Defence Sales Organisation.

Army Board. The Army Board is chaired by the Secretary of State for Defence and delegated by the Defence Council to administer the activities and personnel of the Army.

Army Reserve See **Regular Reserves.**

ASLC: Accruing Superannuation Liability Charge. An estimate of the cost of providing future superannuation protection for all personnel currently in pensionable employment.

Assessment Centre. The formal process used by the MoD to assess suitability of civil servants for promotion into junior management (Band D) and middle management (Band B) grades.

Assets. Can be either financial or non-financial. Financial assets include monetary gold, bank deposits, IMF Special Drawing Rights, loans granted bonds, shares, accounts receivable, and the value of the government's stake in public corporations. Non-financial assets consist of fixed capital (such as buildings and vehicles); stock, land and valuables.

ASTA: Aircrew Synthetic Training Aids. A Full Mission simulator that replicates all aspects of a real flying mission, allowing pilots to match the aircraft and its weapons against interactive attacks, whilst experiencing the pressures and demands of high speed jet flight. A Cockpit Trainer, a lower level device, is primarily used to introduce the pilot to the cockpit environment and procedures.

ASTOR: Airborne Stand-Off Radar. A new capability which will provide a long range all weather theatre surveillance and target acquisition system capable of detecting moving, fixed and static targets. Has an In-Service Date of September 2005 and full Operational Capability is to be achieved by 2008.

AWE: Atomic Weapons Establishment. One of the largest high technology research, design development and production facilities in the UK. Its primary task is to produce and maintain the warheads for the UK's independent nuclear deterrent.

BAES: British Aerospace Systems. An international company engaged in the development, delivery and support of advanced defence and aerospace systems in the air, on land, at sea and in space. It designs, manufactures and supports military aircraft, surface ships, submarines, fighting vehicles, radar, avionics, communications and guided weapons systems.

Balance Sheet. A financial statement showing the assets, liabilities, and net worth of a business on a specified date.

Band B. A grade in the civilian rank structure immediately below the Senior Civil Service.

Battalion. An Army fighting unit, usually comprising around 650 personnel, commanded by a Lieutenant Colonel. See Regiment.

Berlin Plus arrangements. Arrangements negotiated between the European Union and NATO to allow for the EU to have access to NATO's assets and capabilities so that NATO can support the EU, so that there's full transparency between the two organisations and so that we cooperate with the most efficient, the most effective mechanisms possible so that resources are used in the most efficient way.

BOWMAN. A tri-Service tactical communications and information system.

BNFL: British Nuclear Fuel plc. An international nuclear energy business, involved in fuel manufacture, reactor design and services, as well as decommissioning and environmental services; cleaning up the legacy of the Cold War.

Brigade. An Army Brigade is a collection of units that have been formally grouped together for a specific purpose, commanded by a Brigadier. A fighting Brigade will contain a mix of Infantry, Cavalry, Tank and Artillery units together with supporting specialist capabilities. The composition of a Brigade will differ depending on its responsibility but usually contains about 5,000 soldiers.

BTEC. Vocational qualifications to prepare students for employment or for progression to higher education, often taken as an alternative to A-levels.

BVRAAM: Beyond Visual Range Air-to-Air Missile. The next generation air-to-air weapon, also known as Meteor, which will provide Typhoon with the capacity to combat projected air-to-air threats throughout the life of the aircraft and contribute to the superiority requirements of UK and NATO operations.

Capability Reviews. A Cabinet Office initiative, launched in early 2006, aimed at improving the capability of the Civil Service to meet today's delivery challenges and be ready for tomorrow's. The Reviews will help departments to identify where they need to improve and what support they need to do so. The reports on these reviews will be published, with clear assessments of current performance and key actions to be taken to improve. Capability Reviews supersede Performance Partnership Agreements.

CAS: Chief of the Air Staff. Professional head of the Royal Air Force, member of the Defence Council and Defence Management Board, the Air Force Board and the Chiefs of Staff Committee, and Chair of the Air Force Board Standing Committee. Currently held by an officer of the rank of Air Chief Marshal.

CBRN: Chemical, Biological, Radiological and Nuclear materials. Unconventional materials potentially capable of use in weapons of wide area impact, often collectively known as Weapons of Mass Destruction.

CBW: Chemical and Biological Warfare. The use of chemical and biological weapons in conflict. Possession and use of Chemical and Biological Warfare is illegal under the Chemical Weapons Convention and the Biological and Toxin Weapons Convention.

CDL: Chief of Defence Logistics. Head of the Defence Logistics Organisation TLB. Member of the Defence Council and Defence Management Board, Acquisition Policy Board and Investment Approvals Board.

CDP: Chief of Defence Procurement. Head of the Defence Procurement Agency TLB and member of the Defence Council and Defence Management Board, Acquisition Policy Board and Investment Approvals Board.

CDS: Chief of Defence Staff. The professional head of the UK Armed Forces and principal military adviser to the Secretary of State for Defence and the Government. Member of the Defence Council and Defence Management Board, and Chairman of the Chiefs of Staff Committee.

CFE: Treaty on Conventional Armed Forces in Europe. A treaty which established comprehensive limits on conventional military equipment in Europe (from the Atlantic to the Urals) mandated the destruction of excess weaponry and provided for verification and inspection.

CFER: Consolidated Fund Extra Receipt. Receipts realised in excess of amounts authorised as Appropriations in Aid of the supply Estimates, or of kinds which HM Treasury does not allow Departments to use in aid of expenditure. Such receipts are surrendered to the Consolidated Fund as Extra Receipts.

CGS: Chief of the General Staff. Professional head of the Army, member of the Defence Council and Defence Management Board, the Army Board and the Chiefs of Staff Committee, and Chair of the Executive Committee of the Army Board. Currently held by an officer of the rank of General.

CJO: Chief of Joint Operations.
a) the senior joint military operational commander, of the rank of Vice Admiral, Lieutenant General or Air Marshal, responsible for running all military operations other than those so large that a more senior officer is required, or those undertaken predominantly by one Service such that it makes sense for the operation to be commanded by the operational TLB led by that Service (CINCFLEET, Land Command, or Strike Command). Military assets are assigned to CJO only for the duration of the operation.

b) the Top Level Budget organisation managed by the CJO, including the Permanent Joint Headquarters, the Sovereign Base Areas in Cyprus and British forces in Gibraltar and the Falkland Islands.

CINCFLEET: Commander-in-Chief Fleet.
The Royal Navy's principal operational commander, of the rank of Admiral, and a member of the Admiralty and Navy Boards.

CINCLAND: Commander-in-Chief Land.
a) The Army's principal operational commander, of the rank of General, and a member of the Army Board and Executive Committee of the Army Board.

b) Top Level Budget Organisation managed by CINCLAND responsible for the delivery of trained expeditionary armed forces to CJO at agreed readiness states.

CINCSTRIKE: Commander-in-Chief Strike.
a) The Royal Air Force's principal operational commander, of the rank of Air Chief Marshal, and a member of the Air Force Board and Air Force Board Standing Committee.

b) Top Level Budget Organisation managed by CINCSTRIKE responsible for the delivery of trained expeditionary air power to CJO at agreed readiness levels.

CIS: Communication and Information Systems.

Civil Contingencies Act. The Act, and accompanying non-legislative measures, will deliver a single framework for civil protection in the United Kingdom capable of meeting the challenges of the twenty-first century. The Act is separated into two substantive parts: local arrangements for civil protection and emergency powers. It became an Act of Parliament on 18 November 2004.

CMS: Common Military Skills. Core military skills in which recruits are trained in the first stages of their training.

COBRA: Counter-Battery Radar. A 3-D phased radar system designed to locate enemy artillery at very long ranges.

Commission. The legal authority of an Officer's appointment to the Armed Forces. Precise terms vary according to Service and specialisation within each Service.

Conflict Prevention. Early warning, crisis management, conflict resolution, peacemaking, peacekeeping, and peace-building activity and an associated strengthening of international and regional systems and capacity.

Corps:
a) An organised collection of Regiments or groupings of soldiers that share a common area of specialist expertise to ensure common practice and that common interests can be catered for efficiently.

b) An Army fighting unit comprising two or more divisions with associated specialist supporting units, commanded by a Lieutenant General.

COS: Chiefs of Staff Committee. The Chiefs of Staff Committee is chaired by the Chief of the Defence Staff. It is the main forum in which the collective military advice of the Chiefs of Staff is obtained on operational issues. The PUS attends the COS Committee.

Cost of Capital Charge. An annual non-cash charge applied to each department's budget. It is 6% of the net assets of the department and is used to make departments aware of the full cost of holding assets.

CSA:

a) **Chief Scientific Adviser.** The Ministry of Defence's senior expert scientific advisor, recruited externally, Head of Science Innovation and Technology TLB, member of the Defence Council and Defence Management Board and Chair of the Investment Approvals Board.

b) **Customer Supplier Agreement.** An agreement, usually between TLBs, detailing in terms of quality, quantity and timeliness the outputs required from the supplier to enable the customer to meet its defence outputs.

CSP: Civil Service Pension scheme.

CTLB: Central TLB. The Central Top Level Budget organisation has responsibility for the MoD Head Office, covering Defence policy as well as Departmental policy on the equipment programme, resources, finance, personnel and security, as well as a range of non-Head Office functions. The Central TLB provides a diverse range of corporate services for the MoD as a whole. These include pay, estate management, bill payment, consultancy services, accountancy, some training, statistical analysis, central IT systems, public relations, defence exports and policing. The Central TLB's remit also encompasses the management of Service housing and the provision of medical services.

CTP: Career Transition Partnership. A partnering arrangement between Right Management Consultants and the Ministry of Defence to successfully deliver enhanced resettlement services to all ranks from the Armed Forces.

Current expenditure on goods and services is the sum of expenditure on pay, and related staff costs, plus spending on goods and services. It is net of receipts from sales. It excludes capital expenditure, but includes expenditure on equipment that can only be used for military purposes since that is counted as current expenditure. It differs from final consumption in that capital consumption is not included.

Current prices. Prices prevailing at the time.

CVR(T): Combat Vehicle Reconnaissance (Tracked). A light tank used for reconnaissance.

DAC: Defence Audit Committee. The Defence Audit Committee is a subcommittee of the Defence Management Board, chaired by an independent non-executive member of the DMB. It reviews and constructively challenges the adequacy of internal controls, risk management and assurance processes within the Ministry of Defence. In particular it reviews the Department's assurance arrangements and Statement on Internal Control contained within the Departmental Resource Accounts (the DRAc) annually and reports on these to the Accounting Officer.

DARA: Defence Aviation Repair Agency. In 1999, DARA brought together the RAF Maintenance Group Defence Agency (MGDA) and the Naval Aircraft Repair Organisation (NARO). It is the largest Government owned aerospace repair facility within Europe, delivering one-stop-shop aerospace support to the MoD, overseas governments and Industry. DARA became a Trading Agency of the MoD in April 2001.

DASA: Defence Analytical Services Agency. DASA was created in July 1992 and provides National Statistics on Defence and other corporate information, forecasting and planning and consultancy, advice and research services to the MOD.

DBA: Defence Bills Agency. Primarily responsible for paying bills submitted to the Ministry of Defence by defence contractors.

DCSA: Defence Communication Services Agency. Provides telecommunications and related services to the MoD and is part of the DLO. Not to be confused with the DSCA.

DE: Defence Estates. Manages and maintains the MoD's estates in the UK and abroad. Previously part of the Central TLB, but from 1 April 2005 a Top Level Budget Organisation in its own right.

Defence Aim. The Defence Aim is set out in the MoD's Public Service Agreement. It is to deliver security for the people of the United Kingdom and the Overseas Territories by defending them, including against terrorism, and act as a force for good by strengthening international peace and security.

Defence Balanced Scorecard. The Defence Balanced Scorecard is a framework that helps the DMB to translate strategy into operational objectives that drive both behaviour and performance. This strategy is articulated in the Departmental Plan, which sets out the department's top level strategic objectives, including our Public Service Agreement (PSA) targets. The Defence Balanced Scorecard tells the DMB how well Defence is doing in terms of the objectives that underpin the plan. Untimately this assessment tess the DMB whether Defence is 'succeeding' and gives them an insight into the department's ability to achieve the Defence vision.

Defence Budget. Under Cash Accounting, the amount of money planned to be spent during a financial year. Under Resource Accounting and Budgeting (RAB), the sum of resources planned to be consumed during a financial year. See Resource budgeting.

Defence Council. The Defence Council is the senior Departmental committee. Chaired by the Secretary of State it provides the formal legal basis for the conduct of Defence in the UK through a range of powers vested in it by statute and Letters Patent.

Defence Estate. The Defence estate comprises over 4,000 built and rural sites in the UK covering some 240,000 hectares. It includes 21 major Armed Forces training areas, 39 minor training areas, 289 Sites of Special Scientific Interest (SSSI), 48 special protection areas, over 650 statutorily protected buildings and almost 1,300 scheduled monuments.

Defence Mission. The objectives of the Ministry of Defence are to provide the capabilities needed: to ensure the security and defence of the United Kingdom and Overseas Territories, including against terrorism; to support the Government's foreign policy objectives particularly in promoting international peace and security.

Defence Technology Centre: DTC. Centres of excellence for conducting innovative, cutting edge research for enhanced UK Defence capability. They are exemplars for research collaboration between Government, UK Defence, Small-Medium Sized Enterprises, and Universities.

Defence Vision. The Defence Vision set out by the Defence Management Board, is: *Defending the UK and its interests; Strengthening international peace and stability; A Force for good in the world. We achieve this aim by working together on our core task to produce battle-winning people and equipment that are: Fit for the challenge of today; Ready for the tasks of tomorrow; Capable of building for the future.*

DEFRA: Department for Environment, Food and Rural Affairs. DEFRA is the Government Department responsible for all aspects of the environment, rural matters, farming and food production.

DEL: Departmental Expenditure Limit. DELs are firm plans for three years for a specific part of a department's expenditure. In general the DEL will cover all running costs and all programme expenditure except, in certain cases, spending is included in departmental AME because it cannot be reasonably be subject to close control over a three year period. DELs are divided into current and capital budgets.

Depreciation. Also termed capital consumption. The measure of the wearing out, consumption or other loss of value of a fixed asset whether arising from use, passage of time or obsolescence through technological and market changes.

DERA: Defence Evaluation and Research Agency. On 2 July 2001 DERA was split into two parts: QinetiQ, and the Defence Science and Technology Laboratory (Dstl).

DESB: Defence Environment and Safety Board. Chaired by the Under Secretary of State or, in his absence, the 2nd PUS, provides direction, sets objectives, monitors, reviews and reports on performance with regard to the environment and safety in defence.

Devolved Administrations. The devolved administrations of Scotland, Wales and Northern Ireland have responsibility for certain defined areas of domestic Government in their parts of the UK.

DFAU: Defence Fraud Analysis Unit. A dedicated unit within the Defence Internal Audit organisation to evaluate suspected irregularities, support police authorities, promote risk awareness, record reported fraud and theft, liaise with the Treasury and provide advice on procedures and policy.

DfES: Department for Education and Skills. Government Department responsible for setting education and skills policy in England.

DfID: Department for International Development. Government Department responsible for the UK's development aid and work to get rid of extreme poverty.

DH: Department of Health. Government Department responsible for setting health and social care policy in England, and sets standards and drives Modernisation across all areas of the NHS, social care and public health.

DIA: Defence Internal Audit. The MoD's principal Internal Auditing body, whose primary role is the provision of independent and objective advice on the economy, efficiency and effectiveness of systems and controls at all levels of the Department. It reports directly to the Defence Audit Committee.

DII: Defence Information Infrastructure. A fully networked and managed information system being acquired to support Defence worldwide, underpinning much of the defence Change Programme.

Direct Entry Officers. Army officers (previously called Mainstream officers) who either come direct from civilian life or from the ranks of the Army, commissioned on completion of the 11 month Royal Military Academy Sandhurst (RMAS) Commissioning Course. They will normally be under the age of 29 on entry to RMAS.

DIS:
a) Defence Industrial Strategy. Announced on 15 December 2005, the Defence Industrial Strategy is aimed at ensuring that our Armed Forces are provided with the equipment that they require, on time, and at best value for money. It aims to identify the sustainable industrial base required to retain within the UK those industrial capabilities (including infrastructure, skills, intellectual property and capacity).
b) Defence Intelligence Staff. Organisation that provides timely, all-source intelligence assessments to: guide Departmental decision making on the formulation of Defence policy and the commitment and employment of the UK's military forces; inform decisions on the generation and maintenance of operational military capability, including through the Equipment Programme; and contribute to wider national intelligence collection and assessment

Division. An Army Division made up of two or more Brigades depending on the specific role it is to undertake and is configured in a similar fashion to a Brigade but on a larger scale, commanded by a Major General. 1 (UK) Division and 3 (UK) Division are fighting Divisions. 2, 4 and 5 Division are responsible for administrative support of specific geographical areas within the UK.

DLO: Defence Logistics Organisation. The Top Level Budget organisation formed on 1 April 1999 to bring together the logistics support organisations in the Royal Navy, Army and Royal Air Force and Centre staff. It contains a number of specialist Defence Agencies.

DLTP: Defence Logistics Transformation Programme. A single coherent programme of work incorporating all logistic transformation activities across Defence to achieve improved operational effectiveness, efficiency and flexibility.

DMB: Defence Management Board. The Defence Management Board (DMB) is the highest, non-ministerial committee in the MoD. Chaired by PUS, it is essentially the main corporate board of the MoD, providing senior level leadership and strategic management of Defence. Its role is to deliver the Defence Aim set out in the Public Service Agreement. It comprises the ten non-ministerial members of the Defence Council together with the MoD Finance Director and two non-executive members. It is responsible for the role of Defence, providing strategic direction, vision and values; for Objectives and targets, establishing the key priorities and defence capabilities necessary to deliver the MoD's Departmental objectives; for Resource allocation and strategic balance of investment to match Defence priorities and objectives; and for Performance management, managing and driving corporate performance.

DMS: Defence Medical Services. Comprises the Defence Medical Services Department and the three single Service medical directorates.

DOC: Directorate of Operational Capability. DOC provides an independent source of evaluation and audit within the Armed Forces on a range of issues, including operational lessons learnt studies and appraising the care and welfare of Armed Forces initial training establishments.

DPA: Defence Procurement Agency. The DPA is the Top Level Budget Organisation responsible for the procurement of equipment to meet new requirements. It is also a Defence Agency. It is located mainly at Abbey Wood, Bristol.

DRDL: Devonport Royal Dockyards Ltd. A company which runs and owns the Devonport Royal Dockyards in Plymouth.

DSDA: Defence Storage and Distribution Agency. The Defence Agency that provides the Armed Forces with storage and distribution services.

DSL: Debut Services Ltd. A joint venture between Bovis Lend lease Ltd and Babcock Infrastructure Services to provide property maintenance and capital works projects across Defence.

DSTL: Defence Science and Technology Laboratory. An agency and trading fund of the MoD created from part of DERA on 2 July 2001. It provides specialist scientific and technical support to the MoD.

DTC: Defence Technology Centre. A formal collaborative arrangement between industry and academic experts in a particular technology, funded jointly by participants and the MoD, who work together to generate and enhance the technology vital to the delivery of future UK Defence capabilities.

DU: Depleted Uranium. Uranium is a natural element found in soil, water and mineral deposits. It is a heavy metal, nearly twice as dense as lead, is radioactive and chemically toxic. DU is a waste product, (what is left after the removal of some of the more radioactive parts of natural uranium for use in the nuclear industry) and being a very dense and hard metal is an ideal core for tank shells designed to pierce armoured vehicles.

DUOB: Depleted Uranium Oversight Board. An independent panel of scientists and veterans' representatives appointed to oversee the MoD's depleted uranium (DU) screening programme.

DWR: Deep Waste Repository. A facility for the storage of nuclear waste deep underground.

ECAB: Executive Committee of the Army Board. ECAB conducts the day-to-day business of managing the Army on behalf of the Army Board. It brings together, under the Chief of the General Staff, the Army operational and personnel commanders, and supports the CGS in his executive role, his management and operational advisory roles, and as the professional head of the Army.

Environment Agency. The environmental regulator for England and Wales.

ERW: Explosive Remnants of War. Unexploded ordnance (such as bombs, missiles and artillery shells), which may be primed, fused, armed or prepared for use, and may have been abandoned.

ESDP: European Security and Defence Policy. The European Union has agreed on the establishment of a European Security and Defence Policy to ensure it has the tools to undertake crisis management operations, where NATO as a whole is not engaged, in support of its Common Foreign and Security Policy.

Ethnic Minority. A group within a community which differs ethnically from the main population.

EU: European Union. The framework for economic and political co-operation between 25 European countries. It began as a post-war initiative between six countries pooling control over coal and steel to guarantee a more peaceful future for Europe. It now manages co-operation on issues as wide-ranging as the environment, transport and employment, and has increasing influence in defence and foreign policy.

EUFOR. The EU-led peacekeeping force responsible for security in Bosnia-Herzegovina.

FCO: Foreign and Commonwealth Office. The Government department responsible for UK foreign and security policy.

Finance Director. The MoD's senior finance officer, responsible for all aspects of the Department's financial performance and a member of the Defence Management Board.

Fleet. The Top Level Budget (TLB) organisation managed by Commander-in-Chief Fleet which was formed on 1 April 2006 from the CINC Fleet TLB and Chief of Naval Personnel TLB.

FOI: Freedom of Information. An Act giving a right of public access to recorded information held by public authorities subject to certain defined exemptions.

FRES: Future Rapid Effects System. A project to enhance the deployability of UK Land Forces by delivering a family of medium weight, network capable armoured vehicles, such as armoured personnel carriers, reconnaissance, command and control, and or ambulance vehicles. The project is currently in the Assessment Phase.

FE: Force Element. An Armed Force grouping used for the measurement of readiness. This may be an armoured brigade in the Army, an individual ship in the Royal Navy or an individual aircraft or squadron of aircraft in the Royal Air Force.

Full-Time Equivalent. A measure of the size of the workforce that takes account of the fact that some people work part-time.

Full-Time Reserve Service. Individuals on FTRS fill Service posts on a full-time basis while being a member of one of the reserve services, either as an ex-regular or as a volunteer. In the case of the Army and the Naval Service, these will be posts that would ordinarily have been filled by regular service personnel, in the case of the RAF, FTRS personnel also fill posts designated solely for them.

GDP: Gross Domestic Product. The sum of all output (or income or expenditure) in the economy, excluding net property income from abroad.

GOCNI: General Officer Commanding Northern Ireland.
a) The senior military officer in command of the Armed Forces in Northern Ireland, of the rank of Lieutenant General. He is responsible for military aid to the civil power and counter terrorist operations in Northern Ireland;

b) The joint-Service Top Level Budget organisation managed by GOCNI.

Gurkhas. Citizens of Nepal recruited and employed in the Army under the terms of the 1947 Tri-Partite Agreement. They remain Nepalese citizens but in all other respects are full members of HM Forces.

GWMB: Guided Weapons, Missiles and Bombs. Explodable munitions which incorporate guidance mechanisms.

HCDC: House of Commons Defence Select Committee. The Defence Committee is appointed to examine on behalf of the House of Commons the expenditure, administration and policy of the Ministry of Defence and any associated public bodies.

Headline Goal 2010. The aim, adopted by the European Union at the Helsinki European Council in December 1999, to be able to deploying 50-60,000 troops, capable of conducting the full range of crisis management tasks, within 60 days, sustainable for up to a year, with air and naval support as necessary, before the end of 2003.

Heavy Equipment Transporter. A 120 tonne tractor and trailer unit tank transporter, capable of carrying battle tanks and fighting vehicles straight to the front line at speeds of up to 50 mph on road or off road over harsh terrain.

HMG: Her Majesty's Government.

HNBS: Harrier Night Bombing System.

HOME: Head Office Modern Environment. The HOME programme was a comprehensive Modernisation package using the redevelopment of MoD's Main Building as a catalyst for organisational and cultural change to make the MoD Head Office a better, more streamlined, organisation in which to work and enable it to provide more effective support and leadership for UK Defence capability.

HQ: Headquarters.

HR: Human Resources. Civilian personnel management, organisation and arrangements.

HSE: Health and Safety Executive. The Health and Safety Executive is responsible for regulation of risks to health and safety arising from work activity in Britain.

Hydrographic Office. See **UK Hydrographic Office.**

IAB: Investment Approvals Board. The Investment Approvals Board (IAB) is responsible for central scrutiny of equipment requirements, major capital works and Information Technology projects. It makes recommendations to Ministers on the procurement of major defence equipment. The IAB is chaired by the Chief Scientific Adviser and includes the Vice Chief of the Defence Staff, 2nd Permanent Secretary, Chief of Defence Procurement and Chief of Defence Logistics.

ICT: Information and Communications Technology.

ICT FS: Information and Communications Technology Fundamental Skills.

Industrial staff. Civilian staff paid in certain pay bands often performing manual work.

Insensitive munitions. Munitions incorporating design features to reduce the risk of inadvertent reaction to specified stimuli, such as heat, shock and impact.

In-Service Date. The date on which equipment being procured is expected to be available and supportable in service in sufficient quantity to provide a valuable operational capability.

ISAF: International Security Assistance Force. The NATO controlled peacekeeping force providing security in Kabul since the fall of the Taleban in 2001. More than 30 countries contribute troops.

IS: Information Systems.

Intake. Those entering the Armed Forces or Civilian workforce.

IT: Information Technology.

JPA: Joint Personnel Administration. A modern commercial information system enabling provision of pay, pensions and administration services for military personnel, JPA is being introduced in the RAF in late 2005, the RN in Spring 2006 and the Army in late 2006.

JRRF: Joint Rapid Reaction Forces. A substantial pool of capabilities, composed of all readily available forces, from which tailored force packages of up to Brigade level or equivalent for operations on land, sea and air can be assembled and deployed quickly.

KFOR: NATO Kosovo Force. The International NATO led peacekeeping force whose main role is maintaining a secure civilian environment.

LAN: Local Area Network. Two or more connected computers in a room or building.

Land Command. See CINCLAND.

Locally Entered/Engaged Personnel. Civilian personnel working for one of the Armed Forces or directly for the Ministry of Defence who are recruited at overseas MoD locations normally for work at those locations. Also includes Gurkhas.

LS: Large Scale. Operational deployments of division size or equivalent for warfighting or other operations.

Main Gate. The main investment point for a procurement project, comprising In-depth review timed to coincide with the most critical point of the project – the point at which the "Assessment" phase ends and user requirements, system requirements, time and cost can be set with confidence.

MAMBA weapon locating radar. Mobile Artillery Monitoring Battlefield Radar, a radar system that can instantly track incoming mortars, shells and rockets and will help troops pinpoint the enemy's position for rapid counter attacks.

MANPADS: Man Portable Air Defence Systems. Systems designed for military air defence use, and are surface to air missiles, usually shoulder launched and fired by an individual or more than one individual acting as crew.

MDP: Ministry of Defence Police. The non-regional, national police force headed by a Chief Constable, responsible for providing effective policing of the Defence Estate.

Memorandum of Understanding. A formal signed agreement between partners setting out how they will work together in a process to achieve agreed goals.

MIDIT: Means of Identifying and Developing Internal Talent. The MoD's internal corporate development scheme for civilian personnel.

Military Aid to the Civil Authorities: MACA. The provision of military assistance: in time of emergency such as natural disasters and major emergencies; to provide more routine assistance for special projects or events of significant social value to the civil community in the creation and development of local community projects; of individual assistance by full-time attachment to social service or similar organisations; or for the maintenance of law, order and public safety using specialist capabilities or equipment, in situations beyond the capability of the Civil Power.

Military Tasks. The framework on which the MoD bases its detailed planning for the size, shape and capabilities of the Armed Forces, reflecting the broad types of tasks and operations in which they are likely to be involved.

MoD: Ministry of Defence.

MS: Medium Scale. Operational deployments of brigade size or equivalent for warfighting or other operations.

MND(SE): Multi National Division (South East)

NAAFI: Navy, Army and Air Force Institutes. Official trading organisation of HM Forces, providing retail and leisure services to the Services and their families.

NAO: National Audit Office. The independent organisation responsible for scrutinising public spending on behalf of Parliament, reporting to the Public Accounts Committee. It audits the accounts of all government departments and agencies as well as a wide range of other public bodies, and reports on the economy, efficiency and effectiveness with which government bodies have used public money.

NATO: North Atlantic Treaty Organisation. A regional defence alliance formed in 1949 under the Washington Treaty. Its general aim is to "safeguard the freedom, common heritage and civilisation" of its members by promoting "stability and well-being in the North Atlantic area". Members agree that an armed attack against one shall be considered an attack against them all, and that they will come to the aid of each other. Currently there are 26 member countries with the headquarters in Brussels.

Naval Manning Agency. Created on 1 July 1996 and dissolved as an agency 1 April 2004. Its mission was: to ensure that sufficient manpower is available on the trained strength and deployed effectively in peace, transition to war or war.

Naval Service. The Royal Navy (including QARNNS) and the Royal Marines together.

Navy Board. The Navy Board conducts the day-to-day business of managing the Royal Navy on behalf of the Admiralty Board. It brings together, under the Chief of the Naval Staff, the Royal Navy's operational and personnel commanders, and supports the CNS in his executive role, his management and operational advisory roles, and as the professional head of the Royal Navy.

NCO: Non-commissioned officer. Ratings of Leading Hand and above in the Royal Navy, other ranks of lance corporal and above in the Army and other ranks of corporal and above in the Royal Marines and Royal Air Force.

NDA: Nuclear Decommissioning Authority. The body within the DTI responsible for nuclear clean-up issues.

NDPB: Non-Departmental Public Bodies. Public bodies carry out a wide range of functions on behalf of government. As part of the commitment to transparency and accountability, the Cabinet Office collects and publishes annually information about public bodies as a whole, to supplement information about individual bodies already contained in departmental annual reports.

NEC: Network Enabled Capability. A programme to enhance military capability through the exploitation of information. Implemented through the coherent and progressive development of Defence equipment, software, processes, structures and individual and collective training, NEC will enable the MoD to operate more effectively in the future strategic environment by more efficient sharing and exploitation of information within the UK Armed Forces and with our coalition partners.

NED: Non Executive Director. Non Executive Directors serve on various boards and audit committees within the Ministry of Defence, providing independent scrutiny and advice on defence business from their experience in Industry.

Net Cash Requirement. The amount of actual money that MoD requires from the government in order to fund its activities. The NCR takes account of the movements in working capital levels (debtors, creditors and stocks) but not non-cash costs.

NHS: National Health Service. Set up on 5th July 1948, the NHS provides healthcare for all citizens, based on need, not the ability to pay, and is funded by the tax payer and managed by the Department of Health, which has the responsibility to provide healthcare to the general public through the NHS.

Non-cash items in Annually Managed Expenditure include various notional transactions such as depreciation and cost of capital that appear in the operating cost statement under RAB and which are recorded in AME for the period of Spending Review 2000, rather than in DEL.

Non-industrial staff. All Civil servants who are not Industrial staff.

NPT: Treaty on the Non-Proliferation of Nuclear Weapons. An international treaty to limit the spread of nuclear weapons and the foundation of the international nuclear disarmament and non-proliferation system.

NRA: Net Recoverable Amount.

NRF: NATO Response Force. Giving NATO a significant crisis response capability, the NRF is a powerful multi national military force with land, air, maritime and command elements, designed to stand alone for up to 30 days. It is not a permanent or standing force.

NRTA: Naval Recruiting and Training Agency. The Defence Agency within the 2SL Top Level Budget Organisation responsible for recruitment and training of Royal Navy and Royal Marines personnel.

NRV: Net Realisable Value. The estimated disposal sale value of an item of materiel not expected to be used or sold in the ordinary course of business. The estimated disposal sale value may be nil or scrap in appropriate circumstances, and will be net of any costs incidental to the sale, e.g. agent's fees, to the extent that these are identifiable to individual items or sales contracts and are deducted from the sales proceeds on a net receipt basis.

Nursing Services. Queen Alexandra's Royal Naval Nursing Service, Queen Alexandra's Royal Army Nursing Corps, and Princess Mary's Royal Air Force Nursing Service.

OCCAR: Organisation Conjoint de Cooperation en matiers d'ARmement. An Administrative Arrangement established on 12th November 1996 by the Defence Ministers of France, Germany, Italy and the UK. Its aim is to provide more effective and efficient arrangements for the management of certain existing and future collaborative armament programmes.

OECD: Organisation for Economic Co-operation and Development. The OECD comprises 30 countries sharing a commitment to democratic government and the market economy. Its work covers economic and social issues from macroeconomics, to trade, education, development and science and innovation.

Officer. A member of the Armed Forces holding the Queen's Commission. Includes ranks from Sub-Lt/2nd Lt/Pilot Officer up to Admiral of the Fleet/Field Marshal/Marshal of the Royal Air Force. Excludes NCO's.

Officer cadet. An entrant from civil life to the officer corps of the Armed Forces.

OGC: Office of Government Commerce. An independent Office of the Treasury which aims to work with the public sector as a catalyst to achieve efficiency, value for money in commercial activities and improved success in the delivery of programmes and projects.

Operating Cost Statement. The statement in departmental resource accounts that shows the current income and expenditure on an accrual basis. It is similar to the profit and loss statement on commercial accounts. This is the Public Sector's equivalent of a commercial organisation's Profit and Loss Account.

Operational TLBs. The TLBs directly responsible for the planning and management of military operations and the delivery of front-line capability. Operational personnel are those working in these TLBs plus some other small groups.

OPG: Office of HM Paymaster General. The Office of HM Paymaster General is part of HM Treasury. It is responsible for holding the working balances of Government Departments and other public bodies in accounts at the Bank of England and making them available to the National Loans Fund overnight to reduce the government's borrowing costs, and provides cash flow information to the Treasury.

OSCE: Organisation for Security and Co-operation in Europe. With 55 States drawn from Europe, Central Asia and America, the OSCE is the world's largest regional security organisation, bringing comprehensive and co-operative security to a region that stretches from Vancouver to Vladivostok. It offers a forum for political negotiations and decision-making in the fields of early warning, conflict prevention, crisis management and post-conflict rehabilitation, and puts the political will of the participating States into practice through its unique network of field missions.

Other Ranks. Members of the Royal Marines, Army and Royal Air Force who are not officers. The equivalent group in the Royal Navy is known as "Ratings".

Outflow Those leaving the Armed Forces or Civil Service for any reason. Those who rejoin and then leave again will be counted twice if the time period includes both exit dates.

Outturn and **estimated outturn** describe expenditure actually incurred, or estimated on the basis of actual expenditure to date.

Part-time. Civil servants working fewer than 37 hours a week (36 hours in London), excluding meal breaks.

PCPF: Parliamentary Contributory Pension Fund. The fund of the parliamentary pension scheme.

People Programme: A programme to enable MoD civilians to make the best contribution to the Defence capability. This will be achieved by: maximising our pool of talent and skills; matching people and their skills to the jobs that need to be done, now and in the future; and by raising our collective performance by improving management, training and development throughout the Department.

PPA: Performance Partnership Agreement. A central initiative to oversee Departmental management and co-ordinate Government Business. During 2005 they were replaced by other systems including Departmental Capability Reviews.

PPPA: People, Pay & Pensions Agency. The organisation providing civilian pay and personnel services, including the administration of pensions, the payment of salaries of MoD civilian staff and the payment of fees. Launched on 7 April 2006.

PCRU: Post Conflict Reconstruction Unit. An organisation set up to enhance the Government's ability to plan, develop and deliver effective and co-ordinated post conflict stabilisation activity. The organisation is interdepartmental

PFI: Private Finance Initiative. A system for providing capital assets for the provision of public services. Typically, the private sector designs, builds and maintains infrastructure and other capital assets and then operates those assets to sell services to the public sector. In most cases, the capital assets are accounted for on the balance sheet of the private sector operator.

PPP: Public Private Partnership. An initiative through which the private sector is involved in the delivery of public services by providing management and service delivery expertise and sometimes the provision of assets. Improved value for money is the essential prerequisite, with better quality of service provision a highly desirable addition. It is delivered through several mechanisms including Private Finance Initiative, Partnering, Wider Markets Initiative and Contractor Logistic Support.

PSA: Public Service Agreement. An agreement between HM Treasury and each Government Department setting out each department's aim, objectives and key outcome-based targets. They form an integral part of the spending plans set out in Spending Reviews. Progress against the PSA targets is assessed and reported via the Defence Balanced Scorecard.

PSI: Proliferation Security Initiative. The Proliferation Security Initiative is a global effort that aims to stop shipments of weapons of mass destruction, their delivery systems, and related materials worldwide. It was announced by President Bush on May 31, 2003.

PSG: Professional Skills for Government. Professional Skills for Government is a key part of the Government's Delivery and Reform agenda. It is a major, long-term change programme designed to ensure that civil servants, wherever they work, have the right mix of skills and expertise to enable their Departments or agencies to deliver effective services.

PTC: RAF Personnel and Training Command. The Top Level Budget organisation managed by the RAF's Principal; Personnel Officer, the Air Member for Personnel. PTC provides trained personnel to Strike Command and other TLBs.

PUS: Permanent Under Secretary. PUS is the Government's principal Civilian advisor on Defence and has the primary responsibility for Policy, Finance, Management and Administration in the department. He is the MoD Accounting Officer reflecting his responsibility to the Secretary of State for the overall organisation, management and staffing of the department and financial procedures and other matters. He is personally accountable to Parliament for the expenditure of all public money voted for defence purposes and chairs the Defence Management Board.

PVR: Premature Voluntary Release. Those who leave the Armed Forces voluntarily before the end of their agreed engagement or commission period are said to leave on PVR or VR (Voluntary Release).

PRT: Provincial Reconstruction Team. A combination of international military and civilian personnel based in one of Afghanistan's provinces with the aim of extending the authority of the Afghan central government and helping to facilitate development and reconstruction by contributing to an improved security environment. PRTs also aim to support the reform of the Afghan security sector – disarmament and demobilisation of militias; building an accountable national army and national police force under government control; stamping out the drugs trade; and helping build a legal system.

QARNNS: Queen Alexandra's Royal Naval Nursing Service. The Royal Navy's internal nursing service.

QinetiQ. A defence technology and security company, formerly part of DERA, partially owned by the MoD.

Quick Impact Projects. Programmes aimed at kick-starting local economies and creating employment opportunities in immediate post-conflict environments. Projects are identified and implemented by local groups with international assistance. Examples include the reconstruction and refurbishment of schools in Iraq.

RAB. Resource Accounting and Budgeting.

RAF: The Royal Air Force.

Rank. Grade within the Military structure.

Ratings. Junior military personnel in the Royal Navy.

Real terms figures are amounts adjusted for the effect of general price inflation relative to a base year, as measured by the GDP market price deflator.

Regiment. A formed unit of personnel sharing a common identity and area of expertise, carrying the spirit of the people who have gone before.

Regular Reserves. Former members of the UK regular forces who have a liability for service with the Reserve forces. Includes the Royal Fleet Reserve, Army Reserve and Royal Air Force Reserve as well as other individuals liable to recall.

RES: Race Equality Scheme. The MoD Race Equality Scheme sets out how the Department is fulfilling its obligations under the Race Relations (Amendment) Act 2000.

Resource Accounting. The accounting system that will henceforth be used to record expenditure in the departmental accounts instead of cash accounting. It applies generally accepted accounting practice (GAAP) used in private industry and other Government departments to departmental transactions. Spending is measured on an accruals basis.

Resource Budget. The sum of a department's resource Departmental Expenditure Limit and resource Annually Managed Expenditure. It is the budget for current expenditure on an accruals basis.

Resource budgeting. The budgeting regime adopted for the spending plans set in the 2000 Spending Review. It is derived from resource accounting rules, but there are several differences in treatment between resource accounts and resource budgets.

RFA: Royal Fleet Auxiliary Service. The civilian manned fleet, owned by the Ministry of Defence. Its main task is to supply warships of the Royal Navy at sea with fuel, food, stores and ammunition which they need to remain operational while away from base. It also provides aviation support for the Royal Navy, together with amphibious support and secure sea transport for Army units and their equipment. Its employees are full-time civil servants, but who come under the Naval Discipline Act when deployed to sea under naval command.

RfR: Request for Resources. An accruals-based measure of current expenditure which forms part of a Resource Estimate. It represents the basic unit of Parliamentary control.

RM: Royal Marines. Sea-going soldiers who are part of the Naval Service.

RMR: Royal Marines Reserve. The volunteer reserve service of the Royal Marines. See **Volunteer Reserves.**

RN: Royal Navy. The sea-going defence forces of the UK, including ships, submarines, Naval aircraft and their personnel, and Queen Alexandra's Royal Naval Nursing Service, but excluding the Royal Marines and the Royal Fleet Auxiliary Service (RFA).

RNAS: Royal Naval Air Station. An air base operated by the Fleet Air Arm.

RNR: Royal Naval Reserve. The volunteer reserve service of the Royal Navy. See Volunteer Reserves.

RO-RO Shipping. Ships designed to allow cargo, such as vehicles, to be loaded by being rolled instead of lifted, often with a drive-through concept with bow and stern doors. It is commonly used in the in the ferry trades to transport cars and goods vehicles, but also used to transport military vehicles.

RPC: Regional Prime Contracts. Five regionally-based contracts for the provision of construction and maintenance services on the Defence Estate across Great Britain, where stand-alone arrangements are not appropriate. The objective of Regional Prime Contracting is to achieve better long-term value for money through improved Supply Chain Management, incentivised payment mechanisms, continuous improvement, economies of scale, and partnering.

RRUs: Regional Rehabilitation Units.

SALW: Small Arms and Light Weapons. Personal weapons, such as pistols, rifles and light machine guns.

SC: Supply Chain.

SCS: Senior Civil Service. The senior management of the Civil Service.

SDR: Strategic Defence Review. The Defence Review conducted in 1997-98 which reassessed Britain's security interests and Defence needs and set out objectives designed to enhance the Armed Forces.

SEC: Service Executive Committees. The three committees that conduct the day-to-day business of managing the Services on behalf of the Admiralty, Army and Air Force Boards. They bring together, under the Chief of Staff, the Service's operational and personnel commanders, to support the Chief of Staff in his executive role, his management and operational advisory roles, and as the professional head of his Service.
See Navy Board, The Executive Committee of the Army Board; and The Air Force Board Standing Committee.

Senior Non-commissioned officer. Senior members of the Ratings/Other Ranks, including Warrant Officer (all classes), Charge Chief Petty Officer, Chief Petty Officer, Colour sergeant, Staff Sergeant, Flight Sergeant/Chief Technician, Petty Officer, Sergeant.

SFA: Service Family AccomMoDation. Housing for service personnel with families.

SFOR: NATO Stabilisation Force. The International NATO led peacekeeping force, responsible for security in the Balkans, before handing over to EUFOR in December 2004.

SIC: Statement of Internal Control. The formal statement in the resource Accounts by the Accounting Officer, that effective systems are in place for managing the organisation.

SIT: Science Innovation and Technology. The Top Level Budget organisation managed by the Chief Scientific Advisor providing science and technology advice and solutions.

SLAM: Single Living Accommodation Modernisation. A project to raise the standard of single living accommodation for service personnel by delivering over 30,000 new or refurbished bed-spaces from 2003-2013.

Smart Acquisition. Smart Acquisition is a policy which aims to acquire Defence capability faster, cheaper, better and more effectively integrated. The objectives of Smart Acquisition are to deliver and sustain defence capabilities within the performance, time and cost parameters approved at the time the major investment decisions are taken; to acquire defence capabilities progressively, at lower risk; to optimise trade-offs between military effectiveness, time and whole life cost are maximised; and to cut the time for (key) new technologies to be introduced into the frontline, where needed to secure military advantage and industrial competitiveness.

SNM: Special Nuclear Materials. Plutonium, uranium-233, or uranium enriched in the isotopes uranium-233 or uranium-235.

Sovereign Base Areas. The UK Overseas Territory in Cyprus, which is the joint responsibility of the Foreign and Commonwealth Office and the Ministry of Defence.

SS: Small Scale. Operational deployment of battalion size or equivalent.

SSR: Security Sector Reform. This aims to help developing and transitional countries manage their security functions in a democratically accountable, efficient and effective way by initiating and supporting reform and providing appropriate education and training.

SSRB: Senior Salaries Review Body. The independent body advising the Government on Senior Civil Service pay.

SSSI: Sites of Special Scientific Interest. Protected sites of particular environmental and scientific importance, including wetlands, rivers, heathlands, meadows, beaches, moorland and peat bog.
The Defence Estate contains 289 SSSIs.

STC: Strike Command. The RAF's operational Top Level Budget organisation, providing aircraft and trained aircrews to CJO.

SCAPE: Superannuation Contributions Adjusted for Past Experience.

TLB: Top Level Budget. The major organisational grouping of the MoD. There are three types: "Operational", "Military Support" and "HQ and other support".

TNA: The National Archives is responsible for looking after the records of central government and the courts of law, and making sure everyone can look at them.

Trading Fund. Trading Funds were introduced by the Government under the Trading Funds Act 1973 as a 'means of financing trading operations of a government department which, hitherto, have been carried out on Vote'. They are self-accounting units that have greater freedom, than other government departments, in managing their own financial and management activities. They are also free to negotiate their own terms and conditions with their staff and for this reason their grading structures do not always match that of the rest of the Ministry, and this is reflected in some of the tables. MoD Trading Funds are ABRO, DARA, DSTL, the Meteorological Office, and the UK Hydrographic Office.

UAV: Unmanned Aerial Vehicle.

UKAEA: United Kingdom Atomic Energy Authority. A non-departmental public body, responsible to the Department of Trade and Industry. Its primary task today is managing the decommissioning of its nuclear reactors and other radioactive facilities used for the UK's nuclear research and development programme in a safe and environmentally responsible manner and to restore its sites for conventional use.

UKHO: UK Hydrographic Office. A trading fund agency of the MoD responsible for surveying the seas around the UK and elsewhere to aid navigation.

UOR: Urgent Operational Requirement. Additional capability requirements for specific operations met using a streamlined version of the Department's normal procurement procedures. This provides speedy and flexible procurement of capabilities.

UNFICYP. The United Nations Mission in Cyprus

VAT: Value Added Tax.

VAW: Veterans Awareness Week. A week to raise the profile of veterans. The first took place in July 2005.

VCDS: Vice Chief of the Defence Staff. The deputy to the Chief of the Defence Staff. Joint head of the Central Top Level Budget organisation with the 2nd PUS, and a member of the Defence Council, Defence Management Board, Chiefs of Staff Committee and Investment Approvals Board.

Veterans Agency. Formerly the War Pensions Agency. Responsible for veterans' affairs, including war and service pensions, service records, military graves, medals and welfare issues.

VFM: Value for Money.

Voluntary Release. See **Premature Voluntary Release.**

Volunteer Reserves and Auxiliary Forces. Civilian volunteers who undertake to give a certain amount of their time to train in support of the Regular Forces. Includes the Royal Naval Reserve, the Royal Marines Reserve, Territorial Army and the Royal Auxiliary Air Force. Does not include Royal Fleet Auxiliary Service (RFA). Some Volunteer Reservists undertake (paid) Full-Time Reserve Service.

VOP: Variation of Price. A contractual provision providing for variation in contract prices if inflation over the period of the contract falls outside defined bands.

Vote. An individual Supply Estimate by Parliament. Replaced by Requests for Resources since the introduction of Resource Budgeting in 2001, except for Votes A setting maximum numbers of personnel to be maintained by the Armed Forces.

WAN: Wide Area Network. A computer network covering a large geographic area, such as the internet or a network of bank cash dispensers.

War Pensions Agency. See Veterans Agency.

WEAG: Western European Armaments Group. A group of European countries established in 1993 with the objective of more efficient use of resources through, inter alia, increased harmonization of requirements; the opening up of national defence markets to cross-border competition; to strengthen the European defence technological and industrial base; and cooperation in research and development. The group closed in May 2005 with many of its activities now undertaken by the European Defence Agency.

WPB: War Pensions benefits. A non-contributory financial benefit paid to people who have been disabled as a result of conflict, or to dependants of those killed in conflict.

INDEX

Printed in the UK for The Stationery Office Limited
on behalf of the Controller of Her Majesty's Stationery Office
ID 185714 07/06